THE BASKETBALL MAN

James Naismith

James Naismith. Photograph by Ernie Foote, courtesy of Allen Donnell, Almonte, Ontario, Canada.

The Basketball Man

James Naismith

BERNICE LARSON WEBB

Kappelman's Historic Collections
Lawrence, Kansas

With love and admiration for my parents

CARL AND IDA LARSON

Preface

ONE of the puzzling elements in the search for biographical facts about Dr. James Naismith has been the contradictory nature of descriptions and details furnished by his acquaintances. Through the use of official records and, where necessary, my own judgment, I have attempted to strike out the prejudices, to reconcile the differences, and to combine the conflicting impressions until I have come to what I hope to be a true picture of the man.

In writing this book, I acknowledge gratefully the use of records and other information made available to me by faculty, officials, and librarians at eight colleges and universities—the University of Kansas, Springfield College, McGill University, the Presbyterian College in Montreal, the University of Colorado, the University of Calgary, the University of Alberta, and the University of Southwestern Louisana; by librarians in the Western History Department of the Denver Public Library; by the office staff at the Almonte (Ontario, Canada) High School; by officials in the Douglas County courthouse and the City Hall at Lawrence, Kansas; by members of the Naismith Basketball Hall of Fame Committee; by the pastors and members of various Presbyterian churches; and by officials and members at several branches of the Young Men's Christian Association in the United States and Canada. I am grateful to relatives, neighbors, and acquaintances of James Naismith in Lawrence, Kansas, in Springfield, Massachusetts, in Ramsay Township, Ontario, Canada, and in other communities in the United States and Canada who have favored me with lengthy interviews and correspondence. Particular mention should be made of the time and assistance given me by the three daughters and two sons of the late Maude Sherman Naismith and James Naismith—Margaret Naismith (Mrs. George Bowman) Stanley, Hellen Naismith (Mrs. Leslie H.) Dodd, John (Jack) Naismith,

Ann Naismith (Mrs. Thomas L.) Dawe, James Sherman Naismith—and by Mrs. Florence Naismith, second wife of Dr. Naismith. The collection of clippings, papers, and personal items of the late Dr. James Naismith in the possession of Jack Naismith and Mr. and Mrs. J. S. Naismith as well as official records made available by the head of the college library at the Presbyterian College of Montreal have been of inestimable aid in my research.

I acknowledge also the generous cooperation of Mrs. D. Hollie Lowry, Almonte, Ontario; Allan Donnell, Ottawa, Ontario; and Duke D'Ambra, Lawrence, Kansas; whose interest in this book extended over the several years of research involved in its composition.

Others who should be mentioned are: Forrest C. ("Phog") Allen, J. Neale Carman, Edwin R. Elbel, Fred Ellsworth, May Gardner, Clyde K. Hyder, John Ise, Hugh Means, Mrs. Stanton Olinger, Mrs. Ferne Rumsey Vanderhoof, faculty members of the Department of Physical Education of the University of Kansas, the minister of the First Presbyterian Church, the sexton of Memorial Park Cemetery, office personnel of the New York Cleaners, members of Sigma Phi Epsilon fraternity at the University of Kansas, and residents of the Sprague Apartments, all of Lawrence, Kansas; Mrs. H. C. Rumsey, Kansas City, Kansas; A. O. Duer, Kansas City, Missouri; Mrs. Carl Larson, Oberlin, Kansas; Mrs. Erma D. Shank, Topeka, Kansas; office employees of the *St. Marys Star,* St. Marys, Kansas; Mrs. Hugh Grace, Mrs. William J. Naismith, Mrs. Albert Naismith, Margaret ("Maggie") Naismith, Mr. and Mrs. Robert ("Bert") Young, the office staff of Almonte High School, the cemetery caretakers of the Auld Kirk, all of Almonte, Ontario; John E. Young, Toronto, Ontario; George Wilson, Winnipeg, Manitoba; Mr. and Mrs. L. H. Gulick, Jr., Potsdam, New York; J. Halsey Gulick, South Casco, Maine; Edward J. Hickox, Mr. and Mrs. Edward F. Oakes, and Mrs. Charles E. Silvia, Springfield, Massachusetts; officials in the Office of Athletics, McGill University; H. R. Nixon, the University of Saskatchewan; Robert Taylor, Mr. and Mrs. Leslie Deal, and Walter S. Hopkins, Denver, Colorado; and Mrs. Edith Woods Lindley, Ventura, California.

Introduction

BASKETBALL is played today on neighborhood playgrounds, in grade-school and high-school gymnasiums, in university field houses, and in professional arenas in about 130 countries, by some twenty million individuals each year. The game is one adaptable to varying tastes and circumstances. A pair of gym shoes for each player, a ball, and two hoops are uniform and equipment enough; yet with only a few refinements added to these essentials the same game may draw tens of thousands of spectators into a three-million-dollar field house. Consciously created to fill a specific educational need, basketball has grown far beyond that original purpose and continues to grow year after year, now attracting more players and spectators in more countries than any other game. The eighty-year-old baby among American sports has bourgeoned into a multimillion-dollar international giant that would appall the young Canadian student who brought it into being. In the United States alone basketball is watched by more than 150 million people each year, a record for any competitive sport. Its nearest rival in popularity as a spectator and participant sport is baseball, which, although another indigenous American institution, is perhaps a century older and of relatively obscure origin. Basketball, however, the only major American sport invented in the United States, was first played within the memory of living citizens.

Visiting the Naismith Memorial Basketball Hall of Fame, many persons too young to remember him become curious about the man who created the game of basketball; and those who do remember grow impatient for the telling of his story. In the years that have passed since his death Naismith has become a mere name in the cold print of the encyclopedia, where credit is summarily given for a service rendered. Although no one has given so many people so much pleasure with a single sport as has James Naismith, no full-length biography has been written about him. He was once asked to write a book about himself. When the book was finished, it was the story not of Naismith but of basketball. In it one can catch only glimpses of the good-humored, self-effacing man behind the ten-foot, peach-basket goal.

The Naismith story is one of the most interesting in the history of sports, and it is time that it be told. It is the tale of a man who struggled to live his ideals, taking time to create a game that would bring happiness to the world but scorning the wealth that could have been his had he signed his name to a certain piece of paper.

Time grows short for the telling. The number of persons who can lend their personal reminiscences to enrich such a biography becomes smaller each year. Of Naismith's college classmates and close friends, the last one, A. A. Stagg, most famous of all American football coaches, died in March, 1965, at the age of nearly one hundred two years. In the university town in Kansas where Dr. James Naismith lived and taught for forty-one years, relatively few of his colleagues are left—people who can remember that the inventor of basketball was a warm, human individual whose life and problems were intimately connected with their community and who made their lives the better because of that connection.

His story is not a simple story, for James Naismith was an unusual person. An orphan from the age of nine, he was reared on a farm in Canada by a bachelor uncle only twelve years older than the eldest of the three Naismith children entrusted to his care. Earning a living in the rough-and-tumble of a lumber camp, James defied his guardian and returned to high school to prepare for entrance into McGill University. Before his career was finished, he possessed three earned and two honorary degrees in three widely separated fields: religion, medicine, and physical education.

His story is not a stereotyped success story, for he found fame thrust upon him because of a deed from which he sought no fame. Doctor of Divinity, Doctor of Medicine, and Master of Physical Education, James Naismith earned his greatest renown for the creation of basketball, an act that was no more to him than the fulfillment of an assignment in a YMCA class.

His story is not a quiet one, for James Naismith, a peace-loving man, was often at the center of conflict. In his youth he had to fight against misunderstanding, at home and away from home, to gain the education his restless spirit demanded. During his long career of teaching, he fought against those who tried to corrupt the game he had created into purposes for which he had not intended it. And when international warfare came, he twice volunteered his services on foreign soil, in wars from which both his age and his ministerial training would have exempted him had he wished to take the easy way.

Finally, his story is not a black-and-white one, clear-cut in its implications, for James Naismith was many things to many people. Representative of these contradictions are two sets of conflicting descriptions, one of his physical stature and one of his temperament. Some persons who knew him say decisively that he was a tall man, while others state with equal certainty that he was short. Estimates of his height range, bewilderingly, from five feet eight inches to nearly six feet. Equally bewildering are analyses of his personality. "He was a quiet, unobtrusive man," say some of those who knew him. "He was a dynamic extrovert," say others.

Out of this intriguing collection of details, then, comes the tale of James Naismith, benefactor of his fellow man.

Contents

CONTENTS
Continued

Illustrations

1

Orphans at Bennie's Corners

WHEN John Naismith took his wife, Margaret, and his children from the Naismith farm home near Almonte, Ontario, to a house on Grand Calumet Island in the Ottawa River, over on the Quebec side, he could not have guessed the chain of circumstances that had begun to forge itself during that trip of seventy-odd miles. He could not have foreseen the changed existence that lay ahead for his three children, Annie, James, and Robert.[1]

A sawmill was to be established at Havelock on the river island, and carpenters, lumberjacks, and sawmill hands would be needed. Carpenter and lumberman that he was, John found enough opportunity for work in 1869 and 1870 to justify moving his family from Ontario into the neighboring province of Quebec to set up their household. An interesting bit of James Naismith's boyhood, then, began to evolve around this Quebec sawmill.[2]

The summer and fall of 1870, though, brought a series of events that changed the three and one-half months from mid-July to early November into a nightmare of death and fire for Jim. First, on July 17, Grandfather Young, the sixty-eight-year-old patriarch of the family, died. Then came the fire. A conflagration destroyed the sawmill, and everything in which John Naismith had invested his time and money was gone; everything he had accumulated on Grand Calumet Island was burned.[3]

But the worst was yet to come. When John Naismith moved his family to Grand Calumet Island, he had not, perhaps, realized the inadequacy of the living quarters they would find. Sanitation

1

facilities were primitive in that small lumbering community, and epidemics were not uncommon. True to form, typhoid fever was one of the plagues that struck, and in the early fall of 1870 John was the first of the family to contract the fever.[4]

When the news of John's dread illness came to the relatives around Almonte, brother-in-law William Young's first thought was of his sister Margaret and her children, alone among strangers and far from home. He knew that no one would go near the Naismiths' dwelling when news had spread of the contagion inside it. He told his wife that he was going to Quebec to bring the Naismith youngsters home.[5]

William's wife reminded him that he had children of his own at home to think about and that his impulsive plan was likely to bring typhoid onto them all. She pointed out that Ramsay Township was full of Youngs and Naismiths who might well help instead of him. She argued that Margaret had nine brothers and sisters living and only one of them had so large a family as he had to worry over.[6]

But William remained unconvinced by her. With typical determination, he harnessed horses to the sleigh and set out on his journey through the early October snow to the shack on the Ottawa River where the Naismiths were staying.

When he drove up to the little Naismith house, he did not go inside. He told his sister what to do, and Margaret obeyed, quickly packing bundles of clothing for each of her three children. Putting the little bundles into their arms, she hurried Annie, Jim, and Robbie out to the sleigh and kissed them goodbye.[7]

When Jim looked back from Uncle William's sleigh, the last thing he saw was his mother in the doorway, waving at him. She was a small, lonely figure standing there on that cold Canadian day. Jim's father had not come to tell the children goodbye, for he was lying in bed, ill with a great fever.[8]

Uncle William took the three children home with him. But he could not protect them from the bad news which came before long: their father had died. And less than three weeks later word came that their mother was dead. Both parents had died of the fever—John Naismith on the nineteenth of October and Margaret Naismith on the sixth of November.[9] Annie, Jim, and Robbie did not get to see their parents again, even in death, after the day the three children rode away in their uncle's sleigh. Because of the fear of contagion, the young couple—only thirty-seven years old—were buried quickly and quietly in a cemetery at Fort Coulonge, a town near the river island where they had died.[10]

To add irony to the burden of the family's grief, the day of Margaret Naismith's death was the double birthday anniversary of her two elder children—this year Annie's twelfth and Jim's ninth birthdays.

Many years later, when Jim Naismith was married and a father with a family of his own, word was sent to him in far-off Kansas that the place where his parents were buried was to be flooded upon construction of a dam on the river. Their courtship, their marriage, and the births of their children had all occurred in the Township of Ramsay, County of Lanark, Province of Ontario. Jim, therefore, made a trip to Quebec to have the graves opened and the bones moved home to the Auld Kirk cemetery near Almonte.[11] Then it would be possible to cross over the stile into the churchyard of the Auld Kirk and find their double grave back home in familiar surroundings, with only the mended section at the bottom of the tombstone where the old stone had broken, and the fresh concrete into which it had been set, to indicate that the grave had ever been disturbed.[12]

Telling his youngest daughter about the moving of the grave, Jim confided to Maudann how much he had loved his mother and how deeply affected he had been to look at her remains. Her hair was all that was left of his memory of her. "I touched it, Dimps," he told his daughter, tears in his eyes. "It was long and dark, just as I remembered it."[13]

Now, in the sad autumn of 1870, the little Naismiths went to live permanently with Grandmother Anne Young in the two-story stone house halfway between Bennie's Corners and Almonte. The stone residence and the farm buildings were located across the gully from the Naismiths' home, the white stucco house that John Naismith and his family had left to go to Grand Calumet Island.[14] In a way, Annie, Jim, and Robbie had come back home now—but they would never be able to return to the childhood they had known there.

Grandfather Robert Young had died less than four months before,[15] and Grandmother Young was left with the two of her eleven children—Peter and Jean[16]—who had not yet left the family. The little household was a home without a father, and the orphans must have felt doubly orphaned there.

Sometimes Jim had to fight to hold back his tears when he thought about his dead parents. Then he would run across the farmyard and climb into a grain bin, closing the door. There, crouched in a dusty pile of oats, he would cry for his mother and his father. His mother had told him that she used to play in that grain bin when she was a little girl, when the building was new and the boards were still pale and clean looking. He felt closer to her there than he could have anywhere else.[17]

He missed his grandfather, too. Grandfather Young had been a pious, hardworking Scot, a Presbyterian in religion and a cabinet-maker by trade. As precentor in the church, he had led the congregation in singing at every meeting, and on workdays he showed his skill with axe and saw and plane, with hammer and nails.[18]

Jim had worked with his grandfather and learned from him, even while indulging in a bit of tomfoolery now and then. Jim never forgot the day he took a brace and bit and drilled a hole through the neat stack of new doors that Grandfather had ready for a house under construction. Grandfather took one look at the ruined doors and made a comment to the effect that he was going to whale the living daylights out of his grandson. And, it seemed to Jim, he almost did.[19]

But the clearest memory his strong-minded Scottish grandfather left with Jim was of his habitual words, as the two of them worked together at tasks around the farmyard: "Don't think you can't master it! Do it and make a man of yourself."[20]

But now Grandfather Young was gone. And the sojourn of the young Naismiths here in the stone farmhouse was not to be a happy visit of a few hours or a day. It was an abrupt shift into a new way of life. In this autumn of 1870 the three little orphans left familiar discipline to settle into the routine of a foster home.

2
Scots in Canada

THE new home was an attractive and comfortable one, a house built by Scottish stonemasons whose work would stand for centuries to attest to their skill. There were rooms aplenty and two fireplaces—one in the parlor and one in the back kitchen.[1] But life was not soft; for this was a frontier land, where pioneers had settled only a generation or two before, and the frontier heritage was still part of their descendants' existence.

The Young and the Naismith families (who could both trace their ancestry to the clans of the thirteenth-century Scottish lowlands)[2] were members of the Scottish settlements established in Canada after the Napoleonic Wars. These settlements were made through land grants given to disbanded regiments, to Highland chiefs, and to emigration societies.[3] In the hard times of the second decade of the nineteenth century the government of Britain was persuaded by Scottish members of Parliament to arrange for the settlement of their constituents in particular areas in Canada. The British government, specifying that the emigrants pay their own ship passage, agreed to provide tools, blankets, seed grain, and a loan of £10 a head to tide the settlers over until harvest the next fall. Surveys were made, and Lanark County in the Ottawa Valley of Ontario was one of the counties readied for Scottish immigration.[4]

Accepting the terms of the British government, the immigrants began coming. The Lanark settlement, which included the townships of Lanark, Dalhousie, and parts of Ramsay and North Sherbrooke, was formed of unemployed mechanics from Glasgow and the west of Scotland, the area from which James Naismith's ancestors came. Most of these migrants had served in Canada in the War of 1812–1814. Early in 1820, 900 persons came into the Lanark settlement; and later in the year, 1,876 more arrived.[5]

By January, 1821, the township located around the junction of the Mississippi and Indian rivers—where James Naismith would be born—had been divided into lots and concessions, and a road had been laid out across the center of the township. In the early summer of 1821 one hundred families belonging to the Lanark Society of Settlers arrived in Canada. The immigrants, mostly from Lanarkshire, traveled the last stages of their Canadian journey by boat on the Mississippi River or on foot along an old Indian trail into their new land. They chose their lots, built their cabins, and named the location Ramsay Township in honor of George Ramsay, Lord Dalhousie, who was governor general of Canada from 1819 to 1828 and landlord of the Scottish lands on which many of these people had been tenants.[6]

Money was scarce, and many settlers were unable to repay the government loan they had received for passage to the new country. With that debt against them, they were refused government deeds to their property even after they had fulfilled their homesteading time and completed all other homestead stipulations. The British government, however, responding to petitions drawn up by these homesteaders, at last granted the overdue deeds in 1837.[7]

The Youngs and the Naismiths were among the Scots who at a relatively early date found parcels of land in Ontario to call their own. Robert Young and his two brothers came into the country in 1832, when it was a wilderness of forests and streams; and with Robert was his wife, Annie Mason Young, a pioneer woman who would rear eleven offspring in this environment. The fourth of these eleven children was Margaret Young, born in Ramsay Township in 1833.[8] A few years after the Youngs, John Naismith came over from Glasgow as a nine-year-old lad to live with his father's brother Peter ("Black Pete" Naismith) in Ramsay Township and to work in his uncle's lumber camp. Black Pete had migrated with two brothers from Scotland to the Bathhurst district of Upper Canada and then, in 1832, had moved to a farm in Ramsay Township. Coming here so young, nephew John Naismith found himself in such a wild land as he had never seen before; and his parents, James and Ann Wood Naismith, were more than three thousand miles away.[9]

But the new home of the Youngs and the Naismiths did not long remain an isolated and backward area. Ramsay Township grew under the care of hard-working, devout Scots. The community in which the Young farm was located—on the eighth line—was the most heavily populated part of Ramsay Township, and it was the place where the first schools and churches were built. The eighth line had two thriving settlements in the early days, a few miles apart: Leckies Corners and Bennie's Corners. In 1847 Bennie's Corners (named for the pioneer postmaster in the village) had facilities more than adequate for its population of seventy-five persons: a school, a church, a blacksmith shop, a shoemaker shop, a cooperage, a carriage shop, a general merchandise store, and a post office serving a large part of the township. A mile away, at the ninth line, Alex Sneddan had a fine hotel, where teamsters found a stopping place well known for comfort. Also within reasonable distance were a tannery, a carding mill, a weaving shop, a timber slide and sawmill, and several gristmills. Sawmill and gristmill for grain and flour, of course, usually followed close upon settlement in any district.[10]

Then, unfortunately, the great fire of 1851 destroyed the village of Bennie's Corners, and it was never fully rebuilt. Bennie's Corners in the 1870s, the time of the Naismith children's adolescence, was no longer an important crossroads. It consisted then of a few residences, a schoolhouse, a store, and a blacksmith shop. Gone were the post office—long the focal point of the township— the church, and nearly all the little industries and businesses. Even the cooperage was gone. In the days before steel drums and tin cans, all products were shipped in wooden barrels, and, consequently, every respectable settlement had its own cooperage to supply that everyday need. With crude hand tools the cooper constructed wooden barrels of all sizes, skillfully shaping them to specification. But the cooperage, like most of the other essential businesses of a trade center, had disappeared from Bennie's Corners. Only one important institution would remain in use for more than a century—the school—and here the Naismith children received their grade-school education.[11]

In another part of Ramsay Township, three miles from the Young farmstead, was a settlement of more enduring quality than Bennie's Corners. This was where Jim would attend high school. After Bennie's Corners declined from thriving village to little more than a minor crossroads with a few clustered buildings, industry and population expanded instead in the settlement that eventually came to be known as Almonte. This town, founded in 1882, became the economic, social, and cultural center for the area and an important source of textile goods for the country. One of the first villages in the Ottawa Valley, this textile-manufacturing center grew up where the Mississippi River showed a sixty-two-foot drop in three stages, making a tremendous supply of water power available. At each of these falls a separate community of Scots or Irish, with its own industries and its own town name, originated.[12]

Five years before Jim Naismith's birth—relatively late in the history of this cluster of communities—the three joined into one town, with a new name. After a succession of labels for the settlement as a whole or for its separate communities—Sheppard's Falls, Shipman's Falls, Shipman's Mills, Waterford, Ramsayville, Victoriaville—it was finally named Almonte. Strangely, this Scottish-Irish-Canadian group of settlers, admiring a foreigner far to the south, named their town in honor of the Mexican ambassador to the United States in 1856, General Juan Nepomuceno Almonte.[13]

By the time of the elder Naismiths' deaths in 1870, Almonte's high-grade textile mills—the Rosamond Woollen Company having the second largest woolen mill in the Dominion—marked the town as the "Manchester of Canada." In 1871, indeed, Almonte had a population of 2,080, at a time when only thirty-eight towns in the large province of Ontario had more than 2,000 inhabitants. The bell atop Almonte's Rosamond building announced starting and stopping time for most of the working men in the town, and the economic ruin to be wrought by the introduction of synthetic fabrics lay unseen in the future.[14]

After two decades in this thriving pioneer country, Robert Young built the stone house on the west half of Lot 22, Concession 9, and planted a garden at the edge of the forest.[15] Here Margaret, a favorite of her father's, lived until she married young John Naismith. John had been in Canada since he was nine, living with immigrant relatives. After working for a while in his uncle Pete's lumber camp, he had later taken up carpentry as a trade.[16]

When John grew up and courting time came, he proved to be a man of few and mighty words—thus providing a family anecdote that the young Naismith children learned to ask for, again and again. As the story goes, John walked into the Young home one evening and announced: "I'm going to marry Margaret. Is there anyone here strong enough to stop me?" None of Margaret's brothers protested, nor did Margaret. Her parents when asked, politely enough, were willing. And the couple were married January 19, 1858. With this family tale Jim Naismith came into contact with a legend of his father's strength—a tradition that he would eventually carry on.[17]

If Jim had an interest in pioneer days, this interest must have helped to make him feel that he had roots in Ramsay Township, orphan though he was. Sometimes, of course, it was difficult to adjust to the regime of his foster home. His grandparents had both been born in Scotland, his grandfather in Cabusland in 1802 and his grandmother in Grahnstone in 1805,[18] and they still kept many of their Scottish ways. Back home in Scotland they had spoken the Gaelic tongue, and his grandmother still did, sometimes, with the Naismith children.[19] Imagining his mother's growing-up years on the very farm where he was now living and working helped Jim in his adjustment to a new and sometimes strange existence. It helped make life seem less lonely if he thought of the little everyday activities of his mother—doing chores and walking to school at Bennie's Corners and bowing her head in family prayer. And he pictured her sedate behavior during the solemnity of Sunday, too.

Religion played an important part in the lives of the Youngs, as it did in the lives of all Scot-Canadians, day in and day out. Throughout the week the Youngs conducted family worship morning and night, and on the Sabbath Day—from midnight Saturday through Sunday—they carried on no labor or secular activities. And, of course, they went to church, wherever it might be. The state religion of Scotland was Presbyterian, and one of the first establishments in any Scottish settlement in Canada was a Presbyterian church. But in the days before the settlers had time or money enough to build churches, they held services in schoolhouses or mills or, in summertime, in an open field, where a large rock could be the pulpit. Grandfather and Grandmother Young used to attend church services in a barn, where a visiting minister came to read from a Gaelic Bible and to administer the sacraments. To be sure, the Youngs were not so hidebound about Sabbath observances as some persons were. In certain homes a stern regime was followed: activity ceased early Saturday evening to ensure proper rest for church attendance the next day, because for some householders in Ramsay Township there was a walk of as much as twelve miles between home and church![20]

As a little girl, Jim's mother used to attend services with the Youngs every Sunday at the Auld Kirk, the stone church whose construction was begun in 1834, the year after she was born. The Auld Kirk was a handsome structure, inside and out. Steps led up to the door by which the minister entered the high pulpit at the beginning of the service. There was no organ, as some churches had, but that did not matter. The people wanted their singing to reach the Lord without the help of any instrument except the tuning fork that Robert Young, as precentor, used.[21]

In 1843, though, a great split occurred in the Church of Scotland, and this carried into Canada. Those who opposed any further connection between church and state formed the Free Church. Thus, in almost every community there came to be two Presbyterian churches, a Free Church and an Auld Kirk (Old Church). The Youngs chose the Free Church; and in 1846, when a Free Church was built across the corner from the Auld Kirk, they transferred their worship there. By the time the little Naismiths were living with them the Youngs were attending St. John's Presbyterian Church in Almonte, where their congregation had moved in 1865.[22]

As time passed, the stone farmhouse seemed really like home. But sometimes, when Jim was unhappy, he slipped away into the grain bin to "talk" to his mother. He pretended that she was listening to everything he said to her, and her imagined presence made him feel better.[23]

It seemed as if more than enough grief had touched the Young-Naismith family. But more unhappiness was to come. Slightly more than two years after Jim's parents were buried, Grandmother Young died, on February 3, 1873. Aunt Jean's marriage left the Naismith children to the care of their uncle Peter J.

Young, who was only twelve years older than fourteen-year-old Annie.[24]

In this new household the Naismith brothers and sisters grew up too fast. Jim had already taken over a man's work, and Annie turned housekeeper overnight when their grandmother was buried. A "hired girl"—Maggie Lowe, a neighbor's young daughter—was brought in to help out only during busy periods. They were fortunate to find Maggie. She assisted with the Young housekeeping for years, becoming almost like one of the family. But she eventually married a young farmer and left to live on a neighboring farm.[25]

With or without a hired girl, life was harder for Annie than for Jim. Jim would be able to escape when he became a man, but Annie had assumed the triple role of sister-niece-mother and accepted the full weight of the demands, spoken and unspoken, that her three kinsmen would make on her: Jim, with the quick mind and spirit that should be helped to soar; Peter, the disciplinarian, who would unwittingly bind himself and her to the earth; and Rob, the youngest and frailest of the Naismiths, who still desperately needed mothering.

3

High-School Dropout and Lumberjack

THE household routine went on much as it had before, with Annie Naismith and Uncle Peter Young being caricatures of conventional mother and father figures.[1] P. J., as he was called by his acquaintances, was somewhat the gay blade in his young bachelor days. He would have liked to be the complete dandy, but thrift kept him safely within bounds in his living and spending habits.[2]

And across the gully the white stucco house, the children's old home, stood empty and unused. People in the neighborhood used to call it the White House. Now those who knew the Naismith story said that the house was haunted, and even passers-by who did not know the background came to call it a ghost house.[3]

Annie had completed her grade-school education by now, but Jim and Robbie were still in school. The children cut across the fields to attend grade school at Bennie's Corners, by road nearly three miles away, walking sometimes in sub-zero weather. Jim later attended high school at Almonte, again walking approximately three miles. Before and after school hours, while Annie cooked and cleaned and sewed, Jim and Rob did chores around the farm and worked in the woods. Jim learned to chop trees, saw logs, and drive horses.[4] Sometimes in the evening he practiced on the violin that his mother had been so happy to have him learn to play.[5] The children all had their chores to do, and if they went on an errand or a play-visit to the neighbors, they had to be home at an appointed time. Uncle Peter was a hard master, and Jim, clenching his teeth, learned lessons in independence, initiative, honesty, and ruggedness that he carried through life.[6]

For one thing, Uncle Peter didn't like a coward. He preached, pontifically, "The fear of the Lord is the beginning of wisdom,"[7] but added, practically, that he didn't want to catch his wards being afraid of anything else. Jim learned not to be bothered by anything much in Ontario except, maybe, snakes.[8]

Uncle Peter set great store on reliability and self-reliance. When Jim was sent into the field or the woods with a team of horses, he was expected to do the assigned job without asking for help. If trouble arose, he was depended upon to take care of the emergency himself, whether it was the repair of a broken singletree or something more serious. Many years later Jim recounted an episode from that boyhood in Canada to illustrate his uncle's tough wisdom.

Hauling hay by two-horse sleigh across the frozen river one day, Jim, through haste or laziness, neglected to drive his team to the proper place for crossing. Instead, to save driving a quarter of a mile downstream, he took a shortcut across the river where he knew the ice to be unsafe. Hitting a spring hole before they reached the opposite bank, the two horses broke through the ice. Encumbered by their harness, the valuable team floundered helplessly. Jim, desperately frightened, somehow unhitched the team from the sleigh and, risking his own safety, helped the horses, one after the other, onto the bank. Only after he and the horses, still frightened and trembling, were safe on firm ground did he notice his waiting uncle half-hidden behind him in the trees. Peter Young had quietly watched the whole adventure. Even at that moment the boy must have felt a grudging admiration, mixed with resentment, for this man who could lay such unyielding stress on the virtue of self-reliance. Years later he would write about his boyhood in Canada: "When a boy was sent into the field with a team, he was expected to accomplish the task that he had been assigned. If some emergency arose, he was not expected to go to the house and ask for help; if it were at all possible, he was expected to fix the trouble himself."[9]

Despite the burden of farm duties, there was time for play, if Jim was sure to get home from his outings at the time Uncle Peter had set.

In Bennie's Corners the blacksmith shop, which stood in front of a grove of hard maples, was a gathering spot for the children of the village and surrounding farms. They watched the smithy as he shod horses, shaped and pointed plow blades, fashioned hinges, and made wagon wheels, shrinking steel tires to perfect fit on the wooden rims. Best of all, there was ample space for play in the sugarbush behind the shop. Here, in the youthful games, stunts, and contests in which Jim participated, he worked off his loneliness. A long rope, which was used to hobble the horses brought in to be shod, hung on the wall of the blacksmith shop; and one of the favorite sports of the boys who gathered there was a game of tug-of-war with that rope, which they borrowed from the sympathetic blacksmith. Or they used the smithy's anvil to compete in weight lifting. They enjoyed wrestling and other forms of friendly fighting. They did high jumps, they swung, they climbed trees. Where a tree or boulder served as a convenient base, they played variations of tag and hide-and-seek or tried their skill at duck on the rock—a game in which one boy placed his "duck," a stone, on a boulder as target for fist-sized stones thrown by the other boys. Throughout the fields and beside the creeks and rivers that lay beyond the blacksmith shop, too, Jim and his comrades found space to play. They stalked

imaginary Indians through the trees. They set up games of
lacrosse in the fields. They fished for black bass along clear
streams.[10]

Throughout the seasons they played and grew, and every time
of the year had its own delights. In the autumn fishing was exciting, and hunting was good in the woods. When the great
northern pike were biting, the boys divided their fishing time
between the Indian and the Mississippi rivers, coming home in
the evening with food for the family frying pan. There was a great
variety of hunting to be done, too, for sport and for household
economy. Through the split-rail fences and the hedgerows the
boys went with bows and arrows into the forest that crowded
close around the cultivated land. There they shot squirrels and
sometimes a partridge or a snowshoe hare. When they grew older
they were given guns to hunt deer and Canadian lynx. And sometimes, from necessity, they hunted the packs of dogs that skulked
into the fold to kill the sheep.[11]

There were parties, too, especially in the autumn and winter.
A "bee"—whether an apple-paring bee or a husking bee or whatever—was a time for merrymaking while helping neighbors with
their farm work. For example, at an autumn paring bee the
young people of the neighborhood gathered to pare and quarter
apples for drying over the kitchen stove or on racks above the
fireplace to fill a housewife's pantry or cellar with a supply of
winter food. The housewife was pleased to see many strings of
dried apples suspended from the ceiling of kitchen or attic—later,
when perfectly dry, to be packed away in boxes or paper bags—
for then there was sure to be an abundance of pies, puddings,
and tarts during the months ahead.[12]

During the winter, from November on, snowshoeing and ice
hockey, or shinny, on the river were favorite sports and gave
occasion for evening get-togethers. There were tobogganing and
skating parties and bobsled rides—the sled filled with straw and
with yelling boys and girls. Any of these outdoor social activities
might end with cider and doughnuts and perhaps a singsong in
front of a log fireplace at the home of one of the participants.

In the spring, even before the annual ice breakup occurred and
logs began to move down the Mississippi to the Ottawa River,

"sugaring-off" occurred in the Ontario maple groves. Jim was a useful worker there. Then came the fun—the sugar-making in home kitchens. The making of maple sugar may have been a serious business for the farmer and his wife—one of the most important of domestic manufactures in pioneer days—but it provided a merry time for Jim and his young friends.[13]

For Ontario boys a special sport came along when the countryside thawed out from its winter ice and snow. On spring nights they went out to spear fish on the flooded flat lands, using the light of a pine-knot jacklight to attract and dazzle their game. Employing a method of night fishing learned from the Indians, two boys would go out in a canoe, a lighted piece of pitch pine in the bow or on a platform nearby and their spears at the ready. The younger boys looked up to Jim as a hero when it came to skillful jacklight fishing.[14]

In summer, of course, there was swimming. Jim, who was a powerful swimmer, used to lead a gang of nine boys over the old rail fence, across Anderson's pasture, and through the woods to their favorite swimming spot in the Indian River. They dived, they swam, they stood naked on floating logs, balancing with the skill of lumberjacks.[15]

Playtime was often mixed with serious aspects of living. On summer camping trips the boys of Ramsay Township learned woodcraft and the rough art of survival that nineteenth-century Canadians had to know. They learned to paddle a canoe Indian-style through the rough waters of many a creek and river. They learned to run their boats through the rapids of turbulent streams as well as to manage the arduous portages between navigable passages. These youngsters never forgot that the first settlers in their neighborhood used to travel to Montreal for supplies by means of canoe on the Ottawa River, one man sometimes making the laborious trip alone.[16] There was really no chance to forget, for life around Bennie's Corners and Almonte was still an adventurous, pioneer sort of life in the 1870s and 1880s. These Canadian boys lived in a land not yet civilized enough that Nature had lost all its sinister meaning, and they were, besides, the children of hardy Scotsmen distrustful of softness of body or spirit. Jim, for one, never lost his skill with that typical mode of Canadian transportation—a canoe—even when he had moved on to distant places later.[17]

In all outdoor activities Jim was a leader. He was one of the strongest and most skillful boys in the neighborhood.[18] And even more so with Jim than with the other boys, self-reliance became a way of life. Even in playtime Uncle Peter's stern influence hovered, like a dark driving force, behind Jim. When the other boys of the neighborhood went skating on the river, Jim at first watched from the bank, too proud to ask his uncle for money to buy a pair of ice skates. There was money enough, of course, from the property left by the Naismiths and the Youngs, but P. J. Young did not believe in letting coins jingle in the pockets of children.[19] To solve this dilemma Jim put together his own makeshift skates, sharpening and shaping a pair of old steel files on a grindstone, setting each one into a strip of hickory wood, and strapping them to his boots. He was soon skating on the thick ice of the river as gracefully as his comrades.

Uncle Peter could easily have made the skates himself as a lesson in thrift for Jim. The young bachelor was renowned locally as a clever man with his hands. He could turn out bob-sleds, for example, that far outlasted store-bought goods.[20] But he wanted Jim to learn to take care of himself and, if he needed something that was not available, to design it and make it.

Jim became a clever boy, all right, but at school his monthly report cards did not show the highest marks. In the years before his parents died, his father had signed the good report cards and his mother the poor ones—and there were only two with his father's signature.[21] He didn't always study as hard as he should have, and, too, some subjects seemed harder for him to master than others. He remained a little shaky in spelling all his life, to mention one weak spot. Sometimes he slipped so far as to omit the second "m" in "swimming," even though that sport was one of his favorites.[22] He was very good in penmanship, though, for Thomas B. Caswell, his teacher during some of those early years, said that his pupils would lay a good foundation for education if they learned to write well. The principal of Almonte High School, praising Mr. Caswell's many years of successful work at Bennie's Corners, said that he could always tell a student from Bennie's Corners by his handwriting.[23]

Mr. Caswell taught much more than readin', writin', and 'rithmetic, of course, for a fine education was given to Canadian children in the early days. He instructed the older ones in advanced mathematics, mensuration, Euclid, and Latin grammar.[24] Jim had his share of this learning, even though he did not always remember as much or recite as well as his teacher expected.

True, there was as much emphasis put on good behavior as on memorization of book assignments, and he managed, even when at his best, to break lots of the teacher's little rules. When he was eight years old, for example, and P. M. Monroe was teacher of the Almonte School at Bennie's Corners, a report card his father signed showed only slightly more credits than discredits in "good conduct" rating:[25]

James Naismith in the 3rd Division, is this day reported to be entitled to the following marks for the month of March, 1869:

Credit Marks		Discredit Marks	
Good Conduct	12	Misdemeanor	10
Perfect Recitation	30	Imperfect Recitation	23
	42		33

Annie was much better behaved than Jim, as older sisters are likely to be. Her report card for the same month showed eighteen marks for good conduct and only four for misdemeanors. She knew her lessons better than he did, too, the report showed.[26]

Jim had plenty of playmates. Those were the days when a classroom was crowded. In a one-room rural public school, like the one at Bennie's Corners, a schoolmaster sometimes taught sixty or more boys and girls, ranging from beginners in their first year to tall adolescents ready for high school.[27] Jim may not have been at the head of the class in academic subjects, but he was a leader among his peers in all physical activities, showing signs of becoming a fine athlete.[28]

Jim felt himself a little different from the other children, of course, for he lived in a strange household, with a taciturn young uncle as head of the house and a sister not much older than himself cooking and cleaning for the family.

There was another small item, too. Most of the other children had middle names, which they could write out on their slates in large flourishing letters; but he didn't have any.[29] However, his father used to tell him an exciting story about the origin of the family surname that made up for any lack of a middle name.

In the days of battle between the Scots and the English, the way his father told the tale, an outnumbered band of Scots had to take to their heels, with English soldiers in hot pursuit. One quick-witted Scots lad took refuge in a blacksmith shop. The smith, a loyal Scotsman, had time only to put an apron on the lad and a hammer in his hands and set him quickly to work at an anvil, before an English soldier entered the shop. Paying more attention to the Englishman's questioning of the smith than he did to the work in front of him, the Scottish lad broke the handle of his hammer on the anvil.

"You're nae smith!" the Englishman shouted, leaping at him. Together the blacksmith and makeshift apprentice fought the soldier and saved their lives. Escaping safely, the young Scot assumed as his own the name thus given him, "Naesmith," and passed it on, in one spelling or another, to his descendants.[30]

Lots of boys with middle names didn't have a story to equal that one. It may not have agreed with scholarly explanations of the origin of his family name, but it was an exciting tale, anyway, and worth the telling.[31]

For a short while in 1876 Uncle Peter's little family grew. The minister at the two-year-old St. John's Presbyterian Church in Almonte, William McKenzie, suffered a heart attack while preaching his sermon one Sunday evening and died, leaving three children and a pregnant wife.[32] Out of affection for their deceased minister, the community immediately raised money to build a home for the widow when she had to leave the manse to make way for the incoming preacher.[33] While the new house was being constructed, however, temporary homes had to be found for the McKenzie family. Thus it was that nine-year-old Robert Tait McKenzie—who later became a noted sculptor—and his older brother, William, came to visit a while in the Young-Naismith household.[34] The old stone house with its pleasant garden and trees became a second home to the McKenzie boys, and Jim Naismith acquired a faithful admirer in Tait. To him, Jim was the hero of many of their boyish exploits.[35]

The McKenzies were of Scottish Highland descent, with a long tradition of scholarship, and Catherine Shiells McKenzie was a cultured woman, who had good books as part of the furnishings of her home.[36] The brief sojourn of the bookish McKenzie boys in P. J. Young's house was probably a wholesome influence on Jim Naismith—although in Jim's attitude toward education there were no immediate indications of such an effect.

Having completed his grade-school education at Bennie's Corners, Jim was now in high school, walking three miles each morning to the fine gray-stone building in Almonte, which had been completed in 1875.[37] But he didn't intend to stay in school long. In his second year he dropped out, in the autumn of his fifteenth birthday.[38]

In later years he explained, moralistically, that he had wanted to dissociate himself from the wild crowd with which he found himself bound up.[39] This explanation, however, was probably only part of the truth. Actually, Jim had never acted like a serious student.

In his mid-teens, he saw no particular purpose in acquiring more education than he already had. He'd had enough of school. Furthermore, he felt deeply his obligation to contribute to the support of himself, his brother, and his sister. Lumbering was a major occupation in Canada at that time. Besides, it had an appeal to many young Canadians who were looking for adventure along with the hard work they expected, and Jim was an adventurous boy.[40] During the next few winters, therefore, he worked in logging camps, and in the summers he stayed home to help with the farm work. His schoolbooks were replaced—permanently, his friends assumed—by hay, wheat, and lumber.[41]

Working in the woods alongside men, teen-aged Jim took on some of their rough habits. His inherently gentle nature became camouflaged by the working clothes and working manners of a lumberman. Mixture that they were of French, Indians, half-breeds, and Scots, Canadian lumberjacks had been known since early pioneer times as rough and immoral.[42] Under their influence Jim learned to swear and drink, and began to wear heavy boots nearly all the time. P. J. Young was known around Bennie's Corners as a dapper young man; but Jim acquired none of his uncle's interest in fashionable clothes. Grown too old now to creep into the grain bin to "talk to his mother," Jim was a stout and independent lad with a manly air. Only on Sunday, bowing his head in prayer with a face surprisingly sweet and reverent, did he resemble the boy of a few years before.[43]

There were more than a dozen flourishing saloons in Almonte, at that time a thriving mill town of several thousand people. One day Jim walked into one of these pubs and ordered whiskey. A man standing at the bar beside him, cap pulled low over his eyes, spoke to Jim without turning his head.

"Ye're Margaret Young's son, aren't ye?"

"Aye," Jim replied, reaching for his drink.

"She'd turn over in her grave to see ye."

Jim Naismith set the glass of whiskey down before it reached his lips. He got up and walked out of the saloon, never to return. That night he went back to the grain bin. He did not crouch in the dusty grain and weep. He did not whisper little broken sentences in the darkness, as he once had done. But he made a silent vow to his mother that night that she would never again need to be ashamed of him.[44]

After five years away from school, Jim took a thoughtful look at himself and his future and decided to go back to the school he had left in his fifteenth year. He knew that he needed an education in order to do anything worthwhile in life.[45] He promised protesting Uncle Peter that he would still be a productive member of the family, taking care of all the farm chores before and after school hours. In 1881, at the age of nearly twenty, he started again at the beginning of the second year of high-school study.[46]

Almonte High School at that time had school colors of blue and gold, eight teachers, and a remarkable young principal, Peter Campbell McGregor. The return of a "dropout" to high-school classes would be eased, Jim knew, by the presence of Headmaster McGregor. That wonderful Scottish dominie, lame from an accident in his youth, came to be a legend around Almonte during the many years that he taught school in the community and the twenty-six years that he served as high-school principal. He provided private tutoring during his lunch hour and outside-of-hours classes for pupils who needed extra help. Late into the nights he worked with boys who asked for his time. Because of his efforts Almonte High School moved into the front rank of Canadian provincial schools. More striking, an impressive number of his graduates went on to get a university education and to make themselves known in the world as doctors, lawyers, clergymen, and scientists.[47]

P. C. McGregor and his twenty-year-old student agreed that Jim should aim toward university enrollment. Inspired by the headmaster's special interest in him, Jim worked zealously. Under McGregor's guidance, he did much independent study in Latin and Greek.[48] To his gratification, he completed his high-school courses in two years. Next he passed the Latin and Greek examinations required for university entrance.[49] He was on his way toward taking his place on McGregor's list of distinguished graduates.

It was 1883, and Jim, a brand-new high-school graduate, was nearly twenty-two years of age, when he informed his uncle that he was going to the university. Uncle Peter was opposed to higher education mainly for reasons of expense.[50] Jim's work on the farm and in the woods was good reason for wishing to keep the young man at home. But Jim, now a grown man, was in his own way as strong-willed as the uncle who was by so few years his senior. When Jim thought he was right, his mind could not be changed.[51] At last a compromise pleasing to everyone was reached. Peter Young told his nephew and foster son to go ahead, so long as he returned home summers to work—but only if he came out of college a Presbyterian minister.[52]

Jim had always been a devout boy, and after his early teenage experimentation with bad habits, he had become a moral-enough person to satisfy anyone. And the ministry was a profession that had already taken its place in the Young family. His Uncle Stephen, brother of Margaret and P. J. Young, was a minister.[53] Besides, and most significant, Jim wanted to do work that was useful to mankind. Becoming a minister seemed a fair course for him to take, and McGill University was a good place to undertake his preparation.

James McGill had established McGill University at Montreal, along British lines, for Canadian students of superior ability. By the time Jim Naismith was ready for university enrollment, it had become a national institution. In 1882, when he was making his plans, he found that it had two affiliated colleges in the arts and four in theology and had under its management the Provincial Protestant Normal School. It had faculties of medicine, the arts, and law and applied science.[54] As early as 1855 its Faculty of Medicine, modeled after that of Edinburgh, was recognized as the best in America.[55] In the 1880s, as now, McGill was a vigorous and respected university, the "Harvard of the North."[56]

These facts meant that he would be going into the academic big time. Maybe the thought of the venture frightened him a little, but he went ahead. He obtained a scholarship from McGill University, and in the fall of 1883 he left the farm for Montreal.[57]

Athlete and Scholar at McGill

AT McGill University Jim Naismith was a country boy in a big city for the first time in his life. But, despite the university's national reputation, most of the McGill students *were* country boys. The school's term was, in fact, a short one—seven months— to allow its scholars time to help with seasonal farm work at home.[1] This schedule happily met Uncle Peter's need for Jim at home in spring and summer.

Pushing farm work out of his mind, Jim looked around at his new world. The campus was a wonderful sight. The university buildings appeared to grow right out of Mount Royal itself, the elevation at the edge of the rocky Laurentian Shield from which the French city of Montreal took its name. In 1824, five years before the college was formally opened, its first principal was, appropriately, a man named Mountain, a melancholy minister who later became the Anglican bishop of Quebec.[2]

Jim moved into a room in the Presbyterian College, largest of the several residential colleges on campus, and became a student in the Faculty of Arts of the university.[3] He quietly withdrew with his books, not because he felt out of place but because he had come to the university to learn. Enrolling in the honors classics course, and with a fellowship in hand, he studied as he had never studied before. Although he had always been athletically inclined, he made the difficult decision to eschew sports and spend all his time with academic assignments. Now that he had a course of study aimed toward a career, he was determined to make up for the time he had lost. Four years at college for a bachelor's degree and then the course at theological seminary were little enough time for the learning he needed.[4]

The university itself, although a nonsectarian institution by its charter, nurtured religion. For one thing, there were four theological colleges affiliated with it. For another thing, William Dawson, Bible-reading bachelor and geologist, was principal from 1855 until three years after Naismith left Montreal. Although Dawson was on his first leave of absence in 1883, Jim would soon see in action "the man who made McGill." Dawson tried hard to prevent nonsectarian McGill from becoming merely secular. He had established a tradition of having all the classes come in turn to evening gatherings at his residence, in the course of which he would give a little talk on the Bible and science.[5]

Under the influence of McGill's intellectual and spiritual attributes and the thought of Annie and Peter, proud of him at home, Jim Naismith planned his routine conscientiously. He would study hard. He would quietly watch Mount Royal change through the seasons—reddish brown in fall to brownish white in winter and green in spring—and still he would be poring over his books. When summer came he would be one academic year the wiser and one year closer to enrollment in the seminary. And then, after he became a minister, he told himself, he would be able to do some good in the world.[6]

But the initial fire of scholastic ardor cooled within a short while. Two fellow students helped in the cooling process, convincing Jim, without much difficulty, that he should take part in school athletics.[7] Over the years several stories have outlined the manner in which two juniors persuaded the freshman to modify his scholastic schedule, stories only slightly exaggerated from the incident described in Naismith's own autobiographical reminiscences.

According to Naismith's narrative, when Jim McFarland and Donald Dewar found him bowed over textbooks in his dormitory room one evening, they must have stood before him like the "before and after" illustrations of a body-building course. One young man was a big, healthy specimen of muscles. The other was small and weak in appearance. Both boys urged Jim to join in the athletic program at the university for the sake of his health.

The small chap, from his own experience, warned Jim of the distressing effects that a bookworm's life might bring. "Believe me, Naismith, what McFarland says is true. I wouldn't listen to the fellows either, and you see the results."[8]

Although Jim, tanned and sturdy, was a living ad for physical culture himself, he listened and took stock of the situation. He determined to heed the warning before his shoulders were stooped from leaning over books and his studious frown of concentration had become permanent. He decided to take part in physical activities at the school.

The first thing he did after making his new decision was to head for the gymnasium. Gymnasiums were centers of activity in Canada at that time, gymnastics having enjoyed a continuing popularity from the time of Canadian Confederation in 1867. Besides, McGill University had a widely publicized center for indoor physical education.[9]

The gymnasium at McGill University was a story-and-a-half red-brick building at 19 University Street, unassuming in appearance, with an instructor so renowned that students applauded when he entered the hall. A lover of flowers, horses, and sports, Frederick S. Barnjum was an artist and gymnastics enthusiast who had migrated from England in 1859. Settling in Montreal, he turned from paint and easel as his daily tools to barbell and trapeze, making his name a household word in the field of Canadian physical education. He was influential in the construction of a gymnasium for high-school and university students at McGill, and later, after he came there as a university instructor, he caused McGill to be one of the first colleges in America to recognize physical education as part of the curriculum. His set of gymnastic exercises was adopted in Y.M.C.A.s and athletic associations in Canada and the United States, as well as in physical education departments of schools in Canada and New York.

The McGill gymnasium was well known in Montreal, for the little five-foot-six-inch Barnjum was a natural showman. In his well equipped gym he organized teams of skillful gymnasts and held an annual exhibition, in which a breath-taking ladder pyramid was the main event. Notable citizens in Montreal attended his exhibitions and even dropped in to watch rehearsals, held in the gym after the evening class was over.[10]

At the time that Jim Naismith came to the gymnasium, Barnjum, wearing velvet knickerbockers and black stockings, was a colorful and forceful leader. With bars and clubs and dumbbells, trapezes and rings, bridge-ladder and ladder pyramid, he inspired students so thoroughly that after class hours they practiced handsprings and flip-flops on mattresses in their bedrooms. Here Jim found a new niche in university life, into which he fitted as if it had been made for him. He began to spend a lot of time on the floor of the gymnasium, a large hall with a row of iron pillars down the center, and in the fencing gallery above the main hall. At first he could only watch with awe as an advanced gymnastic team swarmed up fourteen-foot ladders to practice on the pyramid. In the beginning he admired from a distance as Barnjum's best students showed off the insignia of their elite gymnastic club, the "Guards." But soon he was part of it all. He liked Barnjum and his work, and he proved an apt pupil. Before long, it was hard to outdo Jim in the gymnasium. By his junior year he was winning the university's highest honors for his athletic accomplishments.

Thus Jim Naismith began participating in the McGill athletic program, starting in the gymnasium. Outdoor team games followed in due course, and from a certain vantage point it began to look as if he were deserting scholarship for athletics.

Organized athletics were not yet strongly developed at McGill University, but they were faring better there than at most places in Canada. Jim was drawn to all sports going, being particularly intrigued by rugby football, McGill's strong point in team athletics. A combination of English Rugby Union football ("rugger") and association football ("soccer"), Canadian rugby football, like American football, was a hybrid form of rugby. Played under the rules of the Canadian Rugby Football Union, it was gaining interest in Canada at the time Jim came to the university.[11]

And in the fall of 1884, his second year at McGill University, came the Cinderella-like chance that no young athlete could turn down.

One day as he stood, dressed in street clothes, watching a strenuous rugby practice, the center in the group of forwards suffered a broken nose. There was no substitute available among the regulars; and when Sack Elder, one of the two team captains, called for someone to take the injured man's place, Jim threw off his coat and volunteered, even though it was the very first time that he had played.[12] So well did he perform that, after completion of that practice, Sack asked him to play center forward the following Saturday against Queen's University.

That wasn't all. A few days later came the game against Toronto University, an annual contest described as being "for years the greatest event in the College sporting calendar."[13] And in that famous competition Jim Naismith played so successfully that his name was mentioned in postgame newspaper accounts. The McGill University *Gazette* set down the main facts but didn't mention the extent of his inexperience: "A new scrimmage man, Naismith, very ably replaced Matthewson, whose nose had been put off the straight at a previous practice."[14]

That was the beginning. After his first romp on a playing field, Jim began an eight-year love affair with rugby football. From 1884 to 1891—his last three years at McGill University, three years at Montreal's Presbyterian College, and then two years at the International Y.M.C.A. Training School in Springfield, Massachusetts— he never missed playing in a game.

Rugby varsity football, as it happened, was the principal organized sport available to him in Canada during the 1880s. As the *Toronto Globe* explained the situation, "Football is about the only game open to the colleges in this country, for the reason that during the long vacation, when the other games are in season, the students are dispersed, and any effort at continuous practice would be impossible."[15]

Plenty of money, time, and effort were involved in Jim's football career. In rugby football the players supplied their own equipment. The uniform, simpler than today's, of course, did not include helmet, shoulder pads, and knee protectors. But the outfit was, nevertheless, an item of considerable expense to students with little money. The usual costume consisted of a sleeveless front-buttoned jacket over a long-sleeved jersey, knee pants to match, McGill stockings (heavy wool stockings woven in red and white stripes), and heavy boots, with or without bars on the soles. Later a laced-up canvas jacket was adopted as part of the uniform.[16] Not only was the outfitting of a player a do-it-yourself project but practice required an early-to-rise program. The McGill team practiced before breakfast, going out to the playing field on Sherbrooke Street at six or six-thirty, often in severely cold weather.[17] That schedule meant self-discipline, and Jim had what it took.

Rugby football in the nineteenth century was not like the polished football game of today. The fifteen-man line-up in a rugby game of the mid-1880s usually consisted of one fullback, two halfbacks, two quarterbacks, and ten forwards or (scrimmages), but there were other combinations. For example, there might be one fullback, three halfbacks, three quarterbacks, and eight forwards. Jim Naismith, as center scrimmage, was one of the group of forwards. There was no coach; at practice sessions two leaders simply selected their respective teams in the manner of small boys choosing up sides, and then they practiced, without using rehearsed plays, careful formations, and signals. Those were the days when the signal for center scrimmage to snap the ball to the quarterback behind him was a pinch on the leg.[18] A touchdown was called a "try" and counted one point; a field goal counted three points.[19] Little running, no forward passing, and little passing of any other type were utilized, and no linesmen were used to help keep the game orderly.[20]

Facilities for spectators were as haphazard as were the conditions of rugby practice. No stadium and no bleacher seats were provided. Viewers, moving about to obtain a good vantage point, combined the tiptoe expectancy of parade-watchers and the friendly intimacy of a theater-in-the-round audience. Sometimes they even got in the way of the players. Women were included among the followers of rugby football. They attended games, with escorts, both at home and out of town, but their presence was still unusual enough to draw comment. Reporting on a game in which Naismith participated in 1887, one reviewer pointedly wrote: "The lawn was crowded with the friends of the college, a large proportion of whom were ladies."[21]

The ladies, to be sure, didn't have to worry about nasty fits of temper being displayed in front of them by the players. Rules and techniques may not have been so refined as today's, but opponents, nonetheless, were friendlier toward one another. At a game between McGill and its keenest rival, Toronto, played during Naismith's second season on the field, it was typical that "the greatest good feeling existed during the entire game."[22]

Jim Naismith found that rugby was an important game not only among universities in the two provinces of Quebec and Ontario but also in the community of Montreal. The Montreal Football Club used to come out before breakfast to practice with the McGill team, at a charge of one dollar a head for use of the university playing field. In 1885, however, university officials decreed that the sod was being ruined from overuse in the practice sessions of city football and baseball teams. After that the McGill team stopped the prebreakfast sessions with the "towners" but continued to hold rugby football matches on campus with the city team. The public was invited to attend these matches without an admission charge, and men and women seemed to enjoy the spectacles thoroughly. Enthusiastic spectators crowded onto the playing field and sometimes had to be pushed back before a game could continue.[23]

As far as competitors went, Jim was pleased to observe, McGill University had had a variety of rugby rivals in its time. It used to compete regularly against Harvard University, the two teams playing the first intercollegiate rugby football game in the United States in 1875.[24] But play was hampered when differences between changing Canadian and American rules became too great. The two universities even differed on the shape of the ball to be used, McGill playing with a melon-shaped ball and Harvard a round one. Finally in 1881, two years before Naismith came to Montreal, the two rivals broke off their rugby relationship, and McGill concentrated on Canadian opponents.[25]

Games were played with numerous Canadian universities and colleges, and McGill "issued challenges in every direction," matches sometimes being arranged only one day ahead of time. The only regularly scheduled game, however, was the annual contest between McGill University and the University of Toronto, begun in 1881 and played alternately in Toronto and Montreal.[26] On a Saturday morning in November the McGill team would travel by Canadian Pacific Railway to its destination in Toronto, where it would be met at the station by members of Toronto's Varsity Blues. The game, usually beginning at two-thirty or three in the afternoon on the university playing lawn, would be well attended by fans from Toronto and Montreal. Enthusiastic gentlemen and ladies from Montreal often accompanied the McGill boys on their journey. After the game the visiting team would be entertained at dinner, with the captain of the host team at the head of the table, the two sets of opponents singing songs and drinking toasts in an aura of good fellowship. The Rossin House at Toronto University was a favorite place for these dinners. The merrymakers had to stop early, though, in time for the McGill group to take the eight-o'clock evening train back to Montreal.

Such an affair as the McGill-Toronto rugby match was not to be treated casually, and it never was. To give it the respect it deserved, each annual game was preceded by a formally worded invitation, to which a formal acceptance was sent.[27]

Encounters with Toronto and other universities were not always gala affairs in sunny, bracing autumn weather. Rugby football games were often won or lost under conditions that tried an athlete's spirit. Running plays in mud, of course, is something that a football player can expect to do occasionally, and Jim Naismith had his share of it. One Saturday afternoon in 1885, for example, he was among the fifteen McGill men who lost a game to Toronto in drizzling rain and sticky mud. "Their pretty costumes of white jackets and knickerbockers with red and white striped stockings . . . were . . . clean for the first three minutes and then they were the colour of the clay loam that lies under the grass of the College lawn."[28]

More extreme than scrimmaging in a drizzle, however, is playing rugby in a snowstorm, and such an event occurred more than once during Jim's college years. In November of 1886, when he was in his third year of intercollegiate athletics, the weather was particularly unfavorable, and college rugby teams began to disband early in the month. But on November 5 McGill telegraphed Queen's College that its team would arrive in Kingston the next day for a game, "rain or shine." The decision proved unwise, inasmuch as the "rain" turned out to be a blizzard. For hardy spectators who came out to watch hardy rugby players, "the sight of footballers struggling in the snow bank was almost absurd."[29] By half time neither side had scored, and only after the teams had changed goals at half time did the McGill players manage to take advantage of the direction of the storm. With the assistance of a strong wind, they "gradually forced the ball towards their opponents' goal" and scored handsomely, winning ten to nothing.[30]

The big game of the season wasn't called off that year because of weather, either, even if it should have been. The rugby football contest between the McGill and Toronto universities was carried out "in a frightful snowstorm." The ground had four or five inches of snow on it, and, to put it mildly, "the match was played under great difficulties" and, different from usual, with few spectators.[31]

Sometimes the snow got so deep in Canada, though, that a rugby game had to be canceled. That November of 1886, at any rate, it was true. When the time came for Naismith and his red-and-white-stockinged teammates to travel to Ottawa, they did not board the train, and a terse item in the newspapers explained why they failed to show up: "The football match between McGill College and Ottawa City, which was to have been played here to-day, has been declared off on account of the snowfall."[32]

Through these vivid years of school colors and toasts and songs, predawn practices and games in mud and blizzard, Jim Naismith proved to be not only a great rugby center but also an outstanding all-around athlete.[33] On his football jersey he wore proudly the coat of arms of McGill University—three small black stars on a red-and-white shield, with the Latin motto *In Domino Confido*— and took part in all the current university athletics. In addition to intercollegiate rugby, he participated notably in soccer. Mc-Gill University played both intramural soccer matches ("Arts vs. Medicine") and games against city teams ("Town vs. Gown"). Lacrosse, a game he particularly liked, had, like baseball, never been popular at the university, though. To play lacrosse he joined a championship city team, the Montreal Shamrocks, in his senior year. But he liked all athletics. He said that his favorite sports at this time were gymnastics, wrestling, lacrosse, and foot-ball—and these four sports covered a wide range of skills.[34]

Legends grew about his strength and agility, off the playing field and on. Favorite tales concerned his skill in the woodlot or in the grainfields back in Ontario. It was said that after a hard sixteen-hour day in the field he would come in and chin himself with one hand from the beam in the hay loft.[35] Better yet was the story that he could cut a swath of wheat with a cradle, bind it into a sheaf, toss it into the air, and, stooping, cut and bind another before the first one hit the ground. Although he was a modest young man, it did not take Jim Naismith long to make a stir in McGill athletic circles.

Back at Bennie's Corners, affairs were not going so happily as they were at McGill University. Uncle Peter, now passing his mid-thirties, remained a hard taskmaster to the niece and nephew at home. Annie, weighed down by household responsibilities, seemed destined to be an old maid.[36] But it was Robbie who gave Jim his deepest heartache. Jim could be grateful only that he happened to be at home for the Christmas holidays that night when his young brother, then eighteen, fell ill.[37]

The men at the Young farmstead had been working hard in the woods that holiday season. P. J. Young was a lumber contractor with an astute sense for business; he owned options on numerous woodlots, hiring many workers to cut the wood when it was ready to be sold to the mills in Almonte.[38] At that time he had a crew of men working for him, including two of his nephews—Robbie Naismith and Robert Young, son of P. J.'s brother William. On New Year's Eve, 1884, the cousins, eight years apart in age, went

to bed together almost as early as usual, for they knew that Uncle
Peter would not change the five-o'clock hour of arising, winter or
summer, New Year's Day or not. But they didn't sleep much.
Robbie had a stomach ache all night, and when the pain was the
fiercest he kept the other young man awake, too.[39]

When morning came, everyone in the household knew that
Robbie was in great pain. And it was Jim to whom Robbie
turned with a strange and terrible request. During a moment
when Uncle Peter, Annie, and Robert were out of the room and
Jim and his brother were alone, Robbie spoke words that would
haunt Jim, he admitted many years later, for the rest of his life.
"You wouldn't see a rabbit suffer like this and not kill it," he
cried out, clutching from the bed for Jim's hand. "Why don't
you kill me?"[40]

Jim turned away without speaking. But Annie, who had nursed
the family through their little illnesses, knew the home remedy
for stomach ache. Not realizing what the consequences could be,
she gave Robbie a dose of salts. He died within the hour, of a
ruptured appendix.[41]

His only brother gone, Jim returned to Montreal that January
of 1885 and went on about his education.

In the fall of 1885 R. Tait McKenzie, after completing his
schooling at Almonte High School and at the Collegiate Institute
in Ottawa, came to enroll at McGill[42] and became Jim's roommate.[43] It was as if a part of Jim's own family had come to the
city campus. The Young farmhouse had, after all, been like a
second home to Tait, and Tait had tagged after Jim like a wor-
shipful younger brother.

Jim still seemed to Tait like an older brother; and for Jim,
Tait replaced in some measure the younger brother he had lost.
But, with Jim only two years ahead of Tait in college study, they
were more nearly equals now than they had formerly been. A fine
companionship developed between them. Both loyal Scotsmen,
together they joined the Fifth Royal Scots, the regiment later to
distinguish itself on Flanders battlefields in 1916 as the Thirteenth
Royal Canadian Highlanders. Each in red coat and kilt, Jim and
Tait were proud to swagger a bit about the campus, sporty-looking
young fellows, on the day or evening of the weekly march-out.[44]

Usually the leader in dormitory escapades, Jim sometimes led Tait into mischief. When study hours grew oppressive in the west wing, Jim was the one who led "raids" on other dorm inhabitants. More than once he was called before administrative authorities to explain and apologize.

The emphasis put on physical culture by Jim and his classmates was justified by Tait's experiences. During his college years young McKenzie underwent an amazing physical metamorphosis, which was encouraged by an enthusiastic Jim. Tait, physically underdeveloped and delicate when he entered college, set out to strengthen his body systematically through gymnastics. And he succeeded amazingly well.[45]

After Tait began to show an interest in athletics at McGill as keen as Jim's, and a skill almost as great, their friendship arrived at an even more satisfying level than before. Much of their free time togther was spent in the Barnjum gymnasium at 19 University Street. Three evenings a week they stayed after physical education classes to work on gymnastic stunts. Practicing diligently on handsprings, back somersaults, and front somersaults, they became proficient in the simpler forms of tumbling. They stole time from study hours to make surreptitious visits to a local vaudeville theater, where acrobatic stunts were usually included on the program.

They soon worked up an acrobatic "brother act," with Jim, the heavier person, as understander and the lightweight Tait as top man. Their act became a feature at the annual university exhibition, and once, when they went home on Christmas vacation, they performed with startling backstage results, as well as onstage success, as part of the High School Concert program in the Almonte Town Hall. Their performance customarily ended in a Catherine wheel, in which the partners, holding each other's ankles, rolled across the stage together in a series of dives. Accustomed to making their exit in six revolutions across a fairly large stage, they rolled across the small Almonte stage and into the wings, bursting through the door of the girls' dressing room before they, or anyone else, realized what was happening.

The college years passed, filled with stunts and books and athletics. In every sport in which Jim participated, he played the way he knew the game was meant to be played—hard, without holding back. Quick and resourceful, he was canny at outwitting his opponents, but he never stinted on physical energy to let mere cleverness substitute. Tait sometimes saw him so exhausted after a rugby game that he could hardly hold up his head. And he performed as well in individual sports as he did in team games. In 1886, for instance, he outwalked everyone else, winning a silver cup in the one-mile walking championship. His strong point in individual sports, however, was gymnastics. R. J. Wickstead, Esq., M.A., LL.D., in 1882 had set up an annual award of one hundred dollars in medals and prizes for the champion gymnasts at McGill University, giving a bronze medal to a second-year student, a silver medal to a third-year student, and a gold medal to a student in the graduating class.[46] Jim won his share of those trophies. In his junior year at McGill he won the Wickstead Silver Medal for the Junior All-Around Gymnastic Championship, and the peak of his undergraduate athletic career came in 1887, when he won the coveted Gold Medal for the Senior All-Around Championship.[47]

Part of Jim's joy in athletics at McGill University consisted in watching Tait McKenzie's transformation from weakling to champion. So successful was Tait in the gymnasium that he became a member of Barnjum's famous ladder-pyramid team. By the end of Tait's second year he won the Wickstead Silver Medal for the Junior All-Around Gymnastic Championship, as Jim had done two years earlier. As a climax to his gymnastic career, still following in his friend Jim's footsteps, he won the Senior Gymnastic Championship in 1889. His interest extended to other sports, too. Before graduation he was playing on the varsity football team. He became an outstanding hurdler and high jumper, setting a record in the Canadian Intercollegiate High-Jump Championship that stood unbroken for years. He also became expert in boxing, swimming, and fencing.[48] Jim who had known Tait throughout his childhood at Almonte, watched his little playmate's surprising athletic career with delight.

Despite athletic activities, Jim had time for other extracurricular interests, including both student government and undergraduate clubs. Joining the Literary Society, he sang and debated and was mentioned in campus newspaper reports. In his senior year he did some solo work as vocalist in the Society, using the group's familiar repertoire of songs. "Naismith sang Song 88 aided by a chorus," reported one monthly issue of the McGill University *Gazette*. He enjoyed public speaking and was an effective debater. When the Literary Society presented the question "Is Capital Punishment a Justifiable Principle?" for example, he and a classmate named Hall argued on the affirmative side and won. That victory was typical of his performance. He did not give away his personal opinions in his public oratory: he could debate on either side and win.

Some persons who looked at Jim Naismith's impressive athletic record assumed that he had deserted scholarship. They were wrong. As conscientious with his scholastic assignments as he was vigorous in athletic contests and forceful in vocal groups and debate teams, he studied hard and became known—despite occasional dormitory pranks—as a fine student. At the completion of his second year he passed the sessional examinations, an accomplishment that indicated exemplary work. And he was achieving these results at a university where making good grades was acknowledged to be difficult.[49] As a reclaimed high-school dropout, Jim Naismith was setting up an amazing record.

Nor did he neglect preparation for his planned profession. During the summer of 1886, anticipating his work in theological seminary a year ahead and a ministerial career beyond that, he went westward into Manitoba to do three months of missionary work.[50] He returned to McGill in the autumn carrying a new gold pocket watch engraved:[51]

PRESENTED TO
JAMES NAISMITH
AS A TOKEN OF REGARD
FROM HIS FRIENDS IN THE MISSION
FIELD OF GRETNA, MANITOBA
AUG., 1886

In 1887, after four successful college years, he was cited on the Prize and Honor List for having passed for the Bachelor of Arts in Honors in philosophy and Hebrew, Second Rank, and was graduated as one of the top ten in his class.[52] On April 30, 1887, he received his B.A. degree, with a diploma signed by eleven professors and the registrar, and prepared for the next step in his education[53]

He had come a long way from a lumber camp in the north woods, and he planned to go even further. He still thought that the pulpit would be a good goal to aim for.

5

Great Decision at the Presbyterian College

FOUR theological schools—the Congregational College, the Presbyterian College, the Wesleyan College, and the Diocesan College— had been erected in the shadow of McGill University and had been granted affiliation by it.[1] After graduation from the university, Jim Naismith enrolled in the largest and second oldest of these, the Presbyterian College, which had been established in 1873. For living quarters he moved into the Presbyterian Seminary, a part of the college.[2] To finance his theological education, that autumn he accepted an appointment as instructor of physical education in the gymnasium at McGill and found himself with double, and sometimes conflicting, duties as he attempted to reconcile his commitments to religion and to athletics.[3]

As a theological student in the full three-year course of the college, Jim did his part, of course.[4] He not only studied hard but was active in extracurricular religious affairs. He was on the staff of the *Presbyterian College Journal,* the impressive monthly publication sponsored by the Philosophical and Literary Society of the college, a pioneer group in its introduction of theological-college journalism into Canada. With a wide range of subjects in articles contributed by faculty, students, and outsiders (including a French column for French readers), the journal "faithfully supported" Protestantism in Canada and "fearlessly criticized" the conduct of the Roman Catholic Church. (One article in an issue of 1887–1888 was written by a "converted priest from Italy.") During his first two years Jim served as one of the four business managers of the journal. He was active in the Philosophical and Literary Society, and in the Missionary Society. For the preceding several years the latter group had been supporting two native missionary helpers in the South Sea Islands, funds having been contributed by the students themselves, and was currently raising money to build a French mission school in the Montreal suburb of St. Jean Baptiste.[5]

Academically, he was consistently among the top students in the college. At the end of his first year at the seminary, a close runner-up to classmate W. L. Clay, he was awarded the fifty-dollar John Redpath scholarship for second place in his class. Undeniably, Jim Naismith was throwing himself enthusiastically into both altruistic and intellectual activities.[6]

But he was not a model theological student. Although he was brilliant enough to win theological scholarships and religiously dedicated enough to promote Presbyterianism in the South Sea Islands, French Quebec, and Canada in general, he dismayed colleagues and professors by continuing his activity in athletics, both in the gymnasium and outside it.

His fellow students could not forget that he had gone so far as to play with a professional lacrosse team, the well-known Montreal Shamrocks, who later, in 1894, would play the Ottawa Rough-Riders for the professional championship.[7] Naismith thought that lacrosse was the best of all games, but, all the same, it was rough.[8] Adopted as Canada's national game in the year of Confederation, 1867, lacrosse as it was played in Naismith's time was occasionally referred to as "legalized murder."[9] Illustrative of the violence of Shamrock games was "a most unfortunate row," reported by the *Montreal Gazette* in 1870, which involved both spectators and players! "Hinton struck at the Shamrock's lacrosse, and missing it, hit a couple of on-lookers. A row ensued, and poor Hinton was almost immediately struck on the head with a brick or stone, and very badly cut." The fracas became rowdy enough to cause cancellation of the game.[10] And this was the sort of recreation that one of the Presbyterian divinity students fancied!

Jim Naismith's rugby playing caused even more consternation than did his participation in lacrosse. As a divinity student he had given up the Shamrocks, but he seemed to have no intention of giving up rugby football, despite a shocking episode. One Saturday afternoon when Jim played in a hard-hitting game against Ottawa, he became badly bruised. The following morning, as student minister, he ascended into a Presbyterian pulpit with two black eyes,[11] and he still looked strange on Monday morning as he sat in the Reverend John Scrimger's class in Old Testament Literature and Exegesis.[12]

His theological classmates, observing his shiners and reminding him that rugby was the tool of the devil, prayed for his soul, and his professors warned him that ordination was not for such as he.[13] While the Reverend Donald Harvey MacVicar, the venerable white-bearded principal, publicly handed out awards for scholarship to him, Jim was privately advised to leave the evils of the athletic life to devote himself to books and Christian duties.[14]

But the crest on Naismith's football jersey held the motto *In Domino Confido,* and "trust in God" he continued to do.[15] He couldn't really see the theologians' point of view. The clean living of the dedicated athlete and the clean living of a religious man had become synonymous for him; and the longer he combined athletics and religion, the more strongly he sensed the advantages of the former in his way of life.

In the autumn of Naismith's second year at the seminary a young man named Amos Alonzo Stagg came up from Yale University and gave a talk at McGill. He said something that coincided with Naismith's own thinking. He stated that the same qualities were necessary for a good athlete and a good Christian—"namely—enthusiasm, perseverance, and hard work."[16]

But, most important of all in Jim Naismith's religion-versus-athletics conflict, in this second year of his theological study he received a promotion in his after-hours job that provided an opportunity to bring athletics into his life in a way that he had never done before.

Unfortunately, his new job and his new way of life came about through the loss of an influential mentor of his college years, Frederick S. Barnjum, founder and long-time director of the gymnasium on University Street. Although Barnjum, troubled by increasing deafness in recent years and sensitive about his ailment, showed occasional signs of irritability, he had continued as usual to direct the gymnasium. In the summer of 1889, however, as he was working in his garden, he sank down among the flowers and died, supposedly of an apoplectic stroke, before his wife could summon aid.[17]

After Mr. Barnjum's sudden death, his sister took over his physical education work among girls and young women under fifteen, for she had been assisting him capably with younger boys and girls. Jim Naismith, however, was asked to replace him as director of the gymnasium and instructor of male students, working three afternoons and three evenings a week.[18]

Now it would become Jim's duty to issue instructions to gym classes in a commanding voice, as Frederick Barnjum had done for so many years. It would become his privilege to climb the narrow flight of steps to the little four-foot platform that over-looked the McGill gymnasium like a watch tower. It would be-come his right to clang the gong during gymnastic exercises. It was not a job to be taken lightly, for Jim Naismith was replacing the leading physical education teacher in Canada. With some misgivings he accepted the unaccustomed responsibility, assuming his new position in the fall of 1889.[19]

Jim's promotion gave him an opportunity to appoint as his assistant in the gym his old comrade Tait McKenzie. In fact, before Jim had agreed to accept the position he had convinced Tait that he needed him, and his friend had agreed to help. Tait seemed a capable man for the job—and, besides, his personal and professional goals were compatible with Naismith's. He had fol-lowed in Jim's footsteps by combining outstanding athletic accom-plishment in undergraduate days with an interest in professional studies. Now, still interested in athletics and destined later to launch a world-renowned career in athletic sculpture, Tait had received his B.A. degree in 1889 and was enrolled in the first year of medical school at McGill.[20]

Together again in the gymnasium, the two friends were now the ones who must line up classes before the bridge ladder and urge the students on as they grasped rungs and sides and progressed by steps or jumps backward and forward. Jim and Tait were the ones who had to supervise the thrice-a-week barbell drills and the exercises with Indian clubs. They were the ones who had to urge young men toward perfection on the bars—the vaulting bar, the parallel bars, and the horizontal bar. They must do alone all the things that Jim had helped Frederick S. Barnjum do.[21]

Happily, they succeeded. They brought to their work as athletic directors the same zest that had prompted them in their undergraduate days to stay after hours to practice tumbling and to work up their flashy acrobatic act. Consequently, Jim and Tait found that they liked their new job,[22] and the students liked their new directors.[23]

At the same time, paradoxically, Jim continued to excel as a student of theology. At the end of his second year, again outdone only by the one student who had ranked above him the year before, Naismith received the fifty-dollar Peter Redpath scholarship for being second in his class.[24]

But through all his activities his position in the gymnasium became more and more important to him. It was the start of something big, the beginning of genuine accomplishment in the field of physical education. Whether or not he was at first aware of what was happening, his work there helped him change his mind about his career. And at last an incident occurred on the playing field that he would pinpoint as influential in his decision about his future.

During a rugged rugby game early in his senior year in theological school the guard on Jim's left used some angry profanity. Then, turning, he apologized, "I beg your pardon, Jim; I forgot you were there."[25]

These words, Naismith said, helped change the course of his life. From that remark he got the idea that he might help men better through athletics than in the ministry. Although for years afterward he was fond of recalling the episode, however, he was never quite specific as to its precise significance to him. In his book he wrote simply:

Great Decision at the Presbyterian College

This surprised me more than a little. I had never said a word about his profanity, and I could not understand why he should have apologized to me. Later, thinking the matter over, the only reason that I could give for the guard's action was that I played the game with all my might and yet held myself under control.

A few days later . . . I brought up the point that I thought that there might be other effective ways of doing good besides preaching.[26]

This much-quoted incident has received varying interpretations by writers or speakers who have related it. (1) The least likely explanation (and rarely offered): the rugby player used profanity because he had made an error resulting directly from the cold weather, that is, frozen ground, numb fingers, generally uncomfortable playing conditions. Naismith thereupon decided to devote his time to athletics in the hope of devising (as he later did) an indoor sport more pleasing to winter participants than rugby or football. (This theory does not fit in with Naismith's own reference to "personal influence": "It [the rugby incident] set me to thinking about the matter of personal influence, and I talked about it with the Y.M.C.A. secretary.")[27] (2) An incomplete explanation: Naismith realized how great a minister's influence is and how greatly a minister is needed to guide the conduct of athletes. (This theory does not explain why he should consider leaving the ministry.) (3) The most likely explanation: Naismith, who, as he admitted, had heard frequent and fluent profanity in lumber camps along the Ottawa River, saw clearly at that moment the advantage he possessed in knowing so intimately two contrasting worlds—the reverent world of a ministerial student and clergyman and the irreverent world of a rough working man. He recognized the deepened understanding and influence he could bring in formally crossing the boundary from the religious area back into the lay world—by *going* to men on the playing field on their own level of interest in athletics rather than *waiting* for them to come up to him in the pulpit.

Another incident happened that apparently furthered his desire to spread religious influence into sports. A football player nicknamed "Drunken" Donegan once taunted Jim for reading the Bible instead of going out with the other fellows. Although he

knocked Donegan down for using the epithet "sissy," Jim realized
that in influencing men toward upright ways a happy medium
between fisticuffs and pulpit preaching might be the most effective
device.[28] Besides, the attraction of athletics was strong for him,
and the field was one in which he was talented. Apparently he
began to believe that he had been pushed into a course of action
that was not the right one for him.[29]

Among the Presbyterian College faculty only his favorite professor seemed to understand Jim's point of view, but even he did
not approve of an abrupt change. "Naismith, I can't tell you
what you should do," the professor admitted. He advised only,
"Finish the course in theology."[30]

The Young Men's Christian Association, founded in London
nearly a half-century before, was at this time growing rapidly
in the United States and Canada, where North America's first
Y.M.C.A.s had been set up in Boston and Montreal in 1851.[31]
Interested in the varied athletic activities carried on by the
Y.M.C.A. in Montreal, Jim Naismith had often visited the gymnasium there and had become friendly with D. A. Budge, the
general secretary. In the early uncertainty of his decision to
change vocations, Jim told Budge that he was considering giving
up the ministry to work in athletics. He thought that a man who
could play a masterful, clean game and help others learn to play
it had an unequaled opportunity to gain the confidence of young
people, to teach them to become good citizens, and to help them
become worthwhile and happy human beings.

Budge had long been aware of the dual nature of Naismith's
activities at the college. He told the young man about a private,
nonsectarian school at Springfield, Massachusetts, for the education of laymen-leaders of organizations serving youth.[32] The Reverend David Allen Reed, who was leading a successful fight for an
unorthodox idea, wished to strengthen the work of theological
seminaries by training laymen to do Christian work in and outside
of church organizations. Under his leadership the School for
Christian Workers was founded in 1885, being incorporated on
January 28 of that year.[33] In 1890 the Y.M.C.A. established a
training program within the school.[34] The combination of religion and athletics proved so successful that the school was pre-

paring to become by official title the International Young Men's Christian Association Training School, and did so in 1891. In 1887 a department of physical training had been added to the school, with two instructors teaching a full-length academic year and summer courses of four to six weeks.[35] The school's two-year course of instruction carried a dual emphasis on spiritual development and physical development that Budge believed would appeal to a man like Naismith. Graduates from the training school could continue in Y.M.C.A. work, teach in schools or colleges, do church or settlement work, or serve in youth organizations.

At the Presbyterian College, James Naismith continued to be, on the school records at least, the right kind of student to have around. He was an associate editor of the *Presbyterian College Journal* and president of the Philosophical and Literary Society. As active as ever in the Missionary Society, he was its recording secretary. Academically, he was excellent. When eleven men completed the three-year theological course in April, 1890, he was still near the top. For the third year edged out for first place by classmate W. L. Clay, Jim was awarded the Calvin Silver Medal for ranking second in his class and received, in addition, the fifty-dollar Crescent Street scholarship. And, summit of his theological studies, on April 18, 1890, he was licensed, thereby becoming eligible to accept a call to a pastorate.[36]

But long before graduation Jim had decided exactly what he was going to do. Taking the advice of Y.M.C.A. secretary Budge, he would go to Springfield for enrollment in the Training School. He made that decision known to distressed classmates and professors at the Presbyterian College and braced himself for a storm of recrimination.

It took courage—and Tait McKenzie, for one, could detect the conflict and uncertainty in his friend—for Jim to leave the honorable profession of the ministry for the relatively unknown and somewhat disreputable field of athletics.[37] True, there were many organized sports going on in Canada at that time—lacrosse, ice hockey, rugger, soccer, rugby football, baseball, cricket, curling, track and field features were all popular—but for a young minister to turn to physical education as a profession seemed to most persons to be a rash step.[38] To some his decision was shocking, and they told him so.

When Jim announced his new plans to P. J. Young and Annie Naismith, his decision was irrevocable, and the two were keenly disappointed. Sister Annie was particularly hurt.[39] Jim had known that his sister disapproved of his playing lacrosse and rugby. He had known that she believed, with his devout friends at the Presbyterian College, that all sports were the devil's doings. But her opposition had usually remained unspoken. Now, however, when she learned that her brother intended to relinquish his career as Presbyterian minister to devote his life to the mischief of athletics, she spoke out bitterly, saying, "You put your hand to the plough and then turned back."[40]

He went stubbornly on with his new course of action. Bearing the Calvin medal and the Crescent Street award for theological scholarship, he left the Presbyterian College an unordained minister, with classmates and faculty praying for his soul for the last time.[41]

Part of the summer of 1890 he spent at Brantford, Ontario, where he introduced himself into Y.M.C.A. work and also did some preaching "to keep his hand in." He traveled across the border, too, to take a good look at the Y.M.C.A.s in the eastern part of the United States. He spent a few days at the Y.M.C.A. school in Springfield, where he met Luther Halsey Gulick, Jr., head of the physical education department. Gulick did his part to convince Naismith of the importance of the work of a physical director.[42]

The rest of the summer Jim used for a farewell visit to Bennie's Corners and Almonte.[43] Then in mid-September he packed clothes and books, bought a ticket on the Vermont Central Railroad,[44] and traveled to Springfield, Massachusetts, to enroll in the college known as the School for Christian Workers, or, soon thereafter, the International Y.M.C.A. Training School. The Presbyterian ministry had been left behind.

To the relatives and colleagues who thought that Naismith had chosen the primrose path to hell, he explained his actions: "I felt that if the devil was making use of athletics to lead young men to evil, there must be some natural attraction in sports that could be used to lead young men to a good end."[45]

6

Gymnasts South of the Canadian Border

IN September, 1890, James Naismith arrived in the historic mill town of Springfield. He was to find the focus of his activity for the next few years in a downtown building in Winchester Square, at the northeast corner of State and Sherman streets. It was a building erected in 1885 to house the Armory Hill Young Men's Christian Association and the School for Christian Workers, to be known later as the International Y.M.C.A. Training School.[1] In the sixth year of its existence and with an enrollment of fewer than forty students,[2] this school, with its motto of "A sound mind in a sound body," was to become James Naismith's true alma mater. Here was being fostered the idea strong in Thomas Hughes's *Tom Brown's School Days*—that the playing field is the place to build character. Naismith would become one of the men to go out to spread that idea.[3]

In the "Examination for Admission to the Young Men's Christian Association Training School, Springfield, Massachusetts" he answered five questions each in the fields of arithmetic, grammar, and geography. He successfully made up a bill, wrote a sample letter of application, and—even though he was better in the geography of Canada than that of the United States—described the water route from St. Louis to St. Petersburg. Passing the admittance exam, he became a part of Springfield's thriving center of "muscular Christianity."[4]

One of the first students he met upon his arrival at the "Y" school was a short, stocky young American named Amos Alonzo Stagg, formerly a student at Yale's theological school, where he had been star pitcher on the Yale baseball team and star right end on the famed Yale football team of 1888, called the Eli Juggernaut. He was the same Stagg who had compared athletics and Christianity in an address at McGill University two years before. The two young fellows, Stagg and Naismith, who were enrolled for the same purpose at the Y.M.C.A. Training School in that autumn of 1890, understood each other from the start.[5] ("Stagg grasped my hand with a grip that he was accustomed to use on a baseball, and I retaliated with a grasp that I had learned in wrestling.")[6] Jim knew that Lonnie Stagg, like himself, had recently turned away from the ministry for athletics. Stagg, who had decided that because of a tendency to stutter he would never be able to speak effectively enough to be a successful preacher, explained, "I felt specially called to preach, but I decided to do it on the football field."[7] Thus Naismith was reinforced in his own shift from church to gymnasium.

And as Naismith worked with the new superintendent of physical education, Dr. Luther Halsey Gulick, Jr., a son of missionary parents in Hawaii and himself a doctor of medicine, he must have been reassured that he had chosen the right school. Tall, red-headed Luther Gulick, who had been appointed director of the School for Christian Workers in 1887 and had received his degree in medicine from New York University two years later, was a well-educated, intelligent, and enthusiastic young man with progressive ideas, well on his way toward gaining professional status for physical education. He and his assistant, Robert J. Roberts, at first constituted the complete physical education staff of the college, conducting together its first summer school of "Special Training for Gymnasium Instructors" in 1887 and the first academic year of the Gymnasium Department in 1887–1888.[8] They presented, however, two opposing attitudes toward education. Whereas Roberts was slow and methodical, Gulick was quick in action and thought, imaginative and experimental, a teacher who could inspire his followers. As one of his former students commented, "Dr. Gulick was never satisfied with following systems but was always exploring the possibilities of something better."[9] David Allen Reed, founder of the school and president of the board of trustees, recognized his director's creative spirit and, until his retirement from the board in 1892, championed Gulick's liberal ideas.[10]

The three of them—Gulick, Stagg, and Naismith—were all in

their twenties, with Superintendent Gulick, at twenty-five, the youngest. Representing the fields of ministry and medicine, they joined together that autumn of 1890 in the common bond of athletics, each of them to go on to his particular niche of national renown: Gulick to be listed in later decades as a "Pioneer in Modern Physical Training," Stagg as the "Dean of American Football," and Naismith as the "Father of Basketball."[11]

Jim Naismith learned from both of the others, Gulick and Stagg.

In its academic departments the school gave instructions in a variety of subjects—anatomy, physiology, hygiene, physical diagnosis, and elementary physics, as well as the philosophy of exercise, the interrelations of body and mind, and the "control of diseased conditions without medicine"—but there was more than formal course work waiting for Jim here. Luther Halsey Gulick, Jr., interested in the relation of good bodies to good morals, in the relation of bodily training to mental training, taught him a lot by the sheer force of his zestful personality. Jim became imbued with Gulick's idea of "working for *young men,* not simply for their bodies, minds and souls, but for the salvation, development and training of the whole man complete as God made him." Gulick uttered this creed publicly as early as 1891 in an address before a convention of Christian Association workers in Kansas City, but he had put it into practice long before then.[12] He originated the inverted triangle as the symbol of the Body-Mind-Spirit ideal; and in 1891, at his own expense, he founded a Y.M.C.A. school paper, with the name of the *Triangle.*[13] Naismith would be able to say of Gulick half a century after those days in Springfield: "He was one of the few men whose teachings have remained with me and have been a help not only in my profession but in my life as well."[14]

With Amos Alonzo Stagg, Jim found Gulick's principles put vigorously into practice. Although Stagg, leaving the seminary at Yale, had given up a theological profession in favor of athletics, at the same time he had rejected offers of such lucrative positions as pitcher with the New York Giants. He made it clear that he wished to devote himself to a more idealistic cause than professional athletics.[15] And he carried out his ideals in word and deed.

Certain though Jim Naismith was of the propriety of his decision to leave the ministry, there may at first have been troublesome moments for him. When he learned that Gulick was introducing football into the sports system of the school that fall, Jim
must have thought uneasily of his sister Annie, who would be
more certain than ever that he was caught in the devil's clutches.
Perhaps he felt guilty as he got out his rugby uniform for daily
practice on the grounds overlooking Watershops Pond. But when
Stagg was selected to be football coach of the group of "husky
little chaps" Gulick had gathered, Jim's conscience could lighten,
for Lonnie gathered the team together for prayer before each
game. And though Stagg never prayed for victory, the results
he obtained showed that high principles and successful athletics
were not incompatible.

With this first team that he had ever handled, A. A. Stagg
early showed the talent that would make him nationally famous
as a football coach. Taking a group of faculty and students, a half
dozen of whom had never played football at all, he created a team
that scored creditably against schools with enrollments and repu-
tations dwarfing those of the Y.M.C.A. school. The weight of
their opponents also dwarfed Stagg's players. The Springfield
team, which averaged less than one hundred sixty pounds, played
with aplomb against the heavyweights of Harvard, Yale, Amherst,
Williams, Wesleyan, Trinity, and other powerful universities.[16]
After the Springfield boys nearly defeated mighty Yale in a historic
first indoor football game in old Madison Square Garden in the
fall of 1890, they were given the nickname "Stagg's Stubby
Christians."[17]

In the big Madison Square arena, cold as a barn that December
night, the two football teams put on a show that made up for the
tedium of a walking race, a two-mile bicycle run, and a variety
of field games, all crammed into a two-day meet. The football
game was even more entertaining than the lacrosse match that
was played on the same program. The fact that the outweighed
Springfield group used some unorthodox tactics helped to amaze
their opponents and delight the spectators. "Stagg's men rather
dumfounded the Yale men with a novel wedge, which differed
from the ordinary wedge in the way that the players interlocked

their arms and legs. Through this device they managed to force their way twenty-five yards toward their opponents' goal."[18] That game was one in which Naismith and Stagg, as usual, cooperated to build up a score for the "Y." "When it [Yale] lost the ball in the scrimmage, Naismith grabbed it, and, having a clear field, made a clean run to touchdown. Stagg kicked a goal."[19] And they felt the prouder for that touchdown and conversion because Yale Consolidated was using such noted players that season as Pudge Heffelfinger and Harry Williams.[20] For a while, they were exhilarated to see, the score was tied at ten points each, before Yale went ahead to win 16 to 10.[21]

Naismith at center in that autumn of 1890 and Stagg as captain and fullback as well as coach provided the main power of a team that played without substitutes.[22] Naismith played the whole period of every game for two seasons, against men outweighing him from twenty to fifty pounds. As classmate Raymond Kaighn phrased it, Jim was "160-odd pounds of concentrated T.N.T." Broad-shouldered and stocky, with an aggressive jaw and bristling mustache, he looked formidable, and in a football match he was indeed, playing a strong and clever game. Like Stagg an advocate of the strenuous life, he liked the rough-and-tumble of physical contact. But he played fair. There was a gallant sporting spirit in the man, and there were no questionable tactics in his methods.[23]

Early in the career of the Springfield football team Naismith questioned Stagg's placement of him in the line-up. "Lonnie, why do you use me at center?"

Stagg answered, "Jim, I play you at center because you can do the meanest things in the most gentlemanly manner."[24]

Center continued to be Naismith's position. He played full-back for the first time only after Lonnie had left for Chicago in 1892 and Jim had replaced him as captain of the football team as well as football teacher.

Off the football field as well as on, Jim enjoyed the companion-ship of his classmates. There were Canadians as well as Americans in the crowd, for he was not the only young man who had crossed the border to come to the International Y.M.C.A. Training School. Many an exciting discussion went on in the evening among his group, on subjects ranging from religion to women, from hockey to politics. The more people in an argument, whether on his side or not, the better he liked it. He never minded disagreement with his views. He was ardently pro-British and often argued with his American friends about the merits of their Revolutionary heroes. Not easily upset himself, he delighted in stirring his opponents to anger, and chuckled while they ranted at his points of debate. He might have made a good lawyer, some people said.

Jim had lodgings upstairs at the "Y,"[25] sharing a room with Max J. Exner.[26] To complete his living arrangements, he found a place to board close to the school, on Westminster Street, in the home of a widow named Mrs. Sherman. Her late husband, Edwin F. Sherman, had been employed till his death at the nearby Springfield Arsenal. He was a part-time inventor, devising such things as a reaper, a harrow, and a bell punch. He had left to his wife eleven children and a handful of unperfected inventions, with the rights to his masterpiece, a grain harvester, long since sold to the McCormick Harvesting Company. After he had died, his wife did what she could to protect her deceased husband's rights. Carolyn Miner Sherman well understood the pitfalls of the world outside her home, for she came from a family of doctors, master mechanics, and scientists, and her own brother was an inventor. In a businesslike manner, as executrix of the estate, she had taken out a patent on his harrow on January 15, 1889, but she never made any money on the invention.[27]

At the time Edwin Sherman was fatally stricken, two of the Sherman daughters were still living at home—Maude and Florence (or Mabel, as she was known by her family). Maude was working as a secretary in the office of a woman doctor on State Street, where she had been employed since she was about eighteen. Mr. and Mrs. Sherman had not wanted their daughters to work, but Dr. Sprague's office was not far from their home and the doctor was highly recommended. Maude's employment there, however, seemed to be accompanied by disasters for the Sherman family. When she took the cage containing the family's canaries, Molly and Dick, over to brighten the doctor's office, the birds died in a fire that broke out there. And when Mr. Sherman fell ill and Dr.

Sprague was summoned, it was too late for any doctor to save him; he died swiftly of a heart attack.[28]

Because the Shermans lived near the Y.M.C.A. Training School, Mrs. Sherman and Mabel began to board a few students or young teachers to help pay expenses. Jim Naismith was one of the boarders.[29]

He probably would have gotten on particularly well with Mr. Sherman, because Jim was something of an inventor himself. For instance, in the fall of 1891 he invented the first known football headgear. He had a cauliflower ear because of injuries in sports, and he had finally been forced to wear a broad strip of adhesive tape to hold his ears protectively close to his head while participating in football. This expedient was never entirely satisfactory, though, and he kept thinking about the problem. At last he devised a more elaborate headgear for protection. His first model was made of several layers of flannel, fastened under the chin, and a later one was of chamois skin. Despite laughter from the other players, Naismith wore this homemade bonnet, which looked very much like a nightcap with a chin strap.[30] Even this headpiece, improvement though it was over a piece of adhesive tape, was not enough. As someone pointed out, "His headgear didn't really protect the head, it just kept the ears from getting torn off."[31] Naismith's bonnet, however, was a forerunner of the more effective leather and, later, plastic football helmets. The *Dictionary of American Biography,* for one, gives credit to Naismith for designing this innovation in football equipment.[32]

Yes, Jim Naismith was clever at thinking up new things in the field of sports, and his cleverness was put to good use in the Young Men's Christian Association.

The Y.M.C.A. was growing fast—an organization whose officials would be in part responsible for the founding of the Boy Scouts of America, the Campfire Girls, the Police Athletic League, and the National Recreation Association—and the Training School at Springfield was expanding along with the "Y." In the second year of their two-year course, James Naismith and Alonzo Stagg were appointed to the enlarged teaching faculty. Assigned to teach psychology, Bible study, boxing, and one of the classes in physical education, Jim was plunged into one of the school's annoying issues, a problem more difficult than the need for football headgear with which he had been confronted.[33] This was the problem of sustaining interest in gymnasium activities.

Luther Halsey Gulick, Jr., born in Honolulu when his missionary father was serving there, had entered Y.M.C.A. work in the United States during the period of greatest expansion in the "Y." In 1887 there were only 50 physical directors, or superintendents, and 3 assistants in the 168 Y.M.C.A. gymnasiums in America. By 1900 there were 244 physical directors and 22 assistants in 491 gymnasiums. Gulick brought to the field of physical education an interest in the continued general expansion of facilities. Complementing this interest, he brought an understanding of the individual needs of participants and an awareness of the inadequacy of existing indoor physical education programs to meet those needs.[34]

Indoor physical education in the United States at that time consisted chiefly of calisthenics, gymnastics, and drills. To enlarge their programs, physical education teachers introduced German, Swedish, and French gymnastic methods and attempted to adapt them to American needs. Robert Jeffries Roberts, a five-foot-five-inch virtuoso in weight lifting and other feats of strength and endurance, had shown his muscles and his forty-three-inch chest in platform and field exhibitions before coming to the International Y.M.C.A. Training School as an instructor for two years (1887–1889). Here at the Springfield school he introduced body-building exercises based on German methods, utilizing both light and heavy apparatus. Combined with the influence of Roberts in Y.M.C.A. gyms was that of Baron Nils Posse. Posse had brought the Swedish system of educational gymnastics to the United States, and in the summers of 1890, 1891, and 1892 he conducted summer courses for teachers at the Martha's Vineyard Summer Institute. On behalf of the Y.M.C.A. Training School, Naismith went to Martha's Vineyard for a summer to study under Posse, bringing back to Springfield a recommendation for adaptations of this Swedish system. In addition to German and Swedish methods, many principles of the French gymnastic system were also adopted in the gym at Springfield.[35]

Notwithstanding gymnastic innovations—German, Swedish, and

French—a lack of interest in the formal winter physical education program persisted on the part of students. In the late 1870s and 1880s there began to be a high interest in outdoor intercollegiate sports, especially track and football, and participation in Y.M.C.A. programs featuring these games became enthusiastic. But between the close of the football season in the fall and the opening of the baseball and track seasons in the spring there was an empty spot that not even Santa Claus could fill.[36]

Gulick saw the danger of overemphasis on gymnastics—that is, on exercises that involved excessive routine, patience, and attention to detail. He wanted to bring recreative sports into the gymnasium.[37] He preferred, in other words, to cultivate the play instinct in physical training.[38] And even if he had not already been in favor of less drill and more fun, circumstances would have forced him to that way of thinking. By 1891 the need to revamp the indoor physical education program at the Springfield school became imperative. Bored with chinning the bar, and thinking wistfully about the bicycle clubs that would flourish in warm weather, students in gym classes were definitely losing interest in the type of work presented. The training in the Springfield Y.M.C.A. classes was for "Y" supervisory personnel in two different fields, physical education and secretarial work; and the future secretaries were the first of the enrollees to become bored, and articulately so, with the gymnasium routine.[39]

During the summer session of 1891 Gulick had introduced a new course in the psychology of play. In Naismith's third semester at Springfield he, Stagg, and a few other students enrolled in this seminar, for by the fall of 1891 the class was an established one in the curriculum. One of the questions discussed in the class was the need for a new indoor game, simple and interesting, that could be played under the artificial lighting of a winter gymnasium, when outdoor games were not in season. Gulick, using the approach that "there is nothing new under the sun," explained to his students the feasibility of devising a new activity by recombining elements from existent games. Naismith endorsed Gulick's suggestion heartily: "Doctor, if that is so, we can invent a new game." Gulick, outlining certain qualities desirable for such a new game, then assigned to the class the problem of inventing an indoor sport to meet the particular needs of the physical education classes at the Springfield Training School.[40]

A striking trouble spot for Luther Gulick in the autumn of 1891 was a class in the Secretarial Department of the Springfield Training School. This class consisted primarily of mature men, not boys, and the regimentation of an hour spent doing calisthenics, twirling Indian clubs, marching, and working on apparatus bored them to open antagonism. Even tumbling did not appeal. Two instructors in turn, first A. T. Halstead and then Robert A. Clark, both enrollees in Gulick's seminar, had instructed the gym class and had asked for relief.

At a faculty meeting Naismith was generous with suggestions for improving the gymnastic situation. Maybe he talked too much, thinking himself safe with his own full schedule of classes. If so, he wasn't as safe as he thought. Dr. Gulick turned to him in the meeting, stating ("like a bolt of lightning from a clear sky"), "Naismith, I want you to take that class and see what you can do with it." He then, in late November, handed the group over to the reluctant Naismith for a two-week period.[41]

Naismith made excuses to try to avoid the new assignment. He had been teaching boxing, wrestling, swimming, and canoeing; and he did not look forward to exchanging instruction in some of his favorite sports for the task of drilling the group that was beginning to be known as incorrigible. He particularly regretted giving up the canoeing and swimming lessons, for he was a canoeing enthusiast with a love for the water in any form. But Gulick would not be dissuaded, and Naismith grudgingly capitulated. "My fate was sealed," he said.[42] The extent of that fate no one could have guessed at the time.

After one thoughtful look at the new class, which included men as old or older than himself—ranging from twenty-six to thirty years of age—Naismith discontinued the regimented "busy work." In its place he introduced simple games involving maximum physical activity. But his attempt to appeal in this way to the "play instincts" of these men was a mistake. As he quickly admitted, a few minutes of grade-school games like three deep, prisoner's base, and long-ball proved more deadly than directed exercise on the parallel bars. He tried and abandoned sailors' tag,

English rounders, town ball, battle ball, and a modification, with medicine ball, of the child's outdoor game of handy-over, or ante-over. Leapfrog was also unsuccessful.[43]

The seminar in the psychology of play was, of course, directly related to Naismith's problem of the dissatisfied gym class. Gulick challenged his student by suggesting that now was the time to create the new game under discussion in class and to put it to practical use as part of the gym curriculum. He went so far as to outline fourteen requirements for such a game.

With his red-headed director's battle cries of "supple bodies," "team spirit," and "clean fun" nudging him on, Naismith accordingly began to use in the gymnasium some ideas that he had acquired in thinking-out that seminar assignment.[44]

His next step with the gym class was the simple adaptation of an adult outdoor sport for indoor use. He first used the game of cricket, but it proved unsuccessful, as did baseball. He then tried, in rapid succession, indoor modifications of football, soccer, and lacrosse.

In introducing football onto the indoor playing field, he adapted some of the elements of English rugby into the game. For example, the gentle tackling of rugby was substituted for the American all-out attack on the runner; the tackle was made above the hips, the object being merely to stop the run rather than to throw the runner. Gentle handling of a football opponent, however, turned indoor football into a subject of ridicule for the "incorrigibles."

When soccer, which was at that time known as "association football," was played by Naismith's men as an indoor game, they forgot in moments of excitement that they were wearing soft-soled shoes, and they kicked the ball as if they were playing outdoors in regulation uniform. The result was smashed toes and windows. "Instead of an indoor soccer game, we had a practical lesson in first aid," Naismith later commented ruefully.[45]

Lacrosse was the Canadian national game, adapted from the North American Indians' *baggataway*,[46] and Naismith had been proficient at it since boyhood and professional at it since playing with the Shamrocks in Montreal. It had long been one of his favorite team sports. Although he eventually rejected lacrosse as an undesirable part of any physical education program, at that time he considered it ideal in many respects. Adapting it to an indoor form, he introduced it hopefully into the Y.M.C.A. class. Unfortunately, seven members of his class were Canadians and already proficient lacrosse players. They utilized the tricks they had learned in actual lacrosse games, and their tactics proved rougher than anything that had heretofore appeared in the Springfield gym. More than a mere first-aid kit and a glazier were needed this time to repair the damage. Besides the injuries to the beginners, the disgust of the experts at the debacle showed Naismith that indoor lacrosse was the most unsatisfactory experiment he had thus far used to hold the interest of an already dissatisfied class.

The trial period with the recalcitrant gym class dragged on. It was not a time-consuming project, but the attitude of his students nagged at Naismith's conscience and nibbled at his self-esteem, so that he carried a mental load with him after school hours. At last, relieved that his frustrating efforts were nearing an end, and yet disheartened because he knew he had been a failure, he prepared to turn the class over to another instructor after the next day, that final day in the gym that would fulfill his two-week assignment. But, as he wearily climbed the narrow stairs to his office above the locker room after that next-to-last session, he felt his Scottish obstinacy stirring. He had neither completed his seminar project nor mastered a teaching assignment. Squaring his shoulders, he decided to do both before another twenty-four hours had passed.

He was going to give the "incorrigibles" a game to play that they wouldn't forget and that Dr. Gulick wouldn't, either.

7

Peach Baskets at Springfield

DREAMING up a new game for the next day's gym class took more than a pinch of Scottish obstinancy and a touch of bravado; it also took serious thought and planning. Fortunately, some background had already been laid.

Some time after Dr. Gulick had made the assignment, each member of the seminar in the psychology of play had presented suggestions for a new game. None of the schemes was worked out completely enough for adoption as a practicable game. From among the plans, however, Gulick had chosen Naismith's.[1] He helped his student by making up a tentative set of rules, with instructions that Jim work out the details and techniques more explicitly. Now the moment had come, Jim knew, when those details had to be completed.

From his experiments with the new games in his men's physical-training class, Naismith had reached two general conclusions: that a children's game cannot be successfully adapted to an adult situation ("Those boys simply would not come indoors to play 'drop the handkerchief!'" he acknowledged) and that any recognizable modification of a well-known adult game creates both confusion and hostility.[2] Through working with his students he had grown from an initial lack of sympathy with them to a feeling of compassion for these mature men who were rebelling against what they believed to be useless drill. And from his sessions with the class, from the seminar discussions under Gulick, and from private conferences with his teacher, he gradually came to certain generalizations on which to base a new game that would avoid the difficulties of many of his experiments.[3]

The two generalizations that Gulick and Naismith had arrived at were: (1) All team games utilize a ball as the essential item of competition; (2) the difficulty of the game is inversely related to the size of the ball—that is, small balls require intermediate equipment such as a stick or bat, which complicates the game, and large balls tend to simplify a game by serving as the direct object of competition.

Much later, in retrospect, it seemed that the basic principles of basketball and all its accompanying rules were created in one afternoon and night. Actually, it had been many weeks since Gulick had assigned to his class the problem of creating a new game, and several weeks had passed since Naismith had set forth his first tentative plan. Now, on this last day, he spent his spare time making diagrams, testing in his imagination the techniques he would transfer to a playing court. He tried to foresee and forestall the problems that might arise when he put his brainchild into the fumbling hands of a completely inexperienced group of players. As Gulick had predicted, most of the elements of the game turned out to be disguised adaptations from several sports; but it would be a new game to the two teams to whom he presented it, unrecognizable as football or any other sport, and he anticipated awkwardnesses in the playing of it.

Naismith held to Gulick's theory that a judicious combination of elements that made various existent games popular should produce an enjoyable new sport. His need for a game that was interesting, easy to learn, and easy to play caused him, despite his disastrous experiments in the gymnasium, to consider football as point of departure for a new game. Football, or American rugby, was the most interesting team game of the time for American men and a logical starting place for the invention of a new sport, but it had to be transformed beyond recognition—and he had not yet accomplished that transformation. Trouble spots existed. For one thing, he knew by now that because of limitations on space in an indoor playing field, running must be kept to a minimum; and because of a need to eliminate roughness on a wooden or other hard-surface floor, tackling of the man with the ball must be forbidden.

Now, in his little office above the locker room, running his fingers impatiently through his hair, Naismith suddenly recognized the relationship of these two requisites—nonrunning and nontackling—and he snapped his fingers in elation. "If he [the player] can't run with the ball, we don't have to tackle; and if we don't have to tackle, the roughness will be eliminated. I've got it!"[4]

Naismith with peach baskets of the type used in the first basketball game in 1891. Photograph by Duke D'Ambra, courtesy of Mrs. D'Ambra and the Athletic Department of the University of Kansas.

A single idea, then, which met the two requirements of non-running and nontackling, became the nucleus of the game: the player holding the ball must be in a stationary, not a running, position. One by one, in this way, certain stipulations that the sport had to meet were set up. Into these fundamental requirements Naismith fitted the rules of a new game.

On this last day before completion of his first two weeks with the problem gym class, it was time to put his daydreamed plans into practical operation. He must present his new game to the eighteen students in his class the next day and interest them in playing it. The drawback was that it was not ready. True, the techniques that he and Gulick had approved on paper seemed satisfactory. And Naismith's no-run–no-tackle scheme was the answer to the most serious problems inherent in the game. But one essential remained to be worked out. When Naismith attempted to devise a goal suited to this unrecognizable new derivative of football, he found that the paraphernalia of familiar games did not provide him with an acceptable solution. He considered the type of goal used in lacrosse. But it was vertical and made inevitable the rough throwing that he hoped to minimize.

At his desk he puzzled over this last important detail of the game. Suddenly he recalled Bennie's Corners and the old childhood game of duck on the rock that he had played with his youthful comrades through the Canadian summers and winters. Behind the blacksmith shop stood a large rock, about knee-high and a few feet long, on which a stone, or "duck," as large as a boy's two doubled fists would be placed by one of the boys as a target for the others' stones. If the duck was knocked off the boulder, the thrower had to run from the throwing base to retrieve his own stone and then run back to the base, twenty feet or more away, more quickly than the guard could pick up his target duck at the boulder and race to tag the boy. If the duck was not knocked off, the guard had only to catch the boy, without pausing to retrieve the target rock, although the thrower had to retrieve his missile. If tagged before reaching base, the thrower became "It," and the players resumed throwing at a new duck on the rock.

All the young lads would line up, each with his duck in hand,

and try to knock the duck off the boulder, each with his own throwing technique. The most successful players lobbed their stones, for one hurled sharply in a hard, straight line would travel too far to give the thrower time to retrieve it and escape safely to base. Thrown in an arc, the stone would fall down at the side of the boulder, within easier reach than a sharply thrown missile. In this game, accuracy of aim was more important than force.[5]

Jim probably remembered something else, too. He must have recalled how, on cold, wintry days in the old Barnjum gymnasium in Montreal, he had led two teams of McGill off-season rugby players in competitive throwing of a ball into an empty box or basket. They had set the receptable on the floor at the end of the gym. Unfortunately, members on the defensive team crowded around the goal, even climbing into it to sit, in order to keep the opposing side from making a point. With scoring made almost impossible by such tactics, the sport had not been successful.[6] But the memory of that abortive game must have helped him fit the pieces of his puzzle together.

Why Naismith did not write about the Barnjum experience in his book on basketball is conjectural. But—whether it was a box he used, as some sources state, or a pair of peach baskets, as another source states—he did, apparently, speak publicly about that ancestral game of basketball in Montreal. At least one citizen of Naismith's home town has declared his readiness to swear by affidavit that McGill University was the birthplace of basketball. He explains that Naismith in a banquet speech at Almonte in about the mid-1930s told citizens about the indoor area in Montreal where, as gym director, he organized a game with ball and baskets to occupy a group of young athletes during cold weather.[7]

Now, on this cold December day in his office above the Y.M.C.A. gymnasium, he straightened up, realizing that he had stumbled on the answer to the problem of the goal for his new game. It would be an elevated horizontal goal, rather than the vertical goal of lacrosse, placed a little above the players' heads for difficult defense, with the ball thrown in a slight arc to reach it. The position of a relatively small goal parallel to the playing surface would necessitate accuracy rather than force, thus helping to minimize roughness.[8] Although a score would be attained by throwing a ball into a receptacle, danger to the goalkeeper from a hard, direct throw or from a rush of players toward the goal would be obviated.

The diagrams of play he had been visualizing, the rules he had been formulating, fell into place. Basically, the new game borrowed the arrangement of players from the game of lacrosse, the movement of the ball between one player and another from rugby football, and the throwing of the ball at the goal from duck on the rock; and it would be played either with a rugby ball or a soccer ball. The rules would be built around four fundamental features: (1) no running with the ball, (2) no tackling or other rough body contact, (3) a horizontal goal above the players' heads, and (4) freedom of any player (while adhering to the no-contact requirements) to obtain the ball and score at any time.[9]

He hoped that he had all the answers now. He hoped that he had come up with a game that would satisfy all the conflicting needs he had recognized in his students—a game "vigorous enough to attract football men, simple enough so anyone could play it, difficult enough to challenge even the best . . . and yet safe enough to play indoors."[10] It was a big order.

In later years Jim Naismith would laugh when he read a Canadian reporter's highly imaginative version of the childhood-based inspiration for the creation of basketball. According to an article printed in the 1930s, young Jim was playing with the family cat when his mother called him to fill the woodbox. In "the first faultless free throw ever made," Jim threw the cat high in an arc to splash into an old cistern about ten feet away. His mother wailed, "What will such a wicked boy ever come to?" and his father, the account continued, eventually sent him to Springfield to the School for Christian Workers for an ethical education. There, according to the imaginative Canadian newspaperman, Jim, remembering his deadly accurate throw of the cat, tossed a volleyball into the top basket in a pile of peach baskets the janitor had left after raking up leaves on the campus lawn. And thus the game of basketball was born.[11]

But that night above the gymnasium—and long afterward—Jim

would have no time to think about cats and cisterns, existent or not. He had a new and untried game to worry about. And that night he played the game in his sleep.

It was mid-morning of the next day when he knew at last that his game was nearly ready. But there were still a few details to be arranged and a few items of equipment to be found—for instance, the essentials, a ball and two goals.

When he walked into his office he saw a football and a soccer ball lying on the floor. He picked up the latter and, the type of ball for his new game decided upon in that moment, started down to the gymnasium with it, ready now to construct goals for the forthcoming class experiment.

On the way to the gym Naismith found Mr. Stebbins, the janitor, or, as the boys sometimes formally entitled him, the superintendent of buildings. Naismith asked if he had two boxes about eighteen inches square. He probably had in mind the large wooden refuse containers used around the school, but almost anything would do. He knew that Stebbins stored boxes squirrel-fashion.

Mr. Stebbins reflected. "I have two old peach baskets down in the storeroom, if they will do you any good."[12]

When Stebbins brought them, Jim examined the peach baskets thoughtfully. They were round, about fifteen inches in diameter at the top, smaller than the usual peach basket of today. From fifteen inches they tapered to a somewhat lesser size at the bottom. He decided that they would serve his purpose.[13] Now all he had to do was construct a pair of goals out of these peach baskets. He also had to set down on paper a set of formal rules for his brainchild.

With the two baskets and a hammer and nails that he found, Jim went on downstairs to the gymnasium, where a balcony, used as a track for running or as an area for spectators, depending upon the occasion, extended around the sides of the room below. He tacked a basket to the lower rail of the balcony at each end of the gymnasium, about ten feet above the floor. Then he went back to his office.[14]

At his desk he sat down to condense his weeks of planning into a set of rules brief and simple enough that his class could grasp the fundamentals at once and play the game that morning. In less than an hour he wrote with pencil on a scratch pad what he considered the thirteen essential rules of the new game and handed the paper to Miss Lyons, the departmental secretary, to type. The fifty-five-minute gym class was scheduled for 11:30 A.M., and it was nearly that time. Miss Lyons shoved a sheet of paper into the typewriter and began to type the handwritten notes: "1. The ball may be thrown in any direction with one or both hands. . . ."[15]

It was almost class time when Miss Lyons finished typing the second page of rules. Taking the two sheets of paper from her, Jim Naismith went immediately to the gym and thumbtacked to a bulletin board inside the gym door the rules of a game as yet without a name.

As he turned away from the bulletin board, he noticed some of his students heading for their rooms to dress for the gym class. He saw Frank Mahan, a troublemaker from North Carolina, look impatiently at the peach baskets on the balcony of the gym and heard him comment derisively, "Huh! another new game!"[16]

Naismith's spirits sank. Mahan, a tackle on the football team and a ringleader of the gym class, had a psychological influence on his classmates proportionate to his physical strength, which was considerable. And he had rebelled against all the games played in the gym thus far. With pretended optimism, however, Naismith went ahead with his plan for the day. He stopped two of his students, Eugene S. Libby and T. Duncan Patton, the latter a guard on the football team and one of the leaders of the gym group, and asked them to serve as captains of two opposing teams in a game he planned to try out.[17]

The two men had been playing Naismith's games for nearly two weeks, and he was sure they felt by now that he could offer nothing better than had the two previous instructors. Nevertheless, they agreed to head two teams in a game about which they knew nothing.

After outlining the rules of the game and having the captains divide the class into two teams, Naismith chose a center from each team and threw up the ball between the two. He figured that a tossup of the ball between two teams as a method of starting the game would afford little chance for roughness. He admitted later, "I realize now how seriously I underestimated the ingenuity of the American boy."[18] But marred by fouls though it was to be, the historic game began.

The first basketball game in history was played at Springfield, Massachusetts, on a day in December, 1891—possibly December 21[19]—in a Y.M.C.A. gymnasium with a total floor space approximately forty-five feet wide and sixty-five feet long, and a playing field approximately thirty-five by fifty feet.[20] Lights set into the ceiling were dim. Boundary lines of the basketball court were imaginary ones, with Indian clubs, dumbbells, and all the other gymnastic apparatus shoved hastily out of the way against walls and into corners. The equipment was simple—a ball and a pair of peach baskets—with the playing uniform consisting of a pair of gym shoes and the gym uniform that each man was wearing when he walked into class. At that first basketball game the eighteen stalwarts of Naismith's teams, dressed in long gray trousers and short-sleeved jerseys, many of the men wearing a full beard or the walrus mustache then popular, provided a spectacle rare to see and never duplicated after Spalding's sports catalog began listing basketball uniforms in 1901. Indeed, although Naismith later put his exhibition nine into matching outfits of long gray trousers and long-sleeved black jerseys and posed them sedately for a historic photograph, during the first years of basketball any costume might be found on a basketball court. Outfits worn in the gymnasium, on the track, or on the football field were used. Only Spalding, listing a choice of knee-length padded pants, knee-length jersey tights, and short padded pants, did its best to put appropriate wear onto the basketball court.

But in December, 1891, the uniform was long trousers and short-sleeved jerseys—and everybody was too busy to care.

That day in the Springfield gymnasium there were nine players on each team—a goalkeeper, two guards (right and left), three center men (right center, left center, and center), two wings (right and left), and a home man, or goal thrower, stationed in this order from the goal. These nine players were equivalent, in modern terminology, to three guards, three centers, and three forwards. In each of the three general positions represented, any number of men might be placed, for Naismith, intending his game for the use of gym classes of varying sizes, left the number of players unrestricted in his planning. The baskets, because of their shape, sloped forward, and most of the shots were attempted from a crowded area directly in front of the goal, where much fouling occurred among the eighteen men. Although Naismith's rules called for both a referee and an umpire, he served as the sole official in this game, and probably found that more penalizing was necessary than one man could handle fairly.[21] Fouls, indeed, far outnumbered scores in this first trial game of basketball.

Furthermore, because the bottoms were left in the peach baskets, a scoring ball would remain in the basket, ten feet above the floor, until someone got it out. Naismith, undaunted, asked janitor Stebbins to get a stepladder and take care of that problem. Stebbins was on hand with his ladder, therefore, to recapture the one ball that tumbled into a peach basket, effectively aimed by William R. Chase from near mid-court for the single point of the day.[22]

Despite improvisations and difficulties the new game was a success from the first moment. The most rebellious ones in the class immediately became devotees of the sport. At first they played a game without a name. After Christmas, though, Frank Mahan, an impatient Irishman from North Carolina, gallantly offered the name "Naismith ball" for the new creation. Laughingly Naismith fended off Mahan's suggestion, telling him that a name like that would kill any game.

"Why not call it basketball?" Mahan then volunteered.

And Naismith acquiesced.[23]

Thus basketball was christened, soon after its birth, with no one realizing how well known that name would become. Naismith and his players on that winter day in Springfield could not have guessed that the peach-basket game would evolve into one of the most popular and exciting of international sports. They did not know that the basketball shots fired that morning would be "heard around the world." Nor did those Y.M.C.A. students realize that their discontent with a gym class had been a contributing cause to the creation of a famous game.

But one of the players had a hunch that something great had

happened. Mahan, the first to scoff and the first to praise, impulsively stole the basketball rules off the bulletin board after the first game and hid the souvenir in his trunk. A greater compliment that he paid to inventor and game was the return to James Naismith, weeks later, of those sheets of paper. And in February Naismith, apparently convinced that this was an important document, belatedly put his signature on it.

Neither Naismith nor Mahan could know, though, that some day both the British Museum and the Smithsonian Institution would request possession of the original copy of the thirteen rules of basketball.[24] But, as events turned out, Britain could rightly feel proud of her Canadian-born subject, while the United States could be gratified that he chose to become an adopted son.

8

Who's Gone Crazy?

Honolulu-born physician-educator Luther Gulick decided that the Y.M.C.A. should have a new game, and the Canadian minister-athlete James Naismith made up the rules for it. A helpful New England janitor named Stebbins provided the two goals, and an impetuous Irish-American from North Carolina, Frank Mahan, gave the game a name. And eighteen Y.M.C.A. gymnasts, no longer bored, began to play basketball.

News spread at the International Young Men's Christian Association Training School that something new was going on in James Naismith's physical education group, along with a rumor that students were actually having fun in gym class. After Christmas vacation was over, the balcony began to fill with spectators about eleven-thirty in the morning. They had come to watch the new game of basketball that Naismith had invented. At first the gallery held only students from the Training School itself, but soon outsiders were dropping in, for passers-by were many and access to the room was easy. The gym was located in the basement of the building, and a door from the balcony of the gym led directly onto the sidewalk on State Street. Women teachers from the Buckingham Grade School nearby, stopping to watch the last part of a game, sometimes became so interested that they missed lunch. Within two weeks a large audience—as many as two hundred persons—assembled in the Y.M.C.A. gym gallery at noon each day.[1]

The spread of basketball beyond Springfield was rapid. Students going home for Christmas vacation carried the details of the game with them and started basketball in their local Y.M.C.A.s. And going home for Christmas meant the scattering of the student body all over the United States and into Canada. Among the players taking part in that first basketball tryout, to give an example of the geographical spread of "Y" enrollees, Eugene S. Libby represented Redlands, California, Frank Mahan came from North Carolina, and T. Duncan Patton was a resident of Ottawa and Montreal.[2]

On January 15, 1892, in the first edition of the school paper after the creation of basketball, the *Triangle* printed Naismith's instructions and the thirteen formal rules under the headline "A New Game." The *Triangle* was distributed to Y.M.C.A.s throughout the United States, and with this issue the phenomenal dissemination of the game began. Because the Y.M.C.A. was one of the few organizations in the United States that was intensely interested in the physical development of boys and men, most local "Y"s included a gymnasium as part of their regular facilities. When the Y.M.C.A. adopted basketball on a nationwide basis, therefore, it became the agency primarily responsible for the extensive and rapid spread of the game.

From the eighteen members of his class present in the historic first basketball scrimmage Naismith soon organized a team of nine, led by Frank Mahan as captain, for competing against outside teams and for traveling as an exhibition group through a few eastern states. The team accompanied the "Flying Circus," a group of Y.M.C.A. students who put on athletic performances. This group of nine is usually recognized as the first basketball team in history.

Basketball caught on in small towns and in big cities. In April, 1892, it was introduced into New York at the opening of the

Athletic Grounds of the Y.M.C.A. The *New York Times* welcomed it as "A New Game of Ball," offering a subtitled explanation "A Substitute for Football without Its Rough Features." A detailed description of playing field and procedure was given for the benefit of persons as yet unfamiliar with the unusual aspects of the new pastime. Basketball was undoubtedly the only game in the country, for one thing, whose main equipment was a ball, a pair of baskets, and a ladder.

The game is played with an ordinary association football, and the object of each team is to get the ball into its opponent's goal. The field is 150 feet long by about 60 feet wide, and at each end is a post with a basket on top just large enough to conveniently hold the ball. The top of the basket is about nine feet above the ground, and a ladder is necessary to take the ball out after a goal has been made. . . . The time for a match is about forty minutes, played in "halves" of fifteen minutes each, with a rest of five or ten minutes between.[3]

Basketball was probably the only game, too, in which a player stood rooted in his tracks when he had the ball and acted as eager to get rid of it as if it were a hot potato in his hands.

When a player gets the ball he is not allowed to run with it, but must stand and pass it to some other member of his own team within fifteen seconds after he touches it.[4]

Despite a few unusual aspects, basketball was easy to learn. In early games, to bridge the leap from familiar sports to a new game, basketball was sometimes referred to as "basket football" or "football in the gym." A half-period in a basketball game was familiarly identified as an "inning" and a goal as a "touchdown." Further mixing baseball and football terms with the language of the new game, a home man or a wing man, whose job was throwing goals, might be called a "pitcher" or "thrower," and a goalkeeper or a guard might be referred to as a "back."

The Y.M.C.A. of New York, which introduced basketball to the public when it was little more than three months old, continued to promote the game. In 1893 one of the largest "Y"s in the city could state: "Basket ball is the great strong point in the Washington Heights Branch . . . it would seem as though every man is enthusiastic over the game."[5] In the next season, 1894, basketball was played "with more energy than ever before." In fact, imitating the popular bowling leagues of the time, New York and Brooklyn organized basketball leagues in order to play for the championship of the two cities.[6] Championship teams from New York City and its vicinity also played for state honors in basketball.[7]

Lonnie Stagg, away on a two-week trip to the Midwest at the time basketball was born, returned to Springfield shortly afterward. He became so enthusiastic about the new sport that he made some historic stereoptican slides of the original baskets and began playing himself.[8] In March he took part in one of the most famous basketball games in history.

The Central and Armory Hill branches of the "Y" played games on February 12 and March 15, but the big public match was an intramural basketball game at the International Y.M.C.A. Training School on March 11, 1892. Seven instructors—Naismith, Gulick, Stagg, and four others—and seven secretaries (students) played what was said to be the first public basketball game in the college gym at 4:15 P.M. "Lanky, whiskered Dr. Gulick" and "burly, walrus-mustached Naismith," three or four inches shorter than Gulick, were noteworthy performers. But the most conspicuous figure on the floor, according to an account in the *Springfield Republican* of March 12, was Stagg—"resplendent in his old Yale uniform." Stagg's football training hampered him, however; he was constantly charged with fouls because of shoving his opponents, and in return for bruises inflicted, he acquired a black eye. But he scored the only goal for his team, at a time when each goal counted one point, and saved his colleagues from complete disgrace. The students won the game five to one. Pleased though he was by the score, Naismith admitted that he was annoyed by Stagg's roughhouse tactics. He complained, "I wish Lonnie could have made that point without fouling everybody."[9]

According to Naismith himself, this Springfield game and one at the University of Kansas in 1898 made up the only two times that he ever played basketball. "Just didn't get around to playing,"[10] he explained offhandedly. When he did play, he transgressed his own rules by committing an inordinate number of fouls, perhaps because of his background of wrestling, boxing, and football. He seems to have used the same tactics that he criticized in Stagg and intended to keep out of his new indoor game altogether. "Once I even used a grapevine wrestling clamp on a man who was too big for me to handle," he admitted ruefully.[11]

The women of Springfield, tired of being restricted to badminton, cycling, and, sometimes, tennis, yearned to share the men's fun. After Christmas the group of teachers from the Buckingham Grade School that had been dropping in at noon to watch the gym class practice approached Naismith to ask his opinion as to the suitability of the game for girls. Because of his encouragement and his offer of the use of the gym, these teachers organized the first girls' basketball team. To his chagrin they came to practice in high-heeled shoes and long, trailing dresses with leg-of-mutton sleeves, some young women with a hint of a bustle on their derrières and, without doubt, corsets underneath. Despite impediments, however, they played the game enthusiastically; and soon, in more suitable attire, they were playing acceptably, some of them even skillfully.

True, there were undesirable aspects to female basketball competition. Occasionally when he called a foul on a girl, she responded with notably poor grace. But, then, certain ministers whom he had refereed in basketball had done so, too. Naismith came to the rather startling conclusion that women and preachers displayed the poorest sportsmanship of any basketball players he had observed. He excused their weakness by explaining that neither the female sex nor the clergy had had a chance to play games often enough to develop a sporting attitude.

Naismith welcomed women as spectators at basketball games, though, calling their presence a wholesome influence. In contrast, men were not always permitted to watch a female basketball game. When the freshman girls played against the sophomore girls at Smith College in early basketball history, no men spectators were allowed because the girls wore bloomers. As if that touch of femininity were not enough, the Smith girls tied green and lavender bows on the goals and sang "Long, Long Ago" as a pep song. And in another part of the country, female basketeers provided men with even more amusement than did those at Smith College. During a girls' basketball game in Denver, newspaper writers snickered. As one reported afterward, "The ball flew about in a most astounding way," at one point bouncing off the head of a venerable bishop in the audience.[12]

Of course, the 'general status of women's basketball was soon upgraded. For one thing, a change in uniform helped. Bloomers were manufactured that didn't look like bloomers, so that no girl needed to feel immodest playing basketball in front of a man. The woman's basketball guide of 1908 describes the uniform of the well-dressed female basketball player: "The bloomers have the appearance of 'kilt' style skirts, no dividing line being visible." The problem of the dividing line, at least, was thereby taken care of. In addition, long worsted stockings and a modish Peter Pan blouse or, later, a middy blouse with three-quarter-length sleeves helped to make the girls feel decorous. And even before that notable change in uniform, in 1899 the first national basketball rules for women were formulated, to be published in the Basketball Guide in 1901 under the editorship of Miss Senda Berenson.[13] Women were at that moment officially welcomed to the basketball court, as they probably never would be to the gridiron, the ring, and the diamond.

The game proved a natural with everyone. It was a love affair at first sight between basketball and the public. Before basketball was one year old, in October, 1892, Dr. Gulick wrote in the Training School notes: "It is doubtful whether a gymnastic game has ever spread so rapidly over the continent as has 'basket ball.' It is played from New York to San Francisco and from Maine to Texas by hundreds of teams in associations, athletic clubs and schools."[14] A year after introduction of the sport, the Y.M.C.A. *Review* of Herkimer, New York, could ask, "Gone Crazy! Who?" and answer that *everyone* had gone crazy over basketball. "Ministers, lawyers, bankers, editors, merchants, clerks, mechanics, boys, young men, older men, yes, everybody plays basketball now."[15] A report came from Providence, Rhode Island, that "basketball fever is contagious"; and Salem, Oregon, sent word that "the game is all the rage" along the Pacific Coast.[16]

In college circles Yale University has been given credit for organizing the first regular college teams, arranging games in 1896 with Trinity, Wesleyan, and the University of Pennsylvania. In the Middle West the University of Minnesota and the University of Iowa are said by some to have established basketball teams in the closing years of the nineteenth century.[17] Even earlier than these competitions, however—on January 18, 1896—a game planned by Springfield graduates A. A. Stagg and H. F. Kallenberg was played at Iowa City between the University of Chicago and a Y.M.C.A. team sponsored by the State University of Iowa. Some basketball experts list this game as a college contest, because the Y.M.C.A. team sponsored by Iowa State was made up of students from that university. It is said, furthermore, that this was the first collegiate game played with only five men on each team.

Throughout the United States and Canada, and in foreign countries as well, basketball made its appearance and settled down for a permanent stay. As is pointed out in *Annals of American Sport,*

the fact that it was developed within an organization having contacts throughout the world gave it an impetus which carried it far. The members of the first organized team at Springfield became missionaries for the new game in the Mississippi Valley, on the Pacific Coast, and, beyond the Pacific, in China and Japan.[18]

The spread of the game into foreign countries began soon after its origin. The Y.M.C.A. Training School at Springfield was an international one, with students from all over the world. After these foreign men finished their education at Springfield, Naismith observed, they sooner or later returned to their homes; and many American students, too, went abroad to carry on Y.M.C.A. work. They all took with them the game of basketball.[19] He liked to point out that in less than two years basketball had been introduced into more than a dozen foreign countries by Y.M.C.A. men trained at Springfield.[20] Duncan Patton, for example, one of the two captains in the first basketball practice, went to India in 1894.[21]

Some writers, however, refuse to believe that the "Y" did much more than build up the game after it had been carried around the world by other groups. Alexander M. Weyand, for one, minimizes the role of Y.M.C.A. members in spreading basketball to foreign lands. He believes that with the exception of Canadian "Y" students, such influence was probably only local.

Whether the "Y" played the leading role in the international dissemination of basketball or not, other organizations helped. Military and naval forces, arranging games and tournaments both at home and abroad, were important agents in spreading basketball to foreign lands. American soldiers played basketball in China during the Boxer Rebellion in 1900 and in the Philippine Islands even earlier, during the Philippine insurrection.[22] In Canada, Europe, the Far East, the Middle East, South America, Alaska, and on islands in the Atlantic and the Pacific, someone or other soon learned the thirteen rules and assembled the ten, twenty, or hundred players who were interested enough to give the game a try.

The sites of basketball play were far-flung, and the modes of play were modified according to local conditions. The player's uniform might be a loin cloth, an Oriental robe, or a pair of well-tailored slacks. Goals were as varied as costumes. When the Sioux Indians played basketball in South Dakota in 1892, sixteen years after the Custer massacre, the goal posts were small saplings and the baskets were rings made of bent willow branches. The Reverend Ernest G. Hildner, one of the members of the first basketball group, recognized the universality of the game when he saw a crowd of boys in a little village in Mexico playing "dust bowl" basketball with an iron barrel hoop nailed to a tree and a dried gourd as a ball.[23]

Basketball indeed seemed to spread like a contagion. There was definite direction behind the apparently wildfire success of the game, however. Direction was provided by Dr. Luther Halsey Gulick, Jr., who had early recognized the potentialities of the game. He helped James Naismith develop the game, he worked on modification of the rules, and he publicized basketball nationally and internationally. Naismith sat in his office and smiled incredulously as the reports rolled in. He was too modest to admit what he had started. Gulick, however, realized what they, together, had accomplished. But, although Gulick was aware that he was largely responsible for the great success of the game, he never detracted from the honor of a student who had carried out his assignment, and he always made it clear that basketball was Naismith's creation.[24] He recognized as well as the other man did, perhaps, a truth that Naismith put into words many years later: Gulick was the man of vision, who could see the distant goal, but, impatient to go on to further goals, he left the working out of the tedious details to someone else. Naismith considered himself the plodder who had worked out those details.

Plodder or not, he had stirred up excitement aplenty with two peach baskets and a soccer ball.

9

Thirteen Rules and Nine Players

AFTER completion of his two-year course of study at the International Y.M.C.A. Training School in the spring of 1892, Naismith remained for three more years as a full-time teacher. For the first two years after he tacked up a list of thirteen rules and sent two teams of nine men each onto a basketball court he was sole arbiter of basketball rules, having vest-pocket editions of the regulations published annually. The first book, *Rules for Basket Ball,* was edited by him and printed in 1892 by the press of the Springfield Printing and Binding Company; but the job soon grew too large for one man. After the 1893 edition Luther Gulick suggested a clarification and expansion of the rules, and Naismith and Gulick collaborated on a revised edition, the *Official Guide,* published in January, 1894.[1]

Naismith left Springfield in 1895, and he did not attempt to carry with him any of the official responsibilities of the game that he had created. He confined himself thereafter to the hobby of collecting translations of the rules of basketball, eventually acquiring books in nearly fifty languages and dialects, and proudly recording the occurrences of new translations.[2] (A typical memorandum in the Naismith notebooks reads: " 'Y' instructor in Shanghai translated rules into Chinese, 1898.")

After Naismith's departure, Gulick became sole editor of the basketball rules—and that editorship was a weighty job. Control of the new game became almost more than the director of the Y.M.C.A. Training School could handle in his spare time. Gulick's predicament was mirrored in the frustration of other "Y" directors. Basketball was growing so popular that it threatened to monopolize the facilities of Y.M.C.A.s all over the country and to crowd traditional classes off the gymnasium floor and off the schedule. In a strange panic some Y.M.C.A. branches for a short time refused to allow a basketball in the gym, and in some cities, notably Philadelphia, many basketball teams were forced out of the "Y" and into dance halls or any other place large enough to accommodate a basketball game during off-hours. This brief flurry of reaction by a few Y.M.C.A. branches was stifled, of course, by the realization that interest in the "Y"'s new game had increased the membership of that institution as nothing else could have done. The Y.M.C.A. wisely chose to ride the tide of popularity that basketball had created and made a big thing of its famous game.

Gulick, foreseeing the magnitude of policing so irresistible a force, removed the management of basketball from the Y.M.C.A. and placed that responsibility in the hands of an impartial representative body. The Amateur Athletic Union of America was the organization that came to his aid, assuming control of amateur basketball in 1896. Soon other organizations joined in control of the game. In 1908 the National Collegiate Athletic Association assumed charge of college basketball rules, and in 1915 the N.C.A.A. and the A.A.U. formed the Joint Basketball Rules Committee. Basketball, originally a possession of the Y.M.C.A., was on its way to becoming, as it soon did, the property of the world.

The rules of basketball as originally set up were sound ones, providing a permanent backbone for the game. Modifications, extensions, and refinements were inevitable, however, in Naismith's hands, in Gulick's, and then in the more or less anonymous hands of various rules committees.

One of the first revisions to be made in Naismith's original instructions was in the number of players. As Naismith conceived the game, the number of players on a team was flexible, to be decided by calculating the size of the floor space or, more commonly, by dividing any group of prospective players into two teams. Any number from three to forty he considered satisfactory. He said judiciously, "The fewer players down to three, the more scientific it may be made, but the more players, the more fun."[3] But for all practical purposes he felt that his original team of nine men constituted the ideal number. He analyzed the assignment of duties in a nine-man group in the following manner: "It shall be the duty of the goal keeper and the two guards to prevent the opponents from scoring. The duty of the wing men and the home man is to put the ball into the opponent's goal and the center men shall feed the ball forward to the man who has the best opportunity, thus nine men make the best number for a team."[4]

Other athletic instructors followed Naismith's lead in the matter of expansible basketball teams, some overenthusiastically. Ed Hitchcock, Jr., physical director at Cornell University, once divided a class of one hundred into two teams for gymnasium practice. After one trial, he discontinued the arrangement, mainly because of the danger of damage to the building.[5] Naismith's dictum "The more players, the more fun" obviously had flaws.

Limitations were gradually placed on the number of players on a team, although for a few years some degree of flexibility was allowed, with the choice restricted, usually, to five, seven, or nine players, according to the size of the playing field or other considerations. In 1897, however, the number of players on a basketball team was officially set at five.

Scoring rules have varied. Rule seven of Naismith's original thirteen rules specified that three consecutive fouls (that is, without an intervening foul by the opposing side) counted as a goal, or one point, for the opponent. In 1893 the penalty for a single foul was set at one point for the opposing side, and in 1894 the free-throw system for fouls was devised. Today, after intervening refinements, a foul gives a chance for either one or two one-point free throws by the fouled player. The distance from the free-throw line to the goal, at first twenty feet, has been decreased to fifteen feet. The value of a field goal has also changed several times. After various revisions (a goal has counted one point, two points, and three points, shifting indecisively back and forth in value), today a goal from the field counts two points.

The length of the playing time and its division have changed occasionally. The length of the first game was thirty-five minutes— two fifteen-minute halves divided by a five-minute rest period. At one time three periods of twenty minutes each were played. Today most amateur games have four ten-minute quarters, although this allotment of time may vary at different school levels, and professional games are played in four twelve-minute quarters.[6]

At first there were two game officials on the playing floor—a referee for watching the ball and an umpire for watching the men and calling fouls. The number of officials has, at various times, ranged from as few as one to as many as three (one referee and two umpires). Their duties have likewise varied, with some of the early responsibilities of umpire and referee taken over today by timers and scorers.

Audience reaction toward officials is another element that has undergone a slight modification. In early basketball games an unhappy gallery was likely to express its feelings overemphatically against referee and umpire. A newspaper account of the first five-player intercollegiate game stated, undoubtedly with underemphasis, that "the strict officiating was a source of great dissatisfaction to the audience." Oldtimers report that in the early days of basketball the final duty of the team captain was to open a window of the dressing room so that players and officials could leave expeditiously if postgame violence seemed imminent. Officials, reportedly, often did depart in this manner.[7]

A ball and a goal were the basic equipment in the first game of basketball, and in these two items changes are easiest to identify.

The fewest changes in the game of basketball have occurred in the ball itself. For more than two years the official association football, or soccer ball, was used. In the 1893–1894 season the first basketball was made by the Overman Wheel Company, a bicycle-manufacturing firm at Chicopee Falls, Massachusetts. The new, and larger, ball was a sphere with circumference to be no less than thirty inches or more than thirty-two inches. Little change has occurred in the size of the ball since then, although more than the circumference of the ball is now scrutinized. Uniformity in construction, weight, pressure, and bouncing potential is also demanded.

The peach-basket goal, on the other hand, though it has caught the fancy of sportswriters more than any other single detail in the history of basketball, did not long survive.

A basic objection to the peach basket was that it was too frail; also the container was not standard in shape and size in every fruit-growing state. A stronger basket of standard measurements, resembling the Naismith peach basket in size and shape, was a natural successor. Early in 1892 Lew Allen of Hartford, Connecticut, suggested a cylindrical basket of heavy woven wire. Allen shaped a piece of wire about two feet long into a cylinder eighteen inches across, running a few cords across the bottom. The cylinder-shaped basket also eliminated the forward slope of the former truncated-cone peach basket that existed when the latter was nailed against the gallery.

The Allen basket did not solve all problems. Along with correction of the above weaknesses of the original basket, a satisfactory method for retrieving the ball was needed.[8] In early games the object was to throw the ball into the basket in such a manner that it remained there. During Naismith's first eighteen-man experiment with basketball, janitor Stebbins climbed a ladder beside the elevated peach baskets to retrieve the ball after a goal was made. Indeed, a drawing by G. S. Ishikawa, a student at the Springfield Y.M.C.A. school in the 1890s, shows a man in overalls waiting at the top of a ladder while a basketball player below him tips a ball into a peach-basket goal.[9] Of course, when the basket was fastened to the rail of the auditorium balcony, as it was in the Springfield gymnasium, it was a relatively simple matter for someone on the balcony to reach into the basket and retrieve the ball after a goal was scored. Later this procedure was followed. But in those gymnasiums where the basket was fastened to the wall, a ladder continued to be needed to ascend to the goal and recapture the ball. An improvement was made when a hole was cut in the bottom of the peach basket that was large enough for a long pole to be inserted from below to push the ball out, as was also possible with the Allen basket. But this was not enough. Even though goals were scored relatively infrequently in the early days of basketball, excessive time and effort were lost under various systems for retrieving the ball.

Modifying the Allen basket, for the 1892–1893 season the Narragansett Machine Company of Providence, Rhode Island, manufactured a basketball goal with an iron rim and a cord basket. Like the Allen basket, the Narragansett goal was closed across the bottom to hold the ball, but an ingenious method for retrieving the ball was included. A chain fastened to the bottom of the basket passed over a pulley back of the basket. When a goal was scored, the referee pulled the handle of the chain, tilting the basket, and the ball fell out. This basket, with a device resembling an overhead chain-pull on an old-fashioned flush toilet, was welcomed as a clever innovation in Naismith's popular game. In 1906 the introduction of open basketball nets of various types, similar to today's hoop and cord, simplified the whole situation.[10] The net was constructed not to retain the ball but momentarily to check its passage through the circular goal. In 1912 the open-bottom net was made official. From peach basket to webbed ring, the evolution of the basketball goal was from makeshifts, from tricks and gadgets, toward functionalism.

The size and shape of the basketball court has varied over the decades, shrinking and expanding and shrinking again, sometimes regular in shape and sometimes irregular. During the first two years of the game all boundary lines were imaginary, but later, as the lines grew more clearly defined and the rules more authoritative, to strict outer boundaries were added the refinements of numerous inner zones and inner boundary lines. In the same indecisive manner that the fixing of boundary lines was carried out, the area of the court at first fluctuated according to the size and shape of the specific gymnasium in which the game was played. The official basketball court settled eventually, however, to specified limits, rectangular in shape. The A.A.U. in 1910 set the maximum area at 4,000 square feet. Under college rules, the size was specified in measurements of length and width. In 1906 the minimum was set at 70 by 35 feet and the maximum at

90 by 55 feet. By 1939 maximum dimensions were 90 by 50 feet, with a four-foot end zone compulsory when space permitted.

Present rules set up by the National Basketball Committee of the United States and Canada establish the ideal playing court for colleges and adults as 94 by 50 feet, and for teams of high-school age as 84 by 50 feet.[11]

Most of the basic appurtenances of basketball appeared in the first game played. The backboard, however, was an accessory added later, for a practical purpose. It was discovered that enthusiastic fans in the balcony would reach through the railing to assist their favorite team in defensive or offensive action around the goal. Thereupon, a backboard—devised first of heavy screen, then of wood, and later of plate glass to avoid obstructing vision—was erected between goal and spectators.[12] As early as the 1895–1896 basketball season the present backboard size of 6 by 4 feet was fixed.

In playing techniques the greatest innovation was the dribble, which was initiated accidentally rather than having been planned. It was, however, developed so early that Naismith was able to say: "The dribble is really as old as the game, and the changes that have taken place are merely developments." In early basketball, when a player—who was not allowed to advance while holding the ball—was cornered too closely to throw, he would drop the ball and run after it. Theoretically, then, he had let it out of his possession and was permitted to move across the floor after it. Players began to use at first a single bounce and then a series of bounces to maintain control of the ball while moving across the floor. Naismith, favorably impressed by this maneuver, explained its usefulness in the following way:

When a player had possession of the ball and was so closely guarded that he could not pass it to one of his team mates, the only thing that he could do was to lose possession of the ball voluntarily in such a way that he might possibly recover it . . . by rolling or bouncing the ball on the floor.[13]

Basketball teams at Yale in the mid-1890s developed the dribble to such a degree that the Yale style of playing became known as the dribble game. As the technique grew sophisticated, Naismith termed it "one of the finest plays, one of the sweetest, prettiest plays in the whole bunch." When opposition arose at one time to the use of the dribble, he fought against its elimination.[14]

Thus basketball was created—in one place and at one time. Unlike other sports that have recognizable beginnings centuries back—some in the Middle Ages—or have evolved after years of modifications, basketball made a sudden appearance, ready for instant use.[15]

Had James Naismith been able to look ahead eighty or more years during those early days in Springfield, he would have seen that despite the changes and developments in an increasingly popular game, basketball would remain basically the same. Like an adolescent who shoots upward into manhood and yet retains his baby features, basketball has remained recognizably that peach-basket game of thirteen rules. Although more than two hundred rules have been added to the thirteen he formulated one December day in 1891, twelve of those original thirteen rules have remained essentially in force.[16] (Rule number four—"The ball must be held in or between the hands; the arms or body must not be used for holding it"[17]—has little meaning in today's game.) After Naismith had lived with his brainchild for forty-odd years, he took time to point out, with some surprise, the basically unchanged quality of the game. "There have been no changes in the fundamental principles on which the game was founded," he pronounced.

During the decade from 1885 to 1895 many new games were created, but basketball was the only one that caught on and stuck and, more amazingly, did so without major overhauling. Naismith's supporters averred that basketball succeeded because it was "scientifically invented"—a reference to his deliberate calculation of the elements necessary to a successful indoor sport. And the same statement could be validly made today. Although adaptations of the game have come to be played on rollerskates, in swimming pools, and in other exotic situations, the stunts are recognizable versions of the basic sport. (For example, a telephone company in California gives a training course in which aspiring linemen toss a basketball around among themselves while clinging to twenty-five- or thirty-foot poles in order to develop confidence and poise; and a power company in Wisconsin uses the same method with its trainees. Penalty: anyone who misses a catch must climb down to retrieve the ball!)[18]

Of course, one can argue that certain obvious changes have occurred—and Naismith would probably agree. The major changes have come in the greater speed of the game, in the increased skill of the players, and in the type and variety of plays that have been developed to make a flashy spectacle of America's most popular indoor team game.

As decades passed, Naismith admitted that he was thrilled by the skill displayed in modern basketball. When he was seventy years old, he lamented over his youthful, prebasketball days: "Why on earth didn't we have a game like that . . . ?"[19]

A subtle sociological change would come, too, in the objectives of basketball. The ogre known as "leisure time" has grown steadily since the turn of the century, and Naismith's invention has helped to fill the insatiable maw of that modern monster, particularly since the large-scale spread of professional basketball after World War II.[20]

An interesting sidelight in the history of basketball is the occasional argument about its origin. New names, dates, and places continue to crop up. Satisfactory rebuttals to these claims can be found, however—sometimes simply in a clarification of dates, sometimes deductively, from circumstantial evidence or lack thereof.

In 1952 Frank J. Basloe presented a copy of an article from the *Utica Daily Press* of February 19, 1898, which reported that the Y.M.C.A. of Herkimer, New York, had a basketball team in 1891, with Lambert Will as captain. As background for this news article was a story indicating that fifteen-year-old Lambert Will had invented the game of basketball in 1890. Research proved, however, that there was an error of two years in dates recorded in the 1898 newspaper item. Will, therefore, must have "introduced" basketball into the Herkimer Y.M.C.A. in 1892 rather than "invented" it in 1890.[21]

On the opposite side of the United States, for many years credit was given to coeds at the University of California for playing basketball against outside competition as early as the fall of 1891.

But again an erroneous figure came to light. The head of the University of California archives in 1957 proved that an early edition of the university yearbook had been one year in error on the date of that first game.[22]

A third confusion in dates appears to have occurred in a story told about 1940 by Dr. George L. Gabler and published after his death in 1950. Dr. Gabler stated that William Morgan, who later created the game of volleyball, developed a form of basketball in a Y.M.C.A. class in Holyoke, Massachusetts, several years before Naismith presented his game to the Springfield Y.M.C.A. class. In this case because of a lack of proof in dating, either pro or con, refutation is based largely on supposition and deduction. Through cautious interpretation of the facts presented in Gabler's account it would seem that some time after 1891 Morgan developed a modified form of basketball, based on Naismith's game, for a middle-aged businessmen's lunch-hour Y.M.C.A. class.[23]

Going farther afield than Massachusetts, New York, or California for claimants to the creation of basketball, and farther back in time than the nineteenth century, one hears reports from archaeologists digging among Mayan ruins in Central America, where a slight uncertainty in year and month is irrelevant. These researchers say that *pok-ta-pok,* ancient sport of the Maya Indians, contains the basic ideas of basketball. But in view of all available knowledge, Naismith seems to owe no debt to either the Mayas or their successors, the Aztecs, and must be assumed to have created his game independently of any Indian traditions.[24]

The claims put forward for Lambert Will, William Morgan, and the Maya Indians have been put into effective perspective by Alexander M. Weyand in his book *The Cavalcade of Basketball.*[25] But in addition to these claimants, two other groups express dissent to the unqualified statement that James Naismith created the game of basketball in Springfield, Massachusetts, in December, 1891. The views of these two groups deserve thoughtful consideration.

On the Canadian side of the border are persons who insist that the game originated at least two years prior to 1891, when Naismith, for indoor winter sport, taught a physical education class at McGill University to toss balls into receptacles, possibly refuse boxes, on the gymnasium floor. These claimants concede only that the game was perfected and formalized after Naismith went to Springfield.[26]

To Canada, indeed, where Naismith garnered the basic ideas for his game, acknowledgment must be made. Credit should be given the McGill University students for participating in an embryonic game of basketball. Although at least one informant identifies Springfield as the place where refuse boxes were first used in the Naismith game, most evidence indicates that the location was Montreal.[27]

The other major group of dissenters consists of the supporters of Luther Halsey Gulick, Jr., who aver that principal credit for creation of the game of basketball belongs to him. And, undeniably, greater credit must be given to Gulick than to anyone other than Naismith. Without Gulick the game might have been stillborn, and certainly without him it would not have been the immediate success that it was. But, as Gulick himself always insisted, "It's Naismith's game," a game first put into organized play in December, 1891, on a Y.M.C.A. gymnasium floor in Springfield, Massachusetts.[28] Gulick went so far as to publish an open letter in the *Official Guide* of 1904–1905 making it clear to everyone that full credit for the game of basketball belonged to James Naismith. And even today Gulick's son, knowing all the facts, avers, "My father would want Naismith to receive the major credit. This is the way he worked."[29]

Thus stands the record, with counterclaims and their refutation. Considering all the evidence available, the three magic words "Naismith," "Springfield," and "basketball"—the man, the place, and the game—seem by now to form too firm a pyramid to be toppled.[30]

10
Courtship, Marriage, and Westward Ho

BACK in December, 1891, as the Sherman family and boarders sat around the dining table one evening, Jim Naismith mentioned to his landlady and her children that he had invented a new game over at the gymnasium. Widow Sherman and her family were all interested in inventions and inventors because of the work that the late Mr. Sherman had done. They were always a little sad that he had sold the rights to his grain harvester to Cyrus McCormick, instead of becoming rich and famous with it himself.[1]

None of them would have believed that their boarder had invented something that would become familiar to more Americans and Canadians than had McCormick's reaper. And it was likely that Jim Naismith himself was thinking more about pretty, brown-haired Miss Maude Sherman that evening than he was about either the reaping machine or the game of basketball.[2]

But the path of love was not smooth.

Jim Hale, one of the other boarders, had taken a fancy to Maude. When he asked her for the pleasure of her company, she was willing, but her mother demanded that sister Mabel chaperone them, a customary arrangement in those days. Young Hale thereupon appealed to Jim Naismith to accompany them and make it a double date.[3]

Jim Naismith had already been looking with interest at Maude Sherman as she busied herself about the kitchen and dining room after she came home from working in Dr. Sprague's office. In fact, she had caught his attention the moment he first saw her, wearing a black dress with a red rose at the collar. He thought her face was as beautiful as a painting by Raphael. Maude was not so good a conversationalist as the more outgoing and robust Mabel, but she was a good *listening* companion, anyway, a gentle, sweet, and retiring girl. When Hale approached him, however, he agreed to help out the Jim Hale–Maude Sherman romance, disregarding the truth that he wanted Maude himself.[4]

During the first date Jim Hale caught onto his friend's feelings about Maude and decided that Mabel was more the Hale type, anyway. He suggested a rearrangement of partners. The suggestion was tempting to Jim Naismith, but he stalled. He feared that Maude would not want to go out with a hulking football player like him. He was not a tall man, a little less than five feet nine, but he was about seven inches taller than Maude and eight years older. The erect manner in which he carried his broad-shouldered one hundred sixty pounds gave him the appearance of being a larger and more forceful man than he really was. Besides, he had a pair of slightly battered ears that were embarrassing to him—one ear in particular—which he had acquired in his years of football playing without wearing a helmet. Jim's morals were high enough to do any girl honor, but a pure heart might have little chance when coupled with a cauliflower ear. Maude, who had attended a private school for girls in Springfield and knew how to do artistic things like painting in watercolors, was ladylike in manner and dainty in appearance. Besides, she was of aristocratic lineage. It was said that her ancestry could be traced back to the Plantaganets of England.[5]

Despite Naismith's misgivings, the arrangements were finally worked out, after the Christmas holidays, with Jim Hale doing most of the arranging. The four of them—Jim Hale and Mabel Sherman, Jim Naismith and Maude Sherman—were to go out together.[6]

But the afternoon before the double date Jim was banged up in football scrimmage. That evening, when he came home wearing bandages and walking with a limp,[7] he probably feared that he had ruined his chances with Maude. She might go out with a football player, but she would never permit a roughneck to be her escort.

Fortunately, he was wrong. The limp and the bandages did a lot for him. He received solicitous attention from Maude instead of the rebuff he had expected—and romance began to bloom.[8]

For her part, Maude Sherman had always admired the blue-eyed Canadian with the athlete's body and strong, sensitive spirit, and she especially appreciated his thoughtfulness toward her mother. After he created the game that caught the attention of everyone in Springfield, she was impressed. Now, as they talked more and more together, she began to think of him as a genius in a class with her adored father and began to feel proud of him in a proprietary sort of way. She tried to please him the way women know how—wearing the dresses he seemed to admire most on her and doing her hair up in particularly attractive fashion. He liked one dress best of all, one set off with a rose at her throat.

She asked him once, curiously, "Why do you admire this dress so much, James?"

"You were wearing it the first time I saw you," he replied. "I thought you looked like a madonna."[9]

She blushed—and found frequent occasions thereafter to wear the frock. But she did not yet realize the many unaccustomed paths into which love would lead her.

Maude was petite and feminine, not an athletic type of girl, but Jim was eager to have her share his fondness for sports.[10] Jim's enthusiasm about his new game and Maude's growing interest in Jim were reasons enough for her venture onto a basketball floor.

In March, 1892, a girls' basketball tournament was held, marking the first scheduled girls' basketball game. Players included the Buckingham school teachers, a group of stenographers and secretaries from establishments near the "Y," and some wives of faculty or students from the Training School. Maude Sherman found herself among the players—and James was there, watching her. He grew more and more certain that this girl was meant to be a permanent part of his life.[11]

When, after completion of his course at the International Y.M.C.A. Training School in 1892, a chance came to go on the faculty as a full-time teacher, Naismith accepted the position. As it turned out, he would remain there until the summer of 1895, with plenty of time to court his landlady's daughter.[12]

The courtship took somewhat more than two years. Considering that James Naismith had fallen in love with Maude Sherman at first sight, one might call it a lengthy courtship indeed.[13] Yet when he wrote his autobiographical *Basketball,* he crowded his whole romance into a reference to the first women's basketball team and a shy mention of a certain player on it: "One young lady who took a prominent part on the newly organized team was a Miss Sherman, whom I later asked to become Mrs. Naismith."[14]

Maude Evelyn Sherman and James Naismith were married June 20, 1894, in the Hope Congregational Church in Springfield in a fashionable seven-o'clock ceremony. Maude's maid of honor was her niece Caroline, who was slightly younger than Maude and very close to her. James's best man was his boyhood friend from Almonte and Montreal days, Dr. Robert Tait McKenzie,[15] now a specialist in orthopedics at McGill University and house physician to the governor general of Canada, the Marquis of Aberdeen.[16] All in all, the wedding was a beautiful one, as Maude wanted it to be.[17]

As soon as the wedding ring, with *semper fidelis* engraved inside, was on Maude's finger, the couple went northward on a rugged honeymoon trip of the groom's planning. Still attempting to teach his demure little bride an appreciation of the sports and outdoor activities he loved, James took her on a sailboat honeymoon down the Connecticut River to Long Island Sound and on to Nova Scotia. He also took along a collie dog he had acquired for their new home. After the adventurers returned home the bride admitted that she had been seasick the whole trip. The collie, too, had been sick, less discreetly than she, and Maude must have had a difficult time pretending, for her husband's sake, that she liked dogs. The truth eventually came out that she *didn't* like them, and never learned to.[18]

The young couple returned to Springfield to make their first home in a house on Princeton Street, a fashionable district in those days. The marriage was a good one. Love overcame seasickness and all other troubles that came along. Maude and James remained sweethearts through everything. Many years later one of Maude's nieces would comment about the lovers' first meeting and their subsequent life: "When Jim saw Maude the romance was on and it lasted forever."[19]

True, Maude sometimes had adjustments to make. Naismith always retained some of the rough spots he had acquired during a difficult childhood, and the Scottish burr that never quite disappeared from his speech seemed a symbol of that rugged quality in him. He possessed a sentimental and compassionate nature, but he showed a brusque surface, like the coarse tweed coats and heavy shoes he liked to wear—and like his own burly, hairy body.[20]

After his brother-in-law Gardner Mason Sherman slept in the same bed with him one night, the Sherman family remained ever after amused .by Gardner's remark: "I'd as soon sleep with a grizzly bear."[21]

The best-natured of men, Naismith had high spirits that demanded an outlet in argument, and he would dispute on either side of a question for the sheer joy of the conflict. Although he was a deeply kind person, gentler with Maude than with anyone else, he sometimes startled his young wife with his robust sense of humor and the practical jokes in which he delighted.

Maude was proud of her husband's inventiveness, of course— so much like her father's. James had thought up the great game of basketball, she liked to point out, and there were other things, like his famous football helmet. James's proud bride also liked to mention that her husband was responsible for a popular new play in football—the forward pass—copied from the method used for advancing the ball in basketball.[22] This basic basketball technique was borrowed from Naismith's game by football coaches. Some authorities credit James Huff McCurdy with being the first coach to develop football's forward pass and its spiral pass from center.[23] Forrest C. Allen, on the other hand, gives Amos Alonzo Stagg credit for introducing the forward pass into football.[24] At any rate, the technique was incorporated into the pigskin sport by the football rules committee in 1905, and histories of sports acknowledge Naismith as being in some degree or other responsible for this new play.* *A Guide to the History of Physical Education* states unequivocally: "The forward pass of today is a Naismith innovation, and is the most spectacular of all plays on our gridirons."[25]

Both the Naismiths liked New England, and they enjoyed the activities that kept them busy. Among other social events during the first year of their married life in Springfield were the evening

---

* Allen explains: "The forward pass . . . indirectly made Naismith responsible for perhaps the most sensational thrill producer in football today" (*Sports Stories,* p. 110).

meetings that the faculty of the Y.M.C.A. Training School held for the instructors and their wives. The minutes of an instructors' meeting might include the description of a blazing log fire in the fireplace and a storm outside, while men and women sat around munching on apples and popcorn.[26]

Buoyed up by their enthusiasm for their community and for family life, the Naismith household flourished. Happy events were occurring, too. The young couple were pleased to learn that James's good friend Amos Alonzo Stagg was planning to marry in the fall. At the University of Chicago, where Stagg had become the school's first athletic coach in 1892,[27] a basketball-playing coed named Stella Robertson had won his heart.[28]

Most of all, the Naismiths were excited by their own news. Maude had become pregnant a few months after their marriage, and her husband, looking hopefully forward to the birth of a son, was joyful. He was able to share his anticipation with another expectant father, Gardner Sherman, and the two young men easily persuaded each other, far ahead of time, that they should go downtown together to buy baby carriages. Then, too impatient to wait for store delivery, they wheeled the empty perambulators home, price tags dangling.[29]

On the first day of July, 1895, the Naismiths' first child, a daughter, was born. James named her Margaret Mason, using his mother's Christian name and his maternal grandmother's maiden surname, and forgave baby Margaret for not being a boy.

An orphan since he was nine, he was sentimental about family life, and clung to whatever articles or customs he could discover in his ancestral past, from his Scottish kilt to the favorite Scottish names his kinfolk had borne. In the Naismith family, Christian names were carried down in long sequence. A James or a John had existed in nearly every family for generations, and the name Margaret was likewise traditional—until the time of the Ontario Naismiths. John and Margaret, even though they were the names of the parents of the household, had been omitted among the trio of Annie, James, and Robert.[30]

Maude and James Naismith added a tradition of their own. On one of his trips James brought home an antique lamp, a winged figure holding a lamp of lavender-tinted glass. He announced that it was Margaret's, to be handed down to the Margaret of each succeeding generation. The Naismiths set it up on the newel post, and it sat on the newel post of each house in which they lived until Margaret married and took it with her.[31]

James Naismith was happy with his home life and with his job. The International Young Men's Christian Association Training School was growing, with plans to expand its two-year course to three at the beginning of the 1895–1896 academic year.[32] He had been an instructor there since 1891, the year after he first enrolled as a student, and his future seemed secure. Nevertheless, he began looking toward new horizons.

The horizons he had already touched were broad ones. For eight years he had combined religious duties with physical education. First, in Montreal he had been theological student and student minister while an instructor of physical education and a participant in amateur and professional athletics. Then in the Y.M.C.A. Training School at Springfield he had worked for the spiritual and physical development of the young men who came under his guidance. But here a new field began to interest him. Caring for the cuts, bumps, bruises, and other injuries of his charges, he became attracted to the study of medicine. With the example of Luther Halsey Gulick, Jr., physician and physical director, guiding him, he decided to return to school, this time to work for a degree in medicine. He wanted to learn all there was to know about the human body.[33]

In his newly established family there were already three persons for him to support, and there would probably be more. Filling a teaching position and being a family man were demanding responsibilities. But James went ahead with his new plans. He made inquiries about the medical schools of the country and looked for a chance to support himself—preferably in a Y.M.C.A. gymnasium—while attending school. Before long, the perfect opportunity came. During the summer of 1895 he was offered the position of director of physical education in the Y.M.C.A. in Denver, Colorado, the city in which the Gross Medical School was located.[34] The Central Branch of the Denver Y.M.C.A. was the largest branch in the United States,[35] and the Gross Medical

School, founded in 1887, was a well-known institution.[36] To James Naismith, the future looked bright.

Maude had been born in Chicopee Falls, Massachusetts, and had never lived anywhere but in the East.[37] To take her tiny first-born baby and move two thousand miles from home, into the midst of strangers, must have been a frightening prospect. But when her husband told her about the opportunity in Denver, she agreed that the move was the right thing to do.

Thus, they headed west to the Mile-High City, more than half a continent away.

11

Pulpit to Gymnasium to Medical School

"BASKETBALL wasn't merely a dream come true," Frank G. Menke would write decades later when he set down the history of basketball in *The Encyclopedia of Sports*, "it was a miracle wrought when it was felt that all sports miracles belonged to history."[1]

With old dreams and miracles behind him and with a new life opening for him at Denver, James Naismith welcomed the challenges of that new life. He moved his worldly possessions, his wife, and his infant daughter to the capital city of Colorado.

Denver in the second half of the 1890s was a lively young city, concerned about frequent violence in the Rocky Mountain mining towns nearby and proud of the culture available in the opera houses on its own paved streets.

In the mountains, prospectors were still striking it rich; but at established mines, headlines were being made by strikes, fires, and riots. As typically cheerful news, for example, the Nelly V. on Squaw Mountain announced a surface strike of gold that panned freely and assayed nearly seven ounces to the ton. On the depressing side, the same fortnight brought a report from Leadville that the militia had been called out to make arrests during riots at the Coronado and Emmett mines, and State Attorney General Carr had made an official visit to the strike-torn scene.[2]

But in the capital city life was different from what it was in the mountains. On the streets of Denver, trolley cars—signs of progress —clanged busily; and city fathers, intent on civic improvement, advanced arguments for putting fenders on the cars. In theaters, parks, and sports areas people found entertainment to their varied likings. Announcements in the local newspaper "Amusements" column of major events for one week were chosen to appeal to the tastes of both highbrow and middlebrow. The National Stock Company brought a perennial favorite, the dramatized version of *The Count of Monte Cristo,* to the stage of the Orpheum, where it opened on the same Sunday in September that an all-day picnic was held for the cathedral parish at Elitch's park. In addition, the opera *The Mikado* was being presented at the Broadway, and at the Tabor Theater little Miss Imogene Washburn, popular child actress, was appearing in a play. In the spring of 1898 the great Nellie Melba, world-renowned operatic soprano from Australia, came to Denver at the peak of her success.

For athletically inclined persons bicycle riding was a popular sport, including both spectators and participants. Professional bicycle races were being held throughout America at that time, both indoors and outdoors—speed races of minutes' duration and endurance contests that lasted for a day or six days or whatever length of time caught the promoters' fancy. At the Coliseum in Chicago, for instance, purses of $250, $150, $100, and $50 and other "liberal prizes" were given to winners of a twenty-four-hour bicycle race. Denver had its share of this sport, too. For professional cyclists and enthusiastic spectators, races were held at sports tracks. For amateur riders, bicycle paths were constructed throughout the city.

James Naismith's interest was focused, of course, on the Central Branch of the Young Men's Christian Association, located in the Florence Building at Eighteenth and Champa streets in downtown Denver. The Denver organization had approximately two decades of solid work behind it and was growing steadily. It boasted that it was the only resort for young men in Denver that was open seven days a week and was free from demoralizing influence, "furnishing healthful recreation and amusement without temptation, and also furnishing ways for the improvement of the mind."[3]

Well situated and efficiently staffed as it was, the "Y" counted more than seven hundred boys and men who participated daily during the winter months in its various departments.

To improve their minds, students enrolled in the Y.M.C.A.'s educational department. The number in that department alone had grown to 317 by the time Naismith arrived, one of the largest enrollments in any educational institution in Colorado. Thirty-four classes were taught each week in such varied areas as penmanship and spelling; Greek and German (elementary and advanced); electricity, telegraphy, and mechanical engineering; banjo, vocal music, and freehand drawing; and first aid. Classes, held each afternoon and evening until ten o'clock, were divided according to the age and profession of enrollees: boys, young men, students, businessmen. More courses were soon added in art, foreign languages, science, industry, and business. So well attended were the classes that they outgrew their original quarters, and additional rooms were engaged.

In its work of spiritual uplifting, the Y.M.C.A. included weekly Bible and training sessions, morning Sunday School classes, and Sunday afternoon meetings at the Central Branch, as well as religious services at the jail. In the department of relief and employment, "Y" supervisors found jobs or gave temporary assistance to jobless men, sent visitors to the ill, and provided funerals when necessary. In addition the Y.M.C.A. was a social center, holding monthly socials during the winter and eight formal receptions throughout the year. The September reception, celebrating the opening of classes, was a gala affair, with the public invited, refreshments served, and entertainment provided. At the reception in 1896, to give one illustration, the Denver University Glee Club presented its popular "Grasshopper Tragedy," and the Y.M.C.A. Banjo Club performed.

The physical department had been added when the Y.M.C.A. moved to its new quarters in the Florence Building, and Naismith became the first director of physical education, teaching classes and giving all physical examinations. Officials of the Association publicized the arrival of the creator of basketball: "We were very fortunate in securing Mr. James Naismith of Springfield, Mass., as physical director . . . he is a man of wide experience and rare

ability . . . and is the originator of the popular game of basketball."[4]

Naismith's department soon proved a focal point in the
Y.M.C.A.'s triumvirate of body, mind, and spirit, and the gymnasium became a popular spot. Hardly an hour in the afternoon
or evening passed when it was not in use, an average of about
fifty-five persons a day using the gym during his first months as
director. Naismith endeavored to make facilities and programs
even better than they were at the start. His plan to add a shower
bath nine feet square was only one of his several ideas up for
consideration as early as the March after he arrived.

In addition to assuming the position of physical director of the
largest Y.M.C.A. in the country, Naismith lost no time in beginning his medical education. During the September of his arrival,
he enrolled in Gross Medical College of Rocky Mountain University in Denver as a member of the freshman class of 1895–
1896. Like the Y.M.C.A., the medical school was located in
downtown Denver, and thus Naismith's medical classes 'fit neatly
into his busy schedule. More important than its convenient location, of course, was the reputation of the school. Eight years
old when Naismith enrolled, Gross Medical College was recognized as a good institution. After several years of discussion and
voting had gone on, in 1902 the school consolidated with the
University of Denver Medical School in order to avoid duplication of services in the community. This consolidated institution
in turn united with the University of Colorado School of Medicine
in 1911, strengthening still further the position of the three formerly separate medical schools.[5]

At thirty-four years of age a freshman in college once more,
Naismith started with the full load of courses that fall. He had
a thirst for knowledge that had not yet been slaked, and his
studies never became drudgery to him. Those years in medical
school were not easy ones, to be sure. He was directing the
physical education department at the Y.M.C.A.—where his students ranged from boys to middle-aged men—and carrying on his
studies at the same time, a difficult task under any conditions.
But he did all parts of his work thoroughly, for he despised lazy
workmanship of any kind. He took time to referee basketball

games during tournaments held in the "Y" gym, and even managed to invent a new gadget now and then or devise a new way of doing something in the gymnasium or at home.[6] And in the spring of 1896 he completed the first-year study of anatomy, chemistry, physiology, pharmacy, and histology along with the rest of his class.[7]

In the second year his studies grew more difficult. He was enrolled in an impressive array of courses, including pathology, physiology, anatomy, therapeutics, and surgery, as well as in two courses entitled vaguely "Medicine" and "State Medicine." When Maude became pregnant again in the early spring of that year, his current enrollment in a course in obstetrics seemed appropriate.[8]

That spring Naismith was very busy at the Y.M.C.A. Delegates from the Denver "Y" attended the international Y.M.C.A. convention in Mobile, Alabama, in April, 1897. It was voted there to hold the next biennial convention in Denver in 1899, for the Denver association, considered one of the best-managed branches in the country, ranked high throughout the world.

Thus, the "Y" in Denver seemed to be flourishing. But matters were not so good as they appeared. Ironically, a few weeks after international recognition had been bestowed on the organization, the Denver Y.M.C.A. was forced to publish an announcement that took the city by surprise and meant that Naismith, with a daughter and a pregnant wife to support, might soon be out of a job. The directors of the Association admitted to the public for the first time that the Denver "Y" was in danger of closing its doors unless $10,000 was raised at once.

The background of the problem was simple. When the Young Men's Christian Association had moved to Eighteenth and Champa streets in 1893, purchases of $8,700 worth of furniture and equipment were made. Unfortunately, $5,000 of that amount was still owing. Because a financial panic came in 1893 and subsequent times of financial distress followed, the "Y" had been unable to pay. At last, in 1897, the predicament of the Association reached a crisis. Knowing that the "Y" still owed $5,000, tradesmen and merchants began to clamor for their money.

Now it looked as if the "Y" 's educational classrooms, its library and reading rooms, its gymnasium and baths would have to be locked up. Editorialists called the impending closure a disaster for the city.

Because the Y.M.C.A. prided itself on being "a link between the church and the world,"[9] directors of the Association hopefully presented a statement of their financial difficulties at a meeting of the Ministerial Alliance. This step was a turning point in their difficulties. The Alliance agreed to give the help that was needed to save the "Y," and money was raised through ministerial appeals to the congregations of all churches, by subscription, and by various fund-raising campaigns.

Efforts were vigorous, campaigns ranging from simple to elaborate. On the elaborate side, in July the "Y" sponsored a five-day "Around the Circle" excursion through the Rocky Mountains in luxurious Rio Grande Pullmans. The trip (with a stop for a four-hour stagecoach ride thrown in at no extra cost) garnered the Y.M.C.A. forty dollars a head.

Other contributions, too, were generous, for the Y.M.C.A. had always been a credit to Denver. At last, sufficient money was raised to keep the organization from closing its doors. Thus, after a few worrisome months, the "Y" and, along with it, James Naismith's position as its physical director were saved.

Among other advantages, his education at Gross Medical College could go on.

The third and last year in medical school promised to be the most difficult of all. In addition to advanced work in surgery, obstetrics, and medicine and courses in gynecology and pediatrics, he enrolled in an array of courses whose titles he abbreviated in professional manner to confusing syllables such as "larng. and dermg. oph.," "otol. microl. diag.," and "nervous dis. and jurispru."[10] He was coming very near to getting his medical degree.

Students at Gross Medical College came from all over the United States and beyond. In Naismith's class they recorded home addresses from Connecticut and New York on the East Coast, California on the West Coast, and Wisconsin on the north. Three women and two foreigners were included. Representing the female sex, Jennie Bailey had traveled from Michigan to study medicine in Denver, and Julia Kapp and Martha MacVean had come from Ohio and Nebraska, respectively. As foreigners, James Naismith from Canada and Alfred Terry Short from England helped to round out the cosmopolitan quality of the class. And among this heterogeneous group Naismith was a success, academically and socially. He passed all his courses, and in his senior year he was elected to one of the four class offices, becoming the class historian.

Then, before he had yet become a doctor, illness struck his household. His pregnant wife fell very ill with typhoid fever, complicated by pneumonia.[11] Recognizing that her condition was critical, he hired a nurse, and he stayed at the bedside himself as much as he could. Watching her as she lay in the fever, he remembered the double loss of his childhood, and he prayed.

One evening Maude opened her eyes, looking small and lost as she lay alone in the four-poster bed that she and James should have been sharing. She moved her head slightly and looked about. Then, motioning weakly in turn toward each of the four bedposts, she chanted softly:

> One to watch
> And one to pray
> And two to bear
> My soul away.

Tears of grief came to James's eyes as he realized that in her delirium she saw an angel on each of the high bedposts and believed that she was dying.[12]

That night the nurse watched Maude Naismith carefully, although the patient seemed again to be resting quietly. But then a crisis came. Reaching for Maude's pulse, the nurse found none.

She called James Naismith urgently from his fitful nap and told him that his wife was dead.

James looked at Maude, pale and unmoving. In desperation, wanting to awaken her from that terrible quiet sleep, he slapped her face. Then the miracle happened, or so it seemed to the nurse and to the medical student at that bedside. Maude caught a breath and stirred, and the lost pulsebeat appeared again, faint and precious in the thin, blue-veined wrist.[13]

Maude lived. But when at last she recovered from the fever,

the shattering truth was clear. She had suffered an almost complete loss of hearing. When the doctor completed his final examination, he diagnosed her case as one of permanent deafness.[14]

Maude began to learn lip reading. But coming upon her in a city where she still felt herself a stranger, her deafness shut her off from the friendships she had begun to make and the friendships she might have made. Too, her hair turned prematurely white after that illness; and, although it was becoming to her, this new strangeness in her appearance made her even more self-conscious.[15]

Helen Carolyn Naismith, the Naismiths' second child, was born on December 21, 1897. Her date of birth has sometimes been referred to as the sixth anniversary of the birth of the game of basketball.[16] But the baby, unlike the game born approximately six years before her, was a sickly infant, who cried and fretted during the long sequence of nights when her father left his books to walk the floor with her. For months the baby cried every night while he sat up studying, and he had to read difficult passages over and over. He made an especial effort to remain unperturbed and cheerful, however, because he knew that Maude was worried about their situation.[17]

To help her laugh, he made a joke of the baby's incessant crying. "Helen Naismith, she's called? She's a bonny lass, but I'd say she sounds like Hell 'n' Blazes."[18]

After Helen Naismith grew up, her parents told her the story. In commemoration of her father's sense of humor, she changed the spelling of her name, insisting ever after on the doubled *l*. Today, long years after she first rocked crying children and grandchildren of her own, she signs her name Hellen Naismith Dodd. But friends and family like to call her "Hannie" (pronounced "Hahnie").[19]

Joke as he might about "Hellen," however, during those months in Denver, when James Naismith thought of Maude's disability he found little cause for laughter. She was hopelessly deaf. He could only be grateful that she was alive and that he could help to make her life as full as possible.

He did not always succeed in his attempts, though. Battling against the obstruction that her thickened ear drums had thrust between her and the joy and beauty of the outside world, he bought her a hearing aid. Despite his thoughtfulness, she did not like it, and she did not use it much. Instead she turned inward, shutting out the world outside her family and household affairs.[20]

Years later, the first radio that James bought had a pair of earphones. There was hope that with that small electronic gadget Maude might be brought into touch with the world of melody that she had missed so long. He dialed a program of music and adjusted the earphones to her head. His effort was a success. As Maude listened, she began to smile with pleasure.

"This song sounds familiar," she said, tilting one earphone out toward James. "Listen and tell me what it is."

He bent his head besides hers and listened. It was "The Star-Spangled Banner."[21]

But in the spring of 1898 Maude's typhoid fever and pregnancy and James's last year of medical courses were finally past, and Maude's long years of frustrating deafness were still in the future. Their child had been born and was growing. At last, James's second daughter three and one-half months old and Maude alive and smiling at him, graduation time came.

On April 8, 1898, he was granted the degree of Doctor of Medicine from Gross Medical College, and on April 12 commencement exercises were held in the Broadway Theater in Denver.[22] In its color and high spirits the ceremony surpassed any other event in town. The enthusiastic applause of the audience outdid even the ovation given Melba, the great opera singer, the night before.

In the pit an orchestra played. On center stage sat the graduates in caps and black gowns. At the right side of the stage, college faculty and trustees were impressively lined up. Throughout the auditorium of the theater a capacity crowd watched and listened and waited to voice their congratulations. "Every parquet and balcony seat was taken, and there was not a box but what was filled with ladies."[23] And flowers were everywhere: on the stage, in the boxes, and among the audience.

After a long philosophical address on the study of medicine, the degrees were conferred. The audience "lustily applauded," and undergraduates came down the aisle to the stage to pass huge bouquets of flowers among the brand-new M.D.s.

It was a great night for James Naismith. Now he had his medical degree, and it looked as if a happy future lay ahead. At the age of nearly thirty-seven, he was prepared for an enriched career, one in which he could even better than before carry out his avowed purpose of serving humanity.[24]

However, ignoring the lucrative possibilities, he did not intend to become an office or hospital physician. A medical practice and an increased income were not his goals. He wanted only to utilize his years of medical school to supplement his training in physical education. He believed that an efficient mind and a well-functioning conscience could best be developed in a physically fit body, and he wanted to combine a doctor's knowledge and a physical educator's skill to help men achieve this balanced goal. He said that he would never commercialize his knowledge of medicine. Later he would be able to point out with pride, "Though I . . . was ordained as a Presbyterian minister, and have an M.D. degree, I have never held a pastorate, nor have I put out a physician's shingle."[25]

But an accident was to occur in the gymnasium that would put James Naismith into an emotional turmoil, changing the course of his life. It would turn him away from Y.M.C.A. work as a profession and start him on a new path.

One day while he was instructing a class in tumbling, one of his boys made a fatal miscalculation. Attempting a somersault in the air, the boy failed in his timing and landed on his head instead of his feet. Although the student was performing over a well-padded wrestling mat, his fall resulted in death from a broken neck.[26]

The memory of this death in his classroom caused Naismith mental torture. He would leap out of sleep at night, dripping with sweat and, as he described his condition, "shaking like a tree in a windstorm." He would lie awake for hours in the grip of terror, while over and over the dread scene unfolded in his mind like a motion picture.[27]

Rather than lessening as time passed, his attacks began to come more and more frequently. Night or day he might find himself suddenly trembling, sweating, and terrified. He thought that he was going insane. One day he went to the fatal spot in the gymnasium, kneeled, and with tears in his eyes prayed for relief. "Oh, God . . . I need you NOW. I can no longer carry on. . . . If you don't respond and alleviate my suffering . . . I cannot believe that there is . . . DIVINE PROVIDENCE."[28]

A few days later he received a telephone call from Amos Alonzo Stagg at the University of Chicago. Although Naismith had never applied for a position in any college or university, and his friend was well aware of the fact, Stagg had recommended him for the position of Director of Chapel at the University of Kansas. That telephone message seemed to Naismith to be an answer to his prayer. Shortly thereafter, administrators at K.U. followed through by offering him the position, and he accepted it.[29]

He always maintained that this unexpected chance at a professorship six hundred miles away was God's way of proving his existence to a momentarily doubting man.[30] This dramatic new development in his life was more truly a miracle to him than his creation of the game of basketball would ever be.

After he moved his family away, he never went back to Colorado to live, but sometimes, when traveling in the state, he returned to the Denver Y.M.C.A. to kneel and pray at that fateful spot on the gymnasium floor.[31]

12

To the Halls of Fraser and the Banks of the Kaw

DURING the search for a new professor at the University of Kansas in Lawrence nothing miraculous seemed to be going on. James Naismith was the ideal man for a position that was open, and to K.U. administrators that's all there was to the affair.

In 1898 Francis Huntington Snow, president of the faculty (in a position later to be called the chancellorship), was looking for an athletic coach and director of physical education who would also serve as religious director. In early times the job of chapel director at the university had been passed around among the ministers of the town. Then university officials had hired the Reverend Hector Cowan, a graduate of Princeton seminary, to serve as their first paid football coach and to act as their chapel director, as well. This was in 1894, before a Department of Physical Education had been formally organized. Before the beginning of the 1898 athletic season, however, Cowan resigned. K.U., therefore, had vacancies for a football coach, a chapel director, and, in addition, an athletic director and a head for the newly established one-man Department of Physical Education—these positions all, preferably, to be filled by one person.[1]

University authorities were happy to lure Fielding H. ("Hurry-Up") Yost, the illustrious football coach, onto their athletic staff, but were disappointed that Yost was unable, or unwilling, to carry out the religious duties involved. He made it clear that he was willing to lead the K.U. football teams to victory, but he felt that he was not properly qualified to lead the student body in prayer. Anyway, the university had grown to the point that a combination football coach and prayer leader no longer seemed appropriate.[2] An athletic director, on the other hand, could more acceptably be a jack-of-several-trades. The University of Kansas was looking for such a man.

President Francis Snow got in touch with President William Harper at the University of Chicago, asking whether he could recommend someone. Harper asked A. A. Stagg, who was coaching football there, whether he knew a person, like himself, who could direct athletics and pray. Stagg, promptly helpful, recommended James Naismith.[3]

It is said that Stagg's wired reply ran like this: "Recommend James Naismith, inventor of basket-ball, medical doctor, Presbyterian minister, tee-totaler, all-around athlete, non-smoker, and owner of vocabulary without cuss words. Address Y.M.C.A., Denver, Colorado."[4]

In this way, then, it happened that Stagg made a telephone call to Naismith that proved the answer to everybody's prayer. Besides being a solution to Jim's personal problem, the opening at the university would bring together the right man and the right job.

When the proposal came, Naismith, graduate of a theological school, had completed seven years' work as physical instructor at the Springfield and Denver Y.M.C.A.s and carried a medical degree in his portfolio. He was a perfect figure for the role of minister–athletic director. To make everything balance, the University of Kansas was a prestigious place, suitable for a man of his reputation as the creator of basketball.[5]

In 1866, when the University of Kansas opened its doors for the first time, James Naismith was only five years old. The university was almost as old as Kansas, for the pioneers of the state "had no sooner driven down their tent-pins than they began to talk of a college."[6] After the legislature passed a law to organize a state university, a building with eleven rooms was constructed, three stories high and fifty feet square; and faculty personnel were hired to teach a student body of fifty-five. In 1866, in short, "the little frontier town of Lawrence settled down . . . to become the chief center of the intellect for the Western plains."[7] The intention was to create another Harvard or Yale on the Kansas prairie.

In the first September of classes the college possessed only one building, known as North College ("Old North"), three professors, and an Episcopalian minister who served as president of the faculty, the Reverend R. W. Oliver. One of the professors was Francis Huntington Snow, librarian and teacher of mathematics and science.

The beginnings of the University of Kansas were small—and so was its young science teacher, Francis Snow, who measured only five feet six inches in height. But dynamic little Snow was eventually appointed president, and it was he who reorganized the university. A recognized scientist and friend of belles-lettres, he claimed as one of his favorite quotations "Whoso findeth wisdom findeth life"—and acted on it.[8] He founded the College of Arts and the Schools of Engineering, Law, Fine Arts, and Pharmacy. Impressively, he even set up a Graduate School. He saw national scholastic recognition bestowed on the university, too. In 1890 chapters of Phi Beta Kappa and Sigma Xi were established, the first chapters of these honor societies to be formed west of the Mississippi River.

What must have been of great interest to Naismith, a brand-new doctor of medicine, was the fact that premedical instruction had been placed in the curriculum, and a two-year medical course, now in the last stages of organization, would begin in 1899, the year after his arrival. Not to be overlooked was the reputation that the University of Kansas had in the 1890s for being the best institution in the West for the study of electrical engineering, which was then supposedly the greatest of all sciences. And, of course, a point of interest to an athletic director like Naismith was that, with Snow's support, the game of football had been introduced at the University of Kansas, the first intercollegiate football game having been played in the first year of Snow's presidency, 1890.

A Kansas newspaper at the turn of the century summed up the reputation of the university when it commented: "The average Kansas man . . . who has hustled along through hot winds, and drouths, and chinch bugs and low prices . . . doesn't growl much about his school tax, and down in the bottom of his heart he cherishes a hope that [he and his children] may go through the University [of Kansas]."[9]

To add to the other attractions of the University of Kansas, as far as the Naismiths were concerned, Francis Huntington Snow shared certain similarities of background with the professor he was trying to hire. Like Naismith, he had been educated for the ministry, but, again like Naismith, he had come from the East to the West to teach instead of preach. A native of Fitchburg, Massachusetts, he had studied for the ministry at Williams College and Andover Seminary, only later changing his interest from pulpit to classroom.

To a man like Naismith, however, there might appear to be one flaw in Snow's philosophy. Although trained in the old-style fundamentalist religion, Snow had revised his stance. When he became involved in the study of science, he was so impressed by the theory of evolution that he began openly to express unorthodox views. As a result, people began to say that there was an atheist at the University of Kansas.

Despite any rumors of atheism, James Naismith accepted Snow's offer of the chapel-and-gymnasium job at $1300 a year. Thus he gave K.U. students years later a chance to say affectionately, "Dr. Naismith prayed for his salary in '98."[10]

On September 1, 1898, Maude and James Naismith, with their two young daughters, moved to the land of the Jayhawks.[11] They may not have known at first what the jayhawk bird was, and it may be that they never found out for sure. If they asked, they might have been told vaguely that there once was a robber bird in Ireland called a jayhawk. Or perhaps they were told that Illinois pioneers in 1848 "jayhawked" their way—that is, struggled through difficulties—across the continent to California in wagon trains. Or it might be that they were told that the jayhawk was a myth of unknown origin. But, at any rate, they learned that somehow the name "Jayhawk" had become attached to Kansans. In fact, about 1911, some thirteen years after the Naismiths came to Kansas, the University of Kansas gave up the bulldog previously used as its school symbol and adopted the jayhawk for its own.[12] And Maude and James became Kansas Jayhawks.

When the Naismiths arrived, it was only a few days before Maude's twenty-ninth birthday, and James was nearly thirty-seven years old. It seemed time for them to settle down. A house was ready for them at 1219 Tennessee Street, one in the row of residences along the side of the hill on which the university stood.[13] Today three concrete steps come up from the sidewalk to a grass-overgrown brick path that leads back to an empty spot, now squeezed between two houses, where their first home in Lawrence stood.[14] Atop Mount Oread, a stone's throw away, was the university around which most of their married life would center. Mount Oread was not a true mountain, but early settlers from the East had nostalgically given that name to the flat-topped topographical feature which dominated the countryside. To students and townspeople the university campus was known as "The Hill."

The buildings of the University of Kansas looked down eastward to the town at their feet and the fertile valley beyond. To the north and south of campus and city stood the bluffs of the Kaw Valley, blue in the distance. Constructed of blocks of native limestone, the campus buildings were rooted firmly in Kansas soil and in Kansas history. They stood with years of ivy softly creeping from the ground up their pale stone walls.

At the time Naismith came to the University of Kansas there were six imposing buildings at the center of the campus: Chancellor Snow's residence, Spooner Library, Fraser Hall, the Chemistry Building, Blake Hall (for physics), and Snow Hall (for natural history and biological sciences). Fraser Hall was Naismith's first classroom building at K.U. There he led chapel exercises, there he held classes, and there he counseled students.

This edifice, which was called simply "New Building" for the first few years of its life, was named University Hall in 1877 and twenty years later was renamed Fraser Hall. The final choice of name was made in honor of General John Fraser, the fiery Scottish president of the university who, in the second year of K.U.'s existence, began its earliest program of expansion by laying plans for this second building on campus. "New Building" thus had a history almost as old as the university.

Opened, although still unfinished, in 1872, it was the largest and most modern academic building in all America. It had such modern miracles as time signals in the classrooms, which were connected by an electrical system to a central clock, gaslights that were ignited instantly by electricity, electric wires and pipes for laboratory gases concealed within the walls, steam heating, and running water. It is true that plans sometimes look better on paper than they do in execution. Very soon President Fraser complained that despite the new heating system in the handsome structure, "the cold air of winter finds free ingress into the building."[15] Obviously, the two classroom halls—North College and New Building—were overtaxing the heating capacities of the old "boiler house." The *University Courier* was sharp in its criticism: "Some of the rooms are so damp that a great number of students have taken severe colds from having to sit in them during the recitation hours."[16]

By the time Naismith came, a new boiler house had been built and the building was warmer than it had been in the 1870s and 1880s. Too, although some of its first innovations may have ceased working, others had been added. For example, electric lighting had replaced the gaslights, and a stone portico had been installed in place of the wooden steps at the front entrance. The glory of the portico was only slightly dimmed by its history: it had ended up at the west door of Fraser because a stonecutter's mistake kept it from fitting the entrance to the state hospital at Osawatomie, for which it was intended.

Various chancellors, or presidents, helped to enhance the image of New Building. After General Fraser left, the next president of the faculty, the Reverend James Marvin, did his part. What was most important was that he finally got New Building finished. Then he employed workers to grade the grounds, sow grass, and plant lilac bushes. As a practical touch, he ordered the erection of a hedge fence on three sides and a stone wall with an iron gate on the other, in order to keep wandering cows away.

From portico to towers Fraser was a distinguished building and one Naismith could be proud to use during his early years at the University of Kansas. Later on there would even be flags flying from Fraser's twin towers: a United States flag on the south tower and a university flag on the north.

Distinctive in appearance as it was, Fraser Hall was long the familiar patriarch of Mount Oread. To strangers it was a tourist attraction. With its twin towers and red tile roof it was the most outstanding landmark in the town, appearing to the traveler from miles away to be a fairy-tale castle from medieval times perched at the summit of "The Hill." The view from the towers was for visitors to Lawrence what a view from the Eiffel Tower is for tourists in Paris. Two presidents of the United States—Ulysses S. Grant and Rutherford B. Hayes—had walked with their wives up one of the inside tower stairways years before Maude and James Naismith first climbed those steps. One visitor called Fraser Hall the "light house of Mount Oread."[17]

The interior of Fraser was as attractive as the outside, having open, curving stairways with walnut handrails, wood-paneled walls, and louvered interior shutters which softened the sunlight that came through tall classroom windows. And the grandest surprise was the chapel. Nothing less than a 650-seat auditorium with a pipe organ was waiting for Naismith when he arrived at the University of Kansas.

Even before bouncy, energetic little Professor Snow became president, he had made a noted contribution to Fraser Hall. By collecting and selling pieces of Kansas meteorites to astronomers over the United States and by lecturing, he bought a $5,000 organ for the university chapel. Its pipes extending magnificently across the stage, the organ provided music when Naismith led the singing during religious services and provided atmosphere for students who came into the auditorium to study between classes.

Naismith would soon consider the balconied auditorium his special domain, while he prayed and preached and led the students in song, or even while he sat in the auditorium listening to to the U.S. Infantry Band and other visiting groups.[18] But on certain occasions he was to feel a different kind of proprietorship. He soon learned that Fraser Hall was the focal spot of student pranks on Hallowe'en or May Day or at any other time that undergraduates felt the need to do mischief. In the course of events he came to be an unofficial student adviser and, when necessary, a mild disciplinarian.

To hang a skeleton from the ceiling of the chapel was not likely to endanger anyone, or to carry a dean's surrey, piece by piece, up the winding steps to reassemble it in the north tower did not hurt anything but the surrey and the Dean's feelings.[19] These acts were harmless student pranks. But to hoist a class flag atop a pole beside Fraser Hall in the midst of an interclass May Day melee, or to the rooftop of a tower on the building, was a dangerous activity and called for stern attention. The day-long May Day scrap over class flags, traditional since 1891, became so rough, in fact, that in 1904 two freshmen were seriously injured. Although the *University Courier* had stated about the annual riot, "It is just such episodes as those that make college life enjoyable and . . . the object of pleasant memories,"[20] Chancellor Strong did not agree, and the rowdy ritual was terminated.[21]

When Naismith came to the University of Kansas in 1898, the campus was lively. He had made his way in fifteen busy years from Canada's "Harvard of the North," to the "Harvard on the Kaw," but students had not changed much.[22] He did find a marked liberality in the required curriculum, though. Three years before he arrived, the age of permissiveness—or so it seemed in the nineteenth century—came to K.U.'s educational system. Beginning in 1895, juniors and seniors were allowed to study anything they chose from the offerings of twenty departments, provided only that a student enroll in no more than four courses under one instructor.[23]

Liberalized curriculum notwithstanding, for Maude and James Naismith life on the campus would not be strange. However, life in the larger community outside the university would be, for a while. This was a different sort of land than either of them had ever lived in before. Sometimes on hot summer days when dust was deep on the ground, old-timers said, the only cloud in the sky might be a cloud of grasshoppers flying in. Or, if that desolate picture were not enough, one could think uneasily back to the horrors of "bleeding Kansas" in the slave-versus-free conflict of the 1850s and 1860s.

The town of Lawrence was a farming center that had risen from a history of pre–Civil War and Civil War violence. Many had been the conflicts over land rights and over the question of slavery. Thirty-five years before, to give one example, William Quantrill and his Confederate guerrillas had burned the town and murdered one hundred and fifty men, women, and children.[24] Pioneer Cemetery, laid out west of town in 1854 or 1855, within a year after Lawrence was founded, became the burial place for most of these massacred persons. The graveyard, still fenced around with barbed wire and stone, had been unused since the 1880s, though. Restoration of Pioneer Cemetery was seventy-some years in the future, and a new cemetery was in use east of town, where many of Quantrill's victims were to be transferred in order that they not be overlooked and forgotten.[25]

Although the raid would continue to be reenacted bitterly in every pageant of Kansas pioneer life, the wounds were healed now. The Eldridge Hotel, the first building to be burned in that raid, had been built again on the ashes of the old hotel and, prosperous now on Massachusetts Street under its old name, stood, when the Naismiths came, as a symbol of the recovery and reconstruction of the town.

County and town had both recovered from the bloody years of thirty-five and forty years before. Douglas County was now a thriving agricultural area, with Lawrence, the county seat, the heart of it. The Horses and wheat were the twin bases of existence— horses for transportation and for cultivation of the land, wheat for food and for trade. At the sign of the Black Horse, on Massachusetts Street, George H. Smith advertised: "Manufacturer of harness, saddles, bridles, and all kinds of strap work. A large stock of collars, whips, curry combs, brushes, and sweat pads. Repairing a specialty."[26] Down the street a few blocks, on the bank of the Kaw River, where a water wheel had transmitted mechanical power in pioneer days, the Bowersock Milling Company stated succinctly its two specialties: "Hard and soft winter wheat flour. Kansas water power."[27] J. D. Bowersock had early constructed a mill and power plant and later founded a box factory and a paper firm.[28]

Horses and wheat were not all. Lawrence was not just a small trade center with wide, pleasant streets; its agricultural base supported many small industries, and the variegated face of the town showed this mixture of occupations. Livery stables, blacksmith shops, and feed stores shared space and prestige in the town with two violin factories and a flourishing box factory, while manufacturers of soda water and of cider did their part in the economy. A foundry and machine shop rubbed elbows on the advertising pages of the town newspaper with a monument maker and a tannery, while a mattress factory and a shirt factory proved companionable neighbors to makers of nails, barbed wire, and woven fences. Industrious manufacturers supplied bricks for the red-brick sidewalks and streets of the town, brooms for housewives, and cigars for their husbands, and a canning factory was a busy center during the growing and harvesting seasons. Three telephone and telegraph companies—the Missouri & Kansas Telephone Company, the Postal Telegraph-Cable Company, and the Western Union Telegraph Company—gave evidence that Lawrence was an up-and-coming town; and stage entertainments brought in from the outside showed that the residents were not isolated culturally. The Bowersock Opera House on Massachusetts Street, at the corner of Winthrop Street—now nonexistent—provided culture on the south bank of the Kaw River for those who did not wish to ride the AT & SF or the UP to Kansas City, forty miles to the east.[29]

As decades passed and Lawrence grew in population, it shed the little industries of its youth, its economy coming to be concentrated on fewer and larger ones. But when the Naismiths came to the town in 1898, it was young, fresh, and varied.

13
The Basketball Man on Mount Oread

WHEN James Naismith arrived at the University of Kansas in 1898, athletics was not the important item that he had found it at the International Y.M.C.A. Training School in Springfield or at the Denver Y.M.C.A.

True, K.U. had a new athletic field, completed in 1892, which Kansans had planned to be the best of its kind in the West. McCook Field, set in a natural amphitheater on the north edge of the campus, was constructed especially for the field-day programs popular in the 1880s and 1890s, usually held to celebrate at graduation time. In these programs events such as a slow bicycle race (winning speed in 1890: one mile in fifty minutes) and a heavy-hammer throw, held for prizes like a five-pound box of cream candies or a copy of Homer's *Iliad,* were typical. Funny costumes, too, brought squeals of delight. One athlete in 1889 wore "a heavy marino tunic with soiled cotton unmentionables displayed in graceful festoons about his lower limbs, gathered at the knees with trimming of garnet plush, and showing well the elegant proportions of his classic calves."[1] Wrestling, three-legged races, 100-yard dashes and all the rest—the events were particularly popular in the 1880s, hot and windy though the days may have been. During a field meet held June 5, 1880, the *Kansas Review* reported, "At times it was almost impossible to keep the immense crowd within limits. Had it not been for the wind and dust, Field Day exercises would have been the most interesting and pleasant feature of Commencement week."[2]

Nevertheless, not counting the fun and games of field day, the only sport of importance at the University of Kansas was football, and coaching it was a sideline, a part-time profession. In 1891 K.U.'s first football coach, an unpaid one, was primarily a professor of English, E. M. Hopkins, who soon left Kansas and went back to Princeton to get a Ph.D. In the fall of 1892 Professor A. W. Shepard took over. Then, on January 30, 1894, the Reverend Hector Cowan, who was primarily a minister, came to coach.[3] Now Naismith was coming into the athletic department, replacing his predecessors as an even more pronounced jack-of-all-trades. The athletic department as a whole was in a rudimentary stage. In 1890, for example, when the big University of Kansas versus University of Missouri football game was played at the midway point of Kansas City, although a two-coach special railroad train was hired to transport fans, the net result for the K.U. athletic treasury was only one hundred fifty dollars, which was immediately deposited in the safe in Woodward's drug store in downtown Lawrence.[4] It seemed to Jim Naismith in 1898 that little progress had been made in building the importance of athletics during the eight years since then. It was a far cry from the 1890s to the late 1960s, when an amazing variety of athletic facilities would have been developed in the community—even to the extent of an artificial ski slope east of town with snow manufactured from the waters of the Wakarusa River.[5]

Naismith could not see into the future, of course. For a while he felt almost discouraged enough to pack up and return to the Y.M.C.A. But he had already sold his household goods in Denver —and, besides, he was no quitter. Overcoming initial disappointment in the athletic program, he introduced basketball into the Department of Physical Education and into the university and began energetically to build interest in sports as a whole.

Ironically, as Naismith became well aware, he had been invited to the University of Kansas as director of physical education simply because of his religious avocation, not because he had created the game of basketball. Many colleges in those days played the game enthusiastically, but no one paid much attention to the name of the man who had dreamed it up.

If anyone had asked, "Who invented basketball?" the answer

would probably have been, "It's a game the Y.M.C.A. started"; and Naismith, modest as he was, would not have contradicted.

Actually, the coaching of basketball was not even included in Naismith's contract, for there was no K.U. basketball team at that time. There was not even much firsthand knowledge about the new sport. Basketball had been introduced to the women of the university before Naismith came, but it did not catch on. A young woman named Lola Bell brought the game from Radcliffe College, probably in 1897, after her sophomore year at that institution, and taught it to the young females in Lawrence. But Kansans did not appear ready for women to play basketball, and the new game at K.U. died a-borning.[6] As the student yearbook, the *Oread*, stated in 1899, "A few futile attempts had been made to interest the students and faculty in the

---

Naismith (standing at far right) with the first basketball team of the University of Kansas, 1899. Courtesy of the Athletic Department of the University of Kansas.

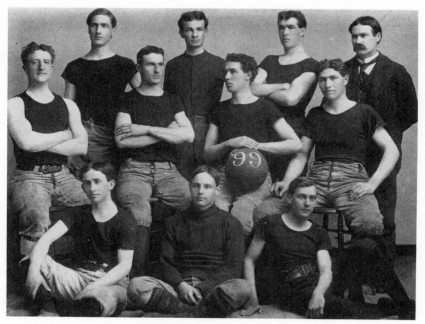

Back row: OWENS, Sub.; HENDERSON, Back; Dr. NAISMITH, Coach. Middle row: AVERY, Sub.; Mgr. EMLEY, Center; Capt. SUTTON, Forward; HESS, Forward. Front row: RUSSELL, Sub.; HOYT, Sub.; YAHN, Back.

game, but without success."[7] When Naismith came, remembered
only was the fact that the adoption of basketball at the university
had been suggested as early as 1896. Thus, he could receive full
credit for bringing basketball into the state of Kansas, in the fall
of 1898, and keeping it alive.

"I organized a basketball team," Naismith said, "the members
of which had never seen a basketball game." He organized eight
teams, as a matter of fact, among his class enrollees and faculty
colleagues.[8] He introduced the game to both campus and town
and soon caught everyone's attention with it. The *Kansas University
Weekly* announced the wild spread of the new sport in its
issue of December 10, only three months after Naismith had come
to the University of Kansas:

A new game has sprung into popularity. It is the game of basket
ball.

Every one who is at all interested in athletics is now talking basket
ball. Yet it does not stop here. Those who hitherto have manifested
no interest in any sports of skill and strength seem now to be enthusiastic over the new game. It is talked at the club; it is discussed in
the corridors; it is practised and played in the gymnasium and on the
campus. Even the professors have become actively interested in the
game and are giving their time of recreation over to this pastime.

At present it appears that the basket ball mania would carry all
before it.[9]

In a few months Naismith's young basketball protégés were
growing eager for something besides intramural competition, and
he organized a varsity team from the best players in class games.
On February 4, 1899, the campus weekly headlined "KU's First
Game." The contest took place between the university and the
Kansas City, Missouri, Y.M.C.A., whose team was already experienced in the "Y" 's pet game. A high point of the event was the
discovery by the Kansas players and fans that one of the Y.M.C.A.
participants was a Jesse James, who, it was reported tongue-in-
cheek, had a connection with the recent train robberies in Missouri. Train robber or not, Jesse James played "a very ungentle-
manly game" and, despite several penalties and numerous warnings by the referee, helped his team steal the match from K.U.[10]

When the contest ended at 9:45 P.M., the score was 16–5. Later in the season, though, when Jesse James did not play, K.U. defeated the Kansas City "Y" 17–14.

The first basketball game to be played on K.U.'s home court came the next week, when K.U. found another neighboring opponent in the Topeka Y.M.C.A. The Topekans traveled a little more than twenty miles to be defeated. The game was played on the Lawrence skating rink, with an attendance of about fifty persons and a score of 31–6 in K.U.'s favor. The University of Kansas had won its first basketball game!

The university was not long restricted to Y.M.C.A. teams for rivals. In this same year of 1899 basketball was introduced into the colleges of the Missouri Valley and neighboring areas, and it quickly became a regular part of extramural college competition. K.U.'s first intercollegiate basketball game occurred the following year, when the Lawrence team traveled across the state line to Lincoln, playing the University of Nebraska on March 2, 1900. Kansas lost that historic game, by an undisclosed score. K.U.'s campus newspaper, the *University Weekly*, reported the exploits of the Nebraskans: "The little northerners tossed baskets so fast that our men lost count and did not linger to find the score after the game."[11] At Lincoln, though, the captain and center of the Nebraska team, who had scored thirty-four points himself, let the final count be known—48 to 8.[12]

This contest revealed something else besides K.U.'s early ineptness with a ball. It showed that officiating at a basketball game was still an unpolished art, not yet refined to a system of whistles and signals manipulated by a disinterested outsider. Naismith, coach of the visiting team, was also a referee at K.U.'s first intercollegiate game, and his approach was blunt and unmistakable. When the Nebraska captain stepped out of bounds, Naismith grabbed him around the waist to inform him of his violation.[13]

Playing facilities for basketball were irregular and impromptu at first. In fact, when Frank Strong became chancellor of the university in 1902,[14] he publicly deplored the lack of physical education facilities.[15] Some of K.U.'s early out-of-town games took place in a hayloft, and at home their arena was, similarly,

a double-duty setup. Before the university had satisfactory court
space on campus, Naismith used to take a group of boys downtown to whatever large floor he could rent. It might be the town
skating rink in the old Armory Building near the Baptist Church
or an empty downtown business building.

The first big setback to K.U. basketball playing came when the
Armory was destroyed by fire. At that time both the Y.M.C.A.
and the Y.W.C.A. were active, and after the rink burned, Naismith was able to use the gym in the downtown Y.M.C.A. during
free hours. This space in the old Gould Building at 937 Massachusetts Street was used until that structure, like the skating rink
before it, burned, the second such misfortune for the basketeers'
playing courts. Then for a few years around 1902 to 1905 the
Y.M.C.A. had its quarters at 924–926 Massachusetts Street, a
location often used by Naismith and his boys. Shortly thereafter
the "Y" moved to permanent quarters on the northeast corner of
Vermont Street, at 16 West Henry, the street later renamed West
Eighth. This handsome building provided offices, a basement
swimming pool, and spacious rooms for sports.[16]

On campus, basketball could be played in old Snow Hall,
predecessor of the present building. But playing conditions were
woefully inadequate. Snow had a court thirty-six feet wide and
eighty-four feet long, with an eleven-foot ceiling and goals about
a foot below the ceiling. In addition to the obstacle of a low
roof, the posts supporting the ceiling were located in a line
down the center of the room, making playing hazardous.

The hazard of supporting columns in the center of a gymnasium was a common problem in the early days of basketball.
This condition existed even in metropolitan areas. In 1894,
for example, the Washington Heights Y.M.C.A. in New York
was one of the few "Y"s in the city whose floor was a delight to
basketball players. One of the largest gymnasiums in New York,
the Washington Heights gym differed from others in the total
absence of poles supporting the ceiling from the floor. "This
gives the boys a large clear floor," officials boasted.[17]

The University of Kansas eventually began to furnish more
adequate facilities than it had previously maintained. The first
step toward improved **quarters for basket**ball was brought about

at Naismith's suggestion. One day he noticed Mr. Crocker, the janitor at Snow Hall, disappear into a hole in one of the basement rooms. Naismith, following, discovered a space about five feet deep between the floor and the foundation below. It occurred to him immediately that one fault of the court could be corrected. Upon his urging, the floor of the court was lowered five feet, to the foundation, to make a sixteen-foot ceiling, with space enough to allow basketball shots to be thrown in an arc. A set of movable steps was constructed to lead down onto the new floor, and these steps were hoisted up into the doorway, after the players had descended, to allow maximum playing space. Only the obstructing center columns would remain to keep the room from being a satisfactory basketball court.

Though it was an improvement, this situation did not continue long. Complaints had been rising near and far about the inadequate basketball court in Snow Hall. No home games were scheduled for the 1906–1907 season, because, as the campus newspaper reported, "No visiting teams will risk their lives among the pillars."[18] At last, sympathetic Chancellor Strong having placed a gymnasium first on his list of proposed construction, in 1906 ground was broken for a physical education building.[19] In 1907 Robinson Gymnasium, new home of the Department of Physical Education, was completed, with the first real basketball court on the campus ready for the 1907–1908 season. Visiting basketball fans and players again flocked to Lawrence, and teams played happily in Robinson Gym until 4,000-seat Hoch Auditorium, nicknamed "the old opera house," was opened in 1927, to be used, among other things, for basketball. Finally, Allen Field House became the home of basketball in 1955.[20]

Naismith was less successful in arousing interest in girls' basketball in Lawrence than he had been in Springfield. The first woman's team was organized at K.U. in 1904, but eleven years after his arrival K.U. women apparently were little interested in athletics. At a meeting of the junior and senior basketball clubs at the beginning of the basketball season in 1909, only four girls appeared. But the zest of the male players easily made up for the apathy of the female basketeers, and the girls cheered excitedly enough as spectators.

In a sense, basketball advanced by its own momentum more than by Naismith's propagandistic efforts, for he never became very excited about the game. True, he considered it a good all-around team sport for young people, superior in many ways to football and other games with the rough physical contact that he had enjoyed in his own younger days.

As a high-school team game, in particular, he gave emphatic recommendation to basketball. In rising progression of praise for outdoor team sports, he stated, "Baseball is good . . . soccer is an excellent game . . . lacrosse is an ideal game." But for an indoor sport he thought that basketball was unsurpassed. "Basket-ball is for the winter months, indoors, what the above games are for outdoors." Basketball developed what he called the best type of athlete—"the wiry, supple, agile man with good arms and shoulders."[21] At the same time, he liked to point out the advantages of more individualized sports. For youngsters he recognized the value of apparatus work in the gymnasium. "When we realize that this is the very best form of training that can be given to high school students it is a wonder that we have not before appreciated it."[22]

For an individual, he considered wrestling better exercise than basketball. For audience enjoyment, he recommended a skillful exhibition of tumbling. And from the standpoint of a coach, he liked best to instruct a couple of eager young people in the art of fencing. Wrestling, tumbling, fencing—to him these sports provided more benefits for spectator and participant than a hundred basketball games.[23]

As a participant, he himself had taken notable part in every sport going around—except basketball. Only once during his time at K.U. did he play the game. Many years later—literally and figuratively at the height of his fame in the season of the 1936 Berlin Olympics—when interviewed on top of the Woolworth Building in New York, he admitted that he had played basketball only twice in his life, at Springfield in 1892 and at Kansas in 1898.[24]

In short, even though basketball was his own creation, he had too many other interests to become obsessed with it. He dutifully attended all the K.U. basketball games, many tournaments in

Kansas City, and some games in eastern cities when he was there on business; but, compared to the shouting fans around him, he was little more than an inconspicuous and mildly interested spectator. People noticed that "Dr. Naismith never yelled at a basketball game."[25]

Basketball steadily grew into an outstanding success at the University of Kansas. About 1905 there was a movement in the United States to tame football by taking the dangerous elements out of it, or even to abolish the game altogether; but basketball went merrily on, at K.U. as elsewhere. After basketball attained an importance equal to that of longstanding sports, a regular basketball coach was hired at the university. Coaching was at first a seasonal profession, with a man coming to oversee a sport for one season. The coach's duties grew, though. In 1909–1910 W. O. ("Bill") Hamilton became a K.U. coach, and in 1912 he was hired as a resident coach on a full-time basis, the first man at K.U. to have the title of head basketball coach.[26]

As far as the coaching of basketball was concerned, Naismith was noticeably uninterested. He had demonstrated that he was better at creating the game than he was at teaching the skills of it, records showing fifty-four games won and forty-four lost under his tutelage. Half a century later people liked to recall that Naismith was "the only losing coach Kansas ever had."[27]

James Naismith, however, never really considered himself a coach. Although technically he was the first of five coaches in the first seventy-odd years of basketball at the University of Kansas, he never believed "coaching" necessary to the game. "Basket Ball is not a game intended merely for amusement," he cautioned, "but is the attempted solution of a problem."[28] The problem, as he saw it, was to find an indoor game that would build bodies and character in young men without boring them. His interest in basketball was directed toward that development, not toward the winning of games. Naismith would not have been unduly excited to know that the University of Kansas would go on to become a powerhouse in Midwestern basketball conferences and in the nation, in 1952 sending five players and their coach to help represent the United States at the Olympic Games.[29] (K.U. was almost number one among U.S. teams that year. The Kansas quintet of champions went into the Olympic finals in Madison Square Garden, only to lose in the last few seconds of the game to the Peoria Caterpillar Diesels, 62–60.)

At the beginning of the twentieth century Naismith did not realize, to be sure, where the basketball bandwagon was heading, but he probably suspected all along that there was coming to be too much hullabaloo about the game.

14
Prayers, Sports, and Students

IT turned out to be fun to be part of the University of Kansas in those years around the turn of the century. Chancellor Francis Huntington Snow was short in stature, physically speaking, but he was dynamic in his effect. He built enrollment from 505 to 1,154 during his tenure, increased the number of books in the library from 14,000 to 38,000, and caused six buildings and twenty acres to be added to the university grounds. Personally, he was what is termed "a character." A favorite anecdote tells about the chancellor and his brakeless bicycle. Coming out of a driveway on the steep east side of Mount Oread now known as the Fourteenth Street hill, he would hoist his feet up on foot rests above the front wheels and shoot down the dangerous incline with his coattails flying.[1]

Under Snow as chancellor James Naismith got along fine. His job at the university, happily, never called for the specialization now necessary in coaching a major modern sport such as basketball. It required, rather, an academic quick-change artist, skilled in several roles. When he came to K.U. in 1898, his job was to act as head and sole instructor of the Department of Physical Education, teaching the required freshman course in hygiene, the gymnastic classes, and other courses that might be offered, as well as overseeing athletics in general. In addition, the point on which he had been hired, he had charge of daily devotional exercises in the student chapel in Fraser auditorium, a large room with balcony, seating 650 persons.[2]

The hour-long chapel program was composed of Bible reading and prayer by Chaplain Naismith, singing and prayer by the students under his leadership, and an address either by a faculty member or a speaker from outside the university. Naismith arranged each program and was often the main speaker himself.[3]

As time passed, the compulsory daily devotional program was changed to one held on alternate days and then to one held weekly at ten o'clock on Tuesday mornings. The next step was to change the rule of compulsory attendance to voluntary participation.[4]

Changes continued, bidden and unbidden. In October, 1902, the first issue of the *Graduate Magazine* was printed, and a new chancellor came along that same autumn.[5] Frank Strong, six feet four inches in height, was a contrast to Francis Snow, with his five feet six inches. He was said to be cold and unbending, too, compared to Snow. But although Strong did not ride a bicycle without brakes down the Fourteenth Street hill, he initiated fifty years of colorful nightshirt parades when he came out of his bed in a nightshirt to lead a student victory march.

He was active in other ways as well. The university already provided many services to Kansas—analyzing foods and drugs, sealing weights and measures, supervising the control of insects, studying underground resources.[6] Now, in his inaugural speech of 1902, Strong announced his plan for increased service to the state; and to implement this approach, he entered descriptions of courses in banking, business, insurance, domestic science, and journalism in the university catalog of 1903–1904.[7] Then, the confidence of the citizenry having been established, he successfully approached the state legislators with proposals for increased budgets. Consequently, he saw a four-year School of Medicine founded on the Lawrence campus and at the university hospital in Kansas City, and, in addition, he managed to get street lights, new buildings, and expanded boundaries on Mount Oread. In scholarly circles, he convinced the directors of the elite Association of American Universities that the University of Kansas should be admitted to membership, in recognition of the quality of its graduate work.

Complementing his involvement in both business and academic matters, he paid due attention to religion in Fraser chapel. By the time Strong came to K.U., Naismith had let the average attendance at chapel exercises diminish to some thirty-five students and five or six faculty members. Whatever Strong's method of stirring up enthusiasm, he soon had the place overflowing, at least temporarily.

Good chapel attendance did not last, though. Greater crowds showed up when the room was used for secular affairs. One such event occurred in November, 1909, when the chapel was borrowed by students and townspeople as a reception center for news from the Kansas-Nebraska football game in Lincoln, Nebraska. As the special correspondent of the *Kansan*—the campus newspaper—sent a running report by direct wire from the University of Nebraska press box, the report was flashed on a screen in the auditorium within one minute of the actual play, and music filled in the half-time and time-out intervals. The room was advertised as being "comfortably warm," and young K.U. women, a definite minority among Lawrence football fans, were given a special invitation to attend the free newscast.

During chapel services themselves the religious content of the programs diminished, with a growing demand for treatment of topical matters. A typical chapel address was Naismith's talk in March, 1911, entitled "Commercialism in Athletics." In discussing the reasons for "commercialism" and its effects, he exhorted against the trend that he felt was destroying the real purpose of sports.

Eventually, regular religious exercises were discontinued, and Naismith no longer had a religious function at the university.[8] Much later, long after his death, handsome Danforth Chapel, with seating capacity for a few dozen persons, was built on the campus, to be used for small weddings and special memorial services. But for a number of years during Naismith's tenure a chapel was not considered a necessity for students.

Naismith was not so much worried about a decline in religion on campus as he was concerned about the way things were going in sports. He was far from the first man, of course, to be upset. In the summer of 1890, in fact, when he was just preparing to come to the United States for an education in athletics, Americans were viewing the field with alarm. An article in the *Atlantic Monthly* pointed out that because of intense competition in American college football in the previous ten years, "a professional spirit has crept in," and "the standard of sport has fallen."[9] The *Atlantic* writer accused sports as a whole of "coming to have the interest of gladiatorial events."[10]

Athletics continued strongly, though. As a member of the University Athletic Board from 1901 until the Board of Regents excluded from membership any faculty member in the Department of Physical Education, Naismith had a good opportunity, particularly during the early years, to make his voice heard in the athletic program.[11] Some of the games familiar to him, such as lacrosse and rugby, were not played at K.U. at that time, but there were plenty of other activities for him to supervise. After he came to K.U., interest in physical education developed rapidly.[12]

Despite his promotion of athletics, he did his best to keep down professionalism, as indicated by his 1911 chapel speech. One of the first things he did upon his arrival at the university was to initiate a program of intramural athletics, which he called "home athletics," and to begin organizing games and tournaments. He was always much more interested in promoting intramural athletics than in managing the ever-growing affairs of intercollegiate sports, just as he was more interested in the welfare of the individual than in the success of the team. Several of his "little projects," happily, bore the seal of university-wide approval.

Among his innovations in the athletic program, fencing had the most accidental beginning. Fencing equipment at the University of Kansas was acquired by chance, in 1896, two years before a fencing instructor, namely Naismith, was available. The university had purchased for its athletic department all the fixtures and equipment—lock, stock, and barrel—of a defunct gymnasium in Atchison, Kansas. Included in the equipment happened to be the masks, foils, plastrons, and other accouterment of a fencing class.[13] The gear looked impressive enough, but no one knew, or cared, much about it. When Naismith came along, though, action began.

Although the University of Kansas had remained uninterested in so frivolous a sport, fencing was becoming popular in Britain and the United States near the end of the nineteenth century, and the Intercollegiate Fencing Association was founded in 1894.[14] Naismith had become adept at the art of dueling before he came to the Middle West, and he liked the sport. Therefore, when he found fencing equipment lying idle in the storeroom of the gymnasium, he promptly dusted it off, organized classes in fencing and broadsword, and became responsible for arousing and maintaining student interest in fencing, with few lapses, throughout his career at the university. His three main fields of coaching in his early years at K.U. were basketball, track, and fencing, the last duty being the one he continued until he was past seventy-five, dueling regularly with his physical education students. A skillful performer as well as a good instructor, he liked to show the fine points of the sport by dueling with a yardstick against a student with broadsword—and winning. He was proud when one of his students, Harold Burdick, continued his fencing activity at Annapolis, where he was on fencing teams that competed against Harvard and Yale.[15]

Naismith was interested in sports for everyone, and one of his earliest projects was the construction on the university grounds of a golf course that was open to students, professors, and townspeople. Located on the north slope of the campus, it stretched from the site of the present administration building to the site of the present athletic stadium. Naismith himself volunteered to give golf lessons in an effort to spread interest in the game. When Chancellor Snow's daughter Edith and her friend May Gardner, both of whom lived on Twelfth Street near the golf course, came to him for lessons, he responded with alacrity. Gratified that he had interested at least two young women in the game, he proudly called them "my prize pupils."[16] But the woman he would probably have most liked to have beside him swinging a golf club did not come to him for lessons. Although Maude would have liked to please James by learning the game, she was busy at home with their two small daughters and, soon pregnant again, was not able to come out.

Interest in golf was great enough that it helped cause the Board of Regents in 1915 to forbid recreational sports on the campus on Sunday. Naismith himself, though the most enthusiastic of golfers, had never intended that the game be played on Sunday. Always a religious man, grown now somewhat overly strict in manners and morals, he believed that secular activity should be sternly curtailed on the Sabbath Day.[17]

Only slightly hampered by the regents' ruling, golf continued to flourish, the Oread Golf Club sponsoring periodic golf "meets." As late as 1928 a fifteen-hole course, with Potter Lake as the center, was in operation. That year, however, the fifteen-hole course was rebuilt as nine holes. Later it was cut to six holes, and then to three. Finally the chancellor's wife planted a row of trees down the middle of the fairway, and today only the vestige of one hole remains. The Lawrence Country Club and its golf course, however, which evolved from Naismith's golf club, became a permanent part of the community.[18]

Perhaps most publicized of his intramural activities was the rowing competition on the Kaw River that he helped organize. The first regatta was held in 1908, with seventy-one entries in the race and a large crowd of spectators on the shore. Then Potter Lake was built in a hollow on the hilly K.U. campus. Originally intended to provide water in the event of a fire in one of the classroom buildings, the lake came to be used for swimming and boating and such competitions as the university canoe regatta. By commencement time, water from melting snow, spring rains, and city water mains had filled the lake, and the Commencement Regatta became an annual affair.[19] Naismith much preferred a canoe to a rowboat. He had grown up in a country where a canoe, even today, is sometimes the only way to travel from one point to another, and he was an expert coach for these Midwestern students.

Throughout all his activities, he never favored his own creation, basketball, over other games. He promoted every phase of athletics. Sometimes his intramural projects spilled over into intercollegiate competition, as, indeed, basketball had done. Track was one of them. By May, 1902, he had fostered enough interest at the upper levels of the administration that seventy-five dollars was appropriated to the Athletic Association by the Board of Regents "for the betterment of track." The money was used to put the track into running condition for the contest against Missouri University on May 17. By 1903 as many as fifty track candidates were running under his direction, and that year the first Missouri-Kansas indoor meet was held in Convention Hall in Kansas City. He was enthusiastic about K.U.'s participation in that group of sports.[20]

By 1904 track had been built up to the point where Naismith needed an assistant. In that year Fay Moulton, the first K.U. athlete to compete in the Olympic Games, coached the track team, and the first interscholastic meet was run. J. P. Hagerman, however, director of the Lawrence Y.M.C.A., served double duty by becoming the first official track coach in 1907. Along with his "Y" duties, university responsibilities took time and attention for a few years. He and Naismith organized the first indoor meet in Robinson Gym in 1909, and, to keep the athletes in optimum condition, a track training table was started.[21]

After an interim without a coach, W. O. ("Bill") Hamilton became Naismith's next track mentor. Hamilton set the goal of a 400-man track squad, and the administration gave assistance to the ambitious coach when it passed a new rule requiring that all male students take track work throughout their first two years in college.[22]

The new coach was as ingenious and enthusiastic as his department head, James Naismith, proving successful enough eventually to become athletic manager from 1913 until his resignation in 1919. He agreed with Naismith that a knowledge of medicine would make him a more capable coach and, therefore, took a summer course in the School of Medicine. Perhaps for Hamilton a little learning was a dangerous thing. Discovering in his studies that showers and tub baths were "enervating," he forbade bathing by his men for three days before the 1912 track meet. Three years later, before the 1915 indoor meet with the University of Missouri, he ordered the training-table cook to feed rabbit to the trackmen to make them run faster. He prescribed "Belgian rabbits plus several of the jackrabbit variety instead of the usual steaks and roasts." He was conscientious enough to worry, though. Aware of the adage "no more brains than a rabbit," he feared that the boys' semester grades would suffer as a result of their diet.[23] Maybe it was poetic justice that they lost the track meet, after all.

Even lacrosse gained a place as part of the athletic program. The national game of Canada was imported by Naismith onto the prairies of Kansas. Although it did not endure permanently at the University of Kansas, for a while it was a popular sport. When Phog Allen and his basketball team posed for a photograph in the campus yearbook of 1908, eight members of the lacrosse team rated a photo of equal importance.[24]

Football was another of Naismith's intercollegiate sports, but it had more startling ups and downs than the rest of his program. Initiated at the University of Kansas in 1890, intercollegiate football ran on enthusiastically for years, causing friendly rivalries with colleges in neighboring states. Competition between the universities of Kansas and Missouri, for instance, resulted in the traditional "big game" of the year for both institutions, attracting large crowds. For many years the annual contest was held in Kansas City, Missouri, a convenient stopping place on the long road between the two universities.

But hard times came to football in the early years of the century, during the presidential administration of Theodore Roosevelt, when the game grew too rough for the public. Roosevelt—Rough Rider, explorer, and African big-game hunter—was an advocate of the strenuous life, but he became alarmed at the casualties in football and threatened to stop the game. For a while the future looked bleak on the playing field.

At the University of Kansas, Chancellor Strong helped to bring football under control by taking the lead in organizing the Missouri Valley Athletic Association and, with it, the Missouri Valley Association of Governing Boards and Chief Executive Officers. Soon football resumed its popularity, and Naismith got on with the game.

As head of the Department of Physical Education, Naismith was in an enviable position. By 1903, as the K.U. administration further extended its leniency in educational rules, the only courses specifically required for graduation were rhetoric, hygiene, and physical education, and the last two of the three required subjects were under his command.[25]

Even so, he managed to introduce new courses into the curriculum. Among them, his favorite was kinesiology, for his work with athletes had caused him to become greatly interested in the working of muscles, tendons, and joints. He liked the gymnastic course, too. He may have neglected ideal organization and orderly progression in the class, but both students and teacher had fun.[26]

Naismith enjoyed both gymnastic instruction and classroom teaching. One of his favorite tricks in the classroom, which he considered a sound teaching device, was to challenge the students with questions; and this resulted in heated arguments.[27] He was a natural teacher, some persons said. Others, however, were not sure that they had learned much in his classes.[28]

The freshman hygiene course was one in which it was difficult to stir up interest. A one-hour course required for every male at the university, Health and Hygiene met in the Robinson lecture room once a week, at 4:30 in the afternoon, an hour when most classes were over and students were tired and impatient to leave the campus.[29] After years without much change in content, the course became known as a "snap."[30] Learning that they could make passing grades without much effort, students devised ways of breaking attendance regulations without penalty. When the official enrollment of a particular class was ninety, at roll call fifty men were likely to be present, with ninety responses of "Present" ringing out, as one young man answered for several of his friends. Professor Naismith probably knew what was going on, but he never let on that he did.[31]

Sometimes, undeniably, the Health and Hygiene lectures had an appeal that was slightly improper. Naismith, ahead of his time in advocating sex education, occasionally introduced into his lectures in the all-male classroom biological points that were inadequately handled in assigned textbooks.

Aside from the question of sexual morality, there was an overall moral quality about much of Naismith's teaching—despite his ignoring of the immorality implied in a dishonest roll call. In spite of the largeness of the Health and Hygiene class, the impatient freshman boys developed a "high respect and deep affection" for this man, "kindly, understanding, and devoutly religious" as they immediately recognized him to be.[32] In other classes, too, his moral earnestness was evident. In his course in Child Development the word "duty" became a key word in his lectures, as he stressed doing the job set before one and doing it right. In his kinesiology course an explanation of bone structure or of nervous tissue often turned into an ethical discourse. In all his teaching there was implicit emphasis on cleanliness of mind and body and on right direction of heart and spirit, as he carried on the theory of Luther Halsey Gulick's Y.M.C.A. teaching that each part of the body is a part of the soul.

There was another kind of challenge in the physical education classroom, also. Remembering basketball's origin, Naismith continued to create new games for his gym students. Before he was through he had dreamed up at least three games worthy of national publication—war-tug, hy-lo, and vrille—but none of them caught on. He even designed a new indoor-outdoor adaptation of basketball. When he created the original game of basketball one December day in 1891, however, he seemed to have used up the magic combination and would never find another one—under either an old name or a new one.[33]

Although he enjoyed classroom teaching, he liked best the method of personal conferences, often finding it more effective to work on a private basis with students than in a formal group session. Particularly satisfying to him were the man-to-man talks that he had with male students. Here he was able to discuss without restraint the implications of the boy-girl relationships so important to the eighteen- and nineteen-year-old freshman boys in his domain. Sex was on the campus, and he met the problem frankly, on his own terms.[34] Whatever the problem—sex or grades or athletic deficiency or parental discipline—he was ready to talk and to listen. Scorning cut-and-dried methods, he had a talent for helping a student to develop his ideas and himself.[35]

Outside the classroom and the office he was available not only for aid with personal problems but also with group activities. Fraternities and their affairs, for instance, took much of his time.

Social fraternities had existed on the K.U. campus since 1873,[36] and Naismith was popular as an adviser and chaperone for the boys, eventually being made an honorary member of Sigma Phi Epsilon in 1923.[37]

But in those early years student escapades made more colorful news for the campus newspaper and more work for Naismith than did tea parties and ice-cream socials. There was plenty of need for a firm but sympathetic faculty adviser, for K.U. students indulged in their share of high jinks. One day in 1882, as Naismith heard the anecdote, when an Easterner had visited the Midwestern campus wearing a silk hat, a senior shot the hat off the man's head. That deed had become a legend by the time Naismith arrived, but other things, like the traditional rivalry of engineering and law students, were still going on. Sometimes in their history the two groups met in a conflict as innocent as a tug-of-war beside Potter Lake, but sometimes they played with bigger toys than a rope.

In 1900, one of the years for giant-sized tricks, the engineering class transported a 5,000-pound boulder onto the campus with "Eng. '01" painted conspicuously on it. For days, law and engineering students alternated in rolling the boulder into competitive positions, until, finally, someone in high authority was needed to settle the growing dispute. Thereupon Chancellor Snow was called in, a man who knew how to stage a more dramatic climax than the two rival classes put together. He simply blew the boulder out of existence with a charge of dynamite, and the trouble was over.[38]

Another choice prank was instigated by engineering students during Naismith's early years at K.U. One night in 1903, irked because the state legislature had granted K.U. $50,000 for a new law building, the engineers hauled an outdoor toilet up the Fourteenth Street hill and placed it in front of Fraser Hall. While innocent law students slept, the engineers labeled the outhouse "Green Hall, the New Law Building" and "Gymnasium in the Basement." They went too far by filling the little structure with hay, for that action gave the "Laws" a chance to have the last word. When law students discovered the hay-filled privy the next morning, they threw in a lighted match and set building and all on fire.[39]

They were clever, those future lawyers. The senior law class of 1904 was especially so. When commencement time neared, would-be graduates decided that, considering all the money they had already spent for their education, it was not necessary to pay the ten-dollar fee required for receipt of a diploma. Their plan received a temporary setback: on graduation day they were handed blank pieces of paper that signaled "no degree." But somehow they won their argument, and the administration later mailed them proper diplomas.[40]

Religion, athletics, classes, and counseling were not all there was for Naismith. Although hired as a minister and an instructor of physical education, not as a physician, for a while he officially used his medical training at the university. During the years before K.U. had the services of a full-time physician, he carried out those duties from his office at the gymnasium.[41] Then, after the university grew larger, he assisted in pioneering a comprehensive health service, before turning over the work to someone else. When Dr. H. L. Chambers was appointed resident university physician in 1909, Naismith helped him initiate a new health program with free medical consultation provided for each student. Then "Doc" Naismith relinquished his practice—in theory, at least.

In actuality, "Doc" continued to use his medical knowledge informally and without fee, and he was often consulted by students and friends. Sometimes, when disaster struck, both Dr. Chambers and Dr. Naismith were called. For example, in the spring of 1911, after the annual farewell meeting of the civil engineering class, a group walked over for a dip in Potter Lake. Newly built that year, the lake was already a popular place for swimming—and on this occasion a tragic one. While twenty students stood helplessly on the bank, one of the boys in the water suffered an apparent heart failure. Both of the doctors hurried to the scene and worked together on the boy, although their efforts at resuscitation were futile.[42]

Much of Naismith's medical work was of a happier kind than emergency calls, though. He was fascinated by the possibility of rehabilitating crippled bodies. "He used to delight in giving special instructions to cripples and help them to use their arms and legs again," his son James explained.[43] "Probably his biggest thrill was watching kids being able to get along without braces after he had worked with them." James added, "He couldn't see a student with crutches or braces without wanting to do something about it."[44]

And do something he did, his main tools being massage, exercise, and enthusiasm. He helped many a boy student, and occasionally a girl, in this way.

His son summed up Naismith's accomplishments in physical therapy by comparing him with the Australian nurse who developed a well-known treatment of polio-affected muscles: "He was doing Sister Kenny work long before she was heard of."[45] Once he worked with success, using osteopathic methods, on a girl with a curvature of the spine.[46]

The university used Naismith for off-campus extracurricular duties, too, notably as a speaker. In Kansas the traveling Chautauqua shows provided an important source of culture and entertainment for citizens from about 1889 to 1930. The University of Kansas had early created a curricular division known as University Extension, intended to provide instruction by mail in a variety of subjects and, in additional ways, to bring intellectual offerings into every Kansas community. While the Chautauqua movement was popular, one of the means by which the Extension Division disseminated education was to arrange Chautauqua lectures by faculty members.[47]

Two representative figures in entertainment and education sent out by K.U. were E. C. Buehler and James Naismith. Professor Buehler, director of speech at the university, not only was a speaker and entertainer but was among the most successful of Chautauqua superintendents, directing programs with versatility and flair for the Redpath Horner Chautauquas.[48] Dr. Naismith, whose intent was more to teach than to entertain, was sent out as a lecturer on the physical development of the child, one of his favorite subjects.[49]

His public addresses were not, of course, restricted to discussions of child development. He liked to talk about athletics and physical education, too. In addition to lecturing on the Chautauqua circuit, on miscellaneous occasions he gave addresses on the origin of basketball, the advantages of gymnastics in high school, the physical development of college athletes, and myriad related subjects to physical education groups either in Lawrence or out of town.[50]

This, then, on the campus and off, pranks and all, constituted the academic atmosphere that Dr. James Naismith found around him in Kansas. He may have wondered whether it was anything like this with his three old friends who, like him, had continued to work in the field of physical education.

Amos Alonzo Stagg was at the University of Chicago, where he had been athletic coach since 1892.[51] Dr. Luther Halsey Gulick, having left the International Young Men's Christian Association Training School in Springfield in 1900, was now employed by the International Committee of the Y.M.C.A., supervising physical work in the Y.M.C.A. of North America. His position as superintendent of the physical department of the Training School had been assumed by Dr. James Huff McCurdy, a faculty member there since 1895. The oldest friend of all, Dr. Robert Tait McKenzie, was also at work in the United States. He had come down from Canada in 1904 to accept a position as Director of Physical Education at the University of Pennsylvania.[52]

The interesting thing about these men was that each embraced two or more professional fields. Stagg, a former divinity student at Yale, managed to mix religion into athletics. Gulick was both physician and physical educator. McKenzie, physician and physical educator, did outstanding sculptures of athletes as an avocation. And Naismith, most versatile of them all—minister, physician, and physical educator—had created the game of basketball. He also seemed, at the moment, to be the busiest one.

15

"I'll Lend No More of My Babies"

JAMES NAISMITH did not stop with playing fields and balls and goals. Ingenious of mind, he invented other things in addition to games, and his innovations and inventions created varying degrees of interest and of laughter.

In the fall of 1909 he caused a stir among university students when he devised an apparatus for testing the effects of alcohol on the nervous system. The basis of his testing instrument was a rod about one-quarter inch in diameter which the subject, standing with feet apart and arms outstretched, was to insert into a hole approximately one-half inch in diameter in the center of a metal block. If the unsteady student touched the metal block with the rod, an electrical circuit would be completed, with evidence of his nervousness recorded on a revolving drum. Professor Naismith enlisted the aid of the Department of Pharmacy, requesting Dean Sayre and Professor Havenhill to prepare samples of alcohol and of an appropriate control beverage, suitably disguised in taste. Naismith's plan was to line up students in Robinson Gymnasium, discreetly administer drinks, measure the resultant condition of the nerves in squiggly lines on graph paper, and make records of those results.[1]

No imbiber himself, James Naismith felt little compunction about recording other people's wobbly lines. In fact, he thought that it was his duty to do so. And that compulsion to immerse himself in statistics extended to other areas.

Records of the victories and defeats of his basketball teams may have been unimportant to Naismith, but records of various conditions of the human body were a passion with him, overflowing his files at the university. His interest in statistics about the bodies of young men dated back to his early college education. By 1890 and before—when Naismith was studying at McGill and the Springfield Y.M.C.A.—many physicians and physical educators had been keeping records of the physical condition of college students. His first professor of physical education, Dr. Luther

Halsey Gulick, Jr., whose influence followed him all his life, was one of these educators. Gulick was keenly interested in anthropometry—the measurement of the human body and its parts—and was striving to make the methods of measurement uniform and to bring something functional out of the measurements. In 1887–1888 he had devised a uniform system for Y.M.C.A. directors to use to secure and tabulate statistical data on physical dimensions of the body. While Naismith was associated with him in the International Y.M.C.A. Training School at Springfield, Gulick published his "Manual for Physical Measurements in Connection with Association Gymnasium Records" (1892) and a series of articles on measurements. He also compiled and published an anthropometric chart.[2]

Much of this work in the late nineteenth century was used to show that the bodily vigor and health of college students had risen perceptibly in the previous ten or twenty years. For instance, as a result of 3,537 measurements taken since 1879, Dr. Dudley Allen Sargent found that each of 248 men in Harvard College in 1890 was stronger than the strongest Harvard man of 1880. Naismith was familiar with Dr. Sargent's work at Harvard, as well as with Dr. R. Tait McKenzie's study under him and McKenzie's subsequent interest in tests and measurements of the human body.[3] In the early decades of the twentieth century Naismith was carrying on this same type of interest in the continuing physical development of college students.

As the instructor of the hygiene class required for all male students at the University of Kansas, he was in an advantageous position for making studies of this type. He proceeded to do so, systematically. Throughout his years at K.U. he insisted on taking various anthropometric measurements of all men entering the university, including those measurements and details of physical health in the record he maintained for each student.[4] There is no evidence that Naismith reported any results to Gulick, or to McKenzie, for comparison. Although he was carrying on a project in which Gulick had earlier done similar work, there was apparently no collaboration between the two friends.

Most current studies of measurements are concerned only with height and weight, assuming that other statistics are reflected to a significant degree in these two, but Naismith meticulously recorded nineteen anthropometric measurements: height, weight, girth of neck, girth of chest contracted, girth of chest expanded, girth of waist, girth of right arm, girth of right arm up, girth of left arm, girth of left arm up, girth of right forearm, girth of left forearm, girth of right thigh, girth of left thigh, girth of right calf, girth of left calf, breadth of shoulders, breadth of chest, and breadth of hips.[5]

Included in the detailed health records that he kept of his students were such items as these:

> Hours in open air: 4 hr.
> Sleep: 9 hr.

Handwritten notes on some of the records showed such personal data as these facts: "carriage erect," "bowels good."[6] Sometimes the facts were even more intimate than this, for Gulick's interest

---

Naismith with the two entering male students at the University of Kansas in 1932 whom he judged to have the finest physiques. Photograph by Duke D'Ambra, courtesy of Mrs. D'Ambra and L. A. Royer, Lawrence, Kansas.

in the sexual development of the adolescent boy had influenced him in this area, too. One of Naismith's daughters, looking at his records after his death, called them a "mid-Victorian Kinsey report."[7]

Statistics continued to fascinate James Naismith all his life. "Doc collects statistics on anything that'll hold still to be measured," was one of the jokes about his activities.[8] Maybe his spelling was not always perfect—he might commit such an indiscretion as leaving out the second "m" in "swimming"—but his notes were copious and often lively.

His zeal for applying a tape measure to the human body extended to his own family. At his son James's birth Naismith measured him—tibia, chest, length, and so forth—calling out the figures to the weary but obedient mother, who lay in bed with pencil and paper. He carried his keen interest in his youngest son's development outside the nursery, too. When little Jimmy was three days old, Professor Naismith brought the baby to the class in child development as an exhibit of an initial stage in the physical growth of a young male. In the warm May classroom the professor marked the naked infant with red and blue chalk to emphasize the main points in the discussion. It was a good lecture, but it was the last one of that type, for Naismith neglected to wash off the red and blue marks before returning the infant to its mother.

"I'll lend no more of my babies," Maude stated firmly.[9]

But she cooperated willingly in home observation of the baby, helping her husband obtain detailed notes at least several times a month on the child's physical and mental development. When Jimmy was a year old, Dr. Naismith was still recording on random scraps of paper the impromptu bits of childish behavior that he gravely justified as scientific data. An example of his notes set down on the back of an envelope reads: "March 20th, tries to drink his bath water by putting his mouth into it like a dog. Also when I give him something to eat keeps it on the foor[*sic*] and then tries to eat it like an animal would."[10]

Finally, after years of teaching the course in child development and of studying babies' idiosyncrasies first-hand, he wrote an article on the physical development of children. Published in the university *Bulletin on Education* in 1930, this article gives an insight not only into the all-inclusive quality of his record-taking, but also into his consideration for the individual whose inches or pounds or intelligence quotient was being recorded.

Critical of current charts of "normalcy," in this article Naismith protested against the use of height as the standard of physical development in school-age children and weight as the basis of classification in many athletic events. In school, labels of "physical precociousness" and "physical retardation" were often given and variations in normalcy disregarded. He favored an individualizing rather than a generalizing diagnosis and a scale of measurement that did something besides compare weight and height.

To provide a composite picture of individuals in separated localities, he collected measurements and tests on more than two thousand children from three states, using information provided by schools in Sioux City, Iowa; Kansas City, Missouri; and Winfield, Kansas. To correct the inequities existing in current systems of measurements, he manipulated these data to set up a compromise between "height age" and "weight age," adding to customary physical measurements a battery of mental and emotional tests. He was thorough, to say the least. He prepared separate sets of charts for boys and for girls aged six through nineteen. In these charts he included not only age and height for both sexes but also muscular development for boys in parts of the body ranging from neck to calf. In addition, he recorded such nonphysical characteristics as "emotional," "aesthetic," "moral," and "religious." These aspects of development were measured by standard tests then available (such as Koh's Ethical Discrimination Test), and results of each of these tests were shown by numbers ranging from six to nineteen, corresponding to the chronological ages covered in his records. He used a total of thirteen tests. Seven of the thirteen items he listed could be measured objectively, and only six depended in part on subjective judgment. He thus prepared an overall picture of development by reducing each of the physical, mental, emotional, social, and scholastic performances to a more or less objective numerical basis.

He pointed out that the preparation of a graph for an individual child based on such measurements and conclusions would help a teacher to assign work that suited the needs of each student. In addition, the child would be able to recognize that instead of being "precocious" or "retarded" for his age, in certain aspects he was simply, for the moment, in a class with boys or girls older than himself and in some aspects with ones younger. In this study, then, as in all his work, Naismith showed an insight into the individual harassed by the demands of an impersonal educational system. Throughout his measuring and testing, he believed that such a systematic diagnosis of the development of each child, with its recognition of individual needs, would help to modify the evils of what he termed "mass production in education."[11]

In addition to exhaustive tabulations of the development of school children, of male college freshmen, and of his own male infant, he did comparative studies of athletes. For example, he compared the average measurements of K.U. basketball players, the measurements of the captain of the K.U. basketball team, and the measurements of the best all-around K.U. athletes in football, baseball, and gymnasium work.[12]

One result of these comparative studies was Naismith's formulation of the idea that basketball helped produce "the tall, agile, graceful and expert athlete rather than the massive muscular man on the one hand, or the cadaverous greyhound type on the other."[13]

While Naismith was overseas during World War I, the United States Army overran K.U., and many of his records, along with the first plate-glass basketball backboard, were destroyed.[14] Still, there were hundreds of record cards left in file cabinets, stacks of dusty cards on top of file cabinets, and piles of notebooks lying around with all the essential data undisturbed.[15] When he returned from France, he calmly resumed his familiar statistical work, with new projects added.

During those years after the war he took great pains to answer charges that basketball was too strenuous a game, charges that Dr. James Huff McCurdy of Springfield College (formerly the International Y.M.C.A. Training School) based on physical examinations and tests. Naismith, in the preparation of his defense, became involved in another series of testing and record-keeping. When the Kansas state high-school basketball tournaments were played at the University of Kansas in the early 1920s, Naismith, assisted by a student in the Department of Physical Education, carried out tests to determine the albumin, sugar, blood, and casts in the urine of players before and after a basketball game. He went on from urinalyses to measurements of time. At the basketball games of the Interscholastic League of Kansas City in the three consecutive seasons of 1925, 1926, and 1927, he made tests timing the periods of activity and of relaxation of each player during a game. He followed this series with similar tests throughout basketball games played at the University of Kansas during the seasons of 1931 and 1932. His several series of time measurements and urinalyses, as well as checks of pulse and respiration, proved to his satisfaction that the periods of strenuous activity in any basketball game are brief and that complete recovery from the effects of these periods of strenuosity is rapid.[16]

He felt strongly enough about the results of these experiments that he published some of them in 1925, and in Cattell's *Leaders in Education* he is cited for his studies of the effects of motor activity on the individual.[17] Perhaps most important to him, he had successfully refuted James Huff McCurdy's claims, he felt, that basketball was too strenuous a game.[18]

But for the most part his accumulation of statistics remained in his files. His younger colleagues admired his meticulous records and complained, "He doesn't *do* anything with them. He just collects them."[19] The ambitious ones thought he should organize, analyze, and publish everything he could, when publication was beginning to be the road to academic promotion. They labeled Doc Naismith a plugger, who failed to draw attention to the duties he was plugging away at.[20]

Eventually something was done with Naismith's exhaustive notes, but it was not until 1949–1950, when three members of the Department of Physical Education at the University of Kansas rescued the pile of records. Repeating his methods and measurements, they carried out a matching study of young men of eighteen to twenty-two years of age then enrolled at K.U. These researchers used fourteen of his anthropometric measurements: height, weight, girth of neck, girth of chest expanded, girth of waist, girth of right arm, girth of left arm, girth of right thigh, girth of left thigh, girth of right calf, girth of left calf, breadth of shoulders, breadth of chest, and breadth of hips. Using his figures as a norm, they were able to publish a comparison of the young men of 1900–1925 with the young men of 1949–1950, showing—whether Naismith's lessons of clean living and hard exercise had any correlation or not—that there had been a significant increase in the size of the average young man in the preceding fifty years.[21]

The years were busy ones and good ones for James Naismith, both on the campus and in the town community. True, the modern need for specialization in a growing university took away from him his formal medical duties and his basketball coaching duties, at the same time that secularization gradually took away his campus ministerial duties. He became a smaller cog in the university mechanism. But there remained a multitude of activities in which, with boundless energy, he involved himself.

In his college classes and in the Sunday School classes that he taught, he found the individuals with whom he could work best. They became the center of his career. The "kindly extrovert," as some of his acquaintances have described him, made a place and a reputation for himself at K.U. and won the love and respect of the Lawrence community.[22]

On February 12, 1911, nearly twenty-one years after he had first stepped inside the doors of an American college, the International Y.M.C.A. Training School, soon to be rechartered as the International Young Men's Christian Association College, let him know that it, too, thought he was doing a worthy job. On this date his former college granted him an honorary master's degree in physical education.[23]

Somewhere along the way the boy without a middle name inadvertently acquired the middle initial "A." The flourishingly abbreviated official signature that he used—"Jas. Naismith"—became mistakenly read as "Ja. A. Naismith." And the mistake was perpetuated. He did not think the matter was worth quarreling over, though.[24]

Despite his academic and professional titles, despite the enlargement of his name by a middle "A," he preferred to refer to himself simply as "Jim Naismith."[25] Even when he donated a basketball award to be given by his home-town high school, at his request the trophy was engraved with the words "Jim Naismith Basketball Trophy."[26] Among his descendants, however, it has become somewhat a point of pride to clarify the orthographic idiosyncrasies of the family: James Naismith never had a middle name or initial, and daughter Hellen Naismith Dodd spells her first name with two *l*s. It was only Naismith himself who remained unconcerned about titles, names, and letters of the alphabet.

16
Home and Community

As soon as the Naismiths arrived at their new home in Lawrence in 1898, James entered into the life of the community as fully as he did into campus activities.

Church affairs were an important part of Lawrence life for the Presbyterian Naismiths. They headed for the First Presbyterian Church downtown at Ninth and Vermont streets about the time that the congregation was ready to pass a resolution "that we will now arise and in the coming year build a new house of worship."[1] And build a new house of worship the zealous congregation did. Despite disruptions caused by the fact that the old stone church was being torn down to make room for the new red brick one on the same site, on January 4, 1899, James and Maude became members of the First Presbyterian Church. Two days later, on January 6, they had the Reverend Willis G. Banker baptize their younger daughter, Hellen. They set down her first name as a sedate "Helen" on the baptismal records, of course, leaving her to double her own *l*s later.[2]

James was soon teaching Sunday School classes that became almost embarrassingly popular. People liked to listen to him—

not only to his "delightful Canadian accent" but also to what he had to say. When he taught the adult male group, favorable comment about his class became so widespread that men of other faiths than the Presbyterian began to attend. These outsiders who crowded the Sunday School classroom did not, however, stay for the church services that followed; so the minister and elders objected to the situation. Naismith thereupon rented a room in a nearby mortuary, where he continued to hold inter-denominational classes for several years.[3]

Later, when he took over a Sunday School class of high-school boys, he found what he considered his real niche. He liked the boys and was popular with them. Besides having a keen sense of humor, he had a way of drawing analogies from his experiences in the athletic world that made his points intelligible to these teen-agers.[4] The boys enjoyed their sessions so much that after they were through high school and were expected to go into the adult Sunday School group, they kept on coming to his high-school class.

Naismith did his best to promote the religious life of college students, too. In 1901 the Disciples of Christ began to support the Kansas Bible Chair on the university campus, using a frame house at Thirteenth Street and Jayhawk Boulevard as head-quarters,[5] and he wanted to do similar work specifically for the campus Presbyterians. In large part through his efforts the pro-gram of service for Presbyterian students at the University of Kansas, carried on through the Westminster Foundation, was begun about 1905, among the first of such programs in the United States. A rented house at 1125 Tennessee Street was used temporarily, and in 1910 Westminster Hall was build on the campus at 1221 Oread Avenue. Naismith, as a member of the Board of Trustees of the Westminster Association, was the most active of any of the Lawrence citizens connected with this re-ligious work.[6] "He had a deep interest in all college life—plus vision."[7] In these words one of his church co-workers explained Naismith's efforts to organize the foundation, erect its head-quarters, hire a university pastor, and institute classes in Bible and religion.

The Young Men's Christian Association was one of the first

places Naismith visited after his arrival in Lawrence. Despite the unfortunate accident that had driven him away from Denver, his participation in "Y" work continued throughout his life. At the Lawrence Y.M.C.A. he provided free instruction in sports, most notably in basketball; he proselytized for members; he donated money. During the first decade of the century, at the time that the large, sports-oriented Y.M.C.A. was settling into permanent quarters in downtown Lawrence, he assisted in opening small branches of both the Y.M.C.A. and the Y.W.C.A. on the university campus.

His influence was not enough, however, to keep the "Y" flourishing permanently. After its period of great expansion ended about 1916,[8] the scope of "Y" work in Lawrence gradually lessened, until the Y.M.C.A. quarters were eventually taken over by the New York Cleaners and the swimming pool was drained to make space for dry-cleaning workers and storage.[9] From 1890, however, when he enrolled at the International Y.M.C.A. Training School, and on through World War I, when he worked with the Y.M.C.A. at the army front in France, the Y.M.C.A. continued to be an important part of Naismith's life. Even after the war he found services to perform. As late as 1938 he went out on a Y.M.C.A. lecture tour that reached into Canada.[10]

Holding to his decision never to hang out a shingle, Dr. James Naismith did not formally practice medicine in the community, but he was recognized as an able physician. He became a member of the Kansas State Medical Society and of the Douglas County Medical Society, serving as a member of the latter organization for forty years. He was treasurer of the Douglas County Medical Society in 1908–1909 and president in 1911.[11]

Maude Naismith, in contrast to her husband, stayed quietly in the background. Always pretty, she had become a woman so attractive that men turned to look twice at her. She liked fashionable clothes and dressed in good taste, having an especial weakness for pretty shoes for her dainty size-four foot. But whether she was aware of her own charm or not, her deafness had deepened her natural shyness, until she hesitated to take an active part in church or community work. After the Naismith children were old enough for Sunday School, James always took them with him, but Maude often stayed at home.[12]

"She's in poor health," the women of the Presbyterian congregation explained understandingly.[13]

As late as 1911, when she should have felt at ease among the campus women, she turned down an invitation sent by the wife of the director at the new Presbyterian student center that James had recently helped to establish. Dr. Naismith went alone to the party.

As gregarious as Maude was retiring, James found a pleasant outlet for his conviviality in male social groups. On the campus he took an interest in the students' social fraternities, giving freely of his time as an adviser to the boys or as chaperone at their parties. When the Kansas Gamma chapter of Sigma Phi Epsilon fraternity was organized at the University of Kansas in 1923, he became chapter adviser, being initiated into the fraternity on April 28, 1923. On July 14, 1928, he was initiated into the member-at-large section of the national chapter of Pi Gamma Mu, the national honor society for the social sciences. He was a member of the Masonic Lodge, to name one of his more important off-campus organizations, where he became a thirty-second-degree Mason in April, 1927.

His favorite group was a more informal one than these, however. He was a charter member of the Saturday Night Club, which was at first a weekly, later a monthly, dinner and discussion group limited to twelve members. He helped to organize it a few years after his arrival in Lawrence. The host at each meeting read a paper on any subject he chose, and the subjects varied widely. Naismith, for example, dipping into his own experiences, discussed such topics as "The Lumberjack," "Politics vs. Religion," "Athletics and Religion," "Religious Intolerance," and "The Development of Character Through Athletics."[14]

Through the years colorful figures existed among the faculty at the university to add variety to life—professors who were remembered by students and colleagues for one reason or another. One was Professor Preyer, who became the subject of a local tale. It was said that when building a home in Lawrence, he had a concert grand piano installed on the third story before the east side of the house was finished. Then there was Dean Skilton, who endeared himself to students by inviting them to his home every spring, performing on his Irish harp as the feature attraction.[15]

Most appealing figure of them all was Professor James Wood Green, whose interest in sports and whose loyalty to K.U. students from 1879 to 1919 resembled Naismith's own attitude. Serving the University of Kansas ten years as chairman of the Department of Law and thirty years as Dean of the School of Law, Green became the only college professor in America to have a life-size statue of himself set up on campus. Furthermore, the great Daniel Chester French, sculptor of the Lincoln Memorial statue, was the one persuaded to sculpt the $45,000 memorial for "Uncle Jimmy." Naismith was around to see decades of green and purple paint splattered on the statue by K.U. engineering students on St. Patrick's Day and by K.U.'s purple-sweatered rivals from the Kansas "Ag" College during each football season.[16]

There was sometimes a grave, even a somber, side to the Naismith activities. Campus, church, and lodge—in the gymnasium, at a sickbed, or in his study—in private trouble or public emergency, Dr. Naismith was available, interested and energetic. He became known as the person to turn to when aid was needed, who always responded to any urgent call. And emergencies did arise.

In the flood of 1903 the Kaw River inundated the community north of the river banks, and Naismith went to North Lawrence to help, in a boat obtained from Dolly Graber's boat livery. Dolly was not making any money that day. Instead of letting boats out for rent, he was loaning them free to rescuers. Naismith chose a boat and got hold of a man who had learned canoeing in Alaska. With his friend in the bow, Naismith labored at the stern, while Maude and his youngest child, two-and-one-half-year-old Jack, stood at the end of Ohio Street above the river, watching. The Kaw, heavy with floating trees and lumber, was running level over the dam, but the two men managed to bring many marooned persons out of their homes and safely to the south shore. Or they brought aid to those who had found a bit of high ground and would not or could not leave it. When word came that a girl was ill with diphtheria in the loft of a flooded barn, Naismith was the doctor who risked his life to go to her.[17]

Maude Naismith had hours of worried waiting and one long moment of anguish. On one of Naismith's rescue trips across the river, his boat went over the dam, and watchers, including Naismith's wife and child, believed that boat and occupants had been lost. But when Naismith appeared back at the south shore, wet and dirty, he was triumphant over good deeds accomplished and a little disappointed that anyone could have believed that he had drowned.

"Don't you know a man's not necessarily lost at sea when he disappears from sight between two waves?" he chided, rolling the *r*s in "necessarily" and "disappears" with more emphasis than usual. "You've got to have faith."[18]

The Naismiths moved several times during their first years in Lawrence, and during those years their third and fourth children, a boy and a girl, were born.

A short time after the family's arrival in town they purchased a skinny, white two-story frame house at the corner of Ninth and Louisiana streets.[19] Here their first son was born on November 3, 1900. Though he was named John Edwin in memory of his paternal grandfather, John Naismith, and his maternal grandfather, Edwin Sherman, the Christian name always used for him was "Jack," even on such official records as his father's petition for naturalization.[20]

The Naismith family had expected the house at Ninth and Louisiana to be their permanent home. But money did not mean much to James Naismith, and he spent little time thinking about balancing the household budget. Before the Naismiths realized what had happened, they had lost the house through failure to keep up the payments.[21]

Back in Ontario, the financial affairs of Uncle Peter and sister Annie were more successful than were James Naismith's. In 1903 P. J. Young, retired before he was fifty-eight years old, sold the farm in Ramsay Township to the Oates family and moved with Annie into the house he bought at 81 Union Street in Almonte.[22] While his nephew Jim reared a family and struggled to keep up payments on a home, P. J. spent his days hunting and fishing and, with his niece, taking part in church work.[23] Both Annie Naismith and P. J. Young were well liked among members of St. John's Presbyterian Church. Annie was a life member of the Women's Missionary Society and a long-time teacher in the Sunday School. P. J.—known as the "Grand Old Man of Presbyterianism" or, for short, "The Apostle Peter"— showed the lighter side of his strong religious nature by serving as a fine entertainer at the social gatherings of the church. The Robert Youngs, James Naismith's grandparents, had always been active in Presbyterian affairs, and their son carried on the family tradition. At the annual memorial service of the church, during P. J.'s middle age, the morning singing was started with the same tuning fork that his father had used when he was precentor of the church; and at the evening tea-meeting the perpetually young P. J. proved to be one of the favorite performers with his poetry recitations, his readings, and his songs. He was often applauded back for encore after encore—usually something Scottish, for he loved Scotland and cherished his Scottish heritage. "He was a fine old gentleman, good company," acquaintances would later reminisce about him.[24]

Down south in Kansas, James Naismith, after he lost his mortgaged home, moved his family a few blocks away, to 847 Vermont Street, later the site of the Lawrence city library and its adjoining parking lot. Then they moved to a two-story frame house at 1108 Tennessee Street, with gingerbread trim on the front porch.[25] The Naismith children may have missed some of the little luxuries other kids had, but nothing really important was lacking. Their father managed to keep them in a house, wherever it was, that *felt* like a real home.

The third and last daughter, Maude Annie, was born October 28, 1904, named for her mother and for her father's sister. Premature at somewhat more than two pounds weight, the baby reflected in her condition the trouble her mother had gone through to bear her.

Deafened before the birth of her second child, Maude Sherman Naismith had been ill during this fourth pregnancy, and after Maude Annie's birth Maude showed signs of a heart difficulty.

But James only grew gentler with his wife; and in the security of her family circle, Maude was a gay and delightful person, not seeming to be an invalid. During the pregnancy he had brought her gifts. She always cherished the wood-burning set he gave her. When Maude Annie was old enough to appreciate them, Mrs. Naismith passed on to her daughter the pieces she had designed with it.[26]

Now, with Maude Annie premature and tiny, James hired a Negro woman to work around the house. She was one of a long series of maids who helped to keep the Naismith household running smoothly, taking care of the smaller children, cooking, and cleaning. She established precedents for the family routine.

Among the Negro maids who worked for the Naismiths, the children would perhaps remember most fondly Auntie Silvers, dark and capable. As Maude Naismith grew frailer in health, most noticeably from the early 1920s onward, she came to depend increasingly on this woman.

"There's a spot left. Get it, Auntie," Maude Naismith would call out; and with her direction and Auntie's labor the house was kept carefully clean.[27]

James helped a lot with the baby himself. Maude Annie was an easy baby to take care of. She was happy and laughed easily. As she grew older, James Naismith seemed secretly to observe that she had a strong will and an independent spirit, somewhat like his. Even the changes in her name bespoke individuality. With Maude Annie, as with Jack, part of the original christened name became altered with use. Many Lawrence friends called her Maude Anne. When she grew up, she shortened the name to Ann, and as her legal signature she took the name "Maudann." But her father called her "Dimps."

Maude Annie was still a toddler when the family moved to the large house at 1635 Massachusetts Street, where a screened sleeping porch at the back gave space for an expanding family.[28] But although Maude Sherman Naismith had been one of eleven children, it seemed that a family larger than her present one was out of the question for her. Pregnancy and childbirth had brought difficulties, and now she suffered from the new weakness with her heart that would always plague her. It looked as if her family must stop with four children.

But it did not. James Sherman Naismith, the second son and fifth child of Maude and James Naismith, was born on May 7, 1913—nine years after Maude Annie—to the disapproval of the neighbors: "What is that man thinking of? And him a doctor, too. That poor little woman is nearly forty-five years old and suffering with a bad heart."[29]

But Maude Naismith was as delighted as her husband and a little awed at her good fortune. "I stole him," she exclaimed about her new baby. "I wasn't supposed to have this one, but I stole him from the angels."[30]

Jack, then nearly thirteen, was pleased, too, dreaming of the comrade he would have in a few years for canoe trips up the Kaw. He hurried up and down the street, knocking on neighbors' doors to report joyfully, "I've got a brother now!"[31]

Jimmy was born in 1913, and then in 1914 the head of the house had a bad case of mumps—and that was all the unusual news there was for a while. The Naismiths were happy here at 1635 Massachusetts Street, happy with one another and with their home. A downtown streetcar line ran along unpaved Massachusetts Street in front of their house, and another one stopped three short blocks away on Tennessee Street. The latter vehicle was the "Gallopin' Goose," the car that labored up Mississippi Street from the north onto the campus every fifteen minutes to rock its way down the south slope of Mount Oread. For twenty-three years the Goose traveled its route, often with Dr. Naismith aboard.[32]

All in all, the Naismiths' Massachusetts Street house was a comfortable one in a convenient location, and it was to be their home for eighteen years. The marriage that had begun so happily in Springfield in June, 1894, continued to be a successful one. James Naismith, with the memory of his own mother idealized during the frustrations of his orphaned boyhood, maintained an old-fashioned reverence for motherhood that was touching. "He kept Mama on a pedestal," his daughters remembered after they grew up.[33]

He taught the children to respect her, he taught the dog to

guard her, and at mealtime he reserved the best pieces of chicken for her plate. He tried to shield her from all knowledge of evil, and because she was partially isolated through deafness and was deeply dependent on him, he accomplished his intent. He succeeded so well that she—bewildered only temporarily by the fact of World War I—believed that the world was good and that James could do no wrong. The only thing faulty with her marriage, she thought sometimes, was that it had brought her to the Midwest. She tried, but she never, really, liked Kansas.

James Naismith had the gift of inspiring admiration in the women who were most intimately associated with him and in some of the men, usually younger than he, who knew him best. Sometimes, nonetheless, it must have been difficult for Maude to believe that her husband was perfect. His attitude toward household finances, for instance, would have been trying for most women.

Throughout most of his marriage he was in demand as a speaker and, after his ordination in 1916, as a minister. In addition to his tours on the Chautauqua lecture circuit in Kansas, he traveled as far away as New York to read papers to assemblages of physical educators.[34] If inadequate reimbursement, or none, was offered for his services, as often happened, he did not worry about it. He was generous to a fault, too. Often, when approached by impecunious students, he loaned money that he could not afford to give. Frequently, therefore, he was forced to borrow from the household fund to make up for his generosity, forgetting, with his typical indifference to finances, to mention to Maude that he had borrowed anything.[35]

Maude Naismith, who liked handsome furnishings and pretty dresses and shoes, was in her way as impractical as her husband about financial matters; and although it was inconvenient to find the grocery purse empty before the end of the month, she could perhaps overlook this little fault in James.

But occasionally, she admitted, he did something thoughtless that ran roughshod over people's feelings. Once, at least, one of his roguish practical jokes proved too rough for her.

One of Maude Naismith's dreams was to own the diamond ring that James had been unable to buy her in the early days of his teaching career. Whenever she mentioned her wish, he answered, "Some day."

At last, one December he ostentatiously measured her finger, and she knew that he was going to give her a ring for Christmas. "The best diamond I can afford," he said as he handed a small box to her on Christmas morning, his eyes twinkling. "It may not be exactly what you had in mind," he admitted, as she tore excitedly at the ribbon. "But the only difference, really, is that the crystalline structure is arranged differently."[36]

When she opened the box she found a ring, her size, set with a small lump of coal. Seeing her stunned look, he roared with laughter. Only after he quieted down to a chuckle did he realize that she was hurt. On another holiday he gave her the real diamond ring she wanted, but she admitted to Maude Annie years later that she never quite forgot the pain of that Christmas morning.

He caused her a different kind of hurt—which sprang from the same careless lack of sensitivity—one chilly night in their cabin in the Colorado mountains. That was the time he put an icy-cold stone into bed to warm her feet, telling her he had heated it in the fire!

To Naismith's credit, he could receive as well as deliver. If the joke was on him, it was funny, all the same. The most famous joke of his career happened the year after he arrived at the University of Kansas, and new crops of students are still hearing about it.

In the fall of 1899 there was a big, awkward clodhopper among the new students who caught Naismith's attention, one George R. Creps, who gave his address as South Cedar, Kansas. Naismith prided himself that he had worked with enough athletes to recognize football talent, and he made the boy his protégé on the athletic field. When time for the Kansas-Nebraska game arrived, Naismith persuaded football coach Fielding H. Yost to put Creps into a football suit and let him make the trip to Lincoln for the experience of watching a real college game. Yost not only took Creps along but, early in the game, put him in to play. In an amazing performance as a linesman the supposed greenhorn won the game for Kansas almost singlehanded—and then disappeared.[37]

The real story eventually came out. The truth was that before Yost had come to the University of Kansas, he had coached at the University of West Virginia, where his star player was a young man named G. R. Krebs. Krebs graduated in the spring of 1899, after Yost was at Kansas. In the fall of 1899 Krebs temporarily changed his address and two letters in the spelling of his name, enrolled in law school at K.U., and hung around the Department of Physical Education until he was "discovered" by Naismith. After that, everything was simple. He got into a football uniform, won the big game of the season for his old coach, secret-weapon fashion, and went back to West Virginia. A good prank had been carried out and nobody was really the worse for it except Nebraska, which had been the idea all along. If Naismith suspected from the beginning what was going on, in those days of unbridled intercollegiate trickery, he refused to spoil anybody's fun by letting on that he knew. On the University of Kansas campus, of course, the joke on Naismith became a legend, and he laughed over it along with everybody else for forty years.[38]

Naismith was an efficient, direct-acting person, who believed in any legitimate timesaving method. "I never take the long way when I can help it," he explained one day as he led a companion across vacant lots in a shortcut from home to campus. Naismith's approach applied to abstract situations as well as to a walk to his classroom. When he saw a problem, he drove directly to a solution, even if, perchance, he created other problems on the way.[39] But despite his timesaving methods, he was so busy with his work on campus and his extracurricular activities that there was less time left for his family than he would have liked.

When he had time to be at home, he was fun, indeed, to have in the family circle. His smile was infectious, and his laugh was deep and hearty. One of the stay-at-home activities was a "family orchestra," with Papa-Jim inexpertly playing the violin and singing in a loud baritone voice. Maude Naismith, who had once enjoyed singing, no longer sang after her illness with typhoid fever and her consequent deafness. She found her artistic outlet in working with watercolors, where deafness was no disadvantage, and remained quietly outside the family music circle. And for Jimmy, understandably, nine years younger than the youngest of the other four children, the family music had to be a spectator sport. But with one of the older girls at the piano, Maude Annie on the trumpet, and Jack on the clarinet, the children helped their father make a joyful noise. "Little Brown Jug" was one of Naismith's favorite songs during these musical evenings. He loved to play and sing out with a deep "Ho! ho! ho!" in the chorus:

> Ho! ho! ho!
> You and me;
> Little brown jug,
> How I love thee.

But on Sundays, in contrast to the rollicking "Little Brown Jug" type of music, the family was permitted nothing but hymns.[40]

In his times at home Naismith liked to read, sometimes aloud. He had learned four languages besides English—Gaelic in the Young household and Hebrew, Latin, and Greek in university courses (he liked to say that he had eleven degrees, including one in music and one in Greek)—and he took up French later, during World War I. Despite this erudition, however, most of his reading was on the light side. His favorite author was Zane Grey, and he bought all the Grey books as they were published. *Riders of the Purple Sage* and *The Lone Star Ranger* leaned companionably against school texts in Greek and Latin on the Naismith bookshelves.[41]

His taste in movies followed his taste in books, and he was as pleased as a child if a Zane Grey picture came to town. Western movies were almost the only thing that could excite him. As fans and sportswriters often observed, Dr. Naismith never yelled at a basketball game. But at a cowboy show he did. An outwardly calm, unperturbable man, he usually held himself in check, but in the moving-picture house he forgot himself completely. At tense moments in Tom Mix adventures he would rise from his seat in his excitement and call out directions to his favorite cowboy and Mix's horse, Tony. Word spread among university students that Professor Naismith put on a good show himself at the Saturday-night movies, and they would follow him into the theater to sit behind him.[42]

He liked Tarzan movies, too. And when *The Perils of Pauline* was running, he took Maude Annie to the Patee Theater every week. Tarzan adventures, cliff-hanger serials—he liked them all. But nothing, including basketball, was so stirring to him as a real shoot-'em-up Western.

Out-of-doors he enjoyed boating and fishing and, a hobby sometimes more eventful than water sports, working with animals. One of his diversions was horses. He had always liked horses, from the time he had ridden them and worked them on the farm in Canada. One of his special tasks back on the farm had been driving the lead team from his uncle's woodlot—a responsible job and one that he enjoyed. He liked dogs, too. He was a natural "dog-and-pony man," as a circus buff would have said, with a knack for training the animals. He would have enjoyed keeping his backyard full of horses and his house full of dogs; but the backyard was not large enough, and his wife disliked dogs.

There was just one dog he taught her to tolerate. When son Jimmy brought Patty home—a half-grown dog, part Airedale and part German shepherd—Maude, looking up from the watercolor of a vase that she was working on, said that she would not have the animal around. And when Patty unabashedly brought home a pan of meat loaf (the owner of which the Naismith family was never able to ascertain), Maude stated firmly that they could not harbor a thief. But in a short time James, boldly bringing Patty into the house, had trained her to take care of his deaf, semi-invalid wife. Maude came to depend increasingly on her canine bodyguard and companion. She knew that Patty not only would protect her from intruders but would let her know when a friend was knocking at a house door and show her which door. A strange comradeship resulted. When Maude Naismith died, the dog, then old, followed her coffin to the grave and had to be removed from the cemetery by force.

Jazzbo, the goat, was another Naismith pet. Named after a

Negro vaudeville performer of the day, he was acquired by James Naismith ostensibly as a pet for young Jim, but actually for Maude Naismith's sake, to keep away the numerous neighborhood dogs. Jazzbo also attempted to keep away the streetcars that ran past the Naismith home. Several times he blocked the streetcar track and defied the motorman, who became painfully familiar with Jazzbo's butting technique. More than once young Jim was called home from school a few blocks away to clear the goat off the track and tether him in the back yard.

Dr. Naismith laughed when he was told about the recurring Jazzbo incidents, suspecting that someone had exaggerated. He found the animal an interesting pet; he liked to play "bull fight" with Jazzbo by waving a rag and then executing fancy footwork when the goat obligingly "charged." Once, however, the good doctor turned his back. While he stooped to pick up the cloth he had dropped, Jazzbo made a running charge that shoved his master sprawling across the yard. "That's the end!" exclaimed Naismith, rubbing *his* and suddenly sympathizing with the streetcar motorman.[43] Shortly thereafter a new home was found for Jazzbo.

Uncle Peter might well have been a part, and an unorthodox one, of the Naismith family had James been able to persuade him to visit. But P. J. Young had stayed away, excusing himself on the ground that with his rough Scottish accent, he would feel out of place among university folk. One summer, however, he did come. Troubled with a cataract on one of his eyes, he decided to come for a medical examination and for a good visit with his American kinfolk. There he had a warm welcome. Although he was known at home as "P. J.," the Naismith children had been taught to address him as "Uncle Peter," and James Naismith affectionately called him "Pete."

With Annie at home taking care of the Almonte property, P. J. swaggered about Lawrence, cutting a fine Scottish figure despite his age and ailment. Known as a sporty chap around Almonte and Bennie's Corners when he was young, he retained many of the sartorial habits of his youth. He wore striped trousers and cutaway coat at every opportunity he could invent. To the end of his life, he was at once "The Apostle Peter" and the fun-loving playboy.⁴⁴ Every night he got down on his knees to pray. Then he would announce, "Now I'll have my hot toddy," and after one drink he would head placidly toward bed.⁴⁵

P. J. was sometimes impish. But taciturn Scottish iceberg of a person when he chose to be, he concealed nine-tenths of his playfulness from the Lawrence townspeople. They thought him peculiar, dignified, and aloof. But his relatives did not trust his dignity to hold up. They were uneasily aware, as his Canadian relatives were, that "you never knew what P. J. was going to do."⁴⁶ With much tolerance, however, and a touch of humor the family was able to live gracefully through his visit.

During Naismith's visits to Almonte he occasionally ran head-on into P. J.'s off-beat jokes. On one of Jim's trips to visit his sister and his uncle he was intrigued to find sitting on the floor in the southeast corner of Uncle Peter's upstairs bedroom a handsome pine box about two and one-half feet wide and seven and one-half feet long, elaborately made and upholstered inside and equipped with a hinged lid. Upon being asked, P. J. Young replied that the box was his coffin.⁴⁷

Whether Naismith took the explanation seriously or not, he told the story straight-facedly to friends, who repeated it. Reporters eventually learned about the eccentric uncle and made good copy out of P. J. Young's coffin. Newspaper accounts, labeling it "Uncle Peter's bed," explained that the thrifty Scotsman had built the box to serve as bed during his lifetime and coffin afterward. They pointed out that he pulled the lid down nights to keep out the chill of the wintry Canadian winds.⁴⁸ Relatives on the American side of the border made the story even more extravagant than the published anecdote. Some of them perpetuated the legend that Uncle Peter, when offended by any one of his Canadian relatives, retreated into his coffin to pout, lying with folded arms until the malefactor apologized. Long after P. J. Young was buried—in whatever box it may have been—this favorite tale about his eccentricity flourished.⁴⁹

When relatives and friends on the Canadian side of the border belatedly learned of the elaborated coffin tale, they denied most points of it.⁵⁰ By that date, it was too late to prove or disprove it. The story had grown to the point where "only his undertaker

knew"—and the undertaker was dead. There *was* a box in Uncle
Peter's bedroom, and P. J. did, it seems, tell Jim Naismith that
it was a coffin. Beyond these details imagination perhaps took
over. All that can be said with certanity is that if Uncle Peter
was a jokester, he was a morbid but startlingly successful one.

17

Spare the Rod

ALMOST everyone liked the Naismith family, especially Dr. Naismith, with his wonderfully unruffled disposition and his modest,
unaffected personality. But some acquaintances predicted that
the kindly professor would have more trouble with his own children at college age than he would ever have with his university
students. He was not a disciplinarian. In his home he preferred
to have peace rather than rules, and he never fussed at anybody.[1]

After the early years of her marriage Maude Naismith was not
robust enough to be a thorough housekeeper, an ambitious cook,
and a proper routinist. Consequently, the house at 1635 Massachusetts Street seemed to be one of haphazard family living, despite the daily help of a Negro maid. As one of the Naismith
neighbors remarked later, "Those kids were raised out of tin
cans. They were like Topsy, they 'just growed.' "[2]

Discipline in Naismith's household was reminiscent of the
routine he had seen in the home of his admired teacher, Luther
Halsey Gulick, Jr., when Jim was a student at the International
Y.M.C.A. Training School. The Gulicks "seemed to residents of
Springfield a casual family and their life somewhat haphazard."[3]

Casualness was a way of life with the Naismiths. James Naismith was not an early-to-bed man, and as his children grew old
enough to put themselves to bed without their mother's assistance, they followed his example. With the exception of Mrs. Naismith, who retired early and left her husband and children to
their own schedules after nine o'clock, the family kept irregular
hours. When the children grew older, they would gather—Papa-

Jim and whichever of his daughters and sons were at home—around the large oval dining table and talk late into the evening. Sometimes they would send out for hamburgers—Maude Annie, in particular, loved hamburgers.[4]

After the children had at last gone to bed, their father would stay up, often playing solitaire in the quiet hours of early morning that he enjoyed, after the witching hour of midnight. He came to find four hours of sleep sufficient, usually sleeping from about 2:00 A.M. until 6:00 A.M. To these four hours he added only a half-hour nap after lunch, always arranging his afternoon class schedule so that he would have that nap-time available. He did not use an alarm clock. He simply lay down, slept thirty minutes, and awakened.

Those who criticized the Naismiths' unregimented existence did not realize that, despite a symbolic neglect of alarm clocks, the family lived by an unarticulated set of rules. They were not regulations like "Brush your teeth after meals" and "Go to bed at nine o'clock," but they were understood, nevertheless, and the children lived within their limits. Naismith's technique of discipline had a clear-cut, simple pattern. Kindness toward everyone was the foundation for his own actions, and he tried to make it the basis for his children's. What seemed laxity in him was only his emphasis on this virtue.[5] Next to kindness was a stress on the high standards of health, including abstinence from liquor and tobacco, that were so important to him. Next in importance to these essentials were the attributes of self-reliance, courage, hard work, tenacity, and responsibility, all of which he taught by precept and by example. To illustrate, he showed by his own actions that he believed strongly in his maxim "It is idleness that breeds mischief."[6]

Even when he did not talk about moral ways of life, he was consistent. Instances of the methods he used on his children—whether unorthodox and startling, whether funny, or whether unwise—were all of a piece. All reflected his emphasis on these high standards. As his son Jim analyzed his father's unobtrusive but determined method of control, "If someone else's kid got in jail, he'd do down and bail him out. If it had happened to be his own child, he would've said, 'You knew better,' and left him there."[7]

On at least one point Naismith was a routinist with all his children. He regularly took them to Sunday School and church even when his wife was unable to go, and he enforced proper behavior on the Sabbath Day. A fun-loving man from Monday until twelve o'clock Saturday night, he was straightlacedly religious on Sunday. He read aloud to the family from the Bible, sometimes in Hebrew. No instrumental music was permitted on that day, with the exception of hymns played on the piano. The comic papers were put away and saved for reading on Monday. Margaret and Hellen took pillows from the parlor sofa and sat sedately on the front porch, but for lively Jack and Maude Annie, Sundays at home were frustrating.[8]

Jack and Maude Annie, born four years apart, were the devil-may-care "twins" of the Naismith family and the principal cause of neighbors' lifted eyebrows. Margaret and Hellen, especially Hellen, were more like their mother than the other children were and acted so demurely that Maude Annie indignantly called them "prim young ladies." Maude Annie and Jack were anything but prim.[9]

Maude Annie was tomboy enough to keep up with her older brother and sometimes to outdo him. As a toddler, she was Jack's special charge in the household's delegation of responsibility, but she grew up to become his comrade and his equal in deviltry.[10] "She could do anything," one of her childhood playmates would later describe her. "She led us all."[11]

Jack was the one who brought a live snake into Dr. Naismith's study, knowing his father's dislike of snakes. It was Jack who inserted an erect darning needle into the seat of an upholstered chair and invited unsuspecting Maude Annie to sit down. But it was Maude Annie who in retaliation crushed Jack's finger in the pitcher pump at the kitchen sink.

Much though James Naismith desired Sabbath propriety, the family members formed a contrast in decorum when they went out to church together on Sunday morning or set forth on a round of visits in the afternoon. While Dr. and Mrs. Naismith and their two older daughters rode handsomely forth in a surrey drawn by a span of horses, Maude Annie and Jack followed behind in a pony cart, whipping their Shetland to a reckless pace.

After Jack and Maude Annie began to grow beyond the kindergarten stage and the sandpile set, Naismith had to put up at least a pretense of conventional discipline, to be sure. He kept a razor strop in the storeroom upstairs for spanking purposes. Although he used it often, mostly on these two younger children, he did not use it wholeheartedly. Sometimes he instructed them to cry loudly for the benefit of the listeners downstairs. The only time he was really stern was the day Maude Annie pretended to faint at the first stroke of the leather. She was a good actress but not good enough for Papa-Jim.

Despite spankings, though, Jack and Maude Annie lightheartedly called their tattling older siblings the "Naismith newspaper" and went on playing devil-may-care pranks. Even after young Jimmy was born and they shared in caring for him, they continued to be good-natured troublemakers.

Although Maude Annie and Jack were called the "Naismith twins," they were different in one way. Jack was a loner at heart—much more so than any of his sisters or his brother. When they were kids at home, Margaret and Hellen and, later, young James went to their mother when they needed to talk to a parent, while Maude Annie took her problems to her father. Jack alone, a combination of rebelliousness and self-sufficiency, turned to no one when he was in trouble, which was often.

Jack was a good-hearted boy. He never wanted to hurt his parents, especially his mother, the sweet and feminine Maude Sherman Naismith. But when he was only seven or eight, his deviltry and his adoration for her were inextricably mixed together. One day, after he had been in a neighbor's peach orchard, stealing fruit, he rushed into the Naismith house in a sudden burst of joy, hugged his mother and spilled out his love for her in one boyish phrase: "You're as soft as a rotten peach."[12]

And he kept on hurting his parents by his escapades and irresponsibility. By the time he was in high school, saucily flunking Latin I every year, Jack was told by his teacher, "If I were Dr. Naismith I'd be ashamed to have a son like you."[13]

Although Jack's usual behavior may not have reflected any

parental discipline, there was one way in which James Naismith was a demanding disciplinarian with both his children and his students. Despite the fact that he was uncomfortable in the role of family law enforcer, he carried over into his everyday life the stern spirit of the gymnasium wherever it might apply. While essentially a kind man, he lived and preached the strenuous life, holding no patience with the hypochondriac, the lazy person, or the crybaby. He scoffed at pain as an admission of either weakness or ignorance, believing that physical exercise was the answer to any infirmity of mind or body.[14]

In his work at the University of Kansas this emphasis was clear. Elmer Verner McCollum, entering the university when Naismith was in his second year of teaching there, was one of the freshmen in the Health and Hygiene class, where both gymnastic work and classroom lectures were part of the course. Gym drills were hard on McCollum because of a hernia that was aggravated by strenuous exercise. Furthermore, his extracurricular duties were heavy. The son of a widow, to pay his way through school he was working four hours each night as a lamplighter—lighting half the gas street lamps in Lawrence at dusk (unless the moon was full) and turning them off again after midnight—thus earning sixty cents a night. He also worked on newspaper routes for the daily *World,* counting out papers for delivery boys and carrying a route himself. In addition to these regular jobs, in season he thinned strawberry plants in the area near the campus later called the "Daisy Field." With all these tasks, he had time for only four hours of sleep each night unless he curled up for a nap on a pile of newspapers at the printing shop. Four hours may have been enough for James Naismith, but not for him. Always tired, he often fell asleep in class.[15]

Thin and exhausted, the young lamplighter at last went to his health instructor for help. Elmer felt that when the situation was explained to Naismith, the professor would prescribe less physical exertion and more rest. But Elmer was disillusioned. Naismith refused to excuse the young man—hernia, overwork, sleepiness, and all—from any of the class requirements, insisting that the exercise would do him good.[16]

McCollum was able to protest effectively only a half-century later. Then, an internationally renowned scientist and perhaps K.U.'s greatest alumnus, he established the Dr. E. V. McCollum Student Aid Fund at his alma mater. The loan fund was set up to eliminate the waste of strength and health involved in a self-financed education and to help students "go to bed and get some sleep when they need it." McCollum wrote a funding check for undergraduate students in 1944 and one for graduate fellows in 1966, and, besides, a ten-story dormitory, McCollum Hall, was opened in 1965 in honor of Elmer and his brother Burton. Symbolically, the handsome new dormitory was erected on the site of the old strawberry patch—so that students can sleep above the field where Elmer used to work. But by 1965, unfortunately, it was too late for Elmer McCollum's accomplishments to soften Naismith's attitude about exercise.[17]

At home, back in those early days in Lawrence, Naismith tried to inculcate the same principles of athletic self-reliance in his children that he did in his students. He taught Maude Annie to swim when she was about six years old, in typical Naismith fashion. He devised a pole with a strap on the end that he fastened to her swim suit, and then he dangled her in the pool in Robinson Gymnasium. She learned all the strokes easily and after several weeks of lessons was performing proficiently. But when the hour came to swim alone, she was afraid to proceed without the aid of her father and the "swimming pole." He let her come out of the water and dress. Then he called her back to the edge of the pool and threw her into the deep end with her clothes on. That time she swam, and she did not call for help.

James Naismith perhaps never realized how strongly the influence of Uncle Peter and Ramsay Township lay upon him. When he threw his daughter into the gymnasium pool that day, he probably was not thinking of the winter day near Bennie's Corners when Uncle Peter stood in the background, silently laughing, while young James struggled alone to pull two horses from the icy river.[18]

Twenty years after Maude Annie's swimming lessons the scene was the Kaw River, and the similarity with that day in the Canadian woods was again strong. Naismith and Maude Annie, now known as Maudann, had gone out together northwest of

Lawrence to the cabin and boat dock that the family owned. Maudann had swum across the river while her father was fishing from the dock. She was on the opposite bank when she saw Tom Dawe, her boy friend from Topeka, arrive. Eagerly, she started to swim to him, straight across the river, instead of diagonally as her father had taught her. The Kaw is always dangerous, and she soon appeared to be in difficulty. Tom quickly began to pull off his shoes, trousers, and shirt, preparing to swim to her rescue. Naismith held him back. "She knew better than to fight the current that way," he said sternly. "Let her save herself. That's the only way to teach her."[19]

While the two men watched, Tom in nervous impatience and Naismith with outward composure, Maudann, a good swimmer, recovered her control and swam to shore. She came first to her father. "Daddy-Boy, you were right," she whispered.[20]

A son gave even greater scope for physical training than did a tomboy daughter. Naismith encouraged Jack to play football in school. He himself trained the boy in blocking tactics and taught him everything else he could about the game, although Jack was not good enough for anything beyond high-school football. Naismith trained Jack in gymnastics, also, and here the discipline was sternest. Jack once fell while trying to do a double reverse turn on the horizontal bar. His father knew that the lad was hurt but did not go to help him up, ordering tersely, "Get up off the floor and go to the office."[21] Then he followed and taped the three broken ribs that he discovered.

Naismith's method was consistent, at least. It was simple, practical, stern. Teaching Jack and some other boys to handle a canoe, he deliberately upset the boat in the middle of the Kaw River and shouted as he went down, "I'm drowning! Save me!"[22] The boys, quick to learn the Naismith lessons, did.

Because of recurring incidents of this type, in some quarters Naismith acquired the reputation of being a fanatic on the subject of physical fitness, exercise, and health regimes. Students, friends, relatives, family—he appeared to line them all up against his own virile standards, unable to sympathize completely with anyone who was frail or ill. But this picture was not entirely valid. His wife, no longer a basketball-playing twenty-two-year-old, proved the prime exception to his rule. The Spartan qualities that he demanded of other persons he did not expect of Maude. In his treatment of her only a mere hint of the vigorous Naismith method appeared. Sometimes when she limped, as she did occasionally because of pain or weakness, he would playfully kick at her from behind and order, "Get your leg up."[23] But this was no more than a reflex action on his part, as a physical education director. He would sooner prescribe setting-up exercises for a madonna than he would subject Maude to his customary rules. Like the old china and glassware he liked to collect, she was precious and breakable.

And there was one other person in his family who received special treatment. That was young James. Soon after his birth the Naismiths found to their dismay that he had been born with a heart lesion. With him, then, rough-and-ready treatment was not apropos, and Naismith knew it. Some of his comments were callous, it is true. To a friend, for example, he said brusquely, "I'd rather have Jimmy dead than an invalid."[24] But whatever his words, he was solicitous about his youngest child's health. Although Maude and James Naismith were careful not to let preschool Jimmy believe that he was less sturdy than his playmates or to realize the extent of their concern for him, they watched him closely. Whenever he seemed to become slightly overheated in summer play, they brought him into the house and set him under a fan. Once when Jimmy was overwriggly and Maude Naismith was overanxious, she tied him in a chair under the fan to make sure that her husband's prescribed treatment was carried out.

The regime Dr. Naismith laid out was apparently a wise one, for by the time Jimmy was six, he appeared to be cured, with his heart lesion healed.

Young Jimmy got the breaks all along. He came into the Naismith household late—only three years before first-born Margaret, a grown-up young lady, eloped from the family group. Jimmy reaped the advantages that a late child in a family of several children sometimes does.[25] Naismith had always been too busy to construct elaborate dollhouses for his daughters or a home gymnasium for his elder son, but for Jimmy he took time to build the finest tree house the neighborhood had ever seen.[26] Sometimes Jimmy stayed up there all day, and his mother would bring out his lunch in a bucket for him to haul up by rope. Both parents, and especially Dr. Naismith, were more lenient with Jimmy than they had been with the older children. Jimmy returned their kindness in full measure. From the time he was about nine years old he was the one who cared for his invalid mother. It was he, not Dr. Naismith, who got up with her at night, who ran her errands, who helped her up and down steps and stairs.

With persons outside his family, too, Naismith showed that he could temper his love of rigorous physical discipline with common sense. When Glenn Cunningham, enrolling at the University of Kansas, became renowned as a middle-distance runner, Naismith took a personal interest in the plucky young athlete. Cunningham was the Kansas farm boy who in 1916, at the age of seven, had come out of a tragic schoolhouse fire crippled. It was Cunningham who, after years on crutches, had learned to walk again and then, miraculously, to run.[27] Although the marvelous rehabilitation of his legs had been accomplished before Naismith met him, the doctor took particular pride in the successful therapy used and in the indomitable spirit of the boy. But almost the only advice Naismith ever gave him was a word of caution when Cunningham was giving his track teammates some pointers on endurance, instructing them in his method of running on one's "second wind." "You'll kill those boys," Naismith said. "They don't have your heart."[28]

The advice sounded strange, coming as it did from the well-known devotee of strenuosity. But Naismith was wise enough to fit the prescription to the person. If he believed that rough stuff was appropriate, that was what he ordered. For his own body it was appropriate, all his life. But for some others' bodies, albeit reluctantly, he modified his instructions. "A man is foolish not to take regular exercise before he's forty and foolish to start strenuous exercise after forty," he said.[29] He liked to catch prospects before they were forty, of course. Always pleased at being asked for help of any kind, he was particularly delighted when it was medical advice that anyone—student, friend, or relative—requested. For most ailments he was quick to recommend the rigorous regime of daily exercise that he always used himself. And often his advice was followed religiously. Dr. Naismith's bedside manner was convincing, and his patients believed what he told them.[30]

Maybe sometimes people thought that his insistence on activity instead of rest and on massage instead of medicines was unorthodox. But they probably thought that his ideas on the care and control of teen-agers were even stranger. The James Naismith theory about runaway children, as a typical solution, was: "Let them go. They'll come home when they're ready."[31]

Jack was the one who took advantage of this dictum.[32] Mature for his age, he ran away repeatedly. But the summer before his fifteenth birthday he had even his father worried. He ran away from home in June, and weeks and then months went by without a word from him or about him. To relieve Maude, James said briskly, "No news is good news. If we don't hear anything, we don't have anything to worry about."[33]

But two and a half months was a long time for the Naismiths, when they could not know that their son was safely at work in the harvest fields near Aberdeen, South Dakota. They could only hope that, wherever he was, he would feel like coming back for the opening of the school term. He did, to their great relief. When he rode a freight car into Lawrence one day late in August, chewing tobacco and growing a fuzzy beard, wheat stubble in his pants cuffs, the welcome they gave him was a mixture of disapproval and joy, but mostly joy.

Naismith always said that the sixteen-to-twenty-one-year-old age group was the neglected segment of American youth, and he liked best to work with this group.[34] His critics liked to say, perhaps unfairly, that he neglected his own children until they were sixteen years old and then discovered that it was too late to do anything with them. Whether he might have worked effectively with Jack at that age was not to be learned, even though he had failed earlier, for Naismith's war service intervened during the two or three years when Jack most needed a father's guidance. When Jack was within months of his sixteenth birthday, in 1916, Naismith entered the United States military service as a chaplain

in the Mexican Border War. The following year he volunteered
for World War service with the Y.M.C.A. and spent nearly two
years away from home. After he returned from France, he tried
to reform the boy. Jack at that stage, however, did not prove the
comradely type.[35] Naismith felt more comfortable going for walks
with Maudann than he did strolling with his son. Nevertheless,
he and Jack went fishing together at favorite spots on the Kaw.
He took Jack along on several of his jaunts into Canada, where
they roughed it, like two comrades together. He took Jack into
the Naismith basement woodworking shop and showed him how
to use the tools there. Jack made a long pipe rack, a lamp, and
some smaller pieces. Both he and his father were proud of his
work, and Jack took the pipe rack and the lamp into his own
home after he was married. But Jack was the first to admit that
for a long while his father thought him a lost cause.

James Naismith adapted his method to the needs of each child.
Sometimes, though, he received credit for teaching lessons of hard
work and virtue when he was really doing nothing but enjoying
himself. The summer of 1922 a local newspaper played up his
good citizenship and salutary influence on youth when it printed
an item telling that he had taken his son Jack and some other
young men from Lawrence out to Chapman, Kansas, to work with
a gang of summer laborers. In truth, the expedition had not
been Naismith's idea at all. Jack and two of his friends were
loaded into a stripped-down roadster, headed west to work on
Kansas road construction, when Naismith, bidding the boys
goodbye, remarked wistfully, "Wish I could go with you."

One of the boys invited, "Well, come along."

"Wait till I get my clothes," Naismith replied, and his wish
promptly became reality.[36]

It was a grand summer. The two Naismiths and their friends
joined a construction gang. While Jack worked on a sand pump
in the river, Naismith drove a team of horses. He had arranged
beforehand that the boys call him "Jim," and no one around
Chapman guessed his real identity. He carried out his little
deception even when some new workmen brought a prostitute
out from Kansas City and his co-workers tried unsuccessfully to
goad "Jim" into visiting her at her quarters.

In spite of practical lessons in hobbies, outdoor life, honest labor, and avoidance of prostitutes, one of the Naismith children remained a rebel, a nonconformist to the Naismith ideals. It was Jack.

Generous and heedless, Jack remained a playboy, following the lead of those who came to college for "fun," flunking out of the university at which his father was a departmental chairman. After Jack's two semesters with an almost straight "F" grade average (he passed Spanish with a "D"), his father helped him get a job as director of physical education for the employees of a steel mill in Joliet, Illinois. Then he went into the teaching of physical education in city schools, first a year in Joliet, then three years in Kansas City, Missouri, before going to Sioux City, Iowa.

Jack knew that he had deeply disappointed his mother by his failure in college. But she had never nagged him, during his two semesters at K.U. or afterward. Her silence hurt him more than a scolding would have—but he felt that she understood without questions or explanations on either side: he was Jack, and he could not change his nature.

After he went to Joliet to work, he let six months pass without writing a letter home. He knew that he was hurting his mother again, and he had not meant to. Impulsively and unannounced, he came home to visit. It was hours past midnight when he reached the house at 1635 Massachusetts Street. His father, late retirer though he was, lay abed sleeping. But his mother, whose habitual bedtime was nine, was sitting alone in a chair in the parlor. Deaf, she did not hear his steps. Jack let himself in the door and, coming quietly behind Maude Naismith, placed his hands over her eyes. Unstartled, she spoke calmly: "Jack? I've been waiting up for you."[37]

Jack believed her. He had realized before then that there was a strange psychic bond between the two of them that distance only made stronger.

With Maudann there was always an undercurrent of the same rebellion that was strong in Jack. After she competed high school her parents sent her to Loretta Academy in Kansas City and to a girls' school in Fulton, Missouri. A coeducational college did not seem the right place to enroll her, for, as her brother Jack, observed, "She's so pretty you have to use a club to keep the boys away."[38] Education at William Woods College in Fulton put some ladylike frills on her, but the freedom of life away from home encouraged her revolt against what she considered the ultrapuritanical attitude of her mother and father. Home from college one vacation, sophisticated in a peekaboo blouse, Maudann joined her father in his study after dinner. Sitting down in front of him, she crossed her legs, pulled out a cigarette, and lit up. Naismith did not hesitate. He put her across his knee and spanked her.

A spanking at college age did not change her much, nor was her father naive enough to believe that it would. All it did was to intensify the admiration that she, and all of his children, felt for him. Forty years after that incident, Maudann, smoking a cigarette in her gift shop in Thayer, Missouri, reminisced proudly about that spanking.

After Maudann left William Woods College and was taking nurses' training in Kansas City in the 1920s, she had a chance to show her father that in certain significant ways his precepts meant something to her.

While she was standing on a ladder counting sheets and pillow-cases in a linen room in the hospital, someone jolted the ladder and she fell, apparently striking her neck in such a way that paralysis of her legs resulted. The doctor told her parents that she might never walk again. Naismith retorted, "Oh, yes, she will."[39]

He worked with her, massaging, exercising, praising. With the encouragement of both father and mother, Maudann grew determined to prove the gloomy prognosis of the hospital doctor wrong. Eventually she forced herself to stand once again unsupported.[40]

One day, when he felt Maudann had grown physically able to take a few steps, James Naismith told his wife that the moment had come to use bribery. They would appeal to their daughter not with a grand promise of future reward but with some small immediate prize enticing enough to cause her to walk. Knowing his daughter's tastes as he did, Naismith laid an appetizing hamburger on the table and offered it to Maudann if she would walk alone across the room to take it.

As Naismith had planned, it was a time of day when Maudann was beginning to feel hungry. But, nonetheless, as she tried to walk toward the hamburger, her legs failed her.

Her father gave her a second chance. This time she walked unsteadily across the room and grasped the hamburger.[41]

Together these three Naismiths had achieved one of their greatest personal victories. Naismith had said, "You can't give up," and Maudann had listened. With the aid of both of her parents the young woman who had been paralyzed learned to walk again. Then, to complete her success story, she went on to graduate from the nursing course in 1924 and later became superintendent of the hospital at Wamego, Kansas.

From each one of his children Naismith learned something, but perhaps he learned the most from the most difficult one—Jack. A few years after Jack ran away to South Dakota, Naismith wrote an article that included an analysis of "the average normal boy after puberty." In that interpretation his experiences with his older son are reflected. Two of his observations about the "average normal boy" seem particularly close to being a description of Jack:

He is in a state of unrest shown in several ways:
(1) His aversion to restraint.
(2) His inclination to wander, a logical outcome of which is the tendency to run away.[42]

One of his remarks obviously includes wishful thinking about the relationship between Jack and his mother:

His reverence for his mother, his interest in the occult and mystic, could be turned to good account.[43]

And another comment reveals an awareness of the influence of Jack's associates on him, from college drinking companions to burly construction workers:

The same incentive that leads him to follow the lead of the braggart debauchee could be used to instill high ideals and develop character.[44]

If James Naismith erred in his methods of rearing children, he did not try to excuse himself. He used to say: "Not only must one do what he thinks is right, he must *think* right."[45] He could only hope that he was thinking right.

18

Chaplain on the Mexican Border

THE years from 1916 to 1919 were momentous and disrupting to the Naismith family. The year 1916 alone held several significant happenings and several sets of emotions—with elopement, ordination, and war came disappointment, gratification, and excitement.[1]

The two older Naismith daughters had always been little ladies, like their mother, and no one had expected Margaret to defy her parents. The Naismiths had long planned that their first-born would graduate from the university at which her father had taught during most of his career, and she had dutifully enrolled and studied for two years. But then, to their disappointment, she eloped with a fellow student. Despite Dr. and Mrs. Naismith's request that she complete her remaining two years of study before marriage, she ran off to wed George Bowman Stanley.

Margaret and George came home the evening of the elopement, late, slipping shyly up the walk onto the side porch. The bride's father met them at the door.

"Well, I've done it," Margaret said bluntly.

Naismith stepped out to her without a word and kissed her. He shook George's hand. "Be good to her." Then he said, "Now you both go in and tell Margie's mother."[2]

After the first feeling of betrayal and disappointment had passed, both the Naismiths adjusted swiftly, needless to say, forgave, and bestowed their blessing. They remembered back with tolerant amusement to the time when the affair had started. Maude Naismith recalled the days when the little Stanley boy used to travel from Kansas City to visit relatives in Lawrence, and she reminded her husband that she had told him to close the gate so that "the nasty little boy next door won't come over and play with my girls."[3]

It was too late to close the gate now. Besides, no one was sure he would have wanted to, even had it been possible. Mrs. Naismith could not blame Margaret for wanting to marry George. He had something of her own husband's sweetness, his sense of humor, his zest for living. George would be kind to Margie, even if he would startle her with such pranks as riding a motorcycle full speed down the stairs from the young couple's second-story apartment.[4]

Everyone soon knew that Mrs. Naismith idolized her new son-in-law, elopement or not, and George Bowman Stanley acquired the family title of "Mama's angel son-in-law." James Naismith, for his part, quickly made practical plans for the young man's future. George returned to the university and his studies, acting as an assistant instructor in the Department of Physical Education, his father-in-law being his supervisor. Perhaps it was in some part Dr. Naismith's influence that inspired George to earn an M.D. degree in 1926.

Something Naismith had waited for longer than Margaret's graduation from college did come true in that year of 1916. Twenty-six years after he graduated from the theological seminary in Montreal, he became an ordained minister.[5]

The main reason for his seeking ordination was his desire to qualify as a chaplain in the United States Army. Although fifty-four years old in 1915—and still a Canadian citizen—he had volunteered for the Kansas National Guard.[6] Europe was in the second year of World War I, and although he did not know it then, the United States was soon to become involved in two wars: the one with revolutionary Mexico and the one in Europe. At any rate, events followed each other in rapid sequence.

On March 18, 1915, Naismith was appointed chaplain in the First Regiment of the Kansas National Guard. With the rank of captain, he served ten days' active training service from August 16 to August 25, 1915.[7] The following spring, on March 9, 1916, the Mexican outlaw Pancho Villa, resentful because the United States had recognized his revolutionary rival, Carranza, as head of the Mexican government, crossed the border into New Mexico, killing United States citizens and destroying property. On March 15, 1916, U.S. troops, commanded by Brigadier General John J. Pershing and known as the Mexican Punitive Expedition, went in pursuit of Villa. The wartime temperature of the United States was high.[8] On April 12, 1916, Naismith was officially ordained as a minister by the Presbytery at Clay Center, Kansas, and his preparations were complete for full military service, whether in Mexico or in Europe.[9]

On June 16, 1916, the Mexicans issued an edict warning the United States to remove all troops from Mexican soil. As a countermove, on June 18, 1916, President Woodrow Wilson called up the entire U.S. National Guard, exhorting it to protect the honor of the nation, and the War Department ordered each state to mobilize its Guard units. On June 19, the day after the national announcement, Naismith was mustered into federal military service. With a full commission as captain in the field staff of the First Regiment, Kansas Volunteer Infantry, he was to work as chaplain during his regiment's service in the Mexican Border War. Sent speedily southward on the Missouri, Kansas, and Texas Railroad in early July of 1916, he became a part of General Pershing's Punitive Expedition.[10]

The military order had come without warning, and he had had no time to arrange his affairs as he would have liked or even to tell his family goodbye properly. Young Jack Naismith meant the farewell to his father to be only temporary, though. As Captain Naismith traveled south, he was unaware that back in Lawrence his most adventurous child was preparing to follow him to war. But that's how it was.

Fifteen-year-old Jack started for Mexico on the fifth of July and got as far west as the small town of St. Marys, Kansas, where he settled down to spend the night in the little park beside the railroad tracks, across the street west from the spot where the bank stood at that time. Unfortunately, the fireworks he heard that night were not firecrackers left over from the Fourth of July celebration the day before, but were exploding nitroglycerine in the bank and gunfire in the streets. The safe in the St. Marys State Bank was blown up and robbed of $2,400 that night, and

Jack, awakened from his sleep in the park, was picked up as a suspect. Vagrant in a strange town, he was a forlorn lad for seven or eight hours. Fortunately, the well-known umpire Ernie Quigley, who knew the Naismith family, got the boy out of jail the next morning and sent him to a relative's farm nearby. Jack, working as a farm hand instead of as a soldier that summer, did not reach Mexico while the Border War was going on.[11]

Meanwhile, his father, writing to Mrs. Naismith on his way through Waco, Texas, on July 7, did not yet know what had happened. Oblivious of the gunfire in Kansas, Captain Naismith continued on to the Texas-Mexican border.[12] National Guard troops were strung out along the entire international boundary— some 1,700 miles from the Gulf of Mexico to the California line— and Captain Naismith was sent to a camp at Eagle Pass, Texas, across the Rio Grande River from the Mexican town of Piedras Negras. There he found much work to do.

Mobilized soldiers usually had no barracks awaiting them at their varied destinations. Campsites had to be cleared and buildings set up.[13] One soldier on the Texas side of the Rio Grande described the conditions that guardsmen found upon arrival:

The men hacked and cut and dug the areas clear . . . the rattlers [were] scared away. But the gnats remained. They swarmed all over the little food we had. . . . We tried to cook a steer over a pit, one day, and the wind blew sand over it until it was uneatable.[14]

In addition to rattlesnakes, gnats, and blowing sand, the Americans had to cope with monotony (unless, of course, the Mexican outlaws came near).

Believe me, it was not fun, day after day to perform the small drill. . . . There was no place to go, nothing to do. The men soon became almost sick at the sight of each other.[15]

Despite his incomplete knowledge of affairs at home, Naismith found time from camp construction, small drill, and monotony to worry about his family. He was particularly concerned about the frailest one of all—his wife—and their youngest child. Margaret, the oldest, was not around home any longer, and a prop of the household had thereby been taken away. He expressed his concern in a hurried, misspelled letter he wrote on July 13 to Hellen, nearly nineteen and the oldest child at home. He addressed her by the pet name "Nel" and used his own family nickname as signature.

To my deal [*sic*] little Nel.
. . . Now Nelie girl you can't realize how I depend on you to take care of mother and Jim. The others can hustle for themselves. Tell Maude for me, I expect her to be her mother's helper too.
Papa Jim[16]

He wrote hurriedly, not taking time to proofread and correct his slips of the pen. But Hellen treasured the letter from her soldier-father and stored it away to keep.

Other activities came along, besides, as they do in wartime. Naismith took part in mock battles and maneuvers that summer, traveling by foot, by horse, and by motor truck. He participated in an overland trek from San Antonio to Austin in hot early September. He even was hurt in the line of duty. On horseback, he sustained a groin injury that later was a factor in bringing on surgery. But most significant during his period of service were his accomplishments at the border camp at Eagle Pass, where from early July till early September he did his part to raise the morals and morale of Uncle Sam's soldiers.[17]

At the time of the military venture of the United States on the Mexican border, the traditional view that liquor and women are necessary parts of army life was beginning to be questioned. The secretary of war, Newton D. Baker, concerned over the military loss incurred through venereal diseases, sent officials to study conditions in the camps and their adjacent civil communities, both at home and abroad. He then made recommendations for the control of prostitution. Thereupon, the Y.M.C.A., influential in promoting federal action of this type, moved into the Mexican campaign to cooperate with the Department of War in a program of sex education for the border troops.[18]

James Naismith, impressed with the work that the "Y" was doing, learned that prostitution was being practiced extensively in most of the military camps along the border, where vice interests from other parts of the country had congregated. He there-upon threw himself into a campaign of his own.

Located outside a small border town, in a camp where several regiments of troops were located, he had ample opportunity for a moral crusade. As soon as the camp was established, organized vice interests moved in to begin construction of a large house of prostitution—actually a long wooden shack partitioned into so-called cribs. When Naismith, with other chaplains in the camp, tried to obtain an injunction against the operation, the district judge refused to act. However, during a temporary absence of the judge, when the building was nearly completed, Naismith helped secure the desired injunction from the judge of a neigh-boring district. Construction of the building stopped abruptly, and an exodus of waiting, out-of-town prostitutes took place.[19]

Although Naismith had helped in a dramatic manner to break up organized prostitution, clandestine prostitution continued to flourish at the edges of the camp, and he never relaxed his battle against it and against uncooperative civil authorities. While many military camps were fighting venereal disease on a medical basis, curing the disease without trying to suppress prostitution, Nai-smith dealt with the cause, emphasizing prevention more than cure. He continued to stake out bounds for soldiers and to close bawdyhouses and saloons to them. He assisted in an educational campaign against venereal disease. He was a pioneer in the use of games to keep soldiers out of trouble, calling his method "practical preaching," or, wryly, "strange preaching."[20]

One of the games he used was his own creation. In the absence of gymnasiums and indoor playing courts, he introduced the soldiers to an outdoor adaptation of basketball, one that he had tried out in physical education classes at the University of Kansas. Here on the Mexican border he laid out a playing field and set up baskets modeled on his work at home. The two goals, about fifty feet apart, were placed a short distance inside the court, without backboards, so that shooting could be done from all sides. This placement kept the ball from going over the end lines as often, and thus interrupting play. Because carom shots were thus eliminated, shooting was more difficult than in conventional basketball, and Naismith optimistically figured that his protégés would become "improved in the game." The rules themselves were practically the same as in basketball except that to start play the men stood sideways to the goals instead of facing their own goal. Naismith said that this position would protect the unsheltered goal posts against possible loosening.[21]

The game served its purpose as a form of outdoor exercise for the border troops, and a description of the playing field and rules was published in a national magazine a few months after he returned home.[22] But his new adaptation of basketball was never used by many persons except physical education students and homesick soldiers.

For homesickness, Naismith was good medicine. He was always available for the small favor and the kindly bit of advice. He helped the boys write letters home, prodding the laggards into sending messages to uneasy parents. His own high moral standards were a wholesome influence, and his brisk good humor provided the light touch that was needed. Although he could become angry, and sometimes did, he rarely showed his anger, and the young men felt at ease with him.

Maybe some people felt more at ease with him than they should have. Maybe his good nature and leniency were a fault. During his four months of military service he came up against both good and evil, and when the evil was directed against him, too often he made excuses for the wrongdoer—even at the cost, once, of his own monthly pay allotment.

On payday, if an officer was not present in the line filing past the long pay table, the adjutant kept the absent officer's money for him until he came to collect it. One payday when Naismith was out of camp, young adjutant F—— withheld the chaplain's allotment, which, as was customary, was in the form of cash, including gold pieces. However, he did not set the amount aside; he spent it. Upon Naismith's return, the adjutant evaded inquiry about the missing pay. When Naismith learned the truth—that his allotment had been stolen—he showed his customary reluctance to be the cause of pain or worry for anyone. As a result, he did not press a demand for his money.

Fellow officers, learning about that affair, urged punitive measures: "For God's sake, Jim, you can't substitute forgiveness for

discipline in a mess like this. This is a case of embezzlement."
But Naismith shrugged off the incident. "He doesn't have the
money any more—what's the use of worrying him about it?"[23]

Honest and fair in his own acts, he had always showed his
greatest anger against injustice in any form; but injustice against
himself he never acknowledged.[24]

Forty-seven years after the expedition against Pancho Villa,
Naismith's major on that tour of duty remembered the chaplain
and spoke about him. On an August afternoon Hugh Means—
now an old man, ex-soldier and ex-judge—sat in his quiet law
office, with cane leaning against his desk, and recalled the hot
days of that other summer and the camp across the Rio Grande
from Piedras Negras. "He was a wonderful man. A pleasant
companion and a good influence on the boys," mused the judge
as he sat gazing out the window onto the sunny Kansas street.
"He was a sweet person. That's the best word I can find to
describe him—sweet."[25]

Judge Means remembered the incident of the stolen pay. His
face changed and his voice grew stern: "That was the only wrong
thing I ever saw Naismith do. His only fault was that he never
wanted to cause anyone trouble. He was a good man, but he was
too good."[26]

Wrong or not in his motives, Naismith lived out his long, hot
summer of Mexican border duty. Then, in slightly more than
four months, his federal military service was ended. In September
he traveled with the First Kansas Infantry one hundred sixty
miles by motor truck from the Mexican border in an overland
convoy to San Antonio on the way to wait for a furlough.[27] On
October 30, 1916, he was discharged from service at Fort Riley,
Kansas.[28] For a little while he would be at home again with his
family in Lawrence.

19

Sex and Games on Home Soil

THE University of Kansas, founded in 1866, was ready to celebrate its golden year in 1916. But the United States was uneasy about the war in Europe, and festivities, therefore, seemed inappropriate. The semicentennial celebration was held down to a nationwide telephone hookup of K.U. students and graduates in three locations—New York, San Francisco, and Lawrence. Off-campus groups of alumni in New York and San Francisco were connected by telephone with a crowd of a few hundred on-campus students and alumni in Robinson Gymnasium in Lawrence, and amenities were exchanged.[1]

Campus celebrations, however, were irrelevant to James Naismith's interests, for he was involved in more important activities. As far as war and the United States were concerned, he was ahead of most of the patriots. He had already been doing his share as a soldier-chaplain. Y.M.C.A. officials, impressed, publicly praised his effectiveness in the campaign against immorality in army life.[2]

As an army chaplain on the Mexican border, Dr. Naismith fought practically single-handed the vice interests and the officials of the community near which his camp was located until he won. . . . He showed in this the same bulldog tenacity for which he was known when he played football against the big teams in the east in earlier days.[3]

But Naismith's Mexican-border service was only a brief, preliminary experience on the outskirts of war. Mustered out of his initial military venture on October 30, 1916, he found grimmer days ahead in far-off places.[4] On April 6, 1917, Congress passed a resolution declaring war against Germany, and the United States was brought into World War I.

As soon as the news reached Lawrence, every whistle in town began to blow a series of long blasts. Student janitor Albert H. Hindman, who was outside of Marvin Hall cleaning chalk out of blackboard erasers, raced downhill to the university power plant to add the foghorn blast of the K.U. steam whistle to the noise.[5] When Naismith heard the raucous serenade and knew that war had begun, he may have had a hunch that he would be playing a role in that conflict.

If so, he was right. But it was to be a role with the Y.M.C.A. rather than with the First Regiment, Kansas Volunteer Infantry.

Military forces were rapidly put into action. The United States Army alone had sixteen National Guard camps, sixteen National Army camps, and eighty or more training centers for officers, aviators, ambulance men, and so forth.[6]

In May, 1917, Newton D. Baker, secretary of war, appointed a National Commission on Training Camp Activities, and Josephus Daniels, secretary of .the navy, soon afterwards appointed an analogous Naval Commission.

The Commissions on Training Camp Activities promoted work in the camps on three principal lines: recreation, education, and restriction. "Recreation" involved a multitude of social and athletic activities in the camps and in communities adjacent to the camps. "Education" included French and German language classes and other instructional opportunities for the soldiers. "Restriction" was part of a morals campaign carried on in and about the camps as well as in nearby industrial communities. The *American Physical Education Review,* in fact, had at first emphasized this third aspect of the work of the commissions: "It is to be hoped that they will be successful in eliminating drink and questionable women from the camps and the vicinity of the camps."[7]

Sex, naturally, was rearing its ugly and fascinating head. Even before the start of World War I, the United States had been involved in a civilian fight against venereal disease, marshaling its forces within the euphemistically labeled "Social Hygiene Movement." Those were the days when syphilis and gonorrhea were politely called "social diseases" and prostituiton was vaguely referred to as "vice." When Dr. Max J. Exner's frank article "Prostitution in Its Relation to the Army on the Mexican Border" was published in the journal *Social Hygiene* at the time the United States was entering the World War, it helped arouse the public. Drawing attention to the accomplishments of the

Y.M.C.A. in its Mexican campaign, Exner's article enlisted support in a campaign directed toward the moral welfare of American soldiers.[8]

The American Social Hygiene Association, aware that the efficiency of a regiment could be reduced by as much as thirty percent because of venereal disease, took upon itself the job of protecting the army and navy against their sexual instincts. The association's activities eventually involved the Medical Corps of the Army, the Medical Corps of the Navy, the United States Public Health Service, the Commissions on Training Camp Activities for the army and the navy, and, by July 9, 1918, the United States Interdepartmental Social Hygiene Board.

The Y.M.C.A. was the first of American civil or social welfare organizations to offer its services to the United States government in the war. President Wilson issued an order giving official recognition to the Y.M.C.A. National War Work Council, which held its first meeting in New York on April 28, 1917, three weeks after war was declared.[9] Among its many activities was a Y.M.C.A. moral-medical crusade: the "Y" was in the forefront of the battle against venereal disease. The Y.M.C.A. International Committee formed a Sex Education Bureau, pledging its cooperation with the federal Training Camp Activities Commissions.[10]

Officials of the Y.M.C.A., judging Naismith's qualifications on the basis both of his work during the Mexican Border War and of his experience at the University of Kansas, asked him to join in the increasingly far-flung program of moral instruction of the National War Work Council. Exner wrote: "Dr. Naismith was well qualified for the task. He had given much study to the subject of social hygiene and had for years done successful work in sex education at the University of Kansas."[11]

Naismith agreed to serve. Now in his fifty-sixth year, he was one of the first persons on the University of Kansas faculty to volunteer for war work.[12] Friends tried to persuade him not to enlist; they argued that he was old enough to stay home. But, as the *Kansas City Star* reported: "They reckoned not on the spirit that is in 'Doc' Naismith."[13]

James Naismith thought differently about war than did his former chancellor, Francis Huntington Snow. In Snow's young

manhood in Civil War years he had been torn between a conscientious abhorrence of battle and a passion to aid the Union
cause. He resolved his conflict by volunteering as a medical aid,
as the poet Walt Whitman was doing, working in hospital and
field service.[14] In 1898, when another war was going on and
Snow was chancellor of the University of Kansas, he stopped
many students from leaving college to serve in the Spanish-
American war. "Boys! don't go. There are plenty of men to go
to the Philippines. Our country needs learned men."[15]

But Naismith, although he chose the Y.M.C.A. rather than the
army, was not a conscientious objector to the act of armed fighting. He believed that war was sometimes a necessary evil. "There
are," he said, "more important things even than the saving of
lives."[16] And now that war had come for the United States he
felt that it was his duty—even though he was still a Canadian
citizen—to help the country in which he had lived since he was
twenty-nine years old.

In accepting the responsibilities of patriotism he had to leave
a wife and four children, not counting married Margaret. The
youngest, son Jimmy, was only four years old; and the older son,
Jack, was now in the 16-to-21-year-old period—the "forgotten age"
that Naismith considered all-important in young manhood. But
Naismith and his wife gave Jack a small red-leather Bible with
the date May 7, 1917, inscribed on the flyleaf and hoped for the
best.[17] Then Naismith turned to the work of the National War
Work Council.

Probably, as the director of the Sex Education Bureau pointed
out, the War Department would not have established its Commission on Training Camp Activities had it not been for the successful sex work accomplished during the Mexican Border War,
when this aspect of Y.M.C.A. work originated. At any rate, the
Y.M.C.A. went into action immediately, with a continuation of
its Border War program.

The "Y" administration appointed a small group of lecturers
early in June, 1917, employing James Naismith on the first camp-
lecture staff. He agreed to travel around the United States to
the various army and navy training camps in an extensive lecture
program aimed at strengthening the moral character of American

military men. By July, eight lecturers, including Naismith, were
giving full time to the work, and additional men were added in
following weeks.

Pamphlets, books, posters, cards, exhibits, slides, and films on
sex education were prepared for use by the lecturers. With the
pamphlet "Friend or Enemy" serving as the first of a long series
of booklets printed for free distribution to men in the armed
forces, the material ranged from the sentimental love story of
"The Nurse and the Knight" to a frank argument for clean living
as a basis for military fitness in "The Stuff That Wins." Films
such as "How Life Begins," which combined biological information with moral pronouncements, were typical. The series of
lectures covered a similar emotional gamut of information,
threat, and appeal.

Naismith successfully carried out his role in this program.
He was an effective lecturer on a subject in which he had long
been interested, and the crowds that gathered about him for
informal question-and-answer periods after the formal lectures
attested to his popularity. In addition, he granted many private
interviews to those men who sought help with their personal sex
problems. The military establishments visited in the Y.M.C.A.
lecture program were widely scattered over the United States,
and Naismith traveled continuously, stopping perhaps a week in
one place. Sometimes he lectured two or three times a day to
audiences of as many as four or five thousand persons.[19]

Organized physical activities as well as lectures were set up by
the Y.M.C.A. in training camps, for "Y" leaders were well aware
of the "play instinct" in men. As one official observed, "The first
thing that American soldiers thought of when they had a little
leisure was to play ball or indulge in some form of athletic
recreation."[20]

Sometimes a spokesman became ecstatic over the therapeutic
effect of a recreational program and the miracles thereby wrought
by the "Y":

The traditional drunken soldier and maudlin sailor are largely products of bad recreation. They are the inevitable result of the one-sided
life forced upon them by the army régime. . . . The Y.M.C.A. and

other agencies are saving our soldiers. They will help . . . to win this war. Thank God for them![21]

But melodramatic statement was not really necessary. By the time the United States entered the World War, nearly three years of evidence had accumulated. The wholesome effect of sports for military men had already been demonstrated from 1914 to 1917 when the Y.M.C.A. had a program of exercise and recreation in the Canadian Corps of the British Army. Y.M.C.A. officials were able to point out that "athletics have real military value . . . in maintaining the *morale* of the army,"[22] and the highest U.S. administrators agreed that fun and games had their place in wartime. The Honorable Newton D. Baker, secretary of war, addressing a meeting of the National Collegiate Athletic Association, commented: "[The] army . . . must have some form of recreation. . . . There is something in athletics that appeals to all healthy young men."[23] And President Woodrow Wilson stated publicly on May 22, 1917, "I hope that sports will be continued . . . as a real contribution to the national defense."[24] Again, on October 23, 1917, in an address delivered at the National Conference of War Camp Community Recreation Service, Secretary Baker expressed faith in the efficacy of athletics in the war training camps. These were things that James Naismith had been saying all his life.

In the first few months of army training the emphasis was on athletic activities for their recreative value, but soon the need for exercise as physical training was evident. Studies showed that twenty-five to thirty-five percent of all men drafted into the army were physically unfit. One army captain was specific in his accusations. "Our physical efficiency tests," he pointed out, "showed whole companies that averaged less than six feet in the standing broad jump."[25] He complained that he had seen regiments go over obstacle courses where not one man could properly vault a four-foot fence with a rifle held in one hand. Further, seldom could he find a man who would step over a two-foot-six-inch hurdle with good form. He summed up, "Most men were sadly in need of training in running, jumping, fence vaulting, wall scaling, hurdling, boxing and wrestling."[26]

The Physical Training Board, which was under the War Plans Division of the General Staff, supervised and coordinated athletic activities that were conducted in military training camps by the Y.M.C.A. and other nonmilitary organizations. "Y" physical directors did their best to supply the physical training that the troops needed. They supervised soldiers in jumping and vaulting, ladder scaling, rope climbing, balancing on fence rails, shelf scaling, lifting and carrying, wrestling, and other exercises—all done to the accompaniment of military commands. In a shadow-boxing drill one might hear: "Company, ATTENTION! MARCH! Front rank about, FACE! On GUARD! STEP! HIT! HIT! STEP! HIT!"[27] The Y.M.C.A. even provided drill in hand-grenade throwing as part of its program.

In order to make participants out of all the soldiers, physical directors used mass athletics. At Norfolk, Virginia, Y.M.C.A. directors supervised setting-up' exercises for fourteen hundred men at one time. At American Lakes 178 basketball teams were scheduled in a league. At Camp Sevier the soldiers staged 125 boxing bouts in two hours. "Y" leaders attempted to see that soldiers took part in everything from football, basketball, baseball, volleyball, and soccer to dodgeball, cageball, pushball, quoits, and tug of war.

At the other end of the scale from mass exercises were informal games for two or more players. Sometimes homesick soldiers made up simple rituals that children might have performed at school recess time. A favorite leisure-time game among certain U.S. troops was one they called "Mike, Where Are You?" To play it, each of two blindfold young men was equipped with a canvas club, about eighteen inches long and an inch and a quarter in diameter, stuffed with cotton batting. One blindfold soldier would call out, "Mike, where are you?" and the other would reply, "Here I am," the object being to locate the opponent by the sound of his voice and then swat him. The game could be played either standing upright or lying on the stomach and maneuvering from that position. Physical director A. E. Metzdorf in Camp Devens reported, "It is very amusing to watch them and affords considerable enjoyment to the onlookers."[28]

Even elementary schools were combining recreation and physical exercise with military spirit. During exercise hour in school gymnasiums children danced the "Army and Navy Quickstep" to the rhythm of a lively march. In the third part of the dance, which was naval in orientation, Figure A was called "Hoisting sails," and Figure B was "Sighting land" ("Bring left hand to forehead . . . stepping obliquely forward on left. . . . Hop on left, counting two. . . ."[29]

Naismith, as might be surmised, was pleased at the national reaction to recreative sports. In his enthusiasm he tried to add new games himself to the military repertoire. One game he originated was hy-lo ball, the rules for which were published in November, 1917. A combination of two sports he had learned in Canada, the game used a soccer ball and rugby goals on a rugby field. It involved much kicking, passing, running, and tackling, before the ball was carried across the goal line or kicked over the bar between the goal posts. Feet, legs, hands, arms, head, and body were all put into use during play; and it took a referee and two umpires, in addition to scorekeepers and timekeepers, to keep the twenty-two participants in order.

But despite all its vigorous activity, hy-lo ball never got off the ground, figuratively speaking; and by the time the rules were published in a national magazine, Naismith was abroad, unable to give it a boost.[30]

Early in his career on the United States sex-lecture circuit, Naismith observed how great was the need for qualified men, and he took steps to extend his participation in the "Y" program. Obtaining an honorable discharge from the Kansas National Guard at Lawrence, Kansas, on July 2, 1917, and obtaining an extended leave of absence from the University of Kansas, he freed himself for service with the Y.M.C.A.[31] That service would take him farther from home and cause a longer absence than any of the Naismiths realized.

20

Rain and Mud and Cold in France

THE First Division embarked from the United States for France on June 14, 1917;[1] and by the end of June, 175,000 American troops were training in France.[2] War had begun for American soldiers on foreign soil, and an urgent need for overseas war service had arisen within the Young Men's Christian Association.

Impressively, Y.M.C.A. officials were in France before the first troops got there. The Y.M.C.A., soon known overseas as the "Y" or the "Red Triangle," set up an international organization in April, having called in Edward Clark Carter from foreign service in India and Great Britain to become Overseas Chief Secretary. Then "Y" personnel set out to take care of the recreational, educational, physical, and spiritual activities of American soldiers, or "doughboys," abroad. The organization would be under the dual control of the National War Work Council of the Y.M.C.A. and General John J. Pershing, commander in chief of the American Expeditionary Forces, the overseas military power of the United States.

As Chief Secretary Carter stated in his address to new "Y" workers: "The Y M C A . . . undertakes . . . to take the place of the American home, the American church, the American school, the American college, the American stage—all that is best in the life of America."[3]

Military authorities gave their approval to the entrance of the "Y" into war service. In the early months of the war, General Pershing sanctioned the cooperation in France of two voluntary welfare organizations—the Y.M.C.A. and the Red Cross—recommending that applications of all other groups be refused. General Order No. 26 of the American Expeditionary Forces, issued in August, 1917, stated in part:

In order to avoid duplication of work by the Red Cross and the Y.M.C.A., the two civil agencies ministering to the welfare of soldiers, the following broad division of activities is prescribed: the Red Cross will provide for the relief work and the Y.M.C.A. will provide for the amusement and recreation of the troops by means of its usual program of social, educational, physical and religious activities.[4]

In outlining the duties of the Y.M.C.A. with the army, emphasis was placed on the physical and recreational aspects of "Y" work. General Pershing's General Order No. 241 stated:

The Commander in Chief directs the attention of all concerned to the importance of encouraging the development of general and competitive athletics and all kinds of appropriate entertainment, for the purpose of keeping up the morale, fostering and developing organization *esprit de corps* and improving the physical fitness of the army.[5]

Further, the order specified that a physical director from a Y.M.C.A. Department of Athletics approved by the commander in chief should be attached to the staff of each division and separate unit and should bear the title of Divisional (or Unit) Athletic Director. After four hours of military training in any day, a soldier with a month or more of training was authorized to be excused by his commanding officer in order to participate in athletic sports.

A few military men did not agree with Pershing and the Y.M.C.A. on the subject of amusement and recreation. An occasional army commander was heard to turn down the proposals of a physical director from the "Y": "Absolutely nothing doing—we are fighting a war—you fellows are crazy—this is not a playground."[6] But the majority of officers were willing to introduce fun and games into the army.

The organizational machinery of the Y.M.C.A. in France was extensive. Within a short time after its entry into overseas work the "Y" was operating a network of banks, post exchanges, retail grocery stores, cafes, hotels and dormitories, garages, machine shops, and motor-transport facilities. Large central warehouses were maintained, from which supplies were sent to smaller warehouses in the division centers for further distribution to appropriate locations. The result of this economic network was a program for American troops that was intended to offset the demoralizing influences traditionally associated with army life. The "Y"'s wholesome activities were provided at the large ports of debarkation, at the training camps, at the front-line billeting locations, and at the leave areas.[7]

Y.M.C.A. administrators were aware of the need for the right kind of man in the right spot in each part of their intricate program. Furthermore, they knew that the real test of the whole program of moral conservation that had begun in the United States would come in France. Therefore, in the summer of 1917 they chose Dr. James Naismith as the man to study moral conditions among the troops of American Expeditionary Forces and to develop a program of sex education there. Although there was as yet no department set up for this work, the "Y" went ahead to select several others of its best lecturers to form his staff of assistants.[8]

Flattered at this confidence in his ability, Naismith agreed. In September, 1917, after nearly four months of traveling and lecturing at military camps in the United States, he sailed for France to continue the work he had been doing on American soil.[9] Although he was the creator of the game of basketball, a game originated in a Y.M.C.A. gymnasium, the "Y" was sending him abroad not as an ambassador of basketball but as a sex moralist.

Aboard ship he set himself to study the French language intensively. His years in French Canada had not given him sufficient speaking knowledge of French for the months ahead of him,[10] and the first thing Y.M.C.A. officials asked a man planning overseas duty was, "Can you speak French?"[11] Study and danger, needless to say, made the ocean trip anything but a pleasure jaunt. The Germans had boasted publicly that their submarines would sink without warning any transports carrying American troops to France, and the Y.M.C.A. men felt as vulnerable as any soldiers.

If he got safely to France, he would have his headquarters in Paris, and a few other Y.M.C.A. workers would be there, men whom he knew. George L. Meylan, for example, came to France the same month Naismith did, and Dr. James Huff McCurdy had been there since August. McCurdy, like Naismith an alumnus of the International Y.M.C.A. College at Springfield and now its director of physical courses, had been granted a six-month leave of absence, later extended, to go to France. He had sailed from New York on August 3, 1917. A representative of the War

Department Commission on Training Camp Activities, working under the National War Work Council of the Y.M.C.A., he was the first director of physical activities with the A.E.F. and Allied troops.

Another of Naismith's friends, Dr. Robert Tait McKenzie, was also in Europe. His area of wartime activity, however, lay on the other side of the English Channel. He had come to England in May, 1915, on leave of absence from his position at the University of Pennsylvania, in order to supervise retraining and rehabilitative treatments for disabled soldiers.[12]

After Naismith arrived in Paris, a month after McCurdy, the two men would be located for a time in a large handsome building at 31, avenue Montaigne. Located just off the central point of the Champs Élysées, this private mansion had originally been the palace built by Napoleon III for his minister of finance. Leased by the "Y" for the duration of the war and three months thereafter, it was opened as administrative headquarters on June 11, 1917. Only after more space was needed would Y.M.C.A. headquarters be moved to 12, rue d'Aguesseau.

Paris was not a holiday resort. Americans found the city cloaked in wartime austerity. At night the streets were so dimly lighted that one was in danger from taxis that were scurrying about. Prices were high; butter and sugar were scarce; and milk was available only for children and ill persons. By October, winter was already approaching and the weather was cold and damp most of the time. Only the Y.M.C.A. personnel who were later sent to Montpellier or some other location in the south of France were happy with French weather. One of them was able to write gratefully, "I am very fortunate to get away from the Paris climate."[13] Naismith was not one of these fortunate ones.

Nor was Paris free from the direct blows of war. Bombing was so frequent, in fact, that Parisians slept through the night raids, and Americans had to learn, too, to become casual about danger. Y.M.C.A. worker Stewart McComber, on leave in Paris, wrote home about one of the German aerial attacks:

The *alerte* was sounded twice that night and there was a terrific bombardment which resulted in some damage to a few dwellings, some injuries and, I believe, two deaths, and . . . destruction of two German planes with their pilots. . . . I got up and looked out of the hotel window and watched the searchlights and the antiaircraft shells bursting so high in the sky that they looked like fireflies; then went back to bed and was asleep when the recall was sounded.[14]

Recreational facilities were available for Y.M.C.A. personnel in the midst of warfare. The month after it opened, on July 22, 1917, the administrative building at 31, avenue Montaigne began double duty as a clubhouse for Americans serving in any kind of war work. Indoors, in addition to offices, it held reading and writing rooms, pool and billiard tables, and shower baths. Outdoors there were tennis courts. Enough Americans congregated there that in its first month as a clubhouse a baseball league was formed, and for the many who requested instruction in the French language, classes were set up in the clubhouse rooms. At first Paris was a restricted area for American troops, but eventually it was opened as a leave area. The great treat then, for the lucky ones, became a trip to the capital city, and 31, avenue Montaigne was one of the places many visited to relax. But for Naismith and McCurdy there would be more work than play in France.

"Alert" signals, antiaircraft guns, and falling bombs were a part of life in Paris, but existence outside the city was even more difficult. Outside Paris—in the ports of debarkation, the permanent training camps, and the temporary camps near the front line—Naismith found much work to do and many adjustments to be made in his way of living. He had been told that service abroad was going to be hard work, and he saw the prediction come true. He had been warned, "There is a great deal of rain and mud and cold in France."[15] He was soon knee-deep in mud and penetrated to the bone by the dampness and cold. Dismal weather encompassed everyone, soldiers and civilians alike. "Y" workers were amused to see children shuffling to school in the little towns of France with wooden shoes as protection against the mud in the streets, dragging their feet in a stiff-legged, stiff-kneed gait so that their shoes would not slip off. Only in the shelter of school or home did they kick off the shoes, leaving felt slippers on their feet.[16]

Naismith found all warnings about the weather true. But he had not realized how penetrating the cold and damp would be or how much of that French mud would be plastered on his own boots as he ranged far out from his Paris office to front-line installations. Strong though he was, he had to admit that living conditions were hard on his health during those long months in France. Outside of Paris, wartime needs had appropriated much of the coal and wood and power that would have made living warm and comfortable. He was resourceful, of course, as the "Y" men were taught to be. When traveling, they wore two pairs of socks for warmth and inserted cork or felt insoles inside their boots for dryness. In addition, they oiled their high, stout boots with mutton lard or bear grease to make them water-resistant. They carried three pairs of long underwear so that they would always have a dry suit available even when there was no fire by which to dry clothing. At night they used several layers of newspaper in their bedding to keep out the cold.

Military in bearing in army garb, Naismith carried out the work of the Y.M.C.A. under army regulations. While overseas, "Y" men wore army officers' uniforms with the exception of the Sam Browne belt. They exchanged salutes with commissioned and noncommissioned officers (but not with privates) in regulation manner. They were subject to court-martial under military law. They were not restricted, however, by army rules concerning relations between officers and men. They were admitted to the officers' mess, or, in line with the Y.M.C.A. policy of good comradeship, they were allowed to eat with a private on equal terms. Naismith accepted all this protocol with good humor.

As soon as McCurdy reached France, he began to organize an extensive program of athletics for the army, and Naismith immediately plunged into that work. Sex was not the first business at hand, as it turned out. Upon his arrival, his first major task, to give him first-hand experience in the program being initiated, was to organize the entire Y.M.C.A. work in a large American camp. After that he set out on a speaking tour, becoming one of the "Y" 's "trained seals," as Y.M.C.A. personnel called the lecturers and entertainers they sent out to American bases in France.

For a time he was officially labeled "athletic inspector and lecturer on recreational topics in the training camps."[17]

There were six principal ports in France where American troopships docked—Brest, St. Nazaire, Bordeaux, Le Havre, La Pallice, and Marseilles—of which Brest was by far the busiest. Workers from the Young Men's Christian Association were on hand at all of these ports to meet incoming soldiers, ready to travel with them from temporary camps to permanent bases; and Naismith and McCurdy were often present, together or separately, when a troopship docked. But the movement of troops was kept secret, for reasons of security, and it was difficult for "Y" men to be Johnny-on-the-spot when a ship arrived. McCurdy complained, "We hear very little here about the coming of troops. We learn that they are at the port of entry, then it's a hustle to get the Y.M.C.A. located for them."[18]

Nevertheless, the "Y" workers did a good job. Even at the beginning, when the first expeditionary unit arrived at St. Nazaire on June 24, 1917, Y.M.C.A. men were at the port waiting for the ship. Sometimes McCurdy found himself so busy that he called Naismith away from other work for assistance. In a letter that McCurdy wrote to his family in the autumn of 1917, he explained the activities that the two of them were carrying out at a French port:

I am here . . . talking to the men at camp and on shipboard. . . . Dr. Naismith sits near me as I write. I had Mr. Carter wire him to come and help out on the speaking. . . . You get a great response from the men when you speak, both at camp and on shipboard. I spoke to-night right down in the bunk room, with three or four in a bunk and men standing in the aisle and on the stairs all around. After speaking there I was whisked out to camp in an auto to speak to another group, already assembled and singing.[19]

During the early weeks of American participation in the overseas war, McCurdy and Naismith did their work without a staff of employees to help out. Typically, they mixed athletics with lectures. McCurdy wrote in a letter a description of his and Naismith's activities among incoming troops at a port in France, "It looks as if I would have a chance to organize a big mass athletic meet for all of the men.''[20] And the mass meet had to be done, as usual, without adequate Y.M.C.A. manpower.

One day in November, 1917, General Charles Summerall shipped into the port of entry of St. Nazaire with a brigade of sixty-four hundred men fresh from training in the United States. The troops had been twenty days at sea. They had been seasick, homesick, crowded, regimented, and, sometimes, frightened. Under a fearful strain throughout the journey, they could not forget that enemy submarines were lurking under the waters of the Atlantic Ocean and that a long, devious route was necessary in order to elude would-be attackers. Now, in port at last, there would be a wait of four more days before the port camp to which they had been ordered would be ready. The town had not yet been "cleaned up" for them as far as venereal disease was concerned, and the General stated, "I am not going to let those men free in this town.''[21]

McCurdy was willing to take over the responsibility for the restless soldiers. "There are [only] two of us here," he replied, "[but] we will set up the program.''[22] A huge athletic meet was hurriedly arranged by McCurdy and Naismith, and with the help of regimental army officers, sixty-four hundred soldiers were soon jumping six-foot trenches and running 220-yard dashes, sixteen hundred men at a time.

Army officials agreed, "The more the merrier." On December 30, 1918, General John J. Pershing issued General Order No. 241: "All Commanders will . . . encourage in every way possible athletic sports and competitions of all kinds, especially those in which the greatest number of participants are actively engaged.''[24]

All Y.M.C.A. directors came to be keen about organizing mass athletic activities. "Our motto," one physical director stated, "has always been to have a thousand players and ten spectators, rather than ten players and a thousand spectators.''[23]

At one of the big athletic rallies arranged by Y.M.C.A. directors, all the regiments in a camp, each with band and flag, formed in turn in columns for running and jumping. Then, at a signal, each regiment charged across the field like a stampede of cattle. One onlooker remarked, "[That] was the most wonderful sight

I have ever seen." Another one exclaimed, "Heaven help the Germans if they ever get in front of that crowd."[25]

Because of the great need for them in France, Y.M.C.A. workers in the United States were channeled into overseas service. Athletic directors who had received military commissions would accompany their contingents to France, announced Dr. Joseph E. Raycroft, the U.S. army athletic director. All kinds of coaches were needed abroad, the sole exception being boxing instructors, who were not to be sent across with the troops because the need for them was greater, it was believed, in training camps at home. Most important, of course, to the success of the Y.M.C.A. abroad were qualified older physical directors. "Drs. Meylan, Naismith and McCurdy are now in France," the "Y" boasted that first autumn, as they searched for more "men of maturity and leadership" like those three.[26] By October 25, 1917, the Publicity Committee of the Y.M.C.A. in Paris was able to state that five of the best-known athletic directors in America had "answered the call." James Naismith was one of the five men listed and one of the first who had volunteered.

The impromptu quality seen at first in "Y" programs was replaced by regular schedules arranged by the hundreds of Y.M.C.A. personnel who were soon reporting for overseas duty. Y.M.C.A. centers were set up at several ports where Americans disembarked, and one was established at the permanent American base twenty-five miles behind the lines of the western front. Fine athletic facilities were constructed wherever possible. At the largest American camp in France—one set up to handle forty-seven thousand men—a half-mile oval running track and a large athletic field were planned even before the camp was completed.

Y.M.C.A. activities were not restricted to athletic displays at debarkation ports and permanent camps. Wherever soldiers were billeted, a "Y" worker was at hand to help out.

Most of the American army consisted of infantry troops located in rural villages near the front lines. Sometimes a thousand soldiers were sent to a village, centuries old, whose normal population was two or three hundred persons. A soldier was crowded in with a French family if he was lucky. More likely, because doughboys might outnumber civilians five to one, soldiers were billeted among the cows and chickens in barns, haylofts, sheds—wherever space could be found for a few men to lie down to sleep. A soldier could jocularly use barnyard landmarks to direct a comrade to his billet: "Two manure piles down the left-hand side." At the front lines, though, the villages in which troops were stationed were often nothing but ruins, with only parts of limestone walls standing. Even the manure piles had been flattened. When Naismith got away from barnyards, he often found soldiers living in dugouts that they had made themselves.

Living was not easy. Among many causes of soldiers' complaints, food was one, for throughout World War I a military diet was crude. Even in a mess hall the meat was sometimes so tough that a jackknife made little impression on it. Often the troops were lucky to have meat at all. On a day-long march, troops were known to have nothing but coffee and hardtack for breakfast and supper, going without lunch altogether. And when Naismith was with American troops, he ate, marched, and slept at they did.

Despite discomforts and danger, however, the doughboys got together in their spare time and started an outdoor game—football, baseball, whatever they could improvise. Sometimes the camp was only a kilometer or two behind the front lines, but "Y" directors kept the boys playing. Once or twice shells dropped so close to a football field that army officials ordered the game in progress to be stopped "for fear the ball might get punctured."[27]

After crossing the submarine-infested Atlantic, training at a base camp, living and fighting at the front line, an American soldier was ready for a rest. French soldiers could go home when they had furloughs; it was said that they commuted to war. But Americans were far away from home, in France "for the duration." They were bored and lonely. "A familiar brand of chocolate, a favorite cigaret, a baseball, a real American canteen girl, or a Broadway comedian" helped to bridge the gap between France and home.[28]

Therefore, at the end of four months' service each American soldier received a week's holiday, and the Y.M.C.A. offered a variety of entertainment. At nineteen leave areas—from Aix-les-

Bains, the first one opened (called "Aches and Pains" by the American doughboy), to Paris, opened as the last leave area on November 1, 1918—extensive programs were carried out. Those programs had tens of thousands of takers, too. Fifteen thousand soldiers a day, for example, gathered at the capital city's popular playhouse the Cirque de Paris.

The Y.M.C.A. brought to the homesick soldier many diversions: entertainment, sports, spiritual guidance, education. Whether at a leave area, a front-line billeting location, a training camp, or a port of debarkation, many of these activities could be provided within the "hut," or local headquarters, the heart of the "Y" program. Sometimes as James Naismith traveled from camp to camp, he might discover that the hut was an abandoned wine cellar. But in a cavern crowded with tired soldiers, chances were good that he would come upon the familiar counter of Y.M.C.A. supplies, a bright spot in the gloom, with a fellow Y.M.C.A. secretary on duty behind the counter.

If the "Y" hut was not a cellar, it might be a dugout or a tent. Or sometimes it was a wooden building shipped to the camp in sections and set up by whatever local labor was available. Often it was an existent building—dance hall, cowshed, or half-demolished home near the firing line.

The big double hut (two standard-size huts set together, with the dividing walls omitted) at Neufchâteau was famous in France for the size and variety of its Parisian entertainments, soldier talent shows, movies, lectures, and athletic contests. In the winter months, when night closed in at half-past four, the Neufchâteau hut, located on the main road to the Toul front, carried the heavy responsibility of combating darkness, cold, and gloom for the soldiers. As a result of directing its multiple activities, in fact, five of its first six secretaries were sent to the hospital, suffering from overwork and exposure.

Before the war was over, the "Y," in carrying out its welfare activities and canteen services, had set up 491 wooden huts and 1,045 tents and had requisitioned thousands of army billets. Naismith himself served a short time as hut secretary in the artillery camp at Coëtquidan.[29]

Whatever the form of the structure, the hut was the focal point

Rain and Mud and Cold in France

of the whole morale-building organization of the wartime
Y.M.C.A., both in America and in Europe. The hut was the
soldiers' club and a "home away from home" for two million
men overseas as well as for more than two million in the United
States. Here was the center of social and economic life for the
military community. For everyone near it the club served as
club, theater, gymnasium, church, school, general store, information bureau, post office, and express agency. In these huts supplies were sold. Cigarettes, tobacco, candy, gum, shaving needs,
writing paper, and postage stamps were stocked in the canteen.
Biscuits and tea were available. Chocolate and cakes were served
evenings at ten o'clock; shower baths and rooms for writing
letters or reading were at hand. Lectures, musical entertainments,
skits and plays from faraway Broadway were presented; and on
Sundays religious services were held. At the hut the "Y" workers
organized card games and athletic contests, spelling bees, and
classes in arithmetic or reading or French, and a library was
open.[30] If a center was large enough, as at Tourny "Y" in the
heart of Bordeaux, there might be a "Mother's Corner," where
one of the women Y.M.C.A. workers was in attendance, ready to
"talk to the boys, admire their sweethearts' pictures, sew on a
button, or mend a torn tunic."[31] Female or male, "Y" personnel
answered questions, gave advice with personal problems, helped
with letters home, furnished wrapping paper and twine for
packages that soldiers wanted to send, and dealt calmly with setbacks, large and small.

Some of the setbacks were funny. One Sunday morning in
a hut in a French village, for example, the roof blew off during
the worship service. Near the front lines, however, the situation
was far from humorous. Y.M.C.A. huts were in constant danger.
In some places a Y.M.C.A. center, under constant bombardment,
was ordered to remain closed during the daytime. A big sign on
the door of a dugout at Villers-Tournell in the Cantigny sector
announced: "This Y M C A is open from dark to daylight only."[32]
Even with these restricted hours, though, danger was ever present.
Shells sometimes struck so close that the candles used for lighting
were blown out. In front of some huts the Y.M.C.A. signs were
shot full of holes.

At Seicheprey a Y.M.C.A. secretary ran a canteen in a wine cellar, operating chocolate boilers with a wood fire and dispensing hot chocolate to weary officers and men. When an enemy shell demolished the cellar and chlorine gas filled it, the secretary, overzealous, ran back into the cellar to salvage a case of condensed milk without stopping to put on his gas mask. Dragged out unconscious, he was pronounced by doctors to be permanently incapacitated and physically unfit for further service.

Brave, indeed, were the workers in the Young Men's Christian Association. "Y" volunteers kept in an office in Paris envied those serving in the field. The closer the latter were to the fighting, the greater the envy. Sometimes the first question a debarking volunteer at a French port asked was, "Can I go right up to the front?"[33] True, many kinds of jobs were available. "Y" workers on duty among combat troops wore permits reading "athletic director," "religious director," "educationalist," "accountant," "mechanic," "chauffeur," and "General Supply Division." But work in offices away from the front had to be done, too.

For Naismith, important work began. On November 6, 1917, the Bureau of Hygiene was set up under the Board of Morals and Morale to handle sex education. McCurdy, as director of Y.M.C.A. physical work with the American Expeditionary Force, appointed Naismith head of the new bureau.[34] With headquarters at 12, rue d'Aguesseau in Paris, Naismith's territory included all the area covered by American troops in France.[35]

As head of the Bureau of Hygiene, Naismith continued the sex lectures he had delivered in the United States, showed films, tacked up propaganda on bulletin boards, arranged exhibits, distributed books and pamphlets among the soldiers, as he had been accustomed to doing in the United States. He was able to make effective use of posters and literature furnished by the Social Hygiene Society of Oregon, which had been a leader in this type of work. Calling his campaign for sexual morality the "clean life" program, he organized clean-life clubs among the soldiers.

Securing as far as possible men with scientific or professional experience, Naismith soon had eight lecturers working under him. Some of them were busy at the ports of debarkation, while others traveled from one muddy end of France to the other.[36] He worked out a coordinated lecture system, to be presented by his staff of lecturers at selected points in France. In it he provided, in the opinion of leaders in the Y.M.C.A. administration, constructive sex education far in advance of anything that had been done in America.

In the outline of his model lecture Naismith used five broad divisions. The first two were devoted to descriptions of the evils of drinking and sexual promiscuity in the army. Entitled "Military Efficiency vs. Debauchery, Alcohol, and Prostitution" and "History of War, Wine, and Women," these lengthy sections were filled with statistics and bad examples from ancient wartimes to the present, showing the need for a new morality in the military service.[37]

In the next part of his lecture he shifted from a dissertation against alcohol and sex to what sounded like a two-division tourist guidebook: "Psychology of the French People" and "Social Relations with the People and Their Opportunities and Dangers." American "Y" workers abroad agreed, wisely, "When in Rome, do as the Romans do." One Y.M.C.A. woman made some suggestions for winning French friends: *"Never* ask anybody to do anything that will make him late for meals. *Never* hurry people; *never* forget to say *'S'il vous plait,'* or *'Merci';* add *'Mon ami'* to all soldiers, *'Mon colonel'* or *'Mon capitaine'* to the officers, *'Monsieur'* or *'Madame'* to civilians; take plenty of time and keep on smiling!"[38] But Naismith added a cynical note. After expressing admiration for the affection, patriotism, and artistic talent of the French people, he warned American soldiers to look out for the unscrupulous individuals who would try to slip drugs into a visitor's wine or beer.

The final part of Naismith's lecture was a flag-waver. Entitled "Here to Make World Safe," this section enumerated the advantages that this "war to end wars" would bring to the world. He concluded on a note of moral victory: one of the triumphs of this war, he asserted, would be a "New Stimulus to Morality."

Naismith was frank in his insistence on sexual morality. Points emphasized throughout his program of sexual abstinence were: "Vigorous physical exercise . . . association with people who live clean lives . . . elimination of vulgar talk, obscene pictures and books . . . refraining from the use of alcohol."[39] He found that group discussions under a competent leader were an effective device in promoting the idea of a chaste life in the military. For the guidance of discussion leaders he and his associate G. E. Johnson wrote two small booklets outlining specific subjects to stimulate discussion. These pamphlets were "The Basis of Clean Living" (January, 1919) and "Suggestive Study for Right Standards" (April, 1919), both published by the Y.M.C.A. headquarters at 12, rue d'Aguesseau in Paris.[40] He used films, including his old standby "How Life Begins" and several others that the Y.M.C.A. and the War Department had been using successfully in the United States. The lectures, films, and literature combined educational and inspirational features, with a strong appeal to Christian principles and familial duty overlaying the informational features.[41] Naismith emphasized, too, the spirit of the athletic training group, with its sporting allegiance to rules. He promoted large-scale repressive measures as well as persuasive discussions. As part of this program of repression, by early 1918 all "disorderly" resorts in France had been put out of bounds to American soldiers.

Of course, army officials realized that high ideals might be inconsistent with existing conditions. Brigadier General A. E. Bradley, chief surgeon of the American Expeditionary Force, declared:

When a man through drink, bad associates or a loss of moral stamina is overcome by his passions and exposes himself to venereal disease, he should at once minimize the probable evil results to the army, to himself, his family and society by obeying the military regulations concerning prophylactic treatment.[42]

And Naismith himself was never an impractical idealist. Although he emphasized prevention rather than cure, he was not blind to facts. Sexual abstinence may have been stressed by "Y" personnel, but in line with army practice he saw that prophylactic stations were kept open at all hours.

Supervision of social hygiene by the Y.M.C.A. was approved by General John J. Pershing and by military authorities serving under him. Chief Surgeon Bradley stated publicly that "sexual indulgence by a vigorous, healthy man is not a necessity for the development or maintenance of his manhood, and . . . abstinence before marriage [is] the best preparation for a happy married life and the only sure way of avoiding disease."[43] Bradley added, "Control of the sexual passions is secured . . . by a full use of leisure time with vigorous athletics, games, reading or study."[44] Naismith and his compatriots were doing their best to fill the soldiers' leisure time in this way.

In addition to his duties in social hygiene, he worked on the Y.M.C.A. committee (J. H. McCurdy, James Naismith, George L. Meylan, D. F. Gardner, A. H. Gleason, W. A. Tener, F. M. West) that made recommendations for an extensive program of recreation in the military training camps of America, on the troop transports traveling to Europe, at the French ports of entry, and in the military camps and leave areas in France. The committee also established an educational program for soldiers. A forty-four-page pamphlet issued in the winter of 1917–1918 was based in part on their work. Bulletin No. 1 of a series of "Recreation Bulletins for the American Expeditionary Forces" outlined specific topics for consideration—not only types of playing equipment and methods of scoring games but also problems of venereal disease among the troops. Even in Naismith's promotion of a recreational program more attention was given to sex than to basketball.

21
Games, Bayonets, and Lofty Ideals

JAMES NAISMITH saw the months of war go on in France and the services of the Young Men's Christian Association expand. In the office in Paris increasing work very soon necessitated more adequate accommodations for the overseas staff of the association. Only two months after he arrived, headquarters were moved from the mansion at 31, avenue Montaigne to an unfinished building at 12, rue d'Aguesseau, a more central downtown location. The French minister's old palace had been left as a clubhouse for Americans. Here at 12, rue d'Aguesseau, James Huff Mc-Curdy's responsibility as Y.M.C.A. representative in France soon evolved into a threefold one. In addition to the organization of Y.M.C.A. athletic and recreational activities and the development of a program of sex instruction carried out by Naismith, supervision of the health of Y.M.C.A. workers in France became his responsibility—all of these duties included in the Department of Athletics, Hygiene, and Health.[1]

To carry out his responsibilities more effectively, McCurdy increased the size of his executive staff in Paris. On January 28, 1918, he appointed Dr. Frederick P. Lord, formerly a professor of anatomy at Dartmouth Medical School, as supervisor of the health of "Y" personnel. Thus, by the winter of 1917–1918 there were three members. McCurdy as director of all physical work in the A.E.F., Naismith as head of the Bureau of Hygiene, and Lord as the full-time medical doctor heading the health section were the three executives of the organization at 12, rue d'Aguesseau, known informally as the Recreation Department. As the work increased, more space and more employees were required. McCurdy took over additional rooms, making a total of five offices in his department: his own, Dr. Naismith's, Dr. Lord's, one for three employees—a stenographer, a nurse, and the newly hired business secretary, George Spencer—and a first-aid room. Outside the office, the association had available a Dr. Cabot for consultation, and in four hospitals space was reserved for ill or wounded Y.M.C.A. workers, men and women.

Gradually McCurdy perfected his Paris department. As director of physical activities in all camps in France, he kept athletic equipment on hand at his central office for distribution, additional space being required for these supplies. And much equipment, indeed, passed through his office. In the winter of 1917–1918 he ordered more than $300,000 worth of baseballs and bats, volleyballs, basketballs, medicine balls, boxing gloves, and all the other paraphernalia that soldiers needed in order to play games. As well as being sent to American army bases, some of the equipment was transported to the American Ambulance Sections with the French army, which were scattered over the whole of the French front. Often on repose for two weeks at a time or longer, ambulance men with nothing to do were eager for the "Y" 's recreational supplies.

By spring, 1918, McCurdy had added G. E. Johnson, E. B. DeGroot, and a man named Gugel to his staff. Johnson's job was to assist Naismith in the "clean life" campaign, DeGroot was to help with athletic supervision, and Gugel was to distribute athletic supplies. Under the supervision of the general staff in Paris were twenty divisional directors throughout France and all the physical directors in individual army camps. Besides, in Paris itself there was always much to do. In addition to the stenographer, the nurse, and the business secretary originally employed, the central office soon needed three more stenographers, an errand boy, and a vehicle driver. An automobile was part of the permanent equipment at headquarters, and two additional autos were available part of the day, one from 10 A.M. till 5 P.M. and one from one o'clock till four or five in the afternoon.

McCurdy, Naismith, and Lord lived and worked together intimately during the intervals when they were in Paris, with less space than they might sometimes have liked and more than enough contact with wounded soldiers and civilians to make them feel close to the trench warfare on the front lines. A passage from a letter that McCurdy wrote home on March 28, 1918, succinctly describes the situation: "I am writing this in the bathroom so as not to wake Dr. Lord who went to bed early. He was up after one a.m. helping with refugees who have come into Paris on account of the battle now in progress."[2]

The Y.M.C.A. was not the only organization actively involved in the welfare of the soldiers. The French equivalent of the American "Y" was "le Foyer du soldat" (the Soldier's Fireside), the French soldier's "home away from home." The organization was created by a French civilian, Emmanuel Sautter, General Secretary of the World's Committee of National Young Men's Christain Associations. He opened seventy-some houses during the early years of the war. Then the American Y.M.C.A. stepped in. When General Henri Pétain, commander in chief of the French armies, ordered Foyers du soldat constructed along the French fighting lines, American money and personnel helped open 1,015 houses between September, 1917, and September, 1918. At the request of General Pétain and Premier Georges Clemenceau of France, the National War Work Council of the Y.M.C.A., putting an American, Dr. George L. Meylan, at the head of the French organization, began the recruitment and instruction of Foyer du soldat workers. At Princeton University volunteers were trained intensively before coming to France to teach the war-torn French soldiers, or *poilus,* "how to play again."[3] Organizing sports and recreation in the Foyers, Dr. Meylan began a program in the French army patterned on that used among American troops.

French Foyers could be impromptu and improvised, as were American Y.M.C.A. huts—tents, dugouts, bombed-out buildings, even the trenches themselves. One of the most interesting was a sloop sunk in the river Aisne by enemy fire. Raised and refurbished, the ship became a floating "fireside."

Headquartered in sunken sloop, trench, or, at the other extreme, ornate town house, American Foyer workers were spread over France. They rode bicycles or motorcycles and sidecars around camps and countryside and wore out the seats of their trousers on the cycles. They traveled to Paris on leave to be outfitted again, to have a week of unaccustomed rest and sleep despite an occasional Parisian air raid, and to visit Y.M.C.A. headquarters. Thus McCurdy and Naismith kept in close touch with activities in the French Foyers.

And the activities were varied. At one end of France Foyer workers might be busy cutting waist-high grass in an Alsatian meadow to make space for a football field, while at the other they might be setting up a game of ninepins or a nighttime boxing match inside a building in Montpellier to entertain the soldiers of many nationalities who congregated there. Often they had to improvise. Physical director E. M. Guest reported to Y.M.C.A. headquarters about indoor entertainment he organized in one of the Foyers. Clearing out a space about ten feet by ten feet in one corner of the room, he surrounded it with rows of benches set in tiers on the floor and on tables. The show he put on sometimes was two Americans wrestling or two Arabs boxing, or sometimes it was a typical game from another country. Two French soldiers might meet in a *combat à coups de polochons,* or pillow fight, with the opponents standing either in barrels or astride a hanging log. Or two blindfold Italians might beat each other around the players' ring with straps. Or an international stunt might be carried out, with representatives from many nations grasping hands and circling around to knock down the bowling pins of the others. Observing that spectators who could not find seats in the cramped arena climbed onto the corner braces and rafters of the roof, Guest wrote wistfully, "This seems to be the limit forced upon us by the overcrowding of the building, and the weather or mud outside."[4] The popularity of impromptu recreational events and the space limitations for spectators caused a physical director oftentimes to complain, in a tone similar to Guest's: "Only a shoehorn could have put another man in."[5]

As far as sexual mores were concerned, Dr. Meylan's aim among French troops in le Foyer du soldat was the same as Naismith's among American troops. In the French army Meylan had to fight the "toleration houses" that were set up with their public women enticing the troops. In a certain camp he found a toleration house filled with soldiers, outside of which were two hundred more anticipating their turn. But he brought in wholesome recreation to triumph over evil. "A week later a great program of sports was planned," as the president of the Athletic Research Society reported happily about Meylan's work, "and on that day not one man was seen waiting entrance."[6]

Le Foyer du soldat and the Y.M.C.A. extended their services to countries outside France, too. In Africa, American directors started programs of physical education in government schools in the French protectorates of Tunisia and Algeria. Centers of le Foyer du soldat were located in Greece in places where the French had taken temporary military possession or at ports where troops landed. Foyer huts were also set up in locations as varied as Belgium in northwest Europe, Czechoslovakia in central Europe, and the Russian port of Vladivostok on the Sea of Japan.

At the time of World War I the French War Department was supervising eight Centres régionnaux d'instruction physique, or schools of physical training, where French youth received pre-military training as noncommissioned officers. In August, 1918, General Cottez, Director of Physical Training in the French army, requested an American physical director for each of the eight schools to serve as an *expert technique*.

One reason for this action was that French military officials were impressed by the results of recreation in the U.S. army. Baseball was one of the American games that intrigued the French. Indeed, in July, 1918, General Cottez recommended that baseball be emphasized in all centers of physical instruction for the French. In his order he included permission for every military unit to employ for one week an American instructor of baseball. Pleased, "Y" workers labeled Cottez's pronouncement the "famous baseball order" and began to teach the game to every French soldier they could lay their hands on.[7]

Foyer or Y.M.C.A., each organization had many demands made upon it and its personnel. In his multitudinous activities James Naismith found this true. But the work was gratifying. He was pleased, for one thing, by the growing interest American and other Allied troops displayed in sports. The adventures and misadventures of basketball, his own brainchild, held his special interest. After organized athletics and team games began in the A.E.F. in the winter of 1917, he was delighted to see the basketball season begin on January 1, 1918, in the Gondrecourt area, running until February 13. In that area an impressive twenty-one teams were formed, playing one night a week in the Y.M.C.A. hut. Records in the Paris office showed that by June, 1918, four thousand games of basketball had been played throughout France. Besides American soldiers in training camps and leave areas, French soldiers in le Foyer du soldat played it. The French, it was said, were very happy with the speed, excitement, and open play of the game.

Not only team games and organized leagues but also individual soldiers and small pastimes drew Naismith's attention. Using the "practical preaching" he had initiated on the Mexican border, he set up counterattractions in camp to keep his boys out of town and out of trouble. One of his devices was a fight ring, set up near the entrance of a camp, where he tried to have a match going at the approximate time the boys were ready to leave for the evening.[8] Boxing and wrestling were popular in the army, and a fast bout was one way to keep soldiers on the post. One physical director reported: "Men told me they had passes to town but would rather stay to see the boxing."[9] Of course, Naismith and his fellow workers did not intend that gambling be allowed to supplement the thrills of boxing, wrestling, or any other sport. As one physical director wrote, "I have worked hard to keep the miserable taint of money away from the boxing ring and have been singularly successful thus far."[10]

Naismith had an opportunity to be creative, too, during the war months. Because sports of all kinds were important to the soldiers, he turned "inventive"—as he called it—in the gymnasium and on the playing court. Or perhaps he just got around to refining games he had already had in mind. At any rate, under the influence of his intimate acquaintance with the French language he created a game called "vrille" (pronounced "vree"). In French the fall of a plane in a tailspin, or a spinning dive, is a "descente en vrille," and to move in a spiral, as a ball in a football game sometimes does, is "vriller." Whatever he may have intended the name to signify, vrille was a simple game played with two to twelve participants and a round ball. Batted with the open hand, or hands, the ball might be any kind that bounced easily, from tennis to basketball, but he preferred that it be a soft leather ball twelve inches in circumference. Victory came to the side that first scored twenty-one points by bouncing the ball into the proper court a sufficient number of times.

The rules for vrille and a diagram of the playing field were published in the *American Physical Education Review* while Naismith was still abroad, in the late winter of 1918–1919. He did not, however, return home to find that his newest game had swept the country. It never, in fact, became popular except with coeds at the University of Kansas.[11]

Despite the services of a capable staff in Paris, James Naismith was no desk man directing activity from afar. In person, he helped organize scheduled or impromptu recreation and entertainment, large and small, for soldiers throughout France. In addition, he always had time to talk to individual soldiers. "Doc"

Naismith, the man with the black mustache and the friendly smile, aided the wounded and encouraged the depressed. He spent much time with troops in the field, often at the front lines. He went out of his way to pay personal visits to men from his former National Guard regiment. Many a University of Kansas student in Company M in the Vosges Mountain area recalled gratefully that Naismith dropped in to say hello.[12] The roads in winter, broken by army trucks, were either rough with ice or very muddy, or sometimes covered with drifted snow, and during the cold months of 1917–1918 Naismith did much walking over those French roads. Once, leaving the train at Mehun, he walked fifteen kilometers through heavy rain and mud, carrying a heavy duffel bag, for the sole purpose of bringing newspapers and other news from home to a group of lonesome Kansas soldiers. Even his thick, bristling mustache was muddy when the rain-soaked Naismith arrived at their billet door and boomed out, "Well, how's my gang?"[13] But he was smiling, wet and dirty though he was. Small wonder was it that doughboys on twenty-four-hour leave often came looking for "good old Doc Naismith" in his Paris office, or in his hotel room, after Paris was recognized by military authorities as a leave area.

Doughboys calling on Doc Naismith were not the only American visitors at 12, rue d'Aguesseau. Dr. Luther Halsey Gulick, Jr., who had been the teacher of both Naismith and McCurdy, was a Y.M.C.A. colleague who came from the United States to be their houseguest. In the late winter of 1917–1918 Dr. Gulick, who had been campaigning in the homeland to recruit Y.M.C.A. workers for overseas duty, came over to survey the moral and physical welfare of the American Expeditionary Force and to observe what McCurdy and Naismith and their cohorts were doing. Gulick was one of the American educators who had directed the great expansion of the Y.M.C.A. from the late nineteenth century until the entry of the United States into World War I. Now an energetic fifty-two year old, he was plagued with a weak heart and a warning from his doctor, but he was still enthusiastic about the "Y" program.

Not realizing that Gulick's physician had cautioned him against travel and strenuous activity, Naismith and McCurdy welcomed the zestful man who had taught them so much when they were students, two years apart, at the International Y.M.C.A. Training School in Springfield. Naismith had looked up to Gulick all these years, following his teachings. With McCurdy, though, there had been for a while more resistance than reverence. Back in the old days when McCurdy worked out in the gymnasium at Springfield, Gulick, a fine gymnast himself, told him, "Mack . . . you are as graceful as a cow, better pack up and go home."[14] But the young man had not packed up and left, and soon Gulick, who changed his mind about Mack, found himself inviting his student to join the teaching staff at the Training School after graduation. Gulick had now decided that awkward McCurdy had more ability as a leader in physical education than most graceful gymnasts could ever hope to have.

While Gulick was in France, the three friends worked together, speaking at meetings in Paris and visiting army bases. On February 26 and 27 they were three of the principal speakers at the Provincial Recreation Convention held at the Hotel du Pavillon in Paris. Gulick spoke the first morning on "Team Play," and Naismith followed that afternoon with a talk entitled "Social Morality Course of Study," while McCurdy's address the next afternoon concluded the two-day series of meetings.

Gulick worked hard while he was there. If Naismith and McCurdy had known the condition of his health, they would not have let him. But he did not tell them, of course, and it was months later before they found out.

One week of Gulick's visit turned into a comedy of errors. McCurdy, hiring a handsome Reo touring car, a driver, and an assistant, took him out to visit army bases near the war front, but the mishaps that the travelers met with were not casualties of warfare. On that trip, which lasted from Tuesday morning until Friday night, the big Reo was the focal point of all misadventures. It sprang a gas leak and stalled twenty miles from the first night's destination; the next day it was inadvertently filled with kerosene instead of gasoline at a fuel stop near the front lines; it (or its driver) became lost in the dark and ended up in the wrong town; its fan and drip pan were smashed on a rock in the road. Finally, the Reo was exchanged for "a good, realistic Ford," and the tour was completed.[15]

In spite of a few days of comic delays, Gulick was quickly introduced to the horrors of trench warfare, which Naismith and his companions had been living with for months. Gulick learned, as they had learned, how battles are fought.

In 1918 armies were facing each other along a front of some three hundred miles across France, separated by only a few hundred yards, and he observed what seemed to be endless battle. While soldiers were on the move across country, they marched to advance, or, if unlucky, they marched to retreat, motor lorries mounted with machine guns shaking off pursuit. The troops used turning movements to evade airplanes as they marched by night and hid by day. When enemy troops came face-to-face after a hard march, "digging in"—the making of trenches—was the only protection against feverishly rapid artillery fire. During an attack, terrific bursts of high explosives and rapid fire from rifles and machine guns came along the ground, and overhead, airplanes hovered. The climax of a confrontation, as men sprang out of the trenches dodging hand grenades and mines in their advance, was hand-to-hand fighting by infantry men with bayonets and knives, while artillery and cavalry stood in readiness to pursue or protect.

To those persons who waited on the western side of the Atlantic Luther Halsey Gulick, Jr., was able to report both on the suffering of the soldiers in battle and on the outstanding work of the Young Men's Christian Association. He got back to the United States in time to deliver an account of his trip at the annual meeting of the American Physical Education Association in April. His views agreed with those of the Y.M.C.A. as a whole. Officials of the "Y" were boasting at that time, "Never since the days of chivalry, when knighthood was in flower, has there been a war in which the health and physique of the common soldier have been looked after as in this one."[16] Indeed, their self-congratulations sometimes sounded exaggerated: "From every city, town and rural community in the land boys have gone to the camps, many of them pale, weak, stooped and awkward. After a few weeks . . . everybody remarks on the change in color, bearing, and evident vigor they exhibit."[17] Also important to the "Y" was the fact that recreation had become a great moral force in the army. "Football has been substituted for vice, and sports for gambling," one official declared.[18]

But "Y" officials were aware of the bloody side of war. Despite the word "Christian" in its name, the Y.M.C.A. frankly declared that war meant the survival of the fittest, and its physical training was intended to help a soldier survive. "Remember war is only a glorified game," one "Y" man commented. "Train for it in the same spirit as you would train for your football cup." But he cautioned, "A game of Rugby football is nothing [compared] to it."[19]

In importance to the Y.M.C.A., footballs and goals were rivaled by the weapons of trench warfare. Bayonet training was developed by Dr. Joseph E. Raycroft, director of athletics in the War Department Commission on Training and Camp Activities, and bayonets became one of the tools that the "Y" used in its training-camp program. When James H. McCurdy, in his position as director of physical activity in the A.E.F., had a choice between gymnasium-type exercises and bayonet drill for the troops, he chose the latter. "I do not object to jiu-jitsu," he said, "but I think it is better at this time to put all power into bayonet exercise."[20] As another Y.M.C.A. administrator said, "The man who can thrust with the bayonet one one-hundredths of a second quicker than the other man will be the one to win."[21]

Explanations of bayonet techniques that were given by Y.M.C.A. leaders were as explicit as those provided in any army training course. Warning that bayonet fighting often occurred in the narrow space of a trench, Luther Halsey Gulick himself pulled no punches when he wrote:

You must get your man in a vital place, the face, throat, upper part of chest, abdomen or groins. A bayonet thrust in all these places is more or less vital, but what is more important they allow of easy penetration and quick withdrawal. If a bayonet fixes in the shoulder blade the foot has to be pressed against the body before the blade can be wrenched out. In a mêlée there is little time for anything but pointing or parrying, and if a blade gets stuck in a bone one is left defenseless.[22]

For James Naismith the choice was clear-cut. Even seeing the blood and wounds caused by armed conflict, he believed more strongly than before that this war was right and good. After he had been in France for more than a year, he wrote back home: "I am fully convinced that the war, dreadful as it has been, will prove a great blessing . . . it is simply . . . a conflict between the two great opposing forces of selfishness and altruism."[23] He had faith in the betterment of society that would come after the armistice and in the willingness of the world to refashion itself. "The burden of reconstruction rests on each society which has for its object the welfare of mankind. I rejoice with them in the great work that lies before them."[24] If bullets had to be used to gain this Utopia, he was willing to see them used.

To use a term popular in the 1960s and 1970s, Naismith in wartime was a hawk, rather than a dove favoring peace. After the war, despite his genuine preference for universal civilian calisthenics over universal military training, he went so far as to outline a program of physical activities and academic education to be used in the compulsory armed service he expected to be set up in peacetime.

But notwithstanding any hawkishness, his personal code of conduct remained mild, pure, and exemplary, and he sought with all his might to propagate it. Promoting the highest moral ideals of behavior, he did his best to carry out President Wilson's goal of sending American soldiers home "with no scars except those won in honorable conflict." And in all this tumult of activity, in war as in peacetime, his own life was a model for his "boys." Across the flyleaf of the little khaki-covered New Testament that he carried he wrote:

> I will be a man
> Strong in body,
> Clean in mind
> Lofty in Ideals.

At first he had written "Sound in body," and then, rewording the phrase, he wrote "Strong in body." Only then was he satisfied to inscribe his signature below this personal creed: "Jas. Naismith."[25]

Meanwhile the war went on—sports, lectures, prophylaxis, artillery fire, battle wounds—with hard work and fatigue playing a greater part in Naismith's life than he had expected. There was, indeed, more than games in wartime, even for the Y.M.C.A. and le Foyer du soldat.

The strain, the constant exposure, the exhaustion of warfare were enough to shatter all but the strongest nerves. Fortunately, Naismith's nerves were strong; but even a stout heart can grow weary.

22

Season of Armistice

In the United States changes had taken place while the war was going on in France. Most distressing to Naismith came the news that his old friend and teacher, Luther Halsey Gulick, was dead.

In the spring of 1918 Gulick had said goodbye to Naismith and McCurdy in France, returning to America to write about his experiences abroad and to carry out an extensive lecture tour. Lectures completed, he went to supervise the summer camp—Sebago-Wohelo—that he had set up in Maine. A part of his duties was to plan the big camp day of sports to be held on August 13, Water Carnival Day.[1]

But when the morning of the thirteenth came, Dr. Gulick lay in his house on top of the cliff at the water's edge, dead in his fifty-third year. The water carnival sports were held, all the same. His widow, Charlotte Gulick, did not let his death interfere. When visitors came to the house that morning, she did not tell them at once that the doctor was dead, for she knew that Luther Gulick would not want his demise to disturb anyone's plans.[2]

Gulick's physician said that his patient died of chronic interstitial myocarditis. Before he had left home for France, friends learned now, medical authorities had given him two months to live, and he had overrun this estimate by more than four months.[3] The year after his death his last book was published, telling about the wartime program of the Young Men's Christian Association at home and overseas. But a posthumous book was small consolation for the loss of this enthusiastic and inventive man—the one who had told James Naismith to create a new game and had helped him perfect it.

Back home at the University of Kansas, military activity was going on full force in the fall of 1918, and, to top the turmoil, an epidemic of influenza struck. Naismith's family, left behind in Lawrence, was embroiled in both patriotic excitement and dread of contagion, as was everyone else. People did not know that the armistice was only a few weeks away.[4]

In September, 1918, K.U. student laborers were hired at thirty-five cents an hour to help erect nine three-story barracks on Mississippi Street for the Student Army Training Corps (S.A.T.C.), and tents were set up on campus for Company M of the Kansas National Guard. Green Hall was converted from law school to army training headquarters. Counting the barracks hastily set up between Marvin and Haworth halls, the military buildings cost about $120,000 and housed twenty-five hundred soldier trainees, nearly as many persons as the three thousand civilians on campus. Freshman caps had given way to military hats, and even students in business suits and neckties could be seen training with wooden rifles in front of Marvin Hall, an army sergeant calling out orders. When the new university cafeteria opened—a student dream for many years—soldiers were allowed first in line at mealtime. Students donated nightshirts for use in the S.A.T.C. hospital. They collected nutshells and fruit pits for the Red Cross, also, as they had long been doing, the Red Cross sending the collections away for manufacture of the carbon in gas masks. Everyone was thrifty. To conserve paper, the daily campus newspaper cut down on publishing. Students and townspeople alike supported the Fourth Liberty Loan drive in order to provide more munitions, ships, and war supplies for their country. (Liberty Loan posters warned, "The Enemy is Watching.") Young men continued to interrupt their education in order to join the military forces and leave the campus to fight overseas. Casualty lists were coming in, and Chancellor Strong, a sensitive man, grieved in the reading of every one, particularly when the name of a former K.U. student appeared.[5]

Scarcely had the S.A.T.C. barracks been completed when influenza hit Lawrence in October. The university was closed for two weeks, and students were forbidden to leave town. For five weeks sleeping quarters in the barracks were converted into sick wards, and some of the young soldiers died of flu before seeing a battlefield. For students who remained well during the height of the epidemic there was not much to do except study. Movie houses, where *To Hell With the Kaiser* had been showing a few weeks before, were closed, and no social functions or public meetings were allowed. Even the annual Thanksgiving Day football game with the University of Missouri was canceled, although intramural games resumed after the university reopened.[6]

But influenza deaths and war fatalities notwithstanding, the armistice was not far away.

Although students and townspeople in Lawrence did not realize in the autumn of 1918 that the war would soon be over, people in France knew that Allied victory must be near. Homesick Americans, particularly, were optimistic. American troops had begun a campaign of intensive fighting in April, 1918, and the turning point of the war suddenly came with the Second Battle of the Marne (July 15 to August 7), in which nine American divisions were involved. At the Battle of Chateau-Thierry, a part of the Marne campaign, the Americans won their first decisive victory of World War I.

A new outlook on the war could be clearly observed in Paris. Naismith had seen the Parisians take all the ups and downs of war stoically. But during the last hundred days of fighting, a change occurred. The phrase "C'est la guerre" was giving place to "Après la guerre"; and when the liberation of Lille came, Parisians let their excitement show.

Lille was the greatest city in France to remain under German occupation throughout four years of war. Not until October 17, 1918, did the Germans evacuate the city and British forces move in. As soon as the good news reached Paris, the War Department filled le place de la Concorde with a display of German guns, planes, and war trophies, and the statue of Lille was covered with flowers and flags. Despite the fact that it rained all day on the following Sunday, there was a parade, and a great demonstration of physical training was held in the Tuileries Gardens.

Naismith's Parisian neighbors were right. Less than a month after Lille was freed, the Battle of the Argonne was won and World War I was over, the armistice being signed on November 11, 1918.

Back in Lawrence patriotic citizens, recovering from influenza, held a wild celebration in the streets when the news was announced, and demobilization of the Student Army Training Corps began in December, two months after their barracks were erected. The flu epidemic, the war, and S.A.T.C. activity at the University of Kansas ended at the same time. Casualty lists ceased to arrive from France, and Chancellor Strong could occupy himself with new problems at the university.[7]

In France the First and Second American armies were scheduled for return to the United States as fast as transport ships could carry them. The largest embarkation center, at LeMans, and all the other centers were crowded. And in the Young Men's Christian Association a new spirit arose.

Officials of the "Y" breathed a sigh of satisfaction and pointed out to the world what they had accomplished. They were certain about the correlation between their program of play and exercise and the outcome of the war.

The American soldier . . . is the fighting man *par excellence.* . . .
No small amount of the credit for this military achievement has been given to the influence of American ideals of physical training and to our widespread participation in sports and games.[8]

Maybe they were right. Even before the American Expeditionary Force had gone to France, the federal administration of the United States had approved the work that the Y.M.C.A. was doing, and during the war the highest military officials in the A.E.F. had cooperated in implementing the Red Triangle's program.

Even with military and moral victory achieved, though, the Y.M.C.A. was not yet to go home. As one of the "Y" directors in France declared two months after the armistice, "There seems to be no let-up in the work over here but the program gets heavier every day."⁹ General John J. Pershing himself would later admit that the "Y" had plenty to do and did it well.

In the field of education, athletics and recreation after the Armistice the Young Men's Christian Association took the lead, without any sort of question, and as a matter of fact about nine-tenths of the welfare work that was carried on in the A E F was carried on under the direction and guidance of the Young Men's Christian Association.¹⁰

Some persons back home put in a good word for those who were still abroad: "Lots of the men who have been over there a year and a half, away from their families, want to come home, and they ought to come home." But the "Y" workers stayed. In fact, the number of its overseas personnel increased after the armistice—from two thousand to six thousand between June, 1918, and January, 1919. The total reached its highest point in April, 1919, when the records showed nearly sixty-four hundred. And James Naismith was one of the "Y" men who stayed.

Things were different now, in more ways than in the strangeness of peace. For instance, empty places had started to show up among Naismith's closest associates. The greatest loss was that of Dr. James Huff McCurdy. After seventeen months abroad, McCurdy relinquished his position. In the winter of 1918–1919, convalescing from a case of pneumonia and "broken in health," as one of his biographers phrased it, by the strain of his experiences in France, he went home to the United States.¹² With postwar work remaining to be done in France, his place as director of athletics there was taken by Elwood S. Brown, a member of the International Committee of the Y.M.C.A.

Outside the Paris office, in le Foyer du soldat another "Y" leader who had come to France as early as Naismith had not managed to stay as long. After seven and one-half successful months in France, Dr. George L. Meylan had gone home to other duties in the United States, giving to Percy R. Carpenter the position of National Secretary of le Foyer du soldat.

After most of the American soldiers had departed, Naismith and his associates were conspicuous figures in their army uniforms. It was flattering to a uniformed "Y" worker to have a French citizen walk up to thank him for American assistance in delivering France from Prussian domination. From civilians to military top hats, the French were interested in the work the Y.M.C.A. had done and was doing. After formal introductions to four French army generals in one week and to two in a single day, one physical director commented, "Shaking hands with generals is a popular sport over here."[13] Even more exciting, occasionally a "Y" man was kissed on both cheeks by a grateful French general.

Perhaps Naismith agreed that the continuing French gratitude was not misplaced. He felt, indeed, that his real labor began only after the warfare had ceased. Problems became intensified in the months of idleness among the troops still remaining in France. The programs of recreation and education now had to be expanded and developed even more strongly than before. In the Department of Athletics alone, four large-scale activities were planned: (1) mass games, for every soldier; (2) A.E.F. championships in competitive sports; (3) physical pageants and demonstrations; and (4) Inter-Allied athletic contests.[14]

Another reason Y.M.C.A. workers remained overseas was that the French had things for them to do. The French high command stated: "We . . . believe that the introduction of an extensive athletic program in France will be an important factor in the physical rehabilitation of the French nation."[15] And the Y.M.C.A. was asked to stay and help carry out that program.

During the war, at the request of the French government, an American physical director had been placed in each of the eight French military schools. Now that the war was over, those eight directors stayed on; and in seven of the centers fifteen thousand demobilized French schoolteachers were learning how to teach American games in the public schools.

Le Foyer du soldat was another organization in which Y.M.C.A. work continued. Premier Georges Clemenceau requested that the Young Men's Christian Association remain from three to five years after the end of the war to train French personnel in Foyer work, and Y.M.C.A. officials agreed to do so. Here, too, "Y" workers could make a postwar report to the folks at home: "The program is getting bigger all the time."[16]

Outside the military schools and the Foyer the French government asked the Red Triangle to help establish a program of permanent playgrounds and athletic fields for both French soldiers and civilians. Y.M.C.A. director Percy Carpenter was selected to work on the French Government Commission for the Reorganization of Physical Education and Social Hygiene, whose attention was to be directed toward the army, the public schools, and the factory system of France.

Y.M.C.A. personnel, feeling like missionaries in a new land, agreed that French civilians, especially the children, needed a program of physical education. Although Paris and some of the other cities had athletic clubs, the smaller towns and rural communities had no organized physical recreation program for any ages. At playtime children idled about with nothing much to do except play a game of hopscotch. If they got hold of a ball, they kicked it around, but they never played catch, as American kids do. Soccer football was the principal organized sport in France, and the French were, therefore, adept at using their feet, but they did not know how to catch a ball properly with their hands. "So . . . the kids hang around the village, and when they get to be seventeen or eighteen they hang around the cafés, and chase the girls,"[17] observed one "Y" physical director, deciding that something should be done about the situation.

Games emphasizing the throwing or striking and the catching of a ball were, therefore, brought by "Y" workers to French playgrounds. Baseball, volleyball, and basketball, in that order, were three of the leading sports used. Perhaps for James Naismith there were elements of both gratification and disappointment here. Baseball had been introduced into France with General Cottez's wartime "baseball order" and consequently had a head start. After the war, volleyball was officially recognized in the public schools, for it was easy to learn and French children were enthusiastic about it. But basketball, although growing in popularity, was more difficult to teach to children than the other two games and, for a while, had to take third place.

Sometimes the trouble was the children, who could not learn

the game easily enough; sometimes it was the adults, who did not treat the game with the respect it deserved; sometimes it was the weather, which was not dependable enough for an outdoor court. Naismith found several obstacles to the wholehearted reception he wanted Europeans to give to basketball.

What he considered a curious manifestation of basketball's development in a major nation occurred shortly after the armistice, when American soldiers sought a competitive game of basketball with British troops. The game turned out somewhat differently than had been desired. Because basketball had been introduced into Britain as a girls' game, men's basketball was not so warmly accepted there as in most other countries, and the British soldiers were unable to furnish a team for competition. Therefore, two American teams, one from the Orly flying field and one an artillery outfit from Bordeaux, played an exhibition game of basketball in the British sector, as a substitute for the aborted international contest.[18]

In addition to an uncooperative human element, the weather in France was often unpredictable. One day during an international program of athletics in Paris, American soldiers played an exhibition game of basketball in the Tuileries Gardens. It rained that day, and half the court was covered with water and an inch of mud. "It was a weird exhibition," one spectator admitted.[19] But it was basketball, and Naismith had to be satisfied.

More exciting to him than these displays of basketball was a small treasure that he found after the armistice in a little book shop on the rue St. Michel in Paris. Browsing through the shelves, he came across a small red book, *Les Sports pour tous* by Ern. Weber, one chapter of which was entitled "Le Basketball." The chapter was a French translation of the basketball rules of 1897.[20] He bought the book and packed it among his European souvenirs.

More poignant was the discovery, after the fighting had stopped, of rusty basketball rings behind a wooded hill southwest of Château-Thierry. Those iron rings were mute evidence that basketball had been played by American marines and infantrymen within range of German guns during the famous Battle of Belleau Wood. He could be proud both of those Americans and of the game that they had, perhaps, risked their lives to play.

But the French and British, at least, had not yet caught on to basketball with the proper enthusiasm.

The grandest showing basketball made in France was in the A.E.F. Championship Games and, following that tournament, the Inter-Allied Games.[21] Naismith had a part in planning the games, and he followed their progress all along.

As early as October 15, 1918, nearly a month before the armistice, plans for peacetime military athletics had begun. As a next step, in November, 1918, plans were made for an interregimental athletic meet to be financed by the Y.M.C.A. and controlled jointly by the army and the "Y." The A.E.F. Championship Games involved semifinals and final elimination matches, which extended through the first five months of 1919. Championships were determined in basketball, football, boxing, wrestling, baseball, golf, shooting, soccer, swimming, tennis, and track and field.[22]

After completion of the A.E.F. Championship Games, the Inter-Allied Games, which were set up by the Y.M.C.A. and the American army, were a fitting climax to postarmistice athletics. Although three-fourths of the Allied troops were gone by the time the competition was held, eighteen nations accepted the invitation sent by General John J. Pershing on January 9, 1919.

The Inter-Allied Games were held at Pershing Field, newly constructed by the Y.M.C.A. and the army in the Bois de Vincennes near Joinville on the site of an old jousting ground used by the knights of Henry of Navarre. For the series of varied athletic competitions, everything from Italian pelota to camel-fighting exhibitions by the Arabs was arranged. To Naismith's pleasure, the high point of the World War basketball season was on the program. Teams selected from the armies of the United States, France, and Italy were to play a basketball tournament.[23] And in this first great demonstration of international military games 875,000 spectators, as it happened, sought admission, half of whom had to be turned away.

Something was happening in the Y.M.C.A., though, that would hinder Naismith's participation in the games. In April, 1919, when army evacuation was proceeding rapidly, the Red Triangle began to reduce its overseas personnel, until by September only one hundred fifty "Y" workers remained in France. During their months abroad hundreds of Y.M.C.A. workers had died or had been wounded or gassed. But now, in the bright springtime after the armistice, it was time for most of those who were left to go home. And James Naismith did just that.

He did not stay in France to view the final competitions of the A.E.F. Championship Games or the two weeks of Inter-Allied Games. He did not remain to see the United States win the international basketball tournament. By the time the flags were flying on June 22, 1919, for the games at Pershing Stadium, he had finished his job and left. Nor was he there when the flags were pulled down on July 6 and the events were declared closed. Nineteen of the most valiant months of his life had been spent in France, but now, at long last, he was back home in Kansas.[24]

23

Sermons in Kansas

AT the University of Kansas, school spirit began to revive in the spring semester of 1919 with the return of youthful servicemen, wearing to classes a strange mixture of army uniforms and left-over high-school garments. The war had ended before the first man of the Student Army Training Corps had graduated, and workers pulled down the last of the S.A.T.C. barracks that spring.[1]

Memorials and tributes were organized. In gratitude for the armistice, the 1919 edition of the campus yearbook, the *Jay-hawker,* was entitled the "Peace Book," and the university proposed to plant a "Hero Grove" in honor of students who had died in the war. In May a giant celebration was planned for the homecoming from Europe of the Kansas-Missouri 35th Division. For the greatest war memorial of all, officials pondered over a choice of grand projects: stadium and athletic field, Student Union building, auditorium, or carillon bell tower.

Remnants of military activity remained, as one might expect. The Red Cross had much work yet to be done, both in the town and at the university, and campaigns for war loans continued. On campus, men students made it clear that they favored the establishment of R.O.T.C. training, and even off-campus news reporters showed interest when Professor H. P. Cady isolated the noninflammable inert gas helium in his K.U. laboratory. But, all in all, the wartime atmosphere faded. Freshman caps, which had been crowded out of style by military hats, took over again. In fact, by April 1 the Student Council got around to disenfranchising any freshman who did not wear his beanie at all times.

Some of the old things, important to Naismith, had changed or were changing. The first building to be constructed at the infant University of Kansas—North College ("Old North")—was torn down in 1919. And Frank Strong, whose term as chancellor totaled eighteen of Naismith's first twenty-two years at the university, was ready to leave his post. Confused by the new faculty committees that had begun to rise up and assume authority, Strong had asked to be relieved of the chancellorship. In compliance with his wishes, the governor of the state and the Board of Administration of the university found a replacement for him in 1920 and let him step down to a professorship in law.[2]

Some people may have thought Chancellor Strong a cold person, but the Naismith family did not. As evidence of his warmth and kindness they cherished snapshots of him walking across the campus hand-in-hand with their small children. One picture was of young Jack in a velvet coat with a lace-trimmed collar, fixed up "fancy" by his mother. (His cherubic appearance that day did not foreshadow the campus escapade a few years later when eleven-year-old Jack stole from the porch of the Strong home the containers of ice cream readied for a university reception.)

To add to Frank Strong's appeal, there were anecdotes, known by almost everyone, that showed his sense of humor—like the one about the viscount's shoes. During Strong's administration James Bryce, first Viscount Bryce, famous British statesman and author of *The American Commonweath,* visited the University of Kansas, staying overnight in the chancellor's home. During the night Strong discovered a pair of shoes sitting outside his guest's bedroom door and realized that the viscount expected a maid or houseman to shine them. Because the Strong home had no servants, Frank Strong picked up the shoes and shined them himself. Later, after the viscount had returned to his own well-staffed home in England, Chancellor Strong told the joke on himself.[3]

Topping even the shoeshine story, of course, and the best-loved remembrance of Strong, was the fact that he had started a tradition at K.U. by wearing a nightshirt in a student parade.[4] But now the man who had become as vivid a symbol of the University of Kansas as Fraser Hall would no longer be in his long-time office.

Among K.U. students the immediate difference between 1919 and wartime days was that they did not need to feel guilty any more about having fun. Extracurricular affairs and social activities came into swing again. Judges of the Mistletoe Vanity Fair contest chose a beauty queen for the 1919 *Jayhawker,* and the *Sour Owl,* campus humor magazine, announced that it was looking for jokes and "snappy" material. Sugar rationing was lifted, and candy stores such as the Olympia Candy Kitchen, Greene's Chocolate Shop, and Von's Candy Store flourished again.

Students renewed their interest in fashion. Men wore golf hats and suit coats with fitted waists, and women wore wasp-waisted outfits with long skirts that plunged down to the tops of their pointed-toe shoes. University girls, showing off their hair in French waves and marcels and puffs, modestly covered their ears. People were horrified when one sorority girl went to a varsity dance with her hair brazenly pulled back. Also shocking to some of the townspeople, the shimmy was danced at the Journalism Jazz dance that spring.

After nineteen months overseas James Naismith came home to this scene of action and was strangely disinterested in it. In April, 1919, he carried back to Lawrence the trinkets, antiques, and works of art he had collected in Paris shops—African bracelets, an antique snuffbox, paintings, and sketches—and the painful knowledge of what war at the front can be.[5] He had had his full share of bursting shells and exploding bombs, both in Paris and in the war-torn countryside. He was thin—so thin, some said, that his family hardly recognized him at first glance—nervous, tense with memories he had brought back, unable for nearly a year to recover from the effects of all he had seen and undergone.[6] To his casual acquaintances the effects were not readily apparent, other than his loss of weight, for he was a person of strong self-control. Only to his wife and children were both outward and inward change evident. But he tried valiantly to adjust. He hung on the wall an unsigned painting, which he had bought in Paris, of the artist Monet at work at an outdoor easel; and he resumed his classroom teaching.

Turning to such relaxation as woodworking, he gradually regained health and good spirits. Ever since the days when he had watched Grandpa Young at work at carpentry and had bored holes through his grandfather's newly made doors, he had been interested in woodworkers' tools. He could do a lot with nothing more than an axe, quickly hewing out the curving front of an ornate buffet or the legs of a dining room chair. Not until after the war, though, after outfitting his home workshop with a fine collection of tools, did he turn woodworking into a full-fledged hobby. He picked up wood in unusual places. From a grove of trees torn up by a Kansas tornado he collected enough wood to make a solid black-walnut sideboard for his dining room. He liked to refinish old furniture as well as make new pieces, becoming a regular customer at antique shops and secondhand stores. He bought a dining table that was said to have survived the burning of the Hotel Eldridge in Quantrill's Raid in 1863, and then he found six old chairs to go with it that had come out of the House of Representatives of an early Kansas legislature.

He returned to his extracurricular professional activities, too. Before the war began he had been a leader in physical education societies. He had delivered papers, and he had served in elective and appointive offices. During early April, 1914, the month in which war was declared in Europe, he served as chairman of a general session at the annual convention of the American Physical Education Association in St. Louis. There he read a paper on "Correlation of Athletics in Colleges and Secondary Schools from the College Standpoint." Even during his service abroad he was one of four members appointed to the national Basket Ball Rules Committee by the Executive Committee of the National

Collegiate Athletic Association. Indeed, he was far from forgotten while he was away. During his sojourn in France, he had had occasion to express his gratitude by letter to a national group for its public recognition of him, as a member *in absentia,* at an annual convention: "Will you kindly convey . . . to the Society of Directors of Physical Education in Colleges, my hearty greetings, my appreciation of their kind remembrance of me at their last meeting."[7]

After the war, never completely separated from the societies he had served, he resumed his duties as if nothing had happened. On April 27, 1919, he was recommended as chairman of a national committee of the American Physical Education Association, and in June he was appointed by the president of the association to that post.

He resumed his practice of attending national conventions, too, even though it was expensive, considering the value of the Midwestern dollar in those days. When the American Physical Education Association Convention was held in New York from April 7 to 10, 1920, headquarters for the annual meetings and for lodging was the Waldorf-Astoria. There the thriftiest procedure a lone delegate could follow was to rent a single room without bath for four dollars a day, or he could go over to the McAlpin for a three-dollar room. New York prices were at least four times as high as the seventy-five cents a day that a delegate paid when he went to St. Louis and stayed at the Hotel Moser.

In addition to his professional memberships, university activities could not help drawing his attention. It was not so important, admittedly, that the Sig Alphs and Phi Delts were penalized for dancing after 1:00 A.M. or that the senior law students burned the University Senate in effigy, but the resignation of "Potsy" Clark as assistant football coach in the spring of 1919 and the opening of Potter Lake for swimming that summer were matters significant, for bad or for good, to a physical education director. In the community of Lawrence as a whole came actions equally worth notice. For instance, at the foot of Ohio Street the river's Kaw Beach was opened to the public in the summer of 1919.

Hobbies and professional activities, university and community affairs helped him to adjust to life once more. He gained weight until he was back to his former one hundred eighty-five pounds, and his hearty roar of laughter began to sound in the Naismith house again.[8]

In some respects, however, he was never quite the same person he had been before. A formal change that the war brought in James Naismith was his move from Canadian to United States citizenship. Although his Scottish-Canadian accent remained, his pro-British attitude, so strong during his days at Springfield, had become modified during the first twenty-eight years that he had lived in the United States. British subject in name, he had become a patriotic American in deed. On September 11, 1918, he filed preliminary citizenship papers by mail with the Clerk of the District Court in Lawrence, Kansas, signing a Declaration of Intention to become a United States citizen and renouncing his allegiance to George V, king of Great Britain and Ireland. Naismith took that initial action while he was still in France. Seven years later, long after he had returned to his home in Kansas, District Judge Hugh Means, his superior officer in the Mexican Border campaign, made the final step legal. On May 4, 1925, Judge Means signed the two certificates of naturalization granting United States citizenship to James Naismith and his wife, Maude Evelyn Naismith.[9]

An even deeper change than that of new citizenship came into his religious outlook. Strangely enough, his modified spiritual approach appeared at a time when church and Bible were gaining status on his home campus. This was a time at the University of Kansas when religion was flourishing. In 1920 the newly formed Council of Religious Workers wrote a constitution for an interdenominational school at K.U. The new institution was housed in brick-veneered Myers Hall, which had originally been the frame house used by the Disciples of Christ for the Kansas Bible Chair. The establishment of the school marked a growing awareness of religion as an essential part of university education. In 1922 course work in the School of Religion became accepted toward a bachelor of arts degree from the university. At first earning only three hours of undergraduate credit, the studies were gradually expanded to a program worth twenty-five hours of undergraduate credit and eventually, in 1966, to a full-fledged graduate program.[10]

This recognition of religion at the university was fine with Naismith, for he remained a devout man. But in his own life he dropped some of the outward trappings of religion. He no longer demanded strict obedience to the Sabbath conventions. In the house at 1635 Massachusetts Street there could now be funny papers and secular music and games on Sunday.[11] Little Jimmy had been too young before the war to remember much about the restricted Sundays; but the older Naismith children remembered too well Papa-Jim's prewar rules, and at first they were uneasy at the change.

James Naismith carried his new liberality into the church itself, not wisely but with startling results. When he introduced a cardboard baseball game into his Sunday School class to stir up interest, with a scoreboard to show each incorrectly answered question about Bible stories as a strike, he threw three strikes against himself with the ruling elders. The church fathers, scandalized at baseball in the church on Sunday, removed him from his post as Sunday-School teacher. The news of Dr. Naismith's disgrace spread swiftly, and other churches in Lawrence competed for his services as a visiting speaker. He went over to the Methodists for a few Sundays, but the Presbyterians, taking a good look at themselves, unbent and asked him to come back.[12]

Although he had undeniably become more liberal in religious matters, he participated in church work more actively and effectively than ever. He very soon gave up Sunday-School classes permanently for something else: the role of preacher. Now an ordained minister, on his return from France he began to fill Presbyterian pulpits in and around Lawrence. He served as substitute pastor wherever and whenever needed—sometimes for weeks, months, or even years at a time. He traveled many miles to little churches in communities to the east, west, north, and south of Lawrence—ones that could not afford to pay a full-time minister. He drove a surrey and later an automobile, or traveled by train. He went southeast to nearby Vinland; to Silver Lake, Rossville, and Delia, approximately forty miles to the west; to Leavenworth, nearly as far to the northeast; and to other Kansas towns as far as sixty miles away. The Naismiths were now rarely seen in the Sunday morning congregation of the First Presbyterian Church at Lawrence, for the Reverend James Naismith was away preaching nearly every Sunday, and Maude did not feel well enough to go alone.[13]

The Presbyterian church at the village of Vinland, the first church at which he filled a long term as part-time pastor, was typical of the small churches at which he served. The village itself was typical, too, except for a certain historical interest that not every town has: it possessed a small, shabby building that was said to be the oldest library in Kansas.[14] And Naismith was interested in antiques!

Naismith went to Vinland on alternate weekends for almost two years during 1919 and 1920, at a time when the church did not have a regular minister, receiving five dollars a visit to pay for his sermon and his travel expenses. When the weather was unreliable he went over from Lawrence on the train Saturday evening, usually staying overnight and eating Sunday breakfast and noon dinner with the Fred Woods family or the Rumseys or someone else who lived within walking distance in town or country from the church. When the weather was good, he drove in his surrey on Sunday morning along the twelve miles of dirt road that wound over and around the gently rolling, wooded hills.[15]

After his ministry at Vinland, in the early 1920s he served as substitute preacher at churches in Rossville and Delia in alternation. Here he received approximately ten dollars a trip. He was earning more than $200 a month at the university (his highest monthly salary at K.U. during his entire career was about $300), but two hundred was not really enough. There were medical expenses for Maude in those years, and, besides, the Naismiths were in the process of building a new house. During the few summer weeks when he was not teaching, those small payments for ministerial services helped to support the family. A note that Naismith wrote to himself on May 20, 1923, as the spring semester neared its end, pointed out that his salary from K.U. at the end of that month would be $262.50. "Save Rossville and Delia payments for living expenses for August and September," he reminded himself in his notes.[16]

To travel to his various pastorates, Naismith gradually made the change from team and surrey to automobile. The family's first car—a secondhand Studebaker Thomas Flyer—he never learned to drive, leaving the chauffeuring to son Jack. While Jack was still at home, he used to drive his father to church when there was preaching to be done. Naismith learned that they usually reached their destination more swiftly and easily in a car than with horses—except when snow was so deep on the road that they were forced to turn back and did not get to church at all. Such a crisis did occasionally occur on wintry Kansas roads in the 1920s.

There were not many automobiles in Lawrence before 1920, but the time eventually came, in the roaring twenties, when Naismith decided that he had to learn to handle an auto. The family car by then was a Model T Ford. Fond as he was of horses, the change from surrey to Ford was, perhaps, a slightly traumatic one for him. He did not learn the new technique easily. He continued to drive as though he were still behind a team of horses, sometimes forgetting himself, pushing in the left pedal instead of the brake to stop, yelling, "Whoa! Whoa!" and pulling upward on the steering wheel as though it were a pair of harness reins.[17] His two sons, grown tired of helping to repair the bashed-out rear wall of the garage, installed an iron rail to cope with their father's equestrian method of braking the Ford. They left the bent steering wheel unrepaired, as a reminder of his errors.

Nostalgic or not at entering the mechanized age, Naismith did so with good humor and good sense. The automobile was convenient, he admitted, and he could travel faster and farther than before to preach. Incidentally, he could work a new automotive-centered type of anecdote into his sermons.

He liked to illustrate his sermons with homely parables from everyday living, and sometimes he tried out spur-of-the-moment lessons on his children when they traveled with him to and from church. As he and Jimmy drove along the highway one Sunday morning in their recently purchased Model T, they noticed occasional rabbits lying dead along the road, animals to whom, alas, automobiles were new. Pointing to one of the dead rabbits, Naismith observed, "Jim, that's an example of a fellow who wouldn't learn from somebody else's experience."[18]

Jim was a trustworthy applause meter, and because he liked the rabbit lesson, it was one that his father used in a sermon or two. Perhaps Jimmy's cooperation as a guinea pig was one of the reasons that Naismith earned a local reputation for keeping even the children of the congregation listening when he talked. Among the kids whose interest he held was, to his pleasure, his son. Young Jim recalled later that he sat in the congregation week after week too enthralled to miss a word of his father's sermons.[19]

Naismith's sermons were popular with both young and old. He spoke in simple, conversational style, without oratorical effects. His listeners, entranced with his Scottish pronunciation, waited expectantly each Sunday morning for the rolling *r*s of his favorite word of emphasis—furthermore. They listened to what he had to say, too. Some persons insisted that the Reverend James Naismith was a spellbinder in his sermons. The secret was that he talked to people on their own level, and he associated the Bible with their everyday living. That's why they listened. Delivered in a soft, pleasing voice, his sermons were thoughtful and practical.[20] Some of his titles were "Arguments Against Prohibition," "Advantages of Fraternal Societies," "Campus Problems," "How to Prevent War," and, on the opposite side of the last question, "Arguments in Favor of War." He talked about basketball and physical fitness, Christ and the Ten Commandments, marriage counseling and divorce, alcohol and temperance, and the relativity of evil.

He kept a little black notebook in which he made outlined notes for his talks. Stuck into the notebook, loose, was a clipping on the psychology of women. One piece of advice in the article was a rule he thought every male should follow: "No man on earth can afford to tell a woman that she is not pretty."[21] But the spirit, rather than the literal quality, of that advice may have been his guide. Perhaps he meant to apply it, somehow, to everyone, not just to women. Perhaps he managed to carry that psychology over into his sermons and into his relations with people.

Popular as his sermons were, Naismith had the same scientific interest in the varying effects of different sermons he preached as he did in the varying measurements of K.U. students. Sometimes he had his congregation evaluate the separate parts of the church service, and from the results of these evaluations he made out charts. From charts—and from Jimmy's reaction to his stories —he plotted future sermons. He referred to this method as a "scientifically religious" one.[22]

He did not try to measure his personal popularity; but if he had, he would probably have found that he was a success at most occupational and age levels. When he traveled to his pastorate by train, the church families with whom he spent Saturday night were always glad to see him arrive. He came like a friend of the family, not like a minister. The children of any family he visited looked forward to his coming because he wanted to hear everything they had been doing at school and at home, and he *listened* while they told him. He never acted hurried or worried about anything. The man of the house, often a farmer, enjoyed having him around because he was so plainly a "man's man." Somehow, though, he appealed as much to every woman whose cooking he ate. A member of his congregation, remembering back after forty years, summed up simply enough one small town's impression of him: "He was a wonderful man."[23]

Maude Naismith usually stayed behind when her minister-husband traveled to his out-of-town pulpits. But when Naismith drove surrey or automobile, instead of taking the train, he liked to take some of the children with him, usually young Jim and Maudann.[24] He and the kids always ate noon dinner with one of the families of the congregation, almost invariably a chicken dinner—or so it seemed, looking back on those meals. Jimmy, for one, grew tired of chicken. After he became a grown man and left home, he stopped eating chicken altogether.

There were compensations galore on those Sundays for any monotony in dinner entrée, of course. Jimmy especially enjoyed the years after all the other Naismith children were grown and scattered from home, and he and his father had the day as their joint property. Driving home together Sunday midafternoon was one of the best parts of the day. Naismith usually bought a treat for the two of them somewhere before they got home. During the years when he preached in towns west and north of Topeka, he and Jimmy always stopped in Topeka on their way home to buy a Coney Island apiece. His father seemed to enjoy their little ritual as much as Jimmy did.

Thus, the preaching years went on. There was more demand for Naismith's ministerial talent than he had time to supply. Sometimes the Presbyterian churches of two neighboring towns would cooperate in obtaining his services. Then he would preach alternate weeks at the two churches, perhaps a few miles apart, with the respective congregations visiting each other's church on the Sunday that the Reverend James Naismith was in the pulpit. During the years from about 1925 or 1926 until 1930 he alternated in this manner between the Presbyterian churches of Silver Lake and Rossville, which were eight miles apart.

Until he was seventy-two years old he continued to preach regularly each Sunday in rural Kansas churches, and was called upon for weddings, baptisms, and funerals when the occasions arose. Even after his retirement from regular ministerial service, he was available until the year of his death for an occasional sermon or ceremony. He did it, he said, because he felt he owed the world more than the world owed him. As if his long career as a teacher were not enough, he saw his work in the church as another way of repaying the debt he owed for his threefold education—in religion, medicine, and physical education.[25]

He kept busy, working off that debt.

24

Forgotten Man at K.U.

BACK at the university, after his return from France, Dr. James Naismith settled at last into the routine of classes.

He saw Hellen receive her bachelor's degree in 1920, with a

major in botany, the first of his children to complete the university curriculum. Margaret had eloped partway through her academic career. Jack, worst of all, had flunked out on his first attempt at higher education. Maudann, who later entered nurses' training after a try at William Woods College, enrolled only one summer at K.U. but did not receive an academic degree from any university. The educational record of the Naismith children proved a sad one for Dr. Naismith. Jimmy was left to try to match Hellen's degree, but he was still in the lower elementary grades. There was going to be another problem for the Naismiths at the university, anyway, long before Jimmy arrived at college age.[1]

That new development in the Naismiths' lives had its beginning in a hayloft two decades earlier. In 1899, in a barn at Independence, Missouri, a red-headed fourteen-year-old high-school boy named Forrest Allen sat on the spectator sidelines in the loft, watching his brother Pete help a Missouri basketball team defeat the University of Kansas. Naismith, who had brought his young K.U. team to Independence, did not know that the boy would grow up to become a lasting part of his life. But the boy did.[2]

A few years later Forrest Allen was playing on the court instead of sitting on the sidelines. In the 1902–1903 season James Naismith saw a tall, red-headed lad playing basketball in Independence with the Kansas City Athletic Club. It was the same boy who had been in the Independence hayloft a few years before. This time he was handling a basketball so skillfully that Naismith would not forget him.

In the 1904–1905 season Naismith was refereeing basketball games in Kansas City, when the Kansas City Athletic Club, with Allen playing again, won two of three games from the Buffalo Germans. The Germans, after winning the Pan American basketball championship in 1901 and the Olympic exhibition in 1904, were touring the United States as "world's champions." Naismith, impressed with young Allen's performance against so renowned a team, urged him to come over to the University of Kansas to study and to participate in athletics.[3]

Allen enrolled at the university at the beginning of the 1905–

1906 term and went straight to the football field. Fulfilling Naismith's faith in his athletic ability, Allen made his mark with students and public that fall as a guard on the notable K.U. freshman football team of 1905.[4]

Football was flourishing at K.U. in those days. Basketball, although a part of the sports program, did not rate the attention that football received as an intercollegiate sport, and Naismith saw no reason why it should. He did not even think that basketball needed a coach.

An incident often repeated in newspaper articles and sports stories shows Naismith's reaction when Baker University at Baldwin City, twenty miles from Lawrence, surprised folks by writing to K.U. to offer Allen a part-time position as basketball coach. The letter came to Naismith, who was highly amused. He called Allen to his office to announce the news.

"I've got a good joke on you, you bloody beggar," he laughed. "They want you to coach basketball down at Baker."

"What's so funny about that?" Allen countered.

Naismith explained indulgently, "Why, you can't coach basketball! You just play it."[5]

Allen insisted, "Well, you can teach them to pass at angles and run in curves."[6]

Allen already had his own ideas about basketball, and he intended to use them. Shrugging off Naismith's ridicule, he set out on the hardwood path. He did not return as a student to K.U. classrooms after the 1905–1906 academic year, nor did he ever complete the requirements for a degree. Instead he took up the coaching of basketball.[7]

During the 1906–1907 season Allen coached at Baker University, dropping in at K.U. occasionally to help Naismith run his basketeers through their practices. For the moment, he was helping out for the experience gained rather than for money. In fact, neither at Baker nor at K.U. did Allen receive a salary, for in order to maintain his amateur status with the Kansas City Athletic Club he did his basketball tutelage without pay. Naismith approved of this setup, for he had always said that basketball was meant to be played for fun. But, at least at first, he refused to consider Allen a basketball coach.[8]

But in 1907–1908, although still unlisted on the payrolls, Allen intensified his activities in the field of basketball.[9] Everyone knew that he was working harder with K.U.'s team than the man officially managing it. Naismith had had charge of the basketball program at K.U. from 1898, and he was the only basketball adviser the university had ever officially employed. But at the end of the 1907–1908 season both Naismith and Allen posed with the K.U. basketball team for an official photograph.[10] Allen was beginning to make himself recognized around a basketball court, and Naismith was losing out.

By the time of the 1908–1909 season Allen had a regular three-part schedule going. He coached basketball at Baker University afternoons, while he worked with the game evenings at Haskell Institute in Lawrence (5:30–7:30 P.M.) and at K.U. (8:00–10:00

Naismith and Forrest C. ("Phog") Allen, 1932. Photograph by Duke D'Ambra, courtesy of Mrs. D'Ambra and the University of Kansas Libraries.

P.M.), thus becoming K.U.'s first nonresident basketball coach.[11] He was now undeniably a professional in the business.

In January, 1909, Allen was hired by the University of Kansas to coach the basketball team for the remainder of the season.[12] The following months were his first real season of basketball coaching at K.U.—and, for a while, his only one. After the 1909 season he left, temporarily, his budding career in athletics. Impressed by Naismith's study of medicine, he departed from Lawrence with a new profession in mind—osteopathy. W. O. ("Bill") Hamilton, former K.U. track coach, took over in 1909–1910 as basketball coach.

To Naismith's credit, he adapted to changing times, agreeing to the need for basketball coaching. Although his original concept of basketball instruction had been to "throw the ball in and let 'em fight over it," he came to realize that there was much more in the game than his thirteen rules could cover.[13] He eventually analyzed his brainchild as a game "easy to play, but difficult to master," elaborating thoughtfully, "Yes, anybody can piddle at it, but to master it—yes, just like life."[14]

But although he came to accept basketball coaching, he remained uninterested in making a big thing out of it for himself, either in 1909 or later.

In 1919, after Naismith had returned from war service in France, his path and that of his protégé Forrest C. Allen joined again, but now the relationship was one between two colleagues. Allen, like Naismith, now had the title "Doctor" in front of his name. During the preceding decade he had attended an osteopathic school in Kansas City, later graduating from osteopathic college at Kirksville, Missouri. Only then had he gone ahead with a career as athletic coach, using his knowledge of osteopathy in the training and the medical care of his players. In 1912, beginning this enhanced profession, he had gone to Warrensburg State Normal College in Missouri as coach of all sports.[15]

Along the line, too, he had picked up a nickname that would in time become nationally known. It seems that he often acted as referee or umpire at athletic events, getting a little extra money and a lot of exercise for his voice by calling out strikes, balls, and fouls. A sportswriter, noticing the similarity between Allen's powerful voice and a foghorn, began calling him "Fog" Allen. In his sports column, however, he whimsically changed the spelling to "Phog," to "doll it up" a little.[16] Henceforth Forrest C. Allen was "Phog" Allen to players, spectators, and newspaper readers.[17]

Phog Allen's reputation in athletics was good enough by 1919 that he was hired as the first Director of Athletics at the University of Kansas, a job that, under the title of "manager of athletics," had previously been Naismith's. Allen came along in time to have a voice in important university decisions. To begin, he supported the vote of the alumni board to build a stadium as one of the war memorials to be established at the university. After that opener, he was influential ever after in athletic affairs.[18]

During the season of 1920, while attempting to hire a permanent football coach, Allen took on the sideline of coaching football. He did not carry on the job long enough to make use of the new stadium in 1921 but long enough to make a success of himself. The record of his football team was good enough to inspire enthusiastic financial contributions to the million-dollar stadium fund.

Track was a sport that he promoted actively. Development of the track program at K.U. had begun under the guidance of James Naismith in the late nineteenth and early twentieth centuries. Now sports director Allen selected Karl Schlademan, one-time DePauw athlete and now coach at Baker University, as his first track coach. Together they set out to make K.U. known outside the Missouri Valley Conference. One of the Allen-Schlademan accomplishments was to push into action a plan originated by John Outland, a K.U. athlete, for a great Midwestern track meet. On Friday, April 20, 1923, a high-school meet was held at K.U., and on April 21 the college division had its turn on the cinder track. With that weekend in 1923, the Kansas Relays had its beginning, soon to become a nationally recognized track event, with K.U. runners like Glenn Cunningham on hand in the 1930s and Jim Ryun in the 1960s. In 1923 the running surface was still a far way from the eight-lane all-weather Tartan track that would one day be laid, and track events would long continue to be plagued by rainy weather. But, nevertheless, Allen had headed that group of sports toward big things.

Basketball coaching was his forte, though. It was a job, held by W. O. Hamilton during Allen's ten-year absence, that had really given Phog his start around Lawrence, in the two years from 1907 to 1909; and he had done a lot with the game since then. Important among the reasons for hiring him now was the fact that he brought with him from Missouri an outstanding record of basketball victories—a record that he was to make even more impressive in the thirty-seven years to come.

Through good fortune and Midwestern propagandistic effort, in the 1920–1921 basketball season the national A.A.U. championship tournament was moved to Convention Hall in Kansas City, making that metropolis for many years the unofficial basketball capital of the country.[19] Attention in national basketball circles was thereby directed toward the Missouri Valley Conference and, in turn, toward K.U., as a member of that basketball league. The timing was good for Allen; from the beginning of his career as K.U. athletic director he would have optimum opportunity to publicize his basketball know-how and his talent as coach. He did so, too, with many years of basketball teams that he coached to high national standings.

From the start the new director of athletics showed his ability to get things done, not only in the teaching of basketball techniques but in anything he handled. In details of administration he was effective and progressive. For one thing, largely through his efforts the University of Kansas organized the first four-year course in athletic coaching to be offered in the general area of the Missouri Valley. Taught by a staff of seven, including Naismith, the course when satisfactorily completed would bring a B.S. degree to the aspiring student.[20]

On a personal level, too, Allen proved an influential person to have around. In 1920 he discovered that neither a picture nor any mention of the man who had created the great game of basketball was any longer included in the basketball rules book. Naismith did not worry over the omission, but Allen did. He protested effectively enough that Naismith's name and photograph were restored to their proper place. Phog was proud of his action. He wrote:

I went back to New York, met with the officers of the National Collegiate Athletic Association and protested vehemently of this injustice to the inventor of the game. Dr. Naismith's name and photograph was placed back on the rule books and later he was made an honorary life member of the Rules Committee.[21]

Strangely enough, this act of loyalty by Allen was the first of many actions that would point up differences in temperament and aims between him and his unassuming old friend.

Athletics was the bread-and-butter of their lives for Phog Allen and James Naismith, but there was a basic difference in their approach, which had become conspicuous in the decade they had been apart. When Allen's book of anecdotes summarizing his life in the sports world was published, his slogan "Play to Win" was blazoned across the opening pages.[22] He trained his teams for hard playing, and he taught them not to lose. Naismith thought it was morally wrong for an athlete not to do his best, but as a coach he had never been interested in winning games for the sake of winning games. Doctor and preacher as well as coach, he had always given precedence to developing the individual player to his full potential. In the appendix of his book on basketball he classified the thirty-six "attributes developed by athletics and games" under six headings: Muscular Development, Skill, Mental, Emotions, Social, Moral. He stressed three purposes in all sports, particularly in basketball: (1) "play for the fun of playing," (2) physical activity as an aid to the organic function of the body, and (3) team participation as a lesson in sportsmanship.

James Naismith said, "Play for the fun of playing." Phog Allen declared, "Play to win!"

To be sure, Naismith wanted his boys to try to win. He declared frankly that sportsmanship was shown as much in fighting for rights as in conceding rights, and winning a game he considered one of the players' essential rights. But he had more important things to stress: "Let us all be able to lose gracefully and to win courteously; to accept criticism as well as praise; and last of all, to appreciate the attitude of the other fellow at all times."[23]

Allen always placed the approval of the spectators high, while Naismith, more interested in the welfare of "his boys," had never been interested in "pleasing the crowd."

Nor could Allen understand the interest that Naismith took in his students and the overwhelming amount of time he gave them off the playing field and outside of the classroom. After his return from the war, Naismith spent more and more time counseling students, advising them about their academic and personal problems. Often he helped someone decide to stay in school who was discouraged and wanted to leave. Sometimes he was too busy to go to class, as students waited outside his office for conferences. His son-in-law George Stanley, teaching in the department as a student instructor, used to substitute for him in the classroom when "Doc" asked him to.

The saying at K.U. about Doc Naismith was: "He's never too busy to help a boy."[24] Students, present and former, came to him all day long, and the doorbell often rang at the Naismith home at night. He became an unofficial dean of men, and when problem or crisis arose, students and officials alike turned to him for help. One night two students went swimming in Potter Lake after the campus guard left at midnight. When one student drowned during that early-morning escapade, James Naismith was one of the first persons called out of bed. It was he, up most of that night, who notified the boy's parents after the body was recovered.[25]

Allen, half curious and half envious, resented Naismith's popularity. "You're wearing yourself out, Doc," he warned the older man.[26] Naismith shrugged and went on listening to the students in his office and in his study at home, advising them and keeping secret their problems and his counsel.

Once when Allen saw one of his basketball players leave Naismith's private office, he asked his colleague point-blank what the boy's trouble was. "If he wanted you to know, he'd have told you," Naismith replied bluntly.[27]

The essential difference between the two men was more important than appeared at first observation. It was a difference of significance to the whole university. Allen and Naismith, as university officials were well aware, stood at opposite poles in a line of action on which the administration must take a stand. Basically, the Naismith-Allen conflict was that of amateur athletics against professional athletics. The one of them with his fetish for victory was promoting the semiprofessionalism in sports that the other believed had no place in an institution of learning.

Those were years when a decision about athletics could be made either way: to play it down or to play it up. Sports were still small-time business. In a basketball auditorium seating a thousand persons, tickets were selling in 1920 for thirty-five cents each. Fifteen cents extra, or one dollar for the season, bought a reserved seat. But there was great enthusiasm for basketball at K.U., and Allen was eager to take advantage of that enthusiasm. He was ready to make basketball big business for the university and to bring all the rest of the sports schedule with it. Naismith was not willing to do that.

In that conflict Naismith fought a losing battle. Allen's ambitions were given a boost and Naismith's way of life was shaken when a change came in the K.U. chancellorship. The new administrator, to Naismith's distress, was ready to endorse a new approach.

In 1920 a second tall chancellor, Ernest Hiram Lindley, six feet two-and-one-half inches in height and prematurely white-haired, replaced Frank Strong. Supported by Governor Allen's determination to push the University of Kansas along the road of change and progress (the slogan: "Rediscover Your University"), the new chancellor quickly acquired a reputation for action. He started innovations with flowers and trees and then worked up to people. His landscaping of the campus was extensive and looked good to everyone. With the help of a clever Belgian gardener, Van Horbeck, he made grass and shrubs flourish on the rocky plot east of Fraser Hall where nothing was expected to grow, and he had rows of elm trees planted all along Jayhawk Boulevard.

But when he dealt in the same determined manner with faculty and staff, feelings were hurt. Like a new broom sweeping clean, he gave a Monday-morning look to the university with his demotions and promotions and hirings. He brought in a new law dean, a dean of men, and a dean of women and made wholesale changes in various departments. He was in part responsible, too, for the creation of the State Board of Regents, with its supervision of all institutions of higher education in Kansas.[28]

Dr. James Naismith, lacking the record of efficient administration that the new chancellor sought, was an easy target. After five years under Allen's progressive new athletic directorship, in 1924 Dr. Naismith was demoted to make more room at the top for the younger, more ambitious man. Dr. Forrest C. Allen assumed the chairmanship of the Department of Physical Education, while Naismith was retained under him as a mere professor in the department.[29]

Once Naismith had been the chapel director and the university physician; then these responsibilities had been taken away from him. Once he had been the manager of athletics for the university, the head of the Department of Physical Education, and the university's basketball instructor. Now the energetic Allen was all of these. The facts that the National Collegiate Athletic Association had paid Naismith tribute by granting him honorary life membership in 1923 and that in 1924 he had been made honorary chairman of the rules committee for life were not enough to make up for his knowledge that his own university had lost confidence in him.

Momentarily Naismith lost his grip on his lifelong philosophy of acceptance and optimism. He could not accept the fact that when progress comes there are persons who must be hurt by it, nor could he find any bright side to the situation. Although he could forgive, he found his demotion difficult to understand. In 1924 Naismith, not yet sixty-three years old, was as erect and vigorous as a man twenty years his junior. Although the thirty years since he had married Maude Sherman in Springfield had added more than twenty pounds to his weight, he looked more like a retired football player than an overage professor. Furthermore, his mind was as keen and young as his body. He was a man of extensive education and high qualifications—a graduate of McGill University, a minister and a physician, the holder of one earned degree and one honorary degree in the field of physical education, and a teacher with more than thirty years of experience, seventeen years of those thirty with the rank of full professor.[30]

Inwardly Naismith was shaken, but to the public he gave no sign of his distress. He descended with dignity to his new status and turned the administrative details of the department over to Allen.[31]

Then he went on teaching his classes, counseling the students who sought him out in his new and smaller office, and went to the movies on Saturday night with Jimmy, since Maudann had grown up and did not go with him any more. He had the satisfaction of seeing the 1925 issue of the *Jayhawker*, campus yearbook, dedicated to him. Perhaps he did not even notice at first glance that the paragraph in the front of the book included an erroneous initial *A* in his name. He was accustomed to having people make that mistake.

Dedication To Dr. James A. Naismith. Twenty-six years at the University as director of Physical Education, father of Basketball, exponent of clean sportsmanship, believer in the Kansas Spirit, a Christian gentleman, and true friend of all K.U. Students.[32]

After he had treasured the yearbook long enough, he sent it to the uncle and the sister who had begun the job of rearing an orphaned boy fifty-five years before. He inscribed a message to P. J. Young and Annie Naismith:

To Pete and Annie who made it possible for me to be of some use in the world.

Jim
August 7, 1926[33]

The new head of the department was a go-getter. Building on the foundations that his predecessor had laid, Forrest C. Allen made people inside and outside the university take notice. In addition to track and football, Allen promoted other forms of athletics, such as wrestling, swimming, and fencing, not to mention the extracurricular sport of golf. But he made a big thing out of one game—basketball. When the coaching staff consisted of nine men, there were two coaches for football, one each for track, wrestling, swimming, and fencing, none for golf, and three for basketball. The fencing instructor was Naismith, and the head basketball coach was Allen.[34]

After four years as director of athletics—time enough to start with freshmen and coach them through their final season of eligibility—Allen had basketball players worth boasting about. The team of 1923, losing only one game the whole season—a noncollege match—won the Missouri Valley Championship and rated national recognition. To top the honors, players Paul Endacott and Charles Black were selected for the All-American team that year and Tus Ackerman was chosen the following year.

James Naismith received one bit of recognition that year for the glory his game had brought to the University of Kansas. He was invited to sit in the team photograph, between Phog Allen and Charlie Black.

During Allen's tutelage of the basketball squad, coach and players worked hard, and University of Kansas teams became outstanding ones year after year. Their record helped the Midwest to remain a basketball center. Despite the claims of such large cities as Indianapolis and New York, Lawrence's neighbor Kansas City was host for fourteen years to the national Amateur Athletic Union tournament, and K.U. played skillfully in those contests. Phog Allen became known as one of the "winningest" coaches of all time. Far in the future, in 1952, he would take some of his championship basketball players to the Olympic Games in Helsinki, Finland, to defeat Russia in the finals and become America's "Coach of the Year."

Throughout the 1920s Allen continued to prosper. The year 1928 was the only one in history when a graduating class was rained out, forced to have baccalaureate and commencement exercises indoors instead of marching through the traditional outdoor ceremonies. For Phog Allen, though, skies remained sunny. In that year the university took time to build a nine-hole golf course around Potter Lake and Marvin Grove, leaving the six-holer behind Marvin Hall for practice. "It's a sporty course," commented Phog proudly about the new layout.[35]

In the spring and fall of 1929 Allen and his athletic program went on, untouched by the nation's financial affairs, as did the whole university. News stories in the *University Daily Kansan* were bland, except when a student did something outstanding with books or brawn or sense of humor, and no one on the tranquil K.U. campus expected the New York Stock Exchange to collapse in October. Feats of Phog's athletes ranged from tomfoolery to broken records. In front of newsreel cameras Adela Hale, captain of the women's rifle team, shot the ashes off a man's cigar to demonstrate her marksmanship. At the track Jim Bausch set a K.U. shot-put record of 50 feet 4 inches, and Jay Wilcox tied a world track mark by running 100 yards in 9.6 seconds. In that same year K.U.'s swimming team began to take part in intercollegiate conference competition. The pool in Robinson Gymnasium was a small rectangular tank, but the swimmers made the most of it.

Even after the national economic crash jolted the nation, Allen and his coaches tightened their belts and continued to build K.U.'s reputation in athletics. And results on the athletic field were what counted in Phog's neck of the woods.

Through all the reorganization of the Department of Physical Education and the rise of Forrest C. Allen, equanimity ruled. Doc Naismith and Phog Allen maintained a friendly relationship that became a tradition in the university and the town. Naismith even took Phog along on a trip to Canada in the 1930s. The arguments between the two men were friendly ones, centered mostly around Allen's efforts to force changes in the basketball rules.[36]

Allen was a radical in his approach to basketball, while Naismith opposed most of the changes introduced after about 1925.[37] Basketball rules may have been destined for a new standardization in 1934, but he was not bending in that direction. He liked the game the way it was, without newfangled changes. He admired the increasing skill of the players, he was quick to admit, but he wanted them to perform within the old rules. "Don't get too far away from the original game," he cautioned. "It was the best game."[38]

True, he did not regard his original creation as immune to man-made changes, but by the 1930s those innovations were coming at him in too rapid and revoluntionary a manner for his comfort. He would have gone so far as to accept the 1932 rules book, but no farther. Perhaps in the 1960s or 1970s he would have bowed tolerantly to inevitable modifications, but he was not ready to do so in the late 1920s and early 1930s.[39]

The new ten-second rule was the pet point of disagreement between Naismith and Allen. People were amused to learn that one day while Allen on the second floor of Robinson Gym was extolling to reporters the advantages of the ten-second rule in basketball, Naismith in his office below was preparing for the press a formal condemnation of the rule. Believing that the blame for stalling should not be placed on the offensive side, he had objected several years before to the rules committee about any regulation compelling the team in possession of the ball to advance beyond the center of the court in any specified length of time.[40] "Play the ball and not the man," he argued. He insisted that the ball should be any player's ball at any stage of the game. "Come and get it," was his challenge.[41]

He explained that this theory was implicit in his original thirteen rules and that if these rules were applied as he had intended them to be, the action would be kept moving satisfactorily in the "wide-open, free-passing game" basketball was meant to be. For that reason, he favored a man-to-man defense rather than a team defense. He scoffed at players who were afraid to "come out in the open." He said that laying down a center line had not stopped stalling on the court, though it had made a horse race of his game.[42] He had never meant that basketball should become so fast. He felt that the series of sprints from one end of the court to the other, intended to speed the game, had created more roughness rather than put an end to delaying tactics. Nor was elimination of the center jump after a goal to his liking. Throwing the ball in at the end of the court instead of throwing it up for a jump was not an improvement, he complained. For whatever his words were worth, Naismith spoke up in defense of the old order.[43]

Admittedly, his words were not worth very much. Basketball was gradually getting away from the intentions of its creator. One indication of the direction of change was the increasing size of the score. It would not be until 1963 that the National Collegiate Athletic Association could report that the "whoa" sign had been put up, at least temporarily. The N.C.A.A. stated that in the past year "coaches across the country deliberately took the race horse out of basketball."[44] Still, the decrease to an average combined score of 138.4 per game for both teams in the 1962–1963 season was not much of a slowdown. It was still a sharp contrast to the score of one-to-nothing in the first session of basketball in history.

A few changes he would have favored, had they been put into effect. For example, to offset the advantage held by tall players he wanted to rotate the jumpers in a set order. Although Phog advocated a twelve-foot basket, Naismith opposed raising the goal.[45] Instead he suggested that in the center jump the referee throw the ball up at varying heights to develop versatile jumpers. Phog, however, did not like this sort of irregularity, and neither did the arbiters of the rules.

Naismith may no longer have had much say-so about the ten-second rule in national basketball or the tactics of the University of Kansas team, but the inescapable fact remained that he was the man who had originated the game. He had created basketball in a few weeks of spare-time figuring. Phog Allen, however, had worked at the game all his life. He pointed out that Naismith had no conception of the fundamentals of coaching basketball. His idea was to throw the ball into the game and let things happen helter-skelter. Phog Allen, though, had put order into coaching. If Naismith was to be called the Father of Basketball, Phog Allen suggested that he himself should be called the Father of Basketball Coaching.

25

The Roaring Twenties and the Depressed Thirties

THE 1920s, heyday for that barnstorming professional basketball team the original Celtics, had some good years for the Naismith family, despite the shock of professional demotion for the head of the household.¹ The nation as a whole was getting along fine. Americans were learning to live with prohibition, gangsterism, and big business, whether they liked it or not.²

At the University of Kansas life went merrily on. Enrollment reached four thousand, and the Student Council decreed that freshman hats were compulsory wear for all male students with less than twenty-four hours of credit. Increased legislative appropriations brought a postwar golden age of construction: war memorials, library, dormitory, laboratories and classrooms, power house, and a new hospital for the Medical Center on the Kansas City campus. Days of prosperity inspired the tradition of "Hobo Day," when students wore tattered clothes and made believe with a lean and hungry look. They whooped it up with rallies like "Doc Yak's Famous Medicine Show," dispensing mock pep pills as they prepared for the annual K.U.–Missouri football game. Potter Lake, once the lively site of Naismith's university regatta and the unhappy scene more than once of his attempts to resuscitate a drowning swimmer, was still "the old swimmin' hole" for university students and townspeople alike. But the diving tower was taken down about 1925, and in the prosperous times of 1927 the city of Lawrence constructed a public pool.³

Naismith continued to be interested in events that were happening in his old home at Springfield, Massachusetts, too. He could be proud of his former site of study and teaching, the International Young Men's Christian Association Training School. Still training "Christian men for leadership in physical education," Springfield College, as it was now called, opened its thirty-third year on September 15, 1920, according to magazine advertisements, although it was thirty-five years earlier that it had had its beginning in the School for Christian Workers.⁴ It now had a four-year undergraduate curriculum and a two-year graduate curriculum that offered work leading to bachelor's and master's degrees, respectively, in physical education. The school possessed four athletic fields, two gymnasiums, a natatorium, a boathouse, and the largest physical education library in existence.⁵

Most important, Springfield College had just received the greatest honor ever granted it thus far—the Olympic Cup of 1920. The International Olympic Cup Committee, since its establishment in 1906, had made the award every four years, at the time of the Olympic Games, to some college or other institution recognized the world over for its contributions to athletics. The work of Springfield's faculty and alumni during the First World War had drawn the attention of Baron Pierre de Coubertin and his committee strikingly enough that they considered the name of Springfield College worthy of being engraved on the international trophy alongside the names of previous winners like the Union des sociétés de gymnastiques de France and the Amateur Athletic Union of the United States.[6] Naismith could feel that his work in the Y.M.C.A. Bureau of Hygiene in France had been one of the reasons for the honor being bestowed on the school.

In the early part of the twenties the Naismiths were financially in satisfactory condition. Jack and Maudann, who now called herself Ann, were both living at home in the large house at 1635 Massachusetts Street. They had jobs, Ann as a nurse at the old McConnell Hospital at 744 New Hampshire Street, and Jack as a physical director in the city schools in Kansas City, Missouri.[7] The Naismiths decided to build a new house, close to the university. The children said that it would be mainly for Papa-Jim and Mama, for the young Naismiths would probably all soon be gone from home, weekends and all. Margie had eloped with George Stanley. Hannie had married Leslie Dodd. (Jack gave the young couple a good send-off by smearing limburger cheese on the muffler of the honeymoon automobile.) And now two more of them, Maudann and Jack, were of marriageable age. That left only Jimmy, who would soon be growing up.

The Naismiths chose a site for the new home. Naismith did the planning, and Jack and his father together did most of the construction with their own hands. As it happened, though, Jack had married before the work was finished.[8]

Before they knew about the demotion that the K.U. administration had in store for the professor, the house was completed. It was an attractive two-story frame residence at 1700 Mississippi Street, and in 1924 Dr. and Mrs. Naismith and young Jim made the move to their new home.[9]

Notwithstanding the joys of a new home, there were family troubles of varying intensities mixed in with the Naismiths' pleasures. One little item was that Maude Naismith was never really as happy in Kansas as she might have been. She was a bit homesick for New England most of her married life. But she was usually either too busy with the children or too unwell to go back for extended visits. And her husband's position at K.U. kept the family living in the Midwest. To compensate, sometimes she nostalgically painted watercolors of ships in a harbor, the way she remembered they used to be back home. "Maybe when I die they'll send me home to Massachusetts to be buried," she said once.[10] Of course, she made it clear that she was joking. But her comment was enough to worry her husband.

A problem of greater significance was Maude Naismith's health, for she had an increasing number of things wrong with her. Besides deafness, she had a weak heart, high blood pressure, and a defective gall bladder. And sometimes she just plain ached, without a definite source of trouble. Worse, another ailment more serious than all these came to light.

When an operation was performed in Kansas City for removal of her gall bladder, the doctors discovered that she had cancer. They diagnosed the growth as a malignancy of slow progression, and they advised against surgery. Ann, now a nurse, tried to reassure her father that there would not be any trouble, that her mother might live for twenty years more without need for further treatment. But James Naismith, who had always treated his wife like a fragile doll, was gentler with her now than ever before.[11]

Because of the condition of Maude's health in the late twenties, even before her operation, James Naismith had to make his trips to Canada without her. Only during the summer of 1926, when Jimmy was thirteen, had both Maude and his youngest son come along with him for a month's visit with relatives on both the Young and the Naismith side of the family. A man of loyalty to friends and kinsmen, Naismith had always kept in close touch with the relatives left behind, making regular trips back to Ontario to visit Uncle Peter and Annie and the others. He always boasted that he had "a hundred and three first cousins" on this side of the Atlantic (ignoring the count of another relative, who insisted that there were only eighty-two cousins), and he wanted his family to meet them.[12] That summer of 1926 he took his wife Maude and son Jimmy with him for a long visit with some of those cousins and with everyone else within visiting distance in Ramsay Township.[13]

Most of the time, however, he had to go alone on his visits, or occasionally with son Jack or with a friend, staying for only a day or two. He often came directly to the farmstead of his cousin Robert Young and wife Lucinda, where fishing was good. He usually arrived unannounced, for he wanted no fuss or preparation made for him. His relatives might look out of a farmhouse window when arising on a summer morning and see Jim's car parked down by the river, where he had been fishing since the early Canadian dawn. The Youngs remembered particularly one day in the summer of 1932. That day Jim and four male companions drove in at noon, when nineteen persons—family and guests—were gathered around the table eating dinner. Intent on going fishing, the Kansas men had driven all night, without letting anyone know that they were coming. But four unexpected guests, three of them strangers, did not perturb Lucinda Young. At the Young table there was always room for a few extra persons. One simply put on extra plates and cups and tableware, moving over to make room for latecomers, whether they were Canadian neighbors or university professors from the United States.[14]

Even without Maude along, Jim Naismith enjoyed himself on those visits to Ramsay Township. He liked to fish the same streams he had fished as a boy and to hike across fields that had been woodland in his youth. If he managed to be there at the time of the annual summer church service, he took part in the anniversary affair. Sitting beside Annie and Uncle Peter on Sunday morning, he listened to the memorial sermon and sang with the congregation the old hymns, pitched to the same tuning fork Grandfather Young had used when he led the church singing in pioneer days. Jim went to the tea meeting in the evening, listening attentively to the so-called concert—which included readings and recitations as well as music—much like the concerts of the old days when his Scottish high-school teacher P. C. McGregor helped "entertain" at social gatherings. Nostalgically, Jim saw that young people still threw conversational candies at one another (mints with "I Love U," "Be Mine," "Dream Boy," and so forth, printed on them) while waiting for the cake and tea to be served, and he observed that the women of the congregation still vied with one another to bake the fanciest cake.[15]

The principal reason for his trips, of course, was to visit Annie and Uncle Peter. Annie Naismith had had a hard life, some people thought. She did not marry, because she was too busy taking care of Uncle Peter, nor did she take time to have as much fun as her American relatives said she should. Her recreation was centered around church activities and her own quiet charitable deeds. She never saw a game of basketball in her life and never quite forgave her brother for leaving the ministry for athletics. He surmised that she was ashamed of him for having created the game.[16] Uncle Peter bought her a Persian-lamb coat and took her with him on a trip to Europe, but her hands bore the marks of her years of toil and her sweet, kindly face sometimes looked tired.

As it turned out, it was fortunate that Maude and James Naismith and their son Jimmy had a good long visit with Naismith's only sister during the summer of 1926, for on March 29, 1929, Annie Naismith died. Preceding in death the uncle she had cared for so long, the eldest of the three orphaned Naismith children went to her reward. A tribute to her published in the *Almonte Gazette* stated: "Her face mirrored a beautiful life, fragrant with kindly words and deeds. We mourn her passing, but realize that heaven will be enriched by her gentle presence."[17]

Jim Naismith paid her an unintentionally ironic tribute of his own. It was with unquestioned love and a notable lack of tact that he made his last brotherly gesture for her. Although years before he had set up a basketball trophy at Almonte High School, which had been awarded annually since 1920, he still insisted it was a shame that so little was being done for basketball in Almonte. With this deficiency in mind, he created for his deceased sister the kind of memorial that would most surely have shocked the living Annie. He set up the Naismith Cup for Inter-form Basketball, to be awarded to Almonte High School girl basketball players.[18] He did not mean it that way, but in Jim's and Annie's lifelong argument over basketball Jim had the final word.

Slightly less than three years after Annie's death, Uncle Peter died, on January 5, 1932. On P. J.'s eighty-third birthday three years before, only a few months before Annie's death, friends in Almonte—mostly young ones—had held a big surprise party for him. The celebration was carried out by members of the Young People's Society of the Presbyterian Church (whose meetings P. J. sometimes mischievously attended) and members of the church choir (to which he had belonged most of his life). The youthful festivities were appropriate, for Annie and Uncle Peter had always been fond of young people.[19] A newspaper article told about the party:

When Mr. Young and his esteemed niece Miss Naismith were having a quiet chat with the minister, the ringing of the doorbell announced the invasion . . . by a band of over 40 young folks. . . . They . . . sang as they marched "For He's a Jolly Good Fellow."

. . . P. J., as he is known . . . is as young in spirit . . . as any member of the Young People's Society, with whom he is a great favourite. He has the rare gift and grace to enter into the joy and fun of an evening with as much zest as the youngest member.[20]

James Naismith was no doubt grateful that his uncle had had that party to remember and doubly grateful that the party occurred while Annie was alive to enjoy it.

Laudatory clippings and sentimental memories laid aside for the moment, the matter of Peter J. Young's will remained to be attended to. Uncle Peter was an unpredictable person, as all his relatives had long known. Jim Naismith could not be sure whether the old man's will would leave him an estate out of love or bestow a curse on him because of his having deserted the ministry forty-two years before.[21]

The terms of the will turned out to be P. J.'s version of a reprimand, and, as it happened, he had accumulated enough worldly goods to make his rebuke felt. His property and savings were considerable for a retired Canadian farmer in the year 1932. When all debts were paid, an estate of approximately nine thousand dollars was left to selected ones among the descendants of his ten brothers and sisters. He had, apparently, two criteria for these selections: those relatives who were in need and those relatives who had done him a remembered favor were bequeathed anything from a gold pocket watch to a sum of money. Jim Naismith, to P. J.'s way of thinking, qualified on neither count.[22]

Finances, of course, had never been a primary consideration with James Naismith.[23] Much more distressing than disinheritance was the truth that within three years he had lost two of the persons who had been closest of all to him for more than sixty years. In losing Annie Naismith and P. J. Young, he had lost not only sister and uncle but his foster parents as well. Now that they were both gone, he felt orphaned for a second time.

His very disregard for money, however, would soon bring on a new crisis. At the moment, to be sure, no one knew that anything was going wrong. Not even Ann knew, although she was in close contact with her father in the late 1920s. In June of 1929, the year that enrollment reached 4,210 at the University of Kansas, she registered as a special student at the university. During that summer, a few months before the great stock-market crash of October 29, she sat as a student in her father's class in kinesiology. "Dimps" helped him grade tests and notebooks and even sat on his knee and twined his hair around her finger as she begged for a good grade for herself. Her professor, as might be expected, was pleased to have her in class and flattered at her attention, and everyone seemed happy at the Naismith house.[24]

In fact, lots of things were going better than usual. For nearly forty years—and markedly so since her operation—Maude had been the center of James's life and his dearest concern. But now, although the children were growing up and leaving home, she found an unexpected antidote for loneliness. Young Edwin Elbel, a graduate of Springfield College, joined the Department of Physical Education in 1928, to become a colleague of her husband's. When the Elbels moved to 1713 Mississippi Street two years later, across from the Naismiths' new house, the two families became good friends. The new friendship proved good for Maude. Mrs. Elbel, aware of Mrs. Naismith's loneliness, began taking the older woman out with her to social functions, and

Maude, despite her frail health, began to take part in outside activities more than she ever had before.[25]

Though she had shied away from doing so in her earlier years in Lawrence, under Mrs. Elbel's sponsorship she joined one of the woman's social groups. When the club met at her home, Maude got out her best silver, her cut glass, her most beautiful teapot. Most of the members were younger women burdened with the labor and expense of rearing small children. Some of them felt slightly resentful that when Mrs. Naismith's turn came to entertain, she was able to serve more elaborately than they. But she, unaware of their resentment, blossomed out as she had never done before.[26]

Then came the thirties. These were the years of depression and dust and economic depths. But at first the decade seemed rosy.

At the University of Kansas athletics, scholarships, and extra-curricular activities continued to progress. University athletes were winning games, particularly in basketball. On the intellectual side, after Solon E. Summerfield established the coveted Summerfield scholarship awards in 1929, each fall saw a new crop of worthy Kansas high-school boys starting on a college career. And the Pioneer found a new home.

In the thirties the Pioneer statue, landmark of the campus, was moved from the end of the boulevard to a more prominent location on the lawn east of Fraser Hall. Representing a prairie pioneer leaning on a shovel as he planted corn in virgin soil, the figure was intended to illustrate "the difficulties and handicaps early Kansans encountered."[27] That explanation made the statue seem to some Naismith devotees like a symbol of the difficulties that he had met and overcome to fashion a threefold career for himself and to create a famous national pastime.

But after Simon Bell had given the statue to K.U. in 1905, succeeding generations of students made up a myth that the Pioneer was resting on his shovel until the day a virgin should walk by: then he would fling a spadeful of dirt at her. Somehow that distorted tale symbolized the misunderstanding and neglect that Naismith's accomplishments had met.

About the time that the Pioneer statue was moved to Fraser

lawn, however, still with no foreshadowing of troubles to come, the thirties began to bring Naismith overdue recognition. On April 1, 1931, he, along with his friends and colleagues Amos Alonzo Stagg and Dr. R. Tait McKenzie, was given the Honor Award of Fellow in Physical Education by the American Association of Health, Physical Education and Recreation.[28] In presenting the award Miss Mable Lee, president of the A.A.H.P.E.R., emphasized his role as teacher of physical education:

Dr. Naismith had a vision, far ahead of his time, of the social values of recreative and competitive athletics and he deserted the ministry, for which he had spent a number of years in preparation, because he saw the great opportunity in recreative physical education for character training of boys and young men.[29]

Another honor came later that same year. During Christmas week in 1931 the Springfield Emblem was presented to him at a meeting of Springfield College alumni in New York. At this presentation Dr. James Huff McCurdy had laudatory words for Naismith's work in social hygiene in France and his efforts toward the character building of youth at home. He commented in summary that "Dr. Naismith represents an ideal in education, in leadership and in inventive ability."[30]

The following year brought more recognition. In January, 1932, James Naismith was invited to New York to deliver to the Society of Physical Education one of the lectures in the third annual Wingate Memorial Lectures series, and his address was published that year in *Aims and Methods in School Athletics*.[31]

In addition to honors came reunions and nostalgia. In the spring of 1932 A. A. Stagg came to Lawrence to referee the second annual Kansas Relays and to reminisce with Jim Naismith about old days at Springfield. Another reunion occurred when Naismith's present university showed its awareness of his place in the world of sports. On February 18, 1933, the thirty-fifth anniversary of his first K.U. basketball team, seven of its members gathered from five states to be guests at a Naismith ceremony between halves of the K.U.–Iowa State basketball game. It was like old times to hear those names called: Avery, Henderson, Hess, Owens, Royal, Sutton, Yahn. That night in February was a good one.

In the Naismith household everything seemed to be going smoothly. Because Jim Naismith had a flair for building things with his own hands, construction continued even after the new house was finished. In his spare hours, and this time without Jack's help, Naismith built a smaller house at 1708 Mississippi Street, two lots away from the Naismith's present home, to be used as rental property. He might make mistakes sometimes in measurements or fitting, but he had fun.

Romance played its part, too. The first evening that Frances Pomeroy, a K.U. student from the Kansas town of Holton, came to the Naismith home she was wearing a black dress with a red rose at the waistline. Although she was with her date, a college friend of young Jim Naismith's, the elder Naismith, recalling the black dress and red rose of his first meeting with Maude Sherman, knew the moment he saw Frances that she was the right girl for his son. Coincidentally, as soon as Frances and young Jim were introduced to each other that evening, they fell in love. They would have felt that way even if they had not had the bond of being fellow students in K.U.'s School of Engineering and Architecture. Their common interest only helped their love affair along.

With such a storybook background as this for their courtship, theirs was a marriage ceremony it was natural that the elder Naismith should perform. On August 11, 1933, young James Sherman Naismith, with a brand-new B.S. degree in chemical engineering, and Frances Pomeroy, who had just received a degree in architecture, were married, the Reverend James Naismith officiating.[32]

Naismith admitted that he would probably always feel sentimental over this marriage. And he did.

The previous time that he had performed a marriage ceremony for one of his children, the union had lasted only three years. With his father officiating at a wedding in the Naismith home at 1635 Massachusetts Street—on sister Hellen's birthday—twenty-three-year-old Jack had married Grace Aking, Ann's roommate at William Woods College. Jack and Grace became the parents of two sons within the next few years. But the marriage failed. Grace went on to other husbands and a career as a writer and associate editor on the editorial board of *Reader's Digest,* still keeping the Naismith name for writing purposes.[33] Jack meanwhile bummed around the country for four or more years, working at a variety of jobs. In the early thirties he came back home to live with his parents.

For the first time in their lives, after years of trying, he and his father became pals. They worked and played and talked together, and they took a few trips together, too. Jack became one of Dr. Naismith's favorite traveling companions, whether on a fishing expedition or an academic visitation of universities.[34] Doc Naismith was having a second chance at fatherhood with Jack.

Like the elder Naismith, Jack enjoyed building things. In that way, too, he fitted well into the household. He and Dell Davidson, groundskeeper at the K.U. stadium, took time to build a cabin on the Kaw nineteen miles upriver from Lawrence, halfway between Topeka and Perry. They finished it during the summer of 1931, and from then on the whole Naismith family used it for summer outings. Screened on three sides, it had a canvas to lower in case of rain and it held three double beds and a cot for Mrs. Naismith.

In the academic term of 1931 Jack enrolled at the University of Kansas to give higher education a second try. Sitting with graying temples in classes in elementary logic and English literature, he strove to prove to his father and mother that he could make good.[35] He studied hard during the week and started to drink on Friday and Saturday nights, because weekend drinking seemed the thing to do in collegiate circles. He was still, as ever, violating Dr. Naismith's moral strictures. But the Naismiths accepted him with much more leniency than they once had allowed.

Jack was still a nonconformist in the classroom, and James Naismith had many a chance to be broad-minded and good-humored. When Jack's English professor assigned the first composition of the semester, she instructed the class, "Write what you know about." Jack wrote a theme devilishly entitled "My Night in a Whorehouse." The contents were innocuous enough, but he was counting on the title to scandalize.

After the professor handed back the papers, Jack took his home to show his father. "You should've been ashamed to write anything like that," Dr. Naismith told him. Jack noticed that his father's mustache was quivering ominously, as it did when he tried to suppress indignation. "I know an old-maid English teacher who doesn't agree with you," Jack retorted stubbornly, pointing to the *A* on the paper.[36] Then Jack saw that the quivering mustache had been hiding a grin.

In 1933 Jack was proud to join Sigma Phi Epsilon, the fraternity to which his father and his brother belonged. There had not been a chapter at K.U. during Jack's first try at college. But now, as a Sig Ep, he was a real college student at last, a credit to the Naismith family.

His college days were busy and successful for Jack, but at home affairs were building up to a shock. He did not pay much attention to family finances, and his father, meanwhile, had not grown any more conscious of the value of money than he had ever been. There was rental money coming from the Simmons family in the house down the street, which made that property a self-paying proposition, and there seemed no need to worry. Naismith lent money freely to students or to friends, never keeping records. He contributed to charities when it took all the change in his pocket, and everyone knew he was an easy mark for any collection that came around. He paid his own travel expenses when he spoke at meetings away from home. He wrote rubber checks, innocently, always sure that he had more money in the bank than he did have. Not believing that the condition could really become serious, he neglected to keep up the payments on the house he was living in.[37]

By the early 1930s the depression had hit the Midwest hard. At the University of Kansas the salaries of faculty members were cut as early as 1931. Chancellor Lindley convinced President Franklin D. Roosevelt's federal policy makers that the National Youth Administration should be inaugurated to help young people earn their way through high school and college, but for most persons there was no helpful governmental agency to keep them on their financial feet. Businessmen suffered losses, and foreclosures of all kinds of mortgages became common. After carrying the delinquent Naismith account for many months, the loaning agency prepared to foreclose.[38]

Then for the second time Phog Allen became a dominant influence in the lives of the Naismiths. The news got around that Dr. Naismith was losing his house, and Allen asked him whether it was true. Naismith admitted that it was. "Do you want to keep that house, Doc?" Allen asked.[39] It was a handsome house. Naismith nodded.

Allen knew how to get things done. By now his salary had grown until it was one-third larger than Naismith's (Allen's $4,000 to Naismith's $3,000), but such figures were beside the point.[40] Allen helped because he wanted to, not because he felt guilty about anything. Going straight to the building and loan company, he took an option on the property at 1700 Mississippi Street.[41]

But Naismith was undecided as to the right course to take. He talked the problem over with Jack, admitting how close the family had now come to forfeiture of their home. The loan company, he explained, was ready to seize their residence. Only Phog Allen could keep the roof over their heads.

"Shall we let the company take it?" he asked.

"Yes," Jack replied.[42] He pointed out that the smaller, rental house was large enough for the Naismiths. There was enough space for an additional second-story room to be built above the back part of the house if, accustomed to spacious homes, they wanted it.

James and Maude Naismith decided to be sensible about their way of life. Most of their children were settled. Son-in-law George Stanley, after a period of teaching at the Manual Training High School in Kansas City, Missouri, had graduated from medical college in 1926. Now he, Margaret, and their children were living in Colorado. Hellen and her husband, engineer Leslie H. Dodd, were living with their family in Dallas, Texas. Ann, pretty and soon to be married, was the superintendent of the hospital in Wamego, Kansas. Jimmy was married, and Jack, due to graduate from K.U.'s School of Education in 1934, showed intent of entering matrimony again. With most of their children gone, a smaller house would really be better for the Naismiths, and it would certainly be easier for Maude to manage than a large one. Therefore, they let the loan company foreclose, without letting anyone help them out of their trouble, and in 1934 they made the move to 1708 Mississippi Street.[43]

Everything was relatively quiet again. News of the growing popularity of basketball in the East provided sufficient spice for the Naismiths at this time.

They had all heard, of course, about the shenanigans of a New York sportswriter named Ned Irish. Partly through his efforts, Madison Square Garden's first doubleheader basketball game was played in 1934. After that pair of games, which brought Notre Dame against New York University and St. John's University against Westminster, basketball became one of the great winter attractions in the New York Garden.[44] Jim Naismith was interested, naturally, although he did not become excited. But then he rarely did show excitement about basketball.

Momentous events in the East soon took on a personal tone, though. In 1935 Springfield College, which had been the International Y.M.C.A. Training School when Jim Naismith brought the first game of basketball into its gymnasium, took occasion to honor him. At the Golden Jubilee commencement dinner in June, 1935, the college awarded him its first Edward Norris Tarbell Medal, which bore the inscription: "Awarded to James Naismith of the class of '91 for distinguished service to his Alma Mater." On the face of the medallion was a replica of the famous forty-six-inch plaque of the hurdlers, "The Joy of Effort," or "Brothers of the Wind," which had been made by Sir Robert Tait McKenzie to be set into the wall of the stadium in Stockholm for the 1912 Olympics.[45]

McKenzie, Naismith's boyhood friend and "Uncle Bob" to the Naismith children, was now a famed doctor, physical educator, and sculptor, who, as a British subject, had been knighted for his services. In their goals of service for youth and humanity and in the breadth of their interests and accomplishments the two men were markedly similar. It was fitting, then, that McKenzie should have sculpted the design, judged to be one of the most compellingly beautiful things he had ever produced, for the medal presented to his friend.[46] The Tarbell Medal, nationally publicized as it was, became one of James Naismith's treasured distinctions.

In the fall of 1935 interest was centered again on occurrences in Kansas. Naismith's illness with pneumonia in early October and Ann's marriage to Thomas Lee Dawe at Wamego on October 19 were upheavals enough to last for the entire autumn season. In truth, some of the family said that Papa-Jim's illness was brought on by the excitement Maude Annie's wedding plans stirred up in the family. Indeed, her marriage was a notable event. Attractive Ann, still single as she approached her thirty-first birthday, had been keeping people guessing for a long time about her plans.

But something more spectacular than weddings, pneumonia, medals, or basketball doubleheaders was brewing by then for the Naismiths. Phog Allen had something in mind for Doc Naismith that was international in scope.

26

One Penny...

AFTER Phog Allen had conceived the idea of saving the Naismiths' home, the notion grew into something much bigger than an effort to keep the mortgage from being foreclosed on a kindly professor's home. Allen noticed that the forty-fifth anniversary of basketball was coming in 1936. Furthermore, thanks in large part to Allen's promotional efforts, basketball was reaching a new milestone by being introduced into the international Olympic Games, which were to be held in Berlin in August of 1936. And the Olympics were the top of the ladder in the sports world.[1]

The ancient Olympic Games had been held every four years, uninterrupted, for nearly twelve hundred years—from the 200-yard foot races of 776 B.C. through many an elaborate gathering. Then in A.D. 394 the games were suppressed by the Roman emperor Theodosius. At last, fifteen hundred years later, they were revived by young M. Pierre de Coubertin of France, and the

First Olympiad of modern times was held in 1896 in Athens. Although basketball was played ten years later at the athletic contests in Athens, these were interim games, not part of the regular Olympic cycle. A more nearly legitimate attempt at a basketball Olympiad came in 1904, when the game was included on the Olympic program in St. Louis, Missouri. Five United States teams competed, the Buffalo-German Y.M.C.A. winning the title. However, because the entrants were confined to United States teams, the 1904 basketball tournament was later officially listed as a demonstration. Not until 1936 was basketball officially recognized as a part of the Olympics.[2]

The stage was set for something big, and Dr. Forrest C. Allen took advantage of the situation. Director of the Division of Physical Education and of Intercollegiate Athletics at the University of Kansas, as well as a championship basketball coach, he was nationally known. His word carried influence in sports circles. This season the proposal he advanced was to honor the creator of basketball during the period of the Berlin Olympics. Happily, when he turned his idea over to the National Association of Basketball Coaches, they accepted it.

A campaign was thereupon begun to pay tribute to Naismith by constructing an appropriate memorial during this Olympiad season. A suggested memorial was, timely enough, the gift of a new home for the Naismiths. After they had lived out their lives in it, the house could then be used as a residence of honor for other outstanding men of basketball. Although basketball can be invented only once, illustrious basketball coaches, beginning, perhaps, with Phog Allen, would be logical succeeding recipients of the award.

Another proposal, however, was approved by the committee. Funds would be collected to send Dr. and Mrs. Naismith to the Eleventh Olympic Games in Berlin, enabling the professor to be present when the game he had created was introduced into the famous international competition. In addition, a trip around the world, an annuity, and a memorial at either Lawrence or Springfield were also suggested, to be provided from the same fund. W. S. Chandler, basketball coach at Marquette University in Milwaukee, became chairman of the national committee in charge of arrangements for the Naismith fund, and Forrest C. Allen was made chairman of the Kansas-Oklahoma committee. Naismith was an honorary member of the Committee of Thirteen formed to direct the American basketball portion of the competition in the 1936 Olympics, and collections for the National Naismith Fund began in the fall of 1935.

February 9–15, 1936, in the heart of the basketball season, was designated "Naismith Week." All over the United States at games held on any of the seven "Naismith Nights" one penny from each ticket sold was to be set aside for the Naismith Fund, which would pay the travel expenses of Dr. and Mrs. Naismith to the Olympics.

The first "Naismith Night" basketball game in the United States was played at Lawrence between the high schools of Lawrence and Ottawa, Kansas, two schools who jumped the gun a bit on the official date by playing in late January. One penny was withheld for Naismith from each of five hundred fifteen admissions, and between halves of the game girls from the school pep organizations held blankets outstretched, into which spectators tossed coins totaling nine dollars and ninety-eight cents. By February 10 a headline in the *Lawrence Daily Journal-World* stated with somewhat pathetic pride: "Local Naismith Fund Receipts Reach $51.40."[3]

But the penny campaign picked up momentum. Chancellor Ernest H. Lindley eulogized Naismith at the University of Kansas–Kansas State College basketball game on February 16: "He is a man whose influence has gone further than that of any other man in Kansas."[4] As if to prove the truth of Lindley's words, games went on all over the United States in high schools, colleges, professional arenas, church basements—and the "Naismith penny" was collected at each one. The campaign caught the fancy of the public. Boy Scouts, Girl Scouts, and other groups added their efforts by passing containers for extra donations during the half-time interval of each game. Newspapers reported that "falling nickels could be heard all over Kansas"—and all over the nation.[5] Even in Canada collections were made. In Almonte, Ontario, high-school students and basketball coach W. J. Saunders collected twenty dollars for their famed native son and proudly mailed the money to the national headquarters of the campaign at Milwaukee. Sometimes the noise of coins dropping into tin containers interfered with speakers at radio microphones who were trying to talk about Naismith. Newspapers and magazines carried articles about the campaign and pictures of the man of the hour.

Trying not to be thrown off balance by the fuss being made over him, Naismith remained humble through it all. At the Naismith Night game in Lawrence, listening to the tinkle of small coins and the bustle of a twenty-minute WREN radio broadcast honoring him, he gave athletes and audience a sample of his philosophy: "Don't be afraid to work for humanity and wait for your reward."[6] Thereupon, the crowd gave him a two-minute ovation.

It takes a lot of persons with pennies, even when some nickels are thrown in, to give a man a trip to Europe. One of the largest amounts collected at any game was $105.35 at the Kansas University–Kansas State College game at Lawrence. The campaign that had begun in the fall was maneuvered on through the spring. While final contests were being held to select the American "masters of the hardwood"—the United States team of fourteen that would go to the Olympic Games—the Naismith fund continued slowly to build up.

At home on the K.U. campus that season of 1935–1936, in addition to teaching, Dr. Naismith was busy serving on the university athletic board, composed then of eight faculty members, four alumni, and two students. Away from the campus he was busy giving talks and officiating at athletic ceremonies. The Department of Physical Education was staffed adequately enough that he could be spared from his teaching for frequent off-campus duties. He was within a year of possible retirement, anyway.

To start the winter, he had visited Canada in January, and as the year went on he became busier. For one thing, there were important basketball games going on, and he was called upon to toss up the opening jump ball at many of them. These commitments kept him traveling fast and far. Near the end of the basketball season, when activity grew intense, there were major basketball tournaments in Denver and in New York, half a continent away from each other and only two weeks apart, and he was invited to open both of them.

Maude Naismith had been in ill health for several years, but the excitement of the tournament season and the prospect of a fabulous trip to Berlin did more for her than medicine could. Writing on March 12, 1936, to thank the Almonte High School for its twenty-dollar contribution to the Olympic Fund, Phog Allen commented about her improved health:

Mrs. Naismith . . . has taken a turn of recovery that is surprising since this proposed trip has been broached to her. She immediately picked up in physical demeanor and never have her friends seen her appear better. She is very happy and expectant and she is sure she is going to Berlin. Dr. Naismith chuckles in his jolly Scotch way and says, "You know she is really so much better, it is amazing and she is going to make it."[7]

Dreaming back to that sailboat honeymoon in 1894, James Naismith, romantic to the end of his life, may have anticipated this climax to his career as being a grand second honeymoon. But Phog Allen's optimism proved mistaken. Maude Sherman Naismith did not have an opportunity to become seasick a second time in the name of love. Four months before she expected to sail, something suddenly and grievously interfered.

The annual tournament of the national Amateur Athletic Union, which had been held in Kansas City for fifteen consecutive years, was moved to Denver in the previous season. Now, in this important year of 1936, the A.A.U. invited Naismith to Denver to be honor guest at the games held March 15–21 to decide the two basketball teams that would represent the A.A.U. in the final Olympic tryouts.[8] He accepted, inviting Maude to accompany him.

But this trip was to be their last one together for a while. As they traveled westward through Colorado, she was stricken with a heart attack. Ironically, it occurred while Phog Allen's letter rejoicing in her good health was on its way to Almonte. Fortunately, the attack was not a severe one, and she was able to convalesce at the home of the Naismiths' daughter Margaret Stanley and her doctor husband in Ordway, Colorado. The catch was that she was not well enough to travel with James to the A.A.U. meet. It was his professional duty to go alone, and he went.

As Naismith had expected, the tournament at Denver was a good one. He was pleased that a well-known A.A.U. team from his own state of Kansas—the McPherson Oilers—was a leading contender. As A.A.U. champions of the Missouri Valley, the Oilers had defeated the Metropolitan College All-Stars in New York on March 11 in the "most brilliantly played and spectacular basketball game" that Madison Square Garden had ever seen.[9] Now in Denver, again playing skillfully, they won the national A.A.U. tournament by defeating the Universal Pictures team from Hollywood.

Naismith enjoyed seeing another tournament team, the Denver Safeways. The Safeways held a double appeal for him. Besides being products of Denver, for three years his home, the players were said to be Y.M.C.A. members. Following that line of reasoning, they would have been "his boys" if he had still been physical director at the Denver "Y." But, to his disappointment, they did not even reach the finals.

Notwithstanding tense games, for Naismith the best part of the tournament was the recognition he received. The honors paid him on opening night were representative of what was happening to him over and over that winter and spring. In Denver's city auditorium a crowd of four thousand basketball fans saw the official opening of play performed by the "Father of Basketball" himself. They viewed the introduction of men he had coached in the Denver Y.M.C.A. in 1895–1898, the formal parade of teams past him, and the presentation of a gold medal to him in tribute to his life's work. And they heard his response: "I only wish I could say with my lips what is in my heart."[10]

Maude's illness marred his night of honor in Denver, though, and all his days thereafter. Talking to reporters, James wistfully mentioned her absence ("I wish Mrs. Naismith could have been here"), and reluctantly he left her behind during the remainder of the tournament season.[11]

Basketball play-offs rolled on throughout the nation. One of the teams in which Naismith was interested got into trouble, though. On March 28 at the Y.M.C.A. national tournament in Peoria, Illinois, the Denver Y.M.C.A. team defeated the Wilmerding, Pennsylvania, "Y" for a place in the final Olympic play-offs. But two days before the play-offs opened in New York, the Denver quintet was informed that it had been disqualified for trying to play both ends against the middle. Their fault was that in March they had entered the A.A.U. tournament at Denver with the name "Denver Safeways" and, defeated, had afterward reorganized as a new team for Y.M.C.A. competition.

One columnist explained their innocent irregularity:

The Denver Safeways didn't keep their shirts on. . . . When they lost out by one point in the quarter-finals of the A.A.U. basketball tourney, they went across the street to the Y.M.C.A., where it seems that they were members, one and all, and won the national Y.M.C.A. title in new suits.[12]

Their changeover was not immediately detected, or at least not immediately pounced on by officials. Only after traveling to New York and working out happily in the West Side Y.M.C.A. gym were they stopped by the ire of the rule makers. The Denver players, whether under the banner of the A.A.U. or of the Y.M.C.A., were out of the race.

Victory and defeat, jubilation and dejection, had their turn with many aspiring quintets. By April 3 eight basketball teams from locations all over the United States had been selected for the Olympic finals. Assembled in Madison Square Garden were five college teams—from the University of Washington, the University of Arkansas, DePaul University of Chicago, Utah State University, and Temple University; two A.A.U. teams—the Hollywood Universal Pictures and the McPherson Oilers; and the Y.M.C.A. team from Wilmerding. The arrangement was that the winner among these eight would place seven men on the Olympic basketball team, the runner-up would contribute five men, and the other six teams would give two outstanding players, making a total of fourteen tall young men to represent the United States in Berlin.

To the disappointment of James Naismith and Forrest C. Allen, the basketball team of the University of Kansas had not quite made it into the play-offs, being defeated by Utah State in a two-out-of-three series of games. But Phog Allen would, nonetheless, travel to Berlin as director-in-chief of the Olympic basketball expedition. He was an important figure during this Olympiad, and, besides, many experts called him the best basketball coach in the country.

Of the eight teams that had reached Madison Square Garden, Naismith was most impressed by the two A.A.U. teams—the Oilers and the Universals. He had his favorite, too. He was proud that the Oilers team from McPherson, Kansas—"colorful giants" and national A.A.U. champions already—was the leading candidate for the Olympic team.[13]

Detracting from the harmony of eight champion basketball teams in motion, a few sour notes were sounded around the gates of Madison Square Garden. Not everyone was as enthusiastic as Naismith about the Olympic Games. The fact that United States athletes would be going to anti-Semitic Germany, country of the Nazis, had aroused protests among anti-Nazi organizations. Threats of picketing the Olympic basketball tryouts were heard, therefore, even though several Jewish men were among the competitors in Madison Square Garden—four in the Temple University group and two on the Universal Pictures squad. The goal of the American anti-Nazi movement was a general boycott of the Olympic Games. In fact, one of the members of the American Olympic Committee, a representative of the Jewish Welfare Board, was a leader in the attempt to have the United States boycott the Games.

The Jewish member, however, was dropped from the Olympic Committee for alleged nonattendance at meetings, and most people preferred to rationalize American participation in a Nazi-sponsored event. They pointed out that when Berlin was chosen in the summer of 1931 as site of the 1936 Olympic Games, the Nazis had not yet come to power.[14] Because of general enthusiasm for the Olympics, the boycott movement did not succeed, and threatened picketing of Madison Square Garden did not hurt basketball attendance.

On the first night of the long-awaited finals a brilliant program was carried out. Experts predicted that competition would be even keener than that to come in the Olympic Games themselves—and the spectators were not disappointed. As one reporter stated: "The show had everything. There even was a touch of sentiment as Dr. James Naismith, 74-year-old physical education instructor who invented the sport forty-five years ago, officially opened the tournament."[15] The huge crowd sat spellbound through six hours of basketball pyrotechnics—the longest basketball program the Garden had ever held—deciding that the affair surpassed even the high expectations held for it.

As for James Naismith, he found the night perfect from the moment he tossed up the ball at 5:30 P.M. and heard himself acclaimed by twelve thousand persons. It was a glorious six-plus hours—through the playing of eight skillful teams and the breathtaking victories of four of them (including the McPherson Oilers) until spectators, players, and officials left the Garden shortly before midnight. He confessed that he was "more pleased and excited than a farm boy at his first circus."[16]

Ironically, midway in the gala opening night of Olympic tryouts in Madison Square Garden, a short distance away the most notorious man in America was executed. Bruno Richard Hauptmann, alleged killer in the famous Lindbergh kidnapping case, made bigger headlines than the tryouts did when he died in the electric chair at 8:44 P.M. in the State Prison at Trenton. A country boy's night at a circus was also a convicted murderer's last night on Death Row.

American kidnapping and Nazi mobilization pushed aside for the moment, after the eliminations of the opening night at Madison Square Garden, four teams came back to play again the second night: both of the A.A.U. teams (McPherson Oilers and Universal Pictures), one of the college teams (University of Washington), and the Y.M.C.A. team (Wilmerding Y.M.C.A.). The outcome in the semi-finals was that the Universals defeated the Wilmerding Y.M.C.A. and the Oilers defeated Washington. The Oilers helped put thousands of basketball fans into a turmoil of excitement that night, and, called "the world's tallest and best team," they were favored to beat the Universals and win the finals.[17]

On the third and final night in Madison Square Garden the

frenzied cheers of thousands of fans urged on a sensationally played game between the two teams. But the Oilers lost to the underdog Universals—the team they had defeated in Denver a little more than two weeks before—by a single, heartbreaking point. The victory of the University of Washington over the Wilmerding Y.M.C.A. that night rounded out the ranking of the top four teams.

The basketball play-offs were over. Final tryouts in twenty-some other sports were yet to come—from fencing on April 29 to yachting near mid-July. Then would arrive the climax—the Olympic Games.

Although disappointed that the Kansas A.A.U. team had not won the national play-offs and that the Kansas University team had not quite reached the play-offs at all, Naismith had other things to think about. His pre-Olympic season of activity was not over.

Honors continued to pour upon him during the pre-Olympic months. Gold medals, citations, honorary memberships piled up in his collection of souvenirs. At K.U., Bernard ("Poco") Frazier, the university's noted sculptor, made a plaster mask of Naismith's face, and amusement was provided when the famous Naismith mustache became stuck in the plaster. Edwin Elbel made a sketch of Naismith, photographic in its likeness, and had reproductions made for Naismith fans.[18] On one of the copies Naismith inscribed an appropriate sentiment—"With kindest regards to Dr. F. C. Allen, the father of basketball coaching, from the father of the game———James Naismith, 1936"—and gave it to Phog Allen.[19] Phog framed the picture and put it on display in his office.

Although Naismith professed a desire to avoid drawing attention to himself, he consented to have cards printed that displayed the three achievements of which, at the moment, he was the proudest.

JAMES NAISMITH, M.D.

INVENTOR OF BASKETBALL

LIFE CHAIRMAN OF RULES COMMITTEE[20]

Meanwhile, the campaign for the National Naismith Fund went on. By late spring a net sum of $4,794.96 had been collected in forty-three states, subtotals showing that Kansas had contributed more than thirteen hundred dollars of the sum. The greatest amount provided by a single game remained the $105.35 collected at the game between the University of Kansas and Kansas State College early in the season. By summer the total amount was enough to send Dr. Naismith to the Olympic Games and on a tour of Europe. There was not enough money, however, to fulfill the grand plans for a trip around the world, an annuity, and a permanent memorial, projects that had all been envisaged at the beginning of the fund-raising campaign. One penny a person might pay for a moment of glory, but it was not enough for a lifetime pension.

27

...And a Moment of Glory

JULY came, the month for sailing to Berlin, and Maude remained invalided. James Naismith had left her behind in 1916 for service in the Mexican Border War, in 1917 for an American tour with the wartime Y.M.C.A., and in 1917–1919 for war work in France; but this peacetime adventure, the greatest journey of his life, was one he wanted to share with her. Their second honeymoon, however, did not happen. When Naismith departed from the port of New York on July 10, he left her behind in Dallas in the care of daughter Hellen Dodd and of son James.[1]

Young Jim was pleased to resume the job of caring for his mother, a task with which he had once been so familiar. But Jim and his wife, Frances, laughed with tender amusement to observe that their husky Negro maid, Big Frances, was the only person Mother Naismith would permit to lift her in and out of the bathtub.[2]

Knowing that Maude was in good hands, James made the most of his vacation. Arriving at Glasgow eleven days after embarking, he first visited relatives in Scotland. Then he traveled south through England. On July 29 he sailed from London on the first leg of his passage to the Continent. In Holland he stopped in The Hague before going by rail to Brussels. After a three-day stay in Belgium, he headed toward Berlin, the great goal, after all, of his whole trip.

The Winter Games, added to the Olympic program in 1924, had been successfully held in February, 1936, at Garmisch-Partenkirchen, in the Bavarian Alps. By now, midsummer, the Berlin committee, sparing no expense in its two years of preparation, had built a sports field and arranged the most spectacular yet of all Olympics, the Eleventh Olympiad, to be held August 1–16 in their magnificent stadium.

When James Naismith arrived in Berlin, the city was overflowing with people and color and sound. Decorations began at the railway stations and extended all the way to the Olympic stadium on the Reich Sports Ground. Oak-leaf garlands and mammoth wreaths hung from the roofs of trainsheds and terminal halls at all the main stations. Each station was surrounded by poles bearing banners forty-five feet long: the flags of the fifty-three competing nations, the Olympic flag (five interlocking rings representing the five continents), and the Nazi flag (red background with black swastika against a white circle). Although the swastika symbol was omitted by the International Olympic Committee from Olympic documents, it was the German national flag and was, therefore, conspicuous everywhere.

The official Olympic highway, colorful with flowerbeds and ornaments, ran for five miles: from the Lustgarten along the street called Unter den Linden—beneath the Brandenburg Gate—on the Charlottenburger Chausee—under the tall trees of the Tiergarten—and between the clipped hedges and double files of sycamores of the Heerstrasse. Along the route, loudspeakers in the form of silver cressets were set one-eighth of a mile apart, and from them Viennese waltzes and quickstep marches alternated with official announcements. The five miles were one long avenue of excitement.

"The opening of any Olympics is a heart-stirring spectacle,"[3] one viewer phrased his reaction; and when the Eleventh Olympiad program began at 4:00 P.M. on August 1, the stadium was jammed for that spectacle. The stands, located on a 325-acre ground, seated one hundred thousand, and the seats were full that afternoon. On the field more than five thousand athletes from fifty-two nations, in their varicolored uniforms, marched in ranks; and in front of them, in native costume, was the Greek shepherd Spiridion Loues, who had won the first Olympic marathon at Athens in 1896.[4]

To open the games, Adolf Hitler ascended ceremoniously into the elevated patron's box. He had become Reichschancellor on January 30, 1933, a year and a half after the site of the 1936 Olympics had been chosen. In 1934, upon the death of aged Reichpresident Paul von Hindenburg, he had combined the offices of Reichpresident and Reichschancellor in himself and assumed the title of "Führer." Now he was the Nazi dictator of Germany. When he entered the stadium a forest of arms outstretched in Nazi salute and a bellow of "Heil Hitler" from spectators and participants greeted him. A little girl in blue, her fair hair bound by a chaplet of flowers, curtsied and handed him a bouquet of roses, and Spiridion Loues presented him with a sprig of wild olive brought from a sacred grove on Mount Olympus. Then Hitler spoke one line: "I proclaim open the Olympic Games of Berlin, celebrating the Eleventh Olympiad of the modern era."[5]

In all the ceremony centered around Hitler, only one gesture was lacking: in neither body nor voice did athletes from the United States join in the salute to der Führer.

After the Olympiad had been officially declared open, blue-jacketed sailors raised the Olympic flag, a trumpet fanfare sounded, and a gun salute went off in the distance. Three thousand white doves were released from hundreds of covered cages, and an orchestra played the "Olympic Hymn." The ceremonies were climaxed by the arrival in the stadium of the final torchbearer from a relay team of more than three thousand men of seven nationalities who had carried a flame across Europe from the ancient field of Olympia, Greece, home of the Olympics. The torch had crossed the Czechoslovakian-German border at 11:45 A.M. the previous day, and German runners had carried it on through the night while the country populace waited up to see it pass. Now the Olympic Flame—the huge torch at the open end of the stadium—was set blazing from the fire of the relay torch, and the Olympic Games began.

People all over the world were following the Olympic news. Back home in the United States the city of Los Angeles lit its own traditional Olympic torch on the same day that the Olympic Flame was lit in the stadium at Berlin. In the presence of consular representatives, Mayor Frank L. Shaw pulled a ribbon that started a flame on the peristyle of the Memorial Coliseum. Lit for the first time since the 1932 Olympic Games had closed, the big torch was to burn for the duration of the 1936 Olympiad.

Despite gray skies and rain showers, the Olympics were a good show. Even der Führer thought so. At the outset he had intended to be present in the patron's box only at the opening ceremony. But never having seen a track and field competition before, he decided to watch one day's events. One day was enough to change his mind. Thereafter his box was never empty except on rare occasions when affairs of state kept him away. At nearly every session he was present to acknowledge the Nazi salutes below him and to watch the Nazi flag hauled to the top of the mast after the victory of each German athlete. His unexpected daily attendance caused "the great disgust" of the secret police, whose responsibility it was to guard him while he sat in an elevated box among a crowd of one hundred thousand or more persons.[6]

Other government dignitaries became regular followers of the games. Hermann Goering, Reich Air Minister, was one of them. One news release showed both Germany and Italy represented together at the stadium: der Führer, Crown Prince Umberto of Italy, Field Marshal Werner von Blomberg, and German officials Rudolf Hess and William Frick posed in a group for a photograph.

Considering the patriotic fervor in Germany, it was not surprising that the Nazis found an excuse to display their flag in two places on the walls of the stadium even though only one flag of each of the fifty-three nations was supposed to be shown. What was surprising, however, was that the American flag showed up three times, outdoing the Nazis. The reason was that three nations officially dropped from competition, and because fifty-three flagpoles had been installed, for a little while three poles were bare. Thereupon, whatever the luck or logic, two extra American flags and one Nazi flag were found to fill the empty spaces.

The Nazi influence did not much disturb James Naismith. But other things were going on that almost turned his journey into a farce. When the Father of Basketball arrived in Berlin, it was discovered that no ceremony had been arranged to honor him at the opening of the basketball Olympics, even though he had traveled from America to see his game being played for the first time in this famous competition. Furthermore, he was denied admittance to the Olympic Games, for his name had been stricken from the pass list. He had been snubbed, his friends charged, by the American Olympic Committee and its head, Avery Brundage.

After the faux pas was made public, steps were quickly taken to straighten everything out. "We managed to get him a pass for all games," reported James Tobin, an Olympic basketball referee from New York and a Naismith supporter.[7] In addition, an appropriate program of tribute was arranged.

Short though the notice was for arranging a special program, Karl Diem, the general secretary of the International Federation of Basketball Leagues, and other officials planned a ceremony that was in keeping with the color and display of the rest of the Olympics. In a miniature replica of the opening-day parade of nations in the stadium, basketball-playing countries honored the Father of Basketball in a demonstration held August 7 in the Hall of German Sports. Speeches of tribute were delivered by important men from the world of athletics, and from a dais Naismith gave an answering address. As a symbol of the peace that prevailed among the nations gathered there, a wreath of olive leaves was given to him.

Fifty-two nations were represented on the stadium field on opening day of the 1936 Olympics, and twenty-two of them brought basketball teams, the largest number entered in any Olympic team competition that year. But the number of participating countries dwindled slightly. The Spanish team, already settled in the Olympic village when civil war broke out in Spain, was called home to join the fighting forces, thus missing the basketball Olympics. When time for the basketball games came, then, only twenty-one teams, each displaying its national flag, could line up on the field in front of Naismith to be addressed by him. He walked by each group of players, met the representative of each, and received the cheers of every nation from Mexico's "Alabeebo" to Japan's "Banzai." When each nation dipped its flag to him, he confessed later, tears came to his eyes. It was his greatest moment.[8]

The whole affair astounded the man who, until recent months, had received little recognition in the United States. Despite the slight given him by the American Olympic Committee, which he tended to minimize and forget, he was having the time of his life. For the first time he realized that he had created a spectacular international game.

True, basketball was an old-timer in the world by now, said to be the most widely played game on the globe next to tennis and soccer, as he well knew. The First International Basketball Conference had been held at Geneva in 1932, and as a result of that conference the Fédération internationale de basketball amateur (FIBA) had been formed on June 18, 1932. But not until now had the originator of basketball felt personally the impact of his game on the world and the extent of his own fame. Basketball, he acknowledged, had gone far beyond his wildest expectations.[9]

After the poignant moments of the honor ceremonies, Naismith tossed up the ball at the first game, between Estonia and France.[10] Remembering the olive wreath of peace presented to him at the pregame ceremonies, he was pleased to see international fun and fair play put into practice, as groups of players shouted happily to teammates in their own languages It was good, for example, to see Japan and China forget their national ill feeling over Manchukuo for the moment and play brisk basketball.[11] He enjoyed the Philippine team, too.

Play briskly everyone did, but the playing court and rules of play were different from those some of the players, including Americans, had been using at home. The court, Naismith did not like; the rules, he did. The Olympic basketball games were played outdoors on a court covered with a combination of sand, sawdust, and salt, where the playing surface became packed when wet and no stops, therefore, needed to be made in the event of rain. As it happened, some of the play took place in a heavy rain.

More to Naismith's pleasure than the rain and the sawdust court were the official basketball rules employed during the Olympics. Amid controversy, rules in the United States and Canada had been undergoing changes in the spring of 1936. But at the Olympics those new rules did not show up, nor did the ones of the previous few years. The Olympic regulations used were the basketball rules in force before 1932. Most notably, there were no center line and no ten-second rule; and the center jump after a free throw was retained. Naismith got to see basketball played as he thought it should be played—with skill and good sportsmanship and without the encumbrance of rules that, he thought, were choking the game in the United States.[12]

The U.S. team fared well under the Olympic rules, defeating Estonia 52–28, the Philippines 56–23, and Mexico 25–10, as well as winning from Spain 2–0 by forfeit. The United States showed its superiority to the world's leading basketball teams. As a happy climax, at the close of the basketball Olympics, Naismith watched the United States team (Johnson, Fortenberry, Ragland, Knowles, Wheatley, Bishop, and Shy), superior in height with some six-foot-eight-inch and six-foot-nine-inch players, defeat Canada in the final game 19–8 to win its first basketball Olympics.[13]

He probably regretted that he could not see both teams win, for he had loyalties on both the United States and the Canadian sides. It was a team from his native Ontario, the Windsor Ford V-8s, augmented by three players from British Columbia, who had won the Canadian championship and had gone to Berlin to the Olympics. As far as loyalty is concerned, though, he felt a certain partiality toward a good many of the teams, for the coaching staffs of the Olympic basketball teams included seventeen graduates of Springfield College.[14]

Basketball was not the only activity that held Naismith's interest, of course. He was at the Olympics to see other sports, too. It was a great year in track-and-field events, for example. Negro Jesse Owens of the United States was on his way to the sports record that helped him to be voted the greatest track-and-field athlete of the half-century in the 1950 Associated Press poll. Owens won the 100-meter race, the broad jump, and the 200-meter race, besides running first leg on the championship U.S. 400-meter relay team. He won four Olympic gold medals and took home four of the tiny potted German oak trees provided as living memorials of 1936 Olympic victories. Although a story persists that racist Hitler refused to shake hands with the great Negro athlete, the probability is that Hitler did not allow an opportunity for handshaking to occur. Whatever der Führer's reaction, Owens dominated the Olympic scene so completely that his name was later hammered into bronze and imbedded in the stone Marathon Gate of the Berlin stadium.

Even more exciting than Jesse Owen's fabulous performance was, for Naismith, the 1,500-meter race. Glenn Cunningham, the middle-distance champion from the University of Kansas and plucky ex-cripple, was one of the leading contenders in an Olympic contest that no one wanted to miss. Counting Cunningham, the glittering competition included five finishers from the 1932 Olympic race, an array unequaled in any other event. One of Glenn's leading competitors was John ("Jack") Lovelock from New Zealand, at that time a medical student at St. Mary's Hospital in London and a 133-pound projectile on the track.[15]

Cunningham was not in his best form, for cold and wet weather in Berlin had hampered his training. A light workout three days before the race had left his once-crippled legs so stiff that his condition was noticeable in his walk. But when the big day came, the young man who had once been told he would never walk again was ready to run against the world's best trackmen.

On August 6 the stands were packed with spectators for the running events. Hitler himself timed his entrance so that he arrived just as the twelve contestants lined up on the red clay track. And it turned out to be a great day for track fans. Cunningham set the pace during much of the 1,500-meter length, but Lovelock, running an almost perfect race, used a terrific sprint to overtake and pass Cunningham in the last lap of the oval track. Fifty yards from the end, Lovelock had the temerity to look around to find out whether his rivals were close, and all he could see worth noticing was Cunningham, eight yards behind. When they crossed the finish line, Lovelock first and Cunningham six yards behind, both had broken the world's record, and all five place-winners that day had broken the Olympic record set four years previously.

Naismith would have liked to see young Cunningham come in first, for every step Glenn ever ran—or even walked—had been won against astounding odds. But Jack Lovelock, too, was the kind of runner Naismith admired—one who had had misfortune strike his legs and had turned that bad luck into good.

When Lovelock was a college student in New Zealand, a broken leg that he had received in a rugby game had ended his athletic career—or so people thought. Forbidden to play rugby or other active games again, he turned to running for light exercise, and here he proved himself a winner. After he had amazingly broken a world track record, however, an operation on one of his knees seemed to mark the end of cinder tracks and medals for him. During the months after his operation, he did not run at all, and it seemed impossible that he could ever compete in a race again. But eventually he did; and today he had won the greatest race of his life.[16]

To Naismith, both Cunningham and Lovelock ran like champions that day in Berlin. And the Finnish distance runners were worth watching, too. All in all, the track events provided the kind of excitement an Olympic spectator would cross the ocean to see.

Elaborate basketball ceremonies and thrilling Olympic races were not the only pleasant memories Naismith stored up in Berlin. To his delight, he was invited one night to dine with Hitler and the coaching staffs of all the Olympic nations. There were other dinners, as well, and other programs to attend. Flags and fanfare—honors and exhibitions—through it all he passed unaffectedly before the dignitaries of international organizations and the high officials of nations.

Then, when the tumult had ceased, when the color and martial music of the Olympic festivities were over, he began to travel about to see Europe at his leisure. He was not, however, finished with ceremonies. In Switzerland, elected honorary president of the International Federation of Basketball Leagues, he had one more ritual in which to participate. Proud of his new presidency but as modest as always, he was embarrased by the huge bouquet of flowers presented to him upon his acceptance of the appointment.

At last he was able to travel quietly for a few weeks along the byways of Europe. He spent the rest of August and the early part of September visiting, in all, fourteen countries. He said that he did not want to see the castles and cathedrals of the past but the living people of the present day. Nor did he trouble himself much with political problems. The fact that Scotland's favorite diversion seemed to be betting on greyhound races was of greater concern to him than a change of government in Spain.

Always interested in the problems of young people, he reached out for the spirit of youth, bringing back with him both pride and anxiety over what he found. He felt an honest worry about the unemployed and idle young persons of Scotland and England and a misplaced admiration for the self-confident German boys whom the government had drilled in physical exercises and disciplined in national spirit from the age of nine. Indeed, he went so far as to call the United States a generation behind Germany in its program of physical and emotional development of young people. Lacking a sense for the deeper implications of economic and political instability, he did not guess, as he sailed for home, that war in Europe was almost exactly three years away.

At home at the University of Kansas, life was continuing without him. While he was away the first summer Band Camp—later to become the nationally recognized Midwestern Music and Art Camp—had been established, and other equally important activities were going on. It was time to go back to work.[17]

Returning to the United States by way of Canada, he traveled to Ontario to visit his relatives around Almonte and Bennie's Corners. They did not realize until later that he was on his way home from the honors of the Olympics, and he did not mention the fact to them.[18]

Back home on September 13, 1936, his moment of glory past, he philosophically commented that his newspaper photographs had found their proper end in the outdoor privies of Lawrence, where periodicals of the past months now lay discarded. Then he quietly settled down to his usual way of life.[19]

28

The Ripening Years

JAMES NAISMITH said that his happiest moment occurred when he saw his game played in the Olympics, but he was not the kind of person to spend the rest of his life dreaming about that single high point.

In his mid-seventies he had not changed much from the youthful professor he was at the turn of the century. In those earlier days when he sat decorously in the surrey beside his wife as they drove out on Sundays, he probably really belonged, much less decorously, in the children's rowdy little pony cart following behind, where life was being lived a bit more boisterously than convention approved. He managed, though, to live in both the world of convention and the world of fun simultaneously. To the end of his days he lived that way, zestfully, even when his appearance belied the truth. To Naismith clean living and exuberance and an occasional touch of humor went hand in hand.[1]

To many persons he seemed a quiet, unassuming individual with the erect carriage of a much younger fellow and the manners of a Victorian gentleman. His daughter-in-law Grace described him in these words:

He looked like the highly moral—but in no sense stuffy—man. that he was. His blue eyes were kind, with crinkles at the corners. He had a heavy mustache, which looked prickly. His head was a bit square, as was his stocky, straight body.[2]

But to his best friends, who had seen his eyes snap and his mustache quiver with indignation, he was more than a moral person with kind blue eyes and a prickly mustache. He was a vigorous, vital man. Even in old age he was quick and energetic in movement, with the firm, brisk stride of a soldier. Sturdy and broad-shouldered, keenly alert, he made a stir, his partisans said, when he passed through a room, becoming the center of interest wherever he was, whether he wanted to or not. He just did not walk quietly.[3]

On the other.hand, some of his acquaintances pointed out that he never attempted to draw attention to himself and was content to sit on the sidelines, chuckling quietly, at a party. They insisted that he never pushed himself into the foreground. This was apparently true. Even those who observed the stir he created recognized his inherent modesty.[4] But sometimes he retired so modestly into the background that it might seem he did so for the pure enjoyment of the sudden recognition that would inevitably ensue.

He related two such incidents in his book *Basketball*. One happened during a visit to Morningside College in Sioux City.

One morning I dropped into the Morningside College gym and found a pick-up basketball game in progress. The boys were in need of a referee for the game, and one of the players glanced over and suggested that they get me to act in this capacity. Another of the boys looked at me and remarked, "Huh! Come on! That old duffer never saw a game of basketball."

That evening I spoke at a banquet, and among the group were three of the boys who had played that morning. When the banquet was finished, the big fellow who had made the remark came up and shook hands. He asked me if I had been in the gym that day, and I told him that I had. A red glow came over his face.[5]

It seemed, indeed, the offender's "red glow" of embarrassment that Naismith savored.

Another incident occurred at a basketball tournament in the Coliseum in Indianapolis.

I was to speak at the final game of the tournament, and arrived at the Coliseum to find that the doors had been closed. There were no seats left, and many people were being turned away. At the door I presented a reserved seat ticket and an official's badge, only to be informed by the guard that he could allow no one to enter. I explained to him that I was to speak there that evening, but he only smiled and shook his head. As I stood there chuckling to myself, a captain of police stepped up to me and asked what the trouble was. I explained my predicament. He asked my name, and when I told him he exploded, "Good Lord, man, why didn't you say so long ago?"[6]

In many ways James Naismith was a paradox. A physically strong man, he was a deeply emotional person and was not ashamed of his feelings, whether they were displayed in tears or in laughter. He was a gentle person but a determined one, whose mind, once set on an ideal, could never be changed. Although a peace-loving man, to him ideas were worth fighting for, whether on a personal level or an international one.

His intimate friends said of him, "Jim is a keg of dynamite waiting to blow up."[7] The beauty of his nature had always been, of course, that he never quite blew. When he grew angry, he walked off his mood and returned to laugh at the thing that had disturbed him. His anger was a snort, and his laughter was a roar.[8]

Fitting with his informality of mood was his casualness in dress. He was still the rough-and-ready man from the Canadian woods who preferred to wear kangaroo-leather shoes with round toes and hooked lacing and rough tweeds even when everyone else was dressed up. Never intent on good grooming, he made striking contrast to his well-dressed wife, yet together they formed a picture of gentility.[9]

"My mother is a lady," her daughters said proudly of Maude Sherman Naismith.[10]

"He's every inch a gentleman," said those who knew Dr. James Naismith well.[11]

Morally he remained a model of clean living and virtue, the honest nineteenth-century man practicing the qualities he had been preaching to twentieth-century boys. The central impulse that ruled his life was the desire to do well whatever job came his way ("We can't work haphazardly at things and expect to get anywhere"), with self-discipline enough to face small daily tasks and courage to face the great ones. He did not try to frame his way of life into a grand set of rules, though. Of philosophers he said scoffingly that they "look at their own insides too much."[12] Still, as a neighbor who knew him insisted, he was as firm as any scholastic philosopher in his assertion that the body is the immediate organ and instrument of the soul. As Naismith explained his belief, "When God breathed in man he gave him a living soul . . . the hands, the feet, as parts of the soul, may be taught goodness too."[13] And through physical exercise he tried to bring goodness to the hands, the feet, and all the other parts of man.

He was a nondrinker, a nonsmoker, and a pious man, even after he forsook the strait-laced Sabbath worship of his middle years. Once in his old age he remarked indulgently to son Jim, "If I thought I'd get as much enjoyment out of smoking as you seem to, I might start myself."[14] But he never did.[15]

He had a reputation for being a nonswearing man, too. When his grandsons were growing up they tried to trick him into profanity, but without success. Even when the set of false teeth that he had worn and hated most of his life fell out of his mouth and skidded embarrassingly on an icy street, his ejaculation was gentlemanly. A favorite exclamation of his was the phrase "Judas Priest!" and a favorite epithet was the adjective "bloody." The latter word was a bit of British profanity that had lost its coarse connotation when he crossed the border from Canada into the United States.[16]

But the belief that he never used any kind of coarse language was a myth. Upon occasion he slipped—as, for instance, when the Model T would not start, despite his use of the hand crank, when he and his family were already late for church. He did not hold his tongue because of passers-by, either.

As the university grew and the size of the faculty expanded, some of his colleagues knew him only from seeing him walk across the campus or stand at the streetcar stop near Robinson Gymnasium, but they had all heard anecdotes. "He's a funny old coot," they remarked carelessly and added, "a fresh-air-and-exercise fanatic."[17] Students often saw him hurrying around the gymnasium even after he had turned over the teaching of his physical education classes to younger men. It was rumored among K.U. undergraduates that the old professor chinned himself in the college gym.

Rumors about James Naismith's physical feats were usually true. From the youthful days of strenuous work on an Ontario farm into an old age of planned exercise, he was always an active and extremely strong person. His daughters and sons had seen examples of his strength in the days when he could pick a recalcitrant Jack up from the dining table by the back of the neck. Too, one of his sons had been present when Doc Naismith lost patience with a clumsy football player and threw the husky athlete into a corner of the gym. Into his old age the Naismith children proclaimed their pride in their father's prowess. "He could kill any man who might attack him," young Jim once said of him. "We never worry about him."[18]

His youngest child conceded that the only sport in which he could outdo his father was track. "I outran him once—when I was sixteen and he was sixty-eight," Jim remembered wistfully. "I felt a tremendous sense of security whenever I was around him."[19]

On the moral side, sophisticated persons grew impatient with Doc Naismith. "He's a do-gooder," a young faculty wife said deprecatingly.[20]

But many of those who had associated closely with him displayed a devotion sometimes reverent. "He's the most completely *pure* man I've ever known," said a colleague who knew him at work and at home throughout the last two decades of his life.[21] When Naismith was a virile, young-appearing man in his early forties, the head of the student health service said, "He's a man I could put into bed with my daughter at night and know she'd get up in the morning as chaste as she was before."[22]

In truth, a quality of inviolable innocence clung to Naismith all his life.

At home, despite his high standards of behavior, he was a hearty person who enjoyed a good story. He was, however, a moral person who felt no need to give constant reminders of his morality. As Lawrence sportswriter Earl Potter put it, he was a "real" fellow. For this reason, Maude Naismith sometimes had to be a censor of family propriety. When some of the grown-up children came home on a weekend visit, the Naismiths gathered around the dining table, and Jack and Ann vied with each other in telling anecdotes and jokes. Maude, being deaf, could not hear the stories that her children told, but she watched the twinkle in her husband's eyes as he listened, and she knew when the jokes had grown rowdy. "Now, James, that's enough," she would admonish, laying her hand on his arm, and that was all she needed to say.[23] Her family recognized and respected her signal.

Purity and high principles brought their penalties, unfortunately. Financial problems plagued the Naismith family off .and on throughout most of their lives. Naismith's creation of basketball brought opportunities, it is true; but he never believed that he deserved money for that creation. Although he could have earned an enormous income with a royalty of, say, a nickel on each admission to a basketball game, when a lawyer tried to convince him that he should attempt to obtain a patent on the game, Naismith sent the man away. Once, urged on by Phog Allen, he weakened and let his name be used as an endorsement of the Rawlings basketball, and this endorsement brought him the only infinitesimal bit of income that he ever accepted for being the creator of basketball. He received small regular payments from the Rawlings company, and his daughter Ann continued to receive checks for a few years after he died. All other offers over the years to "sell" his name were turned down, however, including one from a cereal company advertising on a national radio network.

At long last when the big offer came, the delayed chance of a lifetime, he did not weaken. The opportunity to become wealthy without labor came after introduction of basketball into the Olympic Games had made the nation Naismith-conscious. After his name and face had become well known, a tobacco company offered him a sum reported to be, variously, from seventy-five thousand to half a million dollars for his endorsement of their cigarettes, the money to be paid over a ten-year period.

Naismith did not consult his children, but he called his grandchildren together. He told them that he had been offered an income large enough for the rest of his life for his public approval of a product he believed detrimental to the health of young people. Guided by his comments, his grandchildren made the decision that he should not sacrifice his life's principles for this unexpected fortune. Pleased with the kids, he thereupon gave the cigarette company the negative reply that he undoubtedly had intended all along to give.[24]

Years later, when Hellen Naismith Dodd's son was working as a salesman, the sales manager of the firm gave his employees a training talk with the theme: "Don't underestimate the power of a man's convictions."[25] In the sales manager's reference to a prominent man and a cigarette company, young Mr. Dodd delightedly recognized his grandfather. Impractical about finances to the end of his life, James Naismith left his heirs a heritage greater than money when he showed them how a man can uphold his principles.

The national news magazine *Time* once used his photograph with the text: "Shrewd enough to invent the game, James A. Naismith was not shrewd enough to exploit it." In addition, this caption was printed: "His invention paid him in pennies."[26] *Time*'s phrases were flashy enough to please the public, but for those who knew Dr. Naismith the phrase "not shrewd enough" was faulty. They felt that he knew all along what he was doing.

Some people, including his sons and daughters, admittedly thought that Papa-Jim was impractical and overimpulsive. The Naismith children were proud of their father's mind as well as his moral principles, admiring his high intelligence and inventive talent. But they affectionately called him their "stupid genius" because of the absent-minded blunders he committed. His slips were often no more extraordinary than driving his car up the university hill, parking it behind the gym, and then at the end of the day riding the streetcar home or accepting a ride with a colleague. All that this act of absent-mindedness meant was that Jack or young Jim was sent to bring the car home. But some of the professor's lapses were more startling than this.

One of them happened when he was devising a forerunner of modern tent-camping arrangements. To do this he made up a tent with an open side that fastened to the rear of his Model T. The arrangement worked fine, but when he started to go from the campsite into town for groceries he spoiled the whole setup by forgetting to unfasten the tent from the car. With the stakes jerked out and the tent flapping behind the Ford, only the shouts of onlookers stopped him.

He made a more serious blunder when he built a second-floor sleeping porch onto the house at 1708 Mississippi Street. Maybe he should have stopped with three rooms downstairs and three rooms upstairs, as he originally constructed the house, but he wanted a sleeping porch like the one on the house on Massachusetts Street. Anyway, by now he was an old hand at building houses, and a careful carpenter. Setting in the windows, he made sure that they would be at the same wall level as the other windows on that floor by carefully checking the height at the top. He forgot, however, that the new windows were shorter than the old ones. When installed, they were high above the floor—too high to let in the cool breezes of summer nights at bed level—and that had been the purpose of the new room.

To correct his miscalculation he built a platform for the bed, with steps leading up to it. That monument to absent-mindedness in his bedroom would have been irksome enough, but, to make him feel worse, Maude fell down those steps one night and hurt herself.

Naismith was coaxed into another activity, far removed from his hobby of building houses. Launching Papa-Jim on the project of writing a book about basketball, his family thought that he might at last make some money out of his famous game. But all he accomplished as a budding author was the renewal of his family's resentment against Phog Allen. Before Naismith got his project much beyond the thinking stage, Allen, already the author of *My Basketball Bible,* began his second book. An unacknowledged race developed between the two men, for it appeared that there would be much duplication of material in their finished products.

Working slowly and painfully, Naismith learned that formulating thirteen rules and originating a new game were easier than writing about those accomplishments. Bogged down in problems of sequence and in grammatical constructions, he finally called Jack to his aid. Jack, then in college and fresh from classes in English composition, started working with him.

After a year on the book, they moved out to the cabin on the Kaw to spend the summer writing. Naismith dictated from a notebook full of material, while Jack wrote and rewrote. The manuscript, as it grew, proved rambling and repetitious. Some passages were vague or ambiguous.

When the job of writing a book became too much for the two of them, they went outside the family for help. For one hundred fifty dollars the English professor who had given Jack an "A" on his whorehouse theme began to edit the unwieldy material that they assembled for her. She could at least make all the subjects and verbs agree, put marks of punctuation in the right places, and scold Jack about paragraphs lacking coherence and clarity.

Revising repeatedly, the three of them finally completed the final draft, sure that even though it was not classic prose, it contained a lot of important stuff people would like to know about basketball. Then Jack hired a neighborhood girl to type the manuscript in her spare time. By then the Naismiths felt pretty good about "Jack's book," as they had begun to call it.

Before James Naismith's *Basketball* was finished, however, Phog Allen got his *Better Basketball* off to the publisher. When his book came off the press, he distributed complimentary copies to his friends. The Naismiths, finding a copy of the book inside their screen door one morning, discovered how much of their own story would now be unsaleable.

Mrs. Naismith became angry. Irked at the copy left surreptitiously at their door, she accused, "He's not strong enough to bring it to us in person."

Her husband interposed mildly, "We must allow everyone his weakness."[27]

Jack and the Y.M.C.A. got Naismith's book into print for him. *Basketball: Its Origin and Development* was published in 1941, with an introduction by basketball coach Clair Bee and with the copyright held by the International Committee of Young Men's Christian Associations. But Phog Allen's book had come out in 1937, and while Jim Naismith was reading it, all that he got to see of his own writing was the galley proofs. The very titles of the two books were symbolic of the relationship between the two men: the author of *Basketball* had created a game; the author of *Better Basketball* was the one who had coached that game and refined it.

Besides delayed publication of Naismith's book, there were other things that occurred a little bit late.

When James Naismith returned from his travels in Europe, he was pleased at the amount of money remaining in the Naismith travel fund for his own further use. He paid off the mortgage on his home at 1708 Mississippi Street. Then he and Maude began plans to buy a house in West Hills, the area of handsome homes adjoining the campus on the west. They would be able to live there during his retirement years, when they could spend more time with each other.

Dr. James Naismith reached the age of seventy-five on November 6, 1936, and he, along with six other professors, would be eligible to retire from K.U. teaching on a half-time basis by June of 1937. For some time previous to the spring of 1937 the State Board of Regents, the body governing state-supported schools in Kansas, and the University Senate had been working on a retirement plan for employees at state schools. By the provisions of the plan they drew up, a teacher at the age of seventy-five would be eligible for retirement on a half-time basis. At half-pay he would be unassigned to any specific department but would be left to serve the university in miscellaneous ways. In case of incapacitation, however, he would be retired completely from duties and would continue to receive half-pay. Seven were eligible—Professors Burdick, Corbin, Helleberg, Hopkins, Stevens, Templin, and Naismith—but whether they would actually be granted half-time retirement status depended largely on the annual budget allotment for the University of Kansas. Governor Huxman was to sign the appropriations bill for state educational institutions by late February or early March.[28]

Approval of the bill seemed likely, for state schools were not giving the governor much trouble except for occasional rumblings from a pacifist movement at the University of Kansas. Disturbed by predictions of another world war, pacifists were protesting the existence of the Reserve Officers Training Corps on campus and had even interrupted an R.O.T.C. review with a demonstration. So far they had been successful in gaining minor objectives. When students requested that classes be dismissed for an antiwar rally, however, Chancellor Lindley squelched them. In December, 1936, he issued a statement making it clear "that the University could not spare the time for official cognizance of the Peace Mobilization."[29]

Unworried, James Naismith went on with his plans, including in them the new home he and Maude had chosen—the former residence of ex-chancellor Frank Strong. The prospect of retirement in a fine house on the edge of the campus seemed the crowning touch to a life suddenly full of rewards for labor well done. Maude and James could look forward to their leisure time together, at the conclusion of his thirty-nine years of full-time teaching.

But fate had other plans for them.

The Naismith family had long known that Maude had a weak heart and high blood pressure and had worried over her. Because of the condition of her heart, she was under constant medical care, receiving regular medication in the form of digitalis and, occasionally, nitroglycerine. In addition to identifiable ailments, she had lived for years in constant pain, suffering with an undiagnosed neuralgialike ache that had now grown worse. The active companionship that she and James had shared in earlier times was past. But Maude did not complain about the torments of her body. She had so long ago accepted pain as part of living that it had been transmuted into a sweet resignation. Sometimes in these later days she grew vague, forgetting incidents and names she should have remembered. It was a childlike vagueness, somehow appealing. But, at the same time, she never forgot to be a lady. When she walked, she walked with erect carriage. When she sat, she sat straight and proud in her chair. "Even when she rocked," daughter-in-law Frances said, recalling those months during the Olympic summer when Maude Naismith lived at her son's Texas home, "I never saw her back touch the back of the chair."[30]

When the time came that she could no longer walk from the house, her husband would lift her from her chair and carry her outdoors to the car for the afternoon ride they always took together. Ever since she had missed the trip to the Olympics, James Naismith had wanted her to have some special recompense, and the new house and his retirement seemed a fitting double reward for her.[31]

There was time only for the happy plans, not for the fulfillment of them. On the evening of March 4, 1937, Ann, who lived now with her husband, Tom Dawe, in Topeka, was in Lawrence visiting her parents. For years one of the family had helped Mrs. Naismith walk up the stairs every night and had helped her undress for bed. This night it was Ann who went up the stairs with her mother at bedtime.

Tonight Maude Naismith was feeling unusually good. At the landing she stopped and called back to her husband in the room below. "You think I can't undress myself anymore, don't you, James?" she challenged gaily.[32] Then she pulled her dress off over her head and tossed it down to him. James caught the garment, laughing.

Maude was talkative after she went upstairs. She talked to Ann reminiscently about the life behind her, mostly about her long, happy marriage to James Naismith. "We've had a perfect love," she said softly. "And it has been because of him. There could never be another man like him."[33]

She felt cold after she was in bed. She asked Ann to sleep with her a while, as the mother had once been accustomed to do with the daughter. Ann came into the bed with her and held the older woman in her arms until she was warm and sleeping.

That night Maude Sherman Naismith died in her sleep in the house at 1708 Mississippi Street, from a heart attack. Her funeral was held the following Saturday afternoon at the First Presbyterian Church, where she had been a member for more than thirty-eight years, and she was buried in Memorial Park Cemetery at Lawrence. Even in death her body must remain far distant from the New England she loved. She had long known that it would happen so, for her husband had bought twelve lots in Memorial Park when it opened in 1926.

For James Naismith all had happened too swiftly to seem quite real. Twice in his life he quietly broke down: first when he was removed from his position at the university, and now when his wife died. Each time, suffering silently, he mended his shattered spirit in private, and few persons knew. Maude would never live with him in the new home in West Hills, or anywhere else again, and he had to face the truth. There was nothing for him to do now but to try to go on alone.[34]

29

Alone for a While

DR. James Naismith's half-time retirement came through in June, 1937, but it had turned into a curse rather than a blessing. Maude was not there to share it with him.[1]

The brand-new professor emeritus complained to a close friend, "There's nothing to do. I stay at home and read or stare at myself in a glass. I go out and shop or talk with friends. But I can't forget my wife."[2]

He could have visited his children in turn, but he was a man of regular habits, and he disliked the irregularity that was involved in adapting to various families' schedules.

In travel he found one of his early sources of consolation, and here he turned to A. P. ("Duke") D'Ambra for companionship. D'Ambra was a young friend of long standing, formerly a colleague of Naismith's at the University of Kansas. After four years at K.U. teaching military science and photography (1921–1925), D'Ambra had resigned in 1925 to become a full-time commercial photographer. Naismith had often been called upon to travel on speaking engagements or on miscellaneous matters connected with athletics, and D'Ambra, with a profession well adapted to tours, long or short, had accompanied him on nearly forty of these trips. The two men had traveled together on excursions for pleasure, too, in the Ozarks, in Colorado, and elsewhere. On those trips they shared an intimacy that was not possible in the routine of home.[3] Sometimes they parked at the side of the road, miles from a town or farmstead or spot of scenic interest, simply to talk. They found out a lot about each other, and each liked what he learned.

Their comradeship had begun in an unusual way. When D'Ambra was teaching at the University of Kansas, he had stopped in at Doc Naismith's office in the gym one day, casually mentioning some intestinal trouble he had. Naismith, who was always pleased to offer medical advice to anyone, tackled the problem eagerly. "Constipation? Constipation is for lazy people!" He promptly prescribed, "Fifty kicks and one hundred bends, once daily."[4]

D'Ambra obediently began the home exercises. Soon cured of his ailment and converted to Naismith's vigorous regime, he continued kicking his outstretched fingertips fifty times a day and touching the floor with his hands a hundred times a day in the great swooping and bending motions that his mentor taught him. The day Naismith died, many years afterward, D'Ambra wept, and kept on exercising. Later, when he reached the age of sixty, he moderated the exercises from a daily to a thrice-weekly routine and continued to kick and bend on Mondays, Wednesdays, and Fridays.

Now, in the weeks after Maude's death, Doc Naismith was too old and too lonely to travel alone, and Duke D'Ambra, only forty-seven years old, went with him.[5]

Naismith was pensive those days. He often stopped his automobile beside the road when he had something important to say to his friend—whether a philosophical pronouncement about religion and death or a restatement of his poignant grief for Maude. One day, as they were driving westward across Missouri after a visit to Naismith's daughter Hellen Dodd in St. Louis, he braked his car to a stop under a tall tree and looked at D'Ambra strangely. His companion waited. "If I die before you do, Duke, will you promise not to come to my funeral?"

D'Ambra sat as if frozen for want of words. At last he asked, "Why?"

Naismith explained, "When my wife died, I had to go to her funeral and say goodbye to a corpse. Now what I remember most vividly about Maude is her body lying lifeless in a casket. Memories shouldn't be like that." He paused, then continued, "You and I should remember each other as we are now, smiling and talking. . . . Let's promise to stay away from each other's funeral."[6] He held out his hand to D'Ambra and smiled.

After only a moment of hesitation, D'Ambra reciprocated. The two friends shook hands on the promise.

On June 7, in the late spring after Maude Naismith's death, **James Naismith and Duke D'Ambra** set out on a leisurely five-thousand-mile automobile trip across the United States and Canada to visit various places and people for a month or so.

The father of basketball was "good copy," to use newspaper parlance, in that summer after the Berlin Olympics. Earl Rowe, night sports editor of the *New York World Telegram,* may have thought of basketball as "just a bunch of damn fools running around in their underwear," but most people did not agree.[7] The public liked basketball and was interested in the man who had been featured in all basketball sports stories during the recent Olympiad. D'Ambra, as a self-appointed, unsalaried publicity agent, made a habit of phoning the local sports editor when the two travelers arrived in a town. The resultant interviews furnished photographic setups for D'Ambra and helped to fill some of the lonely gaps in the widower's days. Naismith was not interested in making the headlines, but he liked people and was pleased when anyone wanted to talk with him. In 1937, fortunately, he found himself popular everywhere.

Most of their traveling was done in Canada, where Naismith followed the trail of his "hundred and three first cousins" across the country. He found other interesting trails as well. In Edmonton, Alberta, one Sunday evening in July he was guest of honor at a dinner given by the Edmonton Grads. The Grads were a famous female basketball team organized in 1914–1915 from graduates of the Commercial High School in Edmonton. This team won 502 of 522 games in its twenty-five years under coach J. Percy Page and dominated women's basketball throughout the world in the 1920s and 1930s. Naismith, impressed by the world crowns the girls had won in Paris, Amsterdam, Los Angeles, and Berlin, was flattered to dine with a group that he considered one of the greatest basketball teams of all time.[8]

Another Canadian visit was motivated by current public interest in another famous group of females. In Callander, Ontario, where the world-publicized Dionne quintuplets were then three years old, the travelers stopped to meet Dr. Dafoe, physician for the five little girls. The two Canadians, Dafoe and Naismith, had a long visit, chatting together a much longer time than the busy baby doctor usually allowed for an interview.[9] As usual, D'Ambra wanted to take photos, but this time, to his regret, publicity had to be played down. Although his regular clients in the United States wanted pictures of the Father of Basketball and the Dionne quintuplets together, and would have paid well for any shots he could send, D'Ambra was not allowed to photograph the quints. International News had exclusive photographic rights, and for the first time in his career D'Ambra had to turn down prospective purchasers even though the "picture of the year" was at his fingertips.

Jim and Duke visited Naismith's Ontario relatives, making their headquarters at the farm home of Jim's cousin Bert Young and his wife, Alma. In addition to Naismith's relatives, the two men called on some of Jim's contemporaries, such as his old friends Dr. A. A. Metcalfe, who still lived in Ontario, and Dr. R. Tait McKenzie, who liked to come back home when he could.[10] Jim and Duke found Tait at work sculpting in his summer studio, the Mill of Kintail. The house was a stone gristmill, built in 1830 over a stream north of Almonte and restored a hundred years later by McKenzie.[11]

They stopped for photographs of Naismith's old school at Bennie's Corners, too. The barbed-wire fence around the playground may have been sagging a little, and some of the fence posts were leaning, but the school was in active use. The coat of white paint on the frame building was in good condition, and the front windows patriotically displayed flags of Canada and Britain.

When they were away from their family headquarters near Almonte, Naismith and D'Ambra lived out of doors. They did their own cooking, taking turns. They hiked and hunted. They spent much of their time on streams and lakes, for Naismith was an inveterate fisherman and boatsman, and a skillful one. At White Lake, near Arnprior, they caught trout and pike on a three-hundred-foot copper-wire line with an unbaited spoon hook. They worked and played hard, and Naismith did his share of it all. He had always advocated the strenuous life, and in his old age he was still practicing it.

In their zeal Duke and "Doc," as his friend called him, came close to supplying the biggest Naismith headline of the year. One afternoon, when they were fishing from a boat in White Lake and the big fish were biting greedily, the old master sportsman, through excitement and carelessness, fell out of the boat.

Nearly seventy-six years of age, he was overboard in a deep, cold lake with no life preserver at hand. Furthermore, he was weighed down with all his clothing, including a pair of heavy shoes. There were no other boats on the lake or persons on the shore. D'Ambra was terrified. Naismith, on the other hand, may have lost his balance but not his head. Seizing a fishing line, he held it between his teeth while he swam toward the boat and the oar that the frightened D'Ambra extended toward him. Scrambling aboard and pulling off his dripping clothing, Doc chided D'Ambra for his anxiety: "You know I'm a good swimmer. There wasn't anything to worry about. Stop shaking."

D'Ambra tried to joke "They'd have crucified me if I'd let the father of basketball drown. You're public property, Doc."[12]

Afterward, as Naismith sat naked in the hot summer sun, his clothes drying on the side of the boat, he meditated aloud. He had faith in God, in his fellow man, and in himself, but he was fatalistically ready to accept any eventuality. "Why worry, Duke? When our time comes, it comes. We can't hurry it or hold it back." Then he added softly, "I try to get some comfort out of that when I think of Maude, but I can't."[13]

As their vacation travels went on, Doc and Duke helped each other. D'Ambra happened to have an allergy—which turned out to do Naismith a lot of good. While Doc was busy running tests for allergic reactions, diagnosing, and treating, he perked up and brightened into a strong semblance of his former self.[14]

After the travels ended in July, Naismith returned to the university in his new status of half-retirement. Needing now more than ever something to keep himself occupied, he soon found his time filled. He became an ambassador of good will for the university, in demand as a speaker at various affairs—secular and religious, near and far. He never considered himself effective on the platform, jokingly insisting that he did not have enough funny stories to be a good speaker. But people wanted to hear him.

Frequently outspoken is his public utterances, Naismith did not pretend to represent the views of K.U.'s Department of Physical Education in any of his speeches. In Toronto in the summer of 1937 he criticized the lack of strenuosity in modern athletics. Sticking out his chest, squaring his shoulders, and poking a finger of ridicule at the game of ping-pong as a horrible example, he declared that present-day physical education was making "softies" out of its participants. In December, 1937, at a meeting in St. Louis, he stated publicly that basketball coaches and rules committees were taking his game for a one-way ride on the road to ruin.[15]

Rebel or not against the trends of these latter years, he found honors coming to him in rapid succession for his achievements in medicine, in physical education, and in theology. In December, 1937, his nearly forty years of active participation in the Douglas County Medical Society was climaxed by an honorary life membership, and in January, 1938, he was elected to life membership in the Kansas Medical Society. On February 19, 1938, he was presented a Certificate of Recognition for Meritorious Service in Physical Education in the Young Men's Christian Association. Honor was soon to come as well in his third profession—theology.

The world at that time was filled with war and rumors of war; money had been devaluated; and at the University of Kansas the *Dove,* a liberal journal, was being published. In Spain, Americans were helping out in the Civil War, and one former K.U. student died in 1938 while fighting for the Loyalists. The young man's father thereupon charged the university with harboring a Communist conspiracy. Other local institutions were accused as well, including the Lawrence Y.M.C.A., "that hot-bed of radicalism," as someone called it. The K.U. Board of Regents, the Kansas legislature, and newspaper editorialists throughout the state and beyond grew excited, pro and con. At the university Chancellor Lindley and student leaders defended K.U., and under the leadership of Secretary John L. Hunt, the Y.M.C.A. launched its own protest, instituting debates to argue the charges made against it.[16]

But Jim Naismith would forever be a part of the Y.M.C.A., suspect or not, and that year he even went on tour for a few weeks, lecturing for the organization. In the spring of 1938 the Michigan Y.M.C.A., through its Hi-Y division, called on him for an extensive lecture trip through Michigan and into Canada. He made the 1,650-mile tour with Cliff B. Drurry, field manager of the Michigan Y.M.C.A., spending two weeks addressing audiences at basketball banquets, conferring with basketball coaches, and speaking to Rotary Clubs, Kiwanis Clubs, and Chambers of Commerce in nearly a score of Michigan cities. In March the downtown branch of the Y.M.C.A. in Detroit had a "James Naismith Day," with a dinner, speeches, and demonstration basketball games. A high point of the day was an old-timers' basketball match with Naismith as referee.[17]

A related activity for him was promotion of a basketball memorial. Talk had begun about establishing a basketball Hall of Fame. Someone else suggested a memorial fieldhouse. Disclaiming any personal claim to honor, Naismith gave his support to the idea of memorializing basketball. But if there was going to be a memorial erected for him—a Naismith memorial—he thought that he would prefer a carillon. However, other matters came along and forced this early campaign for a basketball memorial—hall of fame, fieldhouse, or carillon—to wait for later revival.[18]

Busy though they were, the months held moments of sadness, too. One such moment was the death of Sir Robert Tait McKenzie, who had been a "little brother" to Jim when they lived in Ramsay Township, a comrade during the years at McGill University, and best man at the Naismith wedding. McKenzie's death happened at his home in Philadelphia. On April 28, 1938, McKenzie had spent his usual busy day, for he had remained as an adviser at the University of Pennsylvania after his retirement as research professor. But as he was preparing to take his car to meet Mrs. McKenzie, he died of heart failure.[19] With his loss another bit of Jim Naismith's past was gone.

Personal bereavement and political flare-ups notwithstanding, life in the Naismith home and at the University of Kansas went on. By November, 1938, the Communist witch hunt in Lawrence was over, investigation having shown that there were no more Communist or Fascist activities on the campus and environs than seemed normal around an institution the size of the University of Kansas. Naismith, to tell the truth, had never really been disturbed by the furor. He went on making speeches just as before about matters more important to him than Communist threats ever were.[20]

He went on with his travels, too. The Christmas holidays of 1938 he spent at Ordway, Colorado, with the George Stanleys—his daughter Margaret and the man who used to be "Mama's angel son-in-law"—and their children. From there he went to Denver to watch the Denver Safeways play basketball once more. Again one of the nation's leading teams, the Safeways played in the Denver city auditorium. Naismith managed to give some advice to the players and their coach—at least for the benefit of a photographer's publicity shot—and was honored by an invitation to toss up the ball for the opening play of the game.[21]

This same month he made mild headlines again with his public condemnation of the makers of basketball rules. With his old fire he denounced the recent changes in rules. He made it known that the only revisions he would like to see—such as rotation of the jumping order among players—were changes intended to offset the advantage held by the tall player.

The year 1939 came along. Students had settled down to swallowing goldfish in their spare time (one young man downed fifty of them before witnesses), and James Naismith plunged into a season even more exciting than the one before.[22]

In January, 1939, he spoke about basketball on Gabriel Heatter's well-known Columbia-network radio program, "We the People." At half-time of the Kansas-Nebraska basketball game in February, 1939, he was presented a trophy for introducing fencing into the Midwest in 1898 and keeping interest alive in the sport throughout the succeeding forty years. A greater tribute, on April 11, 1939, the degree of Doctor of Divinity, Honoris Causa, was conferred on him at the seventy-second annual convocation of the Presbyterian College of Montreal. This was the college where faculty and graduating class, certain that he was headed for the devil, had prayed for his soul when he had left there forty-nine years before. Naismith hedged modestly upon first receiving news of the planned ceremony, protesting that he would have to buy academic regalia for the occasion. But, as everyone knew he would, he went, proud to have the Reverend W. D. Reid confer the degree on him, while the Reverend Principal F. Scott Mackenzie presided.[23]

Much of Naismith's traveling was done by automobile, with him at the wheel, a situation that caused his friends some concern. D'Ambra was not always available to go with him. Never a good driver, Naismith got by on luck as much as anything else. About his occasional accidents or near-accidents he was maddeningly casual. Understandably, his children worried when Papa-Jim set out on an expedition.

For one of his trips to St. Louis he asked to borrow Jack's car. Jack, remembering the time on the highway to Montreal when he had grabbed the steering wheel from his dozing father in time to avoid a head-on collision with a truck, figured that the Naismith luck would hold. He loaned the car. After the older Naismith's departure, two weeks passed without word from him. At last a card arrived, explaining that he had decided to drive on from St. Louis to New York. From New York, one impulse leading to another, he went on to Canada without telling anyone beforehand. At last he came home and returned the car to Jack, two fenders badly damaged. "Well, it's in perfect shape," he said, self-satisfied, as he stepped out of the car.

Jack silently pointed to the crumpled fenders. Naismith looked surprised. "Oh, that? A couple of taps with a hammer will take care of them."[24]

Meanwhile, between trips Naismith moved into a new home in West Hills, at 1515 University Drive, as he and Maude had planned to do together. The house was large and attractive, with a wide expanse of lawn facing on a quiet street. The residence was conveniently near the campus and was also near some fraternity houses, in whose inhabitants Naismith took a keen interest, as he always had done. Ann and her husband, Thomas Dawe, who was working at a grain elevator in Topeka, moved to Lawrence to live with Naismith. Ann kept house for her father, and Tom drove back and forth to Topeka to take care of his job.[25]

For a while the Dawes' presence brought as much annoyance as it did comfort. Ann was pregnant and not feeling well. With a record of several miscarriages, she was depressed, weeping constantly enough to keep her father and her husband miserable. She was displaying the very lack of self-discipline that had always been repugnant to Naismith. Driven at last to complete impatience during one of her fits of weeping, he spanked her. He was gentle, but it was a spanking, nevertheless.

Ann, startled, stopped weeping and stared at her father in shocked amazement. Then she laughed. It suddenly seemed terribly funny. She was as big as a house, and her father had dared to spank her, anyway. His treatment worked. She did not weep again during the weeks before her first son, Thomas Lee Dawe, Jr., was born.[26]

That spanking did Naismith good, too. It drew the past comfortingly back to him, the past when Maude was alive and the children were small. He felt less alone. But he was still, undeniably, alone, and he sought in his typically direct manner to alleviate that loneliness.

One night, visiting Jack in Kansas City, he announced, "I feel like kicking up my heels. Let's do something risqué."[27] Jack was familiar with the city's lurid spots and obligingly took his father to a burlesque theater. They sat in one of the front rows, where men around them were shouting at scantily clad girls on the stage, "Take it off! Take it off!" Doc Naismith remained unobtrusively silent during the patrons' chant. True to his well-known custom at a basketball game, he did no yelling. But, to Jack's delight, he sat with quiet interest till the end of the show.

Naismith soon found a more socially acceptable way than burlesque to fill his evenings. Before the first anniversary of Maude's death he had begun to seek female company. The first time he went out with a woman he came home grinning like a schoolboy. Jack, who was there, asked, "What've you been up to, Doc?"

The elder Naismith replied proudly, "I had a date."[28]

Among the women who caught his fancy was a poetess thirteen years younger than he, with a Southern accent and a distinguished record of war service. Louisa Cooke, daughter of Colonel Bolivar H. Cooke, moved bravely from Ward-Belmont, a school for girls, in Nashville into the Wild West when she married Harry E. Don-Carlos, who became a federal judge in the Indian Territory. Later her services in World War I paralleled those of Naismith. At first in the United States, as hostess for the War Camp Community Service at Fort Leavenworth, and then in France, as Director of Women in the Dauphiné leave area at Grenoble, she performed so admirably that she was awarded an A.E.F. medal by Douglas County. After the war she and her husband moved to Lawrence, where she displayed the same thirst for knowledge that Naismith always possessed. Because of her interest in creative writing, she enrolled at the University of Kansas, earning a bachelor's degree in 1924 and a master's degree in 1926.[29]

After Harry E. Don-Carlos died in 1933, his widow took a trip around the world. Then, giving up her showplace home at 1605 Tennessee Street, she rented a well-furnished room at the Hearth and devoted her time to culture, community affairs, and writing. She continued with the novels, short stories, and biographies that she occasionally published, and sent feature articles to the *Kansas City Star* and other newspapers, while she continued to enhance her reputation as a poet.[30]

The emeritus professor enjoyed having an appreciative female companion on his arm when he attended a concert or the theater, and Louisa Don-Carlos, in frilled and feathered hat, provided both ornament and intellect. She was knowledgeably interested in drama and music, belonging to the Drama League of Lawrence and a music club, and she was doing research in Kansas history for her latest novel, *The Pride of the Prairie*.[31]

It seemed a little strange to their acquaintances, it must be admitted, that Mrs. Don-Carlos, a Christian Scientist, should be escorted about town by a minister of the Presbyterian church. The lady seemed too forceful a personality, too, for a man who had idolized the quiet and feminine Maude Sherman Naismith. But Mrs. Don-Carlos and Dr. Naismith were a little puzzled that anyone should care about these incongruities.

The only drawback, really, to the friendship was that the public was too curious. Naismith, driving Mrs. Don-Carlos home from an evening in Kansas City on Valentine's Day, 1938, missed a turn and drove his automobile into a ditch. The Naismith luck was operating satisfactorily, and he was able to drive the car home with neither driver nor his only passenger injured. But the accident made news. Although Naismith was accustomed to having his name in the newspapers regularly for the past two years and more, for the first time he was annoyed at publicity. "Why can't I have privacy?" he demanded irritably.[32]

Louisa Cooke Don-Carlos was not the only woman in Naismith's life at this time. There were others—including the memory of Maude Naismith. While he dated the widows of Lawrence he planned a tribute to his late wife. At the annual National Intercollegiate Basketball Tournament in Kansas City in 1938 he presented to the winner a trophy whose form and design he had created as a memorial to Maude Sherman Naismith. He planned to set up a permanent fund for this annual championship trophy, to be perpetuated by a provision in his will.[33]

Another of the women who helped to fill the void in his life was Florence Mae Kincaid, housemother at the Sigma Phi Epsilon fraternity since mid-1937. Both of Doc Naismith's two sons had been members of Sigma Phi Epsilon, and he had long been an adviser to the group. After Maude's death he dropped in at the house even more frequently than before to chat with the boys and help them with their problems. He soon became well acquainted with their housemother, a charming gray-haired woman twenty-two years his junior, who had become a housemother after her husband, a dentist in Beloit, Kansas, died four years before. She had heard about Dr. Naismith when her son, Jack, was a student at K.U. Jack Kincaid, who had been editor of the college yearbook, the *Jayhawker,* and knew everything that was happening on campus, had told her what a wonderful man the professor was.

Mrs. Kincaid proved even better company than the fraternity members. She had a quietly charming way with her group of boys, which Doc Naismith admired, and a talent for making the fraternity house comfortable and homelike. As Florence Mae Kinsley, before her marriage to Dr. F. B. Kincaid, she had trained for concert work in voice, and sometimes in front of the fraternity boys' piano she joined in a duet with Dr. Naismith and his rich baritone.

She had attributes beyond her gift for music and her knack for taking care of a large house full of young people. Important to Naismith, for instance, was her interest in athletics. A keen sportswoman, she rode horseback, played golf, and, in short, enjoyed any game open to a woman. She looked good, too. A tall and attractive woman, she was five feet seven inches in height, being only two inches shorter than James Naismith. Dr. Naismith began taking her out, and people remarked approvingly what a charming couple they made.

Reactions to the romantic events in James Naismith's life varied among his relatives and close acquaintances. Friend Duke D'Ambra was openly pleased that Doc had emerged from his depression enough to invite a woman out, whether it was the local poetess or, for occasional variety, the Sig Eps' housemother. Son Jack was pleased, too, particularly with Florence Kincaid. He thought that she was a perfect mate for Doc. He went so far as to coax his father into writing out a list of qualifications for a wife. Then he pointed out with satisfaction that the attractive housemother filled them to a "T." With helpful remarks to each of the parties concerned, Jack frankly encouraged the romance.

Far away in Dallas, son Jim remained unaware that his father was courting anyone, poetess or housemother, but the Naismith daughters in Colorado and Missouri, kept current by letters from Ann, wrote their disapproval of septuagenarian love affairs. Although Papa-Jim was past his mid-seventies, he was an attractive prospect for any woman from forty onward, and they feared that he was seriously considering remarriage. There was safety in numbers, of course, and they were relieved for the time being that there were several women, instead of just one, who were "interested in Dad." With Florence Kincaid in the running, Louisa Don-Carlos appeared less dangerous a threat to the sanctity of the Naismith family circle than she might otherwise have been.[34]

Heedless of his daughters' opinions, Jim Naismith went on courting. He had been too long and too happily married, it seemed, to remain long alone. He needed a living woman to share Maude's pedestal. Besides, he could not help but realize that he was keeping Ann and Tom away from their own home. Tom could not take care of his grain-testing job properly when he was living more than twenty miles away from it and some days not bothering to drive over to Topeka at all. In typical fashion, Naismith saw a solution, and he acted.[35]

One day when Duke D'Ambra stopped by the Naismith home, Ann told him, "Dad's going to get married."

"That's a good idea," D'Ambra exclaimed.

"I think so, too," replied Ann, accepting defeat with outward equanimity.

"It's Mrs. Don-Carlos, isn't it?" D'Ambra asked as a polite afterthought.

"No," Ann answered shortly. "It's Mrs. Kincaid."[36]

The engagement was almost as great a surprise to Florence Kincaid as it was to everyone else. After her happy marriage to Dr. Kincaid, she had not intended to marry again. The first time that James Naismith asked her, she said, "No." But he kept asking.

Remembering, long afterward, how it happened, she explained gently, "Doctor was very persuasive."[37]

30

Florence and the Doctor

JAMES NAISMITH made one thing clear to his fiancée before they announced their engagement: when he died he wanted to be buried beside Maude. Florence understood. She had had a fine man in Dr. Kincaid, her first husband, and would prefer to be buried in Beloit beside him.[1] After that agreement was made, they relaxed and began to act like an engaged couple.

The first official announcement of their engagement was made at a meeting of the Sigma Phi Epsilon fraternity. Naismith waited upstairs while Mrs. Kincaid told the news to the boys at the close of a regular business meeting. When the young men crowded around him afterward with congratulations and asked whether the tidings were true, he smiled and replied, "She said so, and you can't contradict a lady."

"Why, Doctor!" she protested, flustered.[2]

Afterwards he chided her, "Aren't you going to call me by my first name now?"

She shook her head. "Maybe later."[3]

But she could never bring herself to call him anything but "Doctor."

The Naismith tribe received the announcement of the engagement less happily than the Sig Eps had done. The daughters blamed Jack for encouraging the match, and their father for being a fool. They agreed that Mrs. Kincaid was marrying Daddy-Boy for his reputation and his retirement pay.

For Ann and Tom, of course, life would be simpler now. They could move back into their home in Topeka if Dad had a wife to take care of him, and Tom would no longer have a twice-daily drive to make. But Ann could not be blamed if she felt a little resentment at having a stranger become mistress of the white-columned house that should have been her mother's.

The betrothed couple, disregarding censure, began furnishing the home they would share. As they bustled back and forth between the Sigma Phi Epsilon house and the Naismith residence at 1515 University Drive, neighbors along the street looked on with interest. Sometimes, not knowing that they were being watched, Florence and James held hands.[4] "They look so happy," the neighbors said approvingly.[5] Occasionally he slipped and called her "Maude." But people said it was only natural that he should do so at first.

The pair did not want a long engagement, nor did they want a big wedding. "Let's avoid fuss and feathers," he said as they made their plans.[6] Perhaps he was remembering the publicity incurred when he drove into the ditch with Mrs. Don-Carlos. They agreed, therefore, that their wedding should be kept secret from the public until it was over. Going quietly out of town to avoid attention, he and Florence, both Presbyterians, hurried off to the First Presbyterian Church in Overland Park, Kansas, for a quiet ceremony at noon on June 10, 1939.

The fifty-six-year-old bride was attractive in a bolero ensemble of navy sheer trimmed with white pique and, for head wear, a wide sailor hat of navy straw with white. The nearest approach to "fuss and feathers" came in the corsage she carried of Talisman roses and lilies of the valley and in the organ music that the minister's wife played throughout the ceremony. Among the thirteen guests were two of the five Naismith children, Jack and Ann, and one grandson—Jack's son and namesake. The other three Naismith families lived too far out of state to be present, and the Dawes left their son, Tommy, in Lawrence, rather than bring him along for his grandfather's wedding. One young man from the Sigma Phi Epsilon house was present to represent the fraternity.[7]

Reactions of the persons in the church were varied. The seventy-seven-year-old groom was calm and one-and-a-half-year-old Jack Naismith was noisy in the second pew. Florence was the most nervous of them all. Her voice wavered on the phrase "until death do us part." While the strains of Schumann's "Traumerei" and McDowell's "To a Wild Rose" sounded softly through the church, the Reverend W. K. Waters solemnly spoke the words of the ceremony.

Thus a second June marriage came into the life of the father of basketball.

At the close of the ceremony the groom kissed the bride hurriedly. Mrs. Naismith gave her flowers to the Sigma Phi Epsilon boy's date, who blushed, and Naismith wished the girl luck. Outside the church, amused by the prank someone had played, Naismith tore long pink paper streamers off the bumper of his Chevrolet. With his bride on the seat beside him, he stepped on the starter, to the sound of popping torpedoes and the sight of smoke rising from the hood of the automobile. Barely missing another car as they backed out into the road, the couple set off for a motor trip, heading first to the Southwest, then to the West Coast, and lastly to Canada.

They seemed completely unworried that the number thirteen, as represented in their small group of wedding guests, might prove an unlucky omen for their marriage. Rather, they must have expected good fortune from that number. After all, the thirteen rules Naismith dreamed up in 1891 had proved lucky indeed for a game called basketball.

It was a good honeymoon. Florence soon knew that she had been right to marry the doctor. He was a wonderful man, with the highest ethical principles and the deepest compassion of anyone she had known. Fair in everything he did, he would, she was sure, handle with justice any problems that might arise in their marriage. Naismith, rejoicing that he had found a traveling companion whose enjoyment of the things they did doubled his own pleasure in the trip, told her that she was the kind of pal he had always wanted. When he said that, she sensed that she must make up to him for two lonely parts of his life: a difficult, orphaned childhood and the final sad years of Maude's invalidism and death.

The high point of the visit to California—for Florence was still awed by the notable persons in her husband's circle of acquaintances—was an invitation from the A. A. Staggs to spend the day, through evening dinner, at their home. After retiring from his position as football coach at the University of Chicago in 1932, Lonnie had gone to the University of the Pacific to coach football. Now aged seventy-seven, he was still a successful football coach and a famous man. He and Naismith were eager for another of their too infrequent visits, and the bride was excited at meeting a figure as well known as her husband in the world of sports.[8]

Unfortunately, some unforeseen circumstances intervened, and the Staggs were unable to entertain their Kansas guests. The bridal couple continued up the coast on their honeymoon without having had a visit with Lonnie Stagg, but they told each other that they would come back the next summer.

Combining business with honeymoon, Naismith carried out numerous speaking engagements and visits to fraternities as they traveled northward. In mid-July in Spokane, Washington, he and Florence visited the Athletic Round Table. They attended Kiwanis luncheons and meetings of other civic organizations. In western Canada, Naismith held interviews with notable persons in the field of sports and attended meetings and dinners of basketball associations and other athletic groups. Not to exclude personal affairs, all the way from British Columbia eastward, Jim and Florence visited relatives on the Young and Naismith sides of the family. And wherever he went, with high hat and cane, Naismith was a fine-appearing figure at formal functions. On his honeymoon he did dress up!

Of all the meetings, Florence Naismith afterward remembered best the one in Winnipeg in August. There was a long story behind it.

In March, 1933, Canada's championship basketball team, the Winnipeg Toilers from the Vaughan Street Y.M.C.A., had flown with coach Len Sinclair to Oklahoma to play the Tulsa Oilers. Naismith had come on invitation to address the Canadian team before the game, and he watched with interest the outcome of the Toilers' pilgrimage.[9]

Outclassed by the Tulsa Oilers, the Canadians lost, but they hoped for revenge in a second series of games later in the season. However, they never had a chance to try again. That game in March was the last the Toilers would play. Flying homeward on March 31, their plane crashed in a cornfield near Neodesha, Kansas, killing two of the team and seriously injuring others. The fatal accident occurred less than a hundred miles from the spot where another sports star and good friend of Naismith's, a frequent visitor in the Naismith home, had died in identical manner exactly two years earlier. On March 31, 1931, Knute Rockne, famed Notre Dame football coach, had been killed in a plane crash in a pasture near Bazaar, Kansas.[10]

Now on his honeymoon, Jim Naismith stopped in Winnipeg to visit the remaining members of that famous team from the prairies of Manitoba. Every year the surviving members of the team gathered in Winnipeg for a reunion on the date of the fatal accident, March 31. In addition, they held a memorial service at the Presbyterian church on the Sunday most closely preceding or following that date. Naismith was nearly five months too late for the 1939 reunion dinner, but the Toilers held an out-of-season reunion when they heard that he was in town. Six of them—Wilson, Silverthorne, Penwarden, Samson, Dodds, and Brown—gathered one night to honor him.[11]

Florence had not intended to go to the dinner, for it was an all-male affair. When her husband told her to get dressed, she replied in surprise that she planned to stay in their hotel room that evening.

"I'm not a star basketball player," she put him off laughingly.

"I want you there beside me," he told her. "I want them to know that you belong to me." He knew how to say the things that make a woman feel good and to make her believe that he meant them.

Still she protested. "But it's a stag party, Doctor."

"You are going with me," he said firmly, reaching for the phone to confirm a dinner reservation for her.[12]

She recognized the note of authority she had already come to know, and putting on the dress he liked best, she went with him.

She was grateful that she went, for that night furnished her favorite memory of him. Among all her recollections she would remember him most clearly as he appeared there at the speaker's table. Even though he was overweight now at one hundred ninety-seven pounds, he was erect and distinguished in appearance and his mustache still held many traces of dark hair. He looked big and strong—as indeed he was—with his man-sized eighteen-inch collar and size forty-six coat. He talked to the assembled men about basketball and the good old days when it began. Although never an orator, he was a good speaker when he got started, and he gave a fine speech that night.[13]

She was prouder of him than she had ever been before—and proudest of all because he looked so young and so happy. At nearly seventy-eight years of age, he had been estimated as appearing from fifteen to twenty-eight years younger than he was. Tonight the most flattering estimate seemed justified.

When bride and groom drove away from Winnipeg, one of the doctor's Canadian cousins was there to bid them farewell with a wish that was to them like a wedding gift and benediction: "Long live Jim and beautiful Florence."[14]

The bridal couple returned to Lawrence on September 1 to live in the handsome house at 1515 University Drive. James Naismith's half-time salary was not high. In fact, some full-time professors had not yet regained the cuts in salary incurred in 1931 in the depths of the depression. But he and Florence had enough money for a good life. At the university the administrator who had caused Naismith's heartbreaking demotion fifteen years before was gone. Ernest Hiram Lindley, white-haired go-getter, served at K.U. longer than any other chancellor—nineteen years— but in 1939 he resigned and a native Kansan, Deane W. Malott, came to Mount Oread to take his place.[15] Such a changeover in the university's administration building a few blocks away no longer mattered much one way or another to a retired professor happy with a new wife.

Delighted as they were with each other, however, the past crept in around the Naismiths as it had not done on their wedding journey. Although James's first wife had not lived in that house with him, back in a familiar domestic routine he forgot himself frequently, calling his bride "Maude." She pretended not to notice and kept on addressing him as "Doctor." The children of the first marriage were the strongest reminders of the doctor's earlier life, in visits or by letter. Florence felt a bit uneasy, knowing that the family had been divided in its approval of the marriage and remembering that she was replacing one of the daughters as mistress of the house. Careful not to play the role of usurper in the household, she gave Ann permission to take anything she wanted of her mother's possessions. The young woman took prompt advantage of her stepmother's suggestion.[16]

Naismith made his own decision, however, about one parcel of souvenirs. During Florence's rearrangement of the house, he brought Ann a small locked suitcase.

"Keep this for me, Dimps," he instructed. "Don't open it till after I die."[17]

When Ann opened it after his death, she discovered that the suitcase contained all the letters that Maude Sherman Naismith had ever written to her husband.

When his wife and his daughter were together, Jim Naismith was torn in silent conflict between two sides for whom he felt an equal devotion. Still, for the most part, life was much too full for unhappiness; when he and Florence were alone, he was always an optimist.

Those days were busy ones for the Naismiths. They continued to rearrange and decorate their home to their mutual satisfaction. The doctor spent time in the basement workshop with his woodworking tools, a favorite hobby. Carrying on the interest in collecting antique furniture that he had shared with Maude, he bought and refinished some handsome chairs for his new home. Students dropped in frequently, both the current crop from the campus and alumni who came back to visit with their former teacher. Each afternoon, to fill out his day, he reserved two hours as his private period of relaxation, napping and doing his "relaxing exercises."

Florence disapproved of the latter routine, complaining that his exercises were much too strenuous to relax anyone. He did not change his habits, though. He had long carried out this schedule, asking friends not to phone between three and five in the afternoon because he was busy and Maude, deaf, would be unable to hear the telephone ring. Now, although remarried, he intended to keep on in the old way of doing things.[18]

He had to go to the University of Kansas Medical Center in Kansas City for tests and observation one week soon after he and Florence returned from Canada. An old kidney ailment that had resulted from an injury in a football game in his young manhood continued to flare up recurrently, and surgery was a chore he had been uneasily postponing. The pain had grown increasingly troublesome, however, in the past six months, and he knew he had to go.

After the doctors were finished, he was alone in his hospital room with his youngest daughter. "Is it a cancer, Dimps?" he asked.

Ann looked directly at him. "I'd never lie to you, Dad," she replied and, turning, walked out of the room.[19] In those words she had told him.

Although "cancer" was a word that might have made a weaker man falter, it would make no difference in his and Florence's plans for their future. Florence need not even know for a while. The doctors and the two of his children who had been at the hospital with him, Ann and Jack, were the only persons who knew the truth.

He came home from the Medical Center and told Florence that she was foolish to have worried about him.

Affairs in the world were growing complicated. While antiwar

Jayhawkers at the University of Kansas held rallies for peace and happy-go-lucky ones kicked up their heels at dances, in Europe armed conflict had begun.[20] Ironically, it was only a dozen years after the Union Building had been constructed as a memorial to students who had died in the great "war to end wars."[21] Newspaper headlines told of the sinking of German submarines and merchant ships and of the imminent Allied blockade of Nazi exports. It all seemed far from those August days in Berlin three years before, and ever farther from the evening when he and other notables from the world of sports had been entertained by Hitler. There seemed nothing that Naismith could do, though, except to turn, practical and cheerful, to simple matters at hand.

He and Florence were going to spend the winter season in St. Petersburg, Florida. In his capacity as informal ambassador from the University of Kansas, the doctor worked on his plans for a tour of speaking engagements at Southern fraternities. Then in the spring he and Florence would go to Ontario for a visit.

During the fall when Florence wanted to purchase a fur neckpiece, her husband delayed her. "Wait," he suggested. "I'll buy you one in Ontario next spring."[22] He thought that there were no furs so good as Canadian furs, and he felt much the same way about his Canadian relatives. He was looking forward to introducing Florence to his great tribe of cousins in Ontario. His last trip to Ramsay Township had occurred in 1937, more than two years before, as the honeymoon summer had not been long enough to include this most important part of Canada.[23]

Besides the winter and the spring to anticipate, there were all the years ahead. Some of those years promised to be filled with new honors for him. In October the first contribution for a field house to be constructed at K.U. had been sent to Phog Allen with the stipulation that the building be erected as a memorial to James Naismith and named in his honor. Wesley H. Loomis, Jr., who made the five-dollar contribution,[24] did not guess that the big field house, when finally built in 1955, would be named for Phog Allen instead of Naismith.[25] But at the moment everything looked rosy for Dr. James Naismith.

Fortunately for Jim, he did not suspect the future course of events, either—whether those twenty years away or those of next month. Right now he was full of plans. If Maude's death and his retirement two months afterward had left his life empty, it had filled again with more activity than he had expected would open up to him. He and Florence had not even found time to play golf together, but they were planning to. He looked forward to all the places, people, and events foretokened, grasping eagerly at everything the future offered.

The happy plans were to be rudely interrupted.

Ann, her husband, Tom, and their small son, Tommy, came over from Topeka for Sunday dinner on the nineteenth of November. Conversation at the dinner table turned, as it often did in the Naismith household, to athletics.

Jim Naismith had played many sports and played them hard, and he liked to expound on the advantages and disadvantages of each. Now in his old age, he seemed to have turned against the team games he had always considered tops—football and lacrosse. He no longer favored, as he once had, games depending on excessive bodily contact. Football, although very popular in the United States, did not provide the opportunity for development of agility, speed, accuracy, and muscular control that basketball did, he pointed out. Moreover, it depended too much on brute force. He himself bore the scars of this rough and injurious sport. His recent visit to the Medical Center was a grim reminder.

Basketball, he believed now, was one of the best all-around team sports, emphasizing as it did the recreational element and at the same time aiding physical, mental, and moral development. And it was safer. Quoting the Travelers Insurance Company, he emphasized that it was a nonmaiming sport, safer than one's morning bath. Here he spoke with especial authority, for he had more than once lost his footing when leaving the bathtub, with cracked ribs as a result.[26] "Don't ever let Tommy play football," he begged, glancing fondly at his youngest grandson.[27]

It was shortly after seven o'clock, and the meal was over. He added briskly, "Let me show you some of the statistics I've collected about accidents in sports. I've got them in my study."[28]

He started to rise from the table and fell back into his chair.

Ann recognized the symptoms. A cerebral hemorrhage had struck her father. He was rushed to Lawrence Memorial Hospital, where his condition was immediately listed as critical. Florence called in her own doctor, and the hours of waiting began for the little family group. Through the night the patient lay unconscious, near death. The crisis staggered them all—his children, his bride, his friends.

But at last Jim Naismith opened his eyes. When he regained consciousness, he realized how near death he had been and still was. Alone with Jack, he wept. "I don't want to die."[29]

Then, as if he had chuckled and said, "I was only joking—I really didn't intend to die," he rallied. After a remarkable recovery, he was dismissed from the hospital on Wednesday afternoon, November 22, three days after he had been taken there. He had always had unusually good health and amazing stamina, and these attributes showed up now in dramatic manner.

Convalescing, he talked again about the Naismith plans, which had been interrupted so painfully. He said, "You know, Florence, I feel God's hand has guided me throughout everything I have done in life. And at last, when I thought everything was finished after Maude died, He gave me you. Now He means for us to do so many things together."[30]

Florence cautioned him to modify his plans, but in his dressing gown and out of bed a part of each day, he scoffed at the thought that they might have to give up any part of their program. "I've got too much to do. I don't have time to be ill."[31]

She gave in then to his dreaming. He was stronger than she, and he loved life so deeply that she almost let herself be convinced.

"You're tough," she said admiringly. "You've never let anything conquer you, have you?"[32]

"If it's a weakling you want," he retorted, eyes twinkling, "never marry a Scotsman." Then he added seriously, "You and I don't have anything to say about our living or dying. When it's time for me to die, I'll have to. That's all there is to it."[33]

Friday afternoon, when Florence was giving him an alcohol rub, he laughed, "You'll make a regular sissy of me." He was feeling good and was impatient to be up for longer periods of mild activity.

"You could never be a sissy if you tried," she told him, smiling.[34] She turned away to dampen the washcloth again from the bottle of rubbing alcohol on the dresser. She heard a slight sound from the bed. When she turned back to him, he was unconscious, victim of a second stroke.

Dr. L. K. Zimmer, arriving in haste, advised that the patient was too critically ill to be moved from home to hospital.

Naismith emerged into a state of semiconsciousness in which he was unable to speak intelligibly. When Florence came near him, he struggled desperately to say something to her, which she was unable to understand. Dr. Zimmer, fearing that the futile effort to speak was too great a drain on Naismith's strength, gave instructions that the only attendants at the bedside be the Naismith children, whose presence was less exciting to the patient than that of his wife.

On Saturday Naismith lapsed into a coma from which he did not emerge. At 1:50 in the morning of Tuesday, November 28, at the beginning of the university basketball season, the father of basketball died at his home in Lawrence.[35]

His body was taken to Funk's Mortuary and Chapel at 940 Massachusetts Street, the mortuary where he had taught classes in the days when his church had needed extra space for its Sunday School program. Two days later the body was returned from the undertaker's establishment to the Naismith home, to lie in state from Thursday noon until Friday noon.

The news of Dr. James Naismith's death spread rapidly. In the Duke D'Ambra home, for one, the phone rang frequently, for every news and feature syndicate in America wanted pictures of the Naismith funeral, and D'Ambra had been recognized for years as the Naismith photographer.[36] "Get a picture as the casket is being carried from the Church" and "Get a picture . . . of the notables who may be pallbearers" were typical of the requests that poured in.[37]

But Duke D'Ambra reluctantly turned down all requests for photographs of the funeral. He remembered too poignantly that under a tall tree along a Missouri roadside he had promised James Naismith that he would not attend his friend's funeral. And he recalled that Doc used to say, "A man is as good as his promise. After all, what can you expect from a man who cannot be counted upon to keep his word?"[38]

It was not easy for a professional photographer such as D'Ambra to refuse an assignment. He admitted later, "Misrepresentations had to be used. Some people call them lies."[39] He recalled that it was the second time that he had failed a customer. "Believe it or not . . . Dr. Naismith was involved both times. The other time it was when I could not photograph him with the Dionne quintuplets."[40]

Friday afternoon, December 1, while most of the K.U. students were out of town on Thanksgiving vacation, ten pallbearers carried the casket of Dr. James Naismith into the First Presbyterian Church, while fourteen honorary pallbearers paid their respects. The crowd attending the two-thirty funeral service heard the Reverend Theodore H. Aszman eulogize Naismith as "truly one of God's noblemen," whose life was epitomized in the prayer "Create in me a clean heart, O God, and renew a right spirit in me."[41] Then in the last ceremony to be performed around the body of a man who disliked ceremony, final funeral services were conducted at the grave in Memorial Park Cemetery by the Masonic Blue Lodge No. 6 for their distinguished past master.

To Naismith acquaintances the strangest thing about the funeral services was that Duke D'Ambra, who was known to be in town that day, was not present. They could not understand why one of Naismith's best friends had stayed away.

Only after the funeral and burial were over did D'Ambra go to the cemetery with his camera. After Phog Allen had moved the floral arrangements out of the way and lined up his K.U. basketball players, D'Ambra took a photograph of Allen and the current basketball team at Naismith's grave. There had been only three basketball coaches in K.U.'s history—Naismith, Hamilton, and Allen—and now the first one, the man who had created the game, was dead. The way Phog figured, there should be a final photograph. But even this act caused trouble, for the Naismith family, hearing of it, telephoned their protest at the disarrangement of the funeral flowers.

When the deeds of James Naismith's life were counted after

his death, they were long and varied enough to fulfill the ambitions of three men. Three men he was, indeed—by official title Doctor of Divinity, Doctor of Medicine, and Master in Physical Education.

The list of organizations to which he had belonged and in which he had been an officer reflected his multiplicity of interests. He had held offices and/or memberships in lodge and church organizations, in local and state medical societies, and in several local, state, and national physical education organizations. He was honorary chairman and a life member of the National Basketball Committee of the United States and Canada (national rules committee); he had been honorary president of the Basketball Coaches' Association and of the International Federation of Basketball Leagues.[42] And there were many more societies, offices, and honors. Added to all this was the fact that he had originated basketball, the most popular sport in the world, which would soon be drawing ninety million paid admissions a year and was expanding in both the amateur and the professional fields.[43]

The eulogies delivered reflected the impact his life had made, and tributes were many. Governor Payne H. Ratner wrote to the Naismith family: "I feel that the nation owes a great debt of gratitude to Dr. Naismith for what he has done in behalf of the youth of our country."[44] The headline in the K.U. alumni publication read: "A Master Sportsman Has Completed His Assignment."[45] At Emporia, Kansas, a distinguished University of Kansas graduate composed a tribute. In the *Emporia Gazette* the day after Naismith's death, the renowned editor William Allen White wrote quietly:

The death of Dr. Naismith at the state university closes the life of a notable man who gave something to his generation. It was a game— the game of basketball. . . . Here is a man who has done a real service to humanity. . . . What a privilege it must have been, what a satisfaction for him to realize that he had done something worthy, something to make people happy, something really useful in this vale of tears. He had not a high talent, but he used what God gave him and made his life count. That is all any of us can do. May his ashes rest in peace![46]

A similar note was struck in the obituary in the *Journal of Health and Physical Education:* "Death should have no sting for a life whose devotion to the services [*sic*] of humanity achieved such gratifying results as did Dr. Naismith's."[47] On the K.U. campus the university flag on the tower of Fraser Hall was placed at half-mast. And from Strong Hall, Chancellor Deane W. Malott issued a statement in praise of the late Dr. Naismith: "Many nations of the world . . . will feel the loss of this man."[48] As if to corroborate the chancellor's declaration, from a country already involved in World War II came a lengthy letter of condolence for the widow—signed by Adolf Hitler.

After his family had read and clipped for their scrapbooks the obituaries and tributes from newspapers and journals throughout the United States and Canada, the reading of James Naismith's will was still to be held. Florence had not been aware that the doctor had taken time to change his existing will after they came home from their honeymoon. But he had. In the new will he left all his property to her with the exception of a twelve-hundred dollar share to each of his five children. Jack, griefstricken over his father's death and compassionate toward his widowed stepmother, signed a quitclaim and relinquished his share to Florence.

One ironic detail remained after everything else had been taken care of—the unanswered letter that James Naismith left.

Long years ago he and some of his classmates at the International Young Men's Christian Association Training School at Springfield had formed a club, the Ahikamin Circle of the King's Sons. The comrades held their group together after graduation by means of an annual chain letter. In mid-November, 1939, the small booklet in which each member was to write his annual news arrived at the Naismith home. Jim was too busy at the time to write his Ahikamin letter, and he had laid the missive aside. A few days later he was struck by his first cerebral hemorrhage.

After the funeral, in the space alloted in the booklet for James Naismith's note, his sorrowful children wrote the news of his death and sent the Ahikamin letter on to the next member in line, Amos Alonzo Stagg, whose dinner-party plans for the honeymooning Naismiths had miscarried a few months before.

31

Pattern for a Man

TODAY Memorial Park cemetery stretches like a green rolling park at the east edge of the small city of Lawrence, Kansas, with only a few shafts or memorial stones rising above ground to indicate that this is a burial place. Ducks swim on the pond at the bottom of a west-lying slope. At the far end of the central drive, at the quiet southern end of the cemetery, stands a Masonic shaft, with a group of simple graves circling it. Close to the shaft, in the inner circle of graves, is an unobtrusive double marker, a red granite stone sunk flat into the ground and inscribed with the names of James Naismith and his first wife, Maude, and with their dates of birth and death. Near this double grave a smaller stone marks son-in-law Leslie H. Dodd's grave, with a space left so that the date of Hellen Naismith Dodd's death can be added. A fourth grave is that of Dr. James Naismith's great-granddaughter, Leslie Lynn Dodd, whom he never saw. In the same inner circle where Naismith's grave is located, Duke D'Ambra has had a double stone installed for himself and his wife. In this simple group of graves the father of basketball lies, quietly, with no engraving to mention his famous accomplishment.[1]

As the future advances, forgetful of its heritage, existing reminders of Naismith's past disappear, just as memories of the year-long international celebration of the fiftieth birthday of basketball in 1941–1942 have faded.[2] Among these reminders, K.U.'s Fraser Hall, with its flag-tipped twin towers and its tall, stately interior shutters of fine-grained old wood that opened into the classrooms, is gone. Nothing is left of the chapel where Naismith led college students in prayer, for Frazer was razed in August of 1965 and has been replaced by a new building. Old Robinson Gymnasium is gone, too. This building where he lectured in classrooms, counseled students in his office, and instructed fencers, basketeers, and gymnasts in the gym has been torn down, its functions already taken over in 1966 by a new building with the same name, located down the south slope of the campus. And in the nearby village of Vinland the past has been left behind. The bell is gone from the unpainted steeple tower of the old Presbyterian church where Naismith preached, and the church has been turned into a storage granary. Behind the broken window panes of the church can be seen heaped bags of barley and piles of wheat and corn crowding out the rows of pews that were formerly there. Only two hymnals, lying on top of a small corn-sheller in the sanctuary, remain as vestiges of the past. Inside each hymnal is written: "Presbyterian Church of Vinland. Not to be taken from the church."[3]

But scattered over the American continent are reminders of James Naismith, and others are being built or planned. On the lawn of Naismith's boyhood home, the old Young farmhouse near Almonte, the Historic Sites Committee of the Canadian government erected a plaque on June 26, 1965, to honor its famous Canadian-American. The Highway Department of the Province of Ontario has built a drive to enable passers-by to leave the paved highway and visit this historic landmark.[4] In the town of Almonte a sixteen-by-eighteen-inch bronze plaque on the wall of the high-school gymnasium stands as a memorial to the creator of basketball, who attended school there. Presented by the Almonte Lions Club on June 28, 1953, to commemorate the sixty-second anniversary of the origin of the game of basketball, it hangs modestly, with the erroneous middle initial *A* included, in a new wing of the old stone building.[5] Latest tribute in Ramsay Township, in August, 1970, came the formal opening of the new Naismith Memorial School in Almonte, where a portrait of Dr. James Naismith holds a place of honor.[6]

The place where Naismith would have preferred that any memorial to him be constructed was Lawrence. In this city today there are several small reminders of the great citizen who lived there for forty-one years. The street that passes down the southern slope of the university campus toward the shadow of the huge Allen Field House bears a marker stating "Naismith Drive," while in the main foyer of the field house James Naismith's likeness looks down from a three-by-five-foot oil painting. Nearby stands a university dormitory named Naismith Hall. And in another section of the city, at his office near the duck pond, the sexton of Memorial Park speaks proudly of the Naismith memorial flower garden to be developed in the cemetery.[7]

National recognition of Naismith has been made in a way meant to reach into every American home. On September 25, 1961, announcement was made by federal officials of the forthcoming United States postage stamp honoring the hundredth anniversary of James Naismith's birth; and on the same day a short history of Naismith and of basketball was read into the Congressional Record by the United States representatives from Massachusetts and Kansas,[8] the two states where he had spent his most significant years. The hundredth anniversary of Naismith's birthday was celebrated on November 6, 1961, Basketball Commemoration Day, with the issuance of one hundred million copies of the commemorative postage stamp and by the laying of the cornerstone of the basketball Hall of Fame in Springfield.[9]

Awards have been set up in the name of James Naismith for outstanding high-school and college basketball players in Canada and the United States. One of the most recent awards established in the United States is the James Naismith Trophy sponsored by United Press International in recognition of the College Player of the Year, first bestowed in the spring of 1969 on basketball player Lew Alcindor.[10]

Most ambitious of all Naismith memorials, of course, is the Naismith Memorial Basketball Hall of Fame, officially opened on February 17, 1968, and formally enshrined April 16, 1968, on the campus of Springfield College in Springfield, Massachusetts.[11] After more than thirty years of planning, a shrine bearing his name has been constructed in the city where he created the game of basketball.[12] In this hall a few words engraved on a trophy cup on display reflect the international impact of the man and his game. Emblematic of the Fédération internationale de basketball amateur (FIBA) championships played every four years, this trophy bears the word "Naismith" in English, Egyptian, Arabic, and Chinese.

And, to be sure, every rusty iron basketball hoop fastened ten feet high on a pole, tree, garage, or barn wherever children gather to play, whatever the country, is a memorial to the man and a tribute to the game of basketball.

But perhaps the truest memorial is the imprint that James Naismith's life has left on the people who knew him.

Although Phog Allen has known the honor of being designated America's "Coach of the Year" after taking a basketball team to the Olympic Games in 1952 and although he has had a 17,500-seat field house named for him, still his dearest memory is his acquaintanceship with James Naismith. Old now and unable to walk unaided, Phog keeps in view a treasured possession, showing it proudly to visitors—a picture of Naismith autographed "From the Father of Basketball to the Father of Basketball Coaching."[13]

Among the members of Naismith's family his memory is cherished with an intensity that few fathers gain. His youngest child, namesake James, expressed admiration for his father's character. His adulation was phrased, perhaps unintentionally, in basketball terms: "He was a goal to shoot for in life."[14]

Naismith's long-time friend Duke D'Ambra paid him the greatest tribute of all: "He was my idea of a man. If I could choose a man as a pattern by which to make myself, I'd choose him."[15]

Notes

Many of the notes refer to interviews that the author held with various individuals or groups associated with James Naismith These interviews are listed below with the date and place of the interview. They will be referred to in the notes in shortened form.

Dr. Forrest C. Allen; Aug., 1963; Lawrence, Kans.
Almonte High School, office staff; June 25, 1964; Almonte, Ont.
Auld Kirk Cemetery, caretakers; June 24, 26, 1964; Almonte, Ont.
J. Neale Carman; Aug. 18, 1964; Lawrence, Kans.
Duke D'Ambra; Aug., 1963; Lawrence, Kans.
Mrs. Ann Naismith Dawe; Aug. 13–14, 1963; Thayer, Mo.
Mrs. Hellen Naismith Dodd; Sept. 3, 1963; Westcliffe, Colo.
Allan Donnell; June 24–26, 1964; Almonte, Ont.
Fred Ellsworth; Aug., 1963; Lawrence, Kans.
Miss May Gardner; Aug., 1963; Lawrence, Kans.
Mrs. Hugh Grace; June 24, 1964; Almonte, Ont.
Edward J. Hickox; June 20, 1964; Springfield, Mass.
Mrs. Edna Gardner Lowry; June 24, 1964; Almonte, Ont.
Hugh Means; Aug., 1963; Lawrence, Kans.
McGill University, Office of Athletics officials; June 23, 1964; Montreal, Que.
Florence (Mrs. James) Naismith, Sept. 6, 1963, and Aug. 11, 1964; Seneca, Kans.
Mr. and Mrs. J. S. Naismith; Apr. 18, 1964; Corpus Christi, Tex.
John Edwin ("Jack") Naismith; Aug. 11–15, 1964; Lawrence, Kans.
Mrs. William J. Naismith, Mrs. Albert Naismith, Miss Margaret ("Maggie") Naismith; June 26, 1964; Almonte, Ont.
New York Cleaners, office personnel; Aug., 1963; Lawrence, Kans.
Mr. and Mrs. Edward F. Oakes; June 20, 1964; Springfield, Mass.
Mrs. Stanton Olinger; Aug. 25, 1963; Lawrence, Kans.
The Presbyterian College, head of library; June 23, 1964; Montreal, Que.
Sigma Phi Epsilon fraternity members; Aug. 23, 1963; Lawrence, Kans.
Sprague Apartments residents; Aug. 24, 1963; Lawrence, Kans.
George and Margaret Naismith Stanley; Sept. 3, 1963; Gilman, Colo.
St. Marys Star, office employees; Aug. 19, 1964; St. Marys, Kans.
Mrs. Ferne Rumsey Vanderhoof (by telephone); Aug., 1963; Lawrence, Kans.
George Wilson (by telephone); July and Aug., 1964; Winnipeg, Man.
Mr. and Mrs. Robert ("Bert") Young; June 25, 1964; Almonte, Ont.

CHAPTER 1
Orphans at Bennie's Corners

1. Dawe and Stanley interviews; John Dewar, "The Life and Professional Contributions of James Naismith," p. 4.
2. Dewar, "Life," pp. 4–5.
3. Ibid., p. 5.
4. Ibid.
5. Young interview.
6. Ibid.
7. Ibid.
8. Dawe interview.
9. Young interview; cemetery records, the Auld Kirk, Almonte, Ont.
10. Letter from Edna Gardner Lowry, Aug. 19, 1965, Almonte, Ont.
11. Dawe and Maggie Naismith interviews; Lowry letter.
12. Interview with cemetery caretakers at the Auld Kirk.
13. Dawe interview.
14. *Almonte Gazette,* June 17, 1965, p. 1; Maggie Naismith interview.
15. Cemetery records, the Auld Kirk.
16. The baptismal name of the youngest Young daughter was either Janet (Dewar, "Life," pp. 6–7) or Jane (Lowry letter, Aug. 26, 1965, and John E. Young letter, Sept., 1965).
17. Dawe interview.
18. J. S. Naismith and Lowry interviews; Edna Gardner Lowry, "Early Church History," *A Family Record,* p. 5.
19. J. S. Naismith interview.
20. "James Naismith: Inventor of the Game of Basketball," Watson Collection, University of Kansas.

CHAPTER 2
Scots in Canada

1. Grace interview.
2. Dewar, "Life," p. 2.
3. Christopher Hussey, *Tait McKenzie: A Sculptor of Youth,* pp. 1–2.
4. Lowry, *A Family Record,* p. 7; Lowry interview; Jesse Edgar Middleton and Fred Landon, *The Province of Ontario—A History,* II, 929.
5. Middleton and Landon, *The Province of Ontario,* II, 929.
6. Lowry, "Some Early Ramsay History," p. 1, and *A Family Record,* p. 7; Lowry interview; Middleton and Landon, *The Province of Ontario,* II, 929 and 1150.
7. Lowry, "Some Early Ramsay History," p. 2.
8. Lowry and Jack Naismith interviews; Auld Kirk graveyard.
9. Dewar, "Life," p. 2.
10. Lowry, "Some Early Ramsay History," pp. 1–2, and "Early Church History," p. 5; Edwin C. Guillet, *Pioneer Days in Upper Canada,* pp. 63–71.
11. Lowry, "Some Early Ramsay History," pp. 1–2; James Naismith, *Basketball: Its Origin and Development,* p. 13.
12. Lowry interview; "Almonte, Ontario" (pamphlet); Middleton and Landon, *The Province of Ontario,* II, 1152.

13. Lowry interview; "Almonte, Ontario"; Middleton and Landon, *The Province of Ontario*, II, 1152.

14. Lowry interview; "Almonte, Ontario"; William Canniff, *History of the Province of Ontario (Upper Canada)*, p. 674.

15. Dawe interview; *Almonte Gazette*, June 17, 1965, p. 1.

16. J. S. Naismith interview; Dewar, "Life," p. 2.

17. J. S. Naismith interview.

18. Dewar, "Life," p. 2.

19. Stanley interview.

20. Lowry, *A Family Record*, pp. 2–4, and "Early Church History," pp. 4–6.

21. Lowry, "Early Church History," pp. 4–5, and interview.

22. Lowry, "Early Church History," p. 5, and letter of Aug. 19, 1965, Almonte, Ont.; *Almonte Gazette*, June 17, 1965, p. 7.

23. Dawe interview.

24. Lowry letters, Aug. 19 and 26, 1965, Almonte, Ont.; *Almonte Gazette*, June 17, 1965, p. 1; Stanley interview.

25. *Almonte Gazette*, June 17, 1965, p. 1; Lowry letter, Aug. 19, 1965.

CHAPTER 3

High-School Dropout and Lumberjack

1. This chapter is based in part on the following: Naismith, *Basketball* (chapter one, "Bennie's Corners"), pp. 13–28; Allan Donnell, "Extracts from a Talk to Almonte Lions, May, 1953" and "Basketball and Its Inventor, Dr. James Naismith."

2. Young, J. S. Naismith, and Dawe interviews.

3. Maggie Naismith interview.

4. *Almonte Gazette,* June 17, 1965, p. 1; "James Naismith: Inventor"; Grace Naismith, "Father Basketball," *Sports Illustrated,* Jan. 31, 1955, pp. 64–65.

5. Dawe interview.

6. D'Ambra interview.

7. Donnell, "Extracts," p. 2.

8. Dawe interview.

9. Naismith, *Basketball,* p. 17.

10. Hussey, *Tait McKenzie,* pp. 3–4.

11. Ibid., p. 3; R. Tait McKenzie, "Reminiscences of James Naismith," *Journal of Health and Physical Education,* IV (Jan., 1933), 21.

12. Guillet, *Pioneer Days,* pp. 41, 120–38.

13. Dewar, "Life," pp. 11–12; Guillet, *Pioneer Days,* p. 98.

14. McKenzie, "Reminiscences," p. 21; Guillet, *Pioneer Days,* pp. 110–11.

15. Grady Phelps, "National Ceremony Set for Basketball Founder," *Corpus Christi Caller-Times,* Nov. 5, 1961, p. 19; Hussey, *Tait McKenzie,* pp. 3–4.

16. Hussey, *Tait McKenzie,* p. 3; Edwin C. Guillet, *Pioneer Travel in Upper Canada,* p. 36.

17. Hussey, *Tait McKenzie,* pp. 3, 7.

18. Dewar, "Life," p. 12.
19. Dawe interview.
20. Lowry letter, Aug. 19, 1965.
21. Dodd interview.
22. From inspection by author of Dr. James Naismith's personal papers in the possession of his children, and of his class records in the Department of Physical Education, University of Kansas.
23. Lowry interview.
24. *Almonte Gazette,* Aug. 21, 1969, p. 1.
25. Dewar, "Life," p. 10.
26. Ibid.
27. *Almonte Gazette,* Aug. 21, 1969, p. 1.
28. Dewar, "Life," p. 12.
29. J. S. Naismith interview.
30. Ibid.
31. George F. Black, *The Surnames of Scotland,* p. 623.
32. *Almonte Gazette,* June 17, 1965, p. 7.
33. "The Mill of Kintail & Robert Tait McKenzie" (leaflet); Young interview.
34. Stanley interview.
35. McKenzie, "Reminiscences," p. 21.
36. Hussey, *Tait McKenzie,* p. 3.
37. Lowry interview; interview with office staff of Almonte High School.
38. Bob Hurt, "Basketball Got Away," *Topeka Daily Capital,* Feb. 4, 1962, p. 5C; Grace Naismith, "Father Basketball," p. 65.
39. "James Naismith: Inventor."
40. Guillet, *Pioneer Days,* pp. 84, 92.
41. Jack G. Hammig, "A Historical Sketch of Doctor James Naismith," p. 1; Dewar, "Life," pp. 15–16.
42. Guillet, *Pioneer Days,* p. 86.
43. Dawe interview.
44. Ibid.
45. Grace Naismith, "Father Basketball," p. 65.
46. Hurt, "Basketball Got Away," p. 5C.
47. Lowry and Donnell interviews.
48. "James Naismith: Inventor."
49. Hammig, "Historical Sketch," p. 2.
50. Dawe and Young interviews.
51. Stanley interview.
52. James Naismith, "Basketball—A Game the World Plays," *Rotarian,* Jan., 1939, p. 33; "James Naismith: Inventor."
53. "James Naismith: Inventor"; letter from Edna Gardner Lowry, Aug. 26, 1965.
54. Cyrus Macmillan, *McGill and Its Story, 1821–1921,* pp. 236–38.
55. Hugh MacLennan, ed., *McGill: The Story of a University,* p. 63.
56. Edgar Andrew Collard, *Oldest McGill,* p. 123 and passim; Dewar, "Life," p. 17.
57. Records in registrar's office, McGill University.

CHAPTER 4
Athlete and Scholar at McGill

1. Interview with officials in the Office of Athletics, McGill University.
2. MacLennan, *McGill*, pp. 23, 41.
3. This chapter is based in part on the following: Dewar, "Life," pp. 17–25; Naismith, *Basketball*, pp. 19–28, 41; R. Tait McKenzie, "Frederick S. Barnjum and His Work," *American Physical Education Review* (hereafter *APER*), II (June, 1897), pp. 73–80, and "Reminiscences," pp. 21, 55; *Toronto Globe*: Nov. 3, 1883, p. 16; Nov. 9, 1885, p. 8; Nov. 8, 1886, p. 3; Nov. 9, 1886, p. 3; Nov. 12, 1886, p. 3; Nov. 15, 1886, p. 3; Nov. 7, 1887, p. 2.
4. See also Donnell, "Extracts," p. 5.
5. MacLennan, *McGill*, pp. 49, 70; Collard, *Oldest McGill*, p. 113.
6. MacLennan, *McGill*, p. 23.
7. Donnell, "Extracts," p. 5.
8. Naismith, *Basketball*, pp. 20–21.
9. Nancy Howell and Maxwell L. Howell, *Sports and Games in Canadian Life: 1700 to the Present*, p. 99.
10. See also Fred Eugene Leonard, *A Guide to the History of Physical Education*, p. 397.
11. Howell and Howell, *Sports*, p. 80; Leonard, *Guide*, pp. 398–99.
12. J. G. G. Kerry, "Football in the Eighties," *McGill News*, XXXIV (Summer, 1953), 20–21.
13. *Toronto Globe*, Nov. 9, 1885, p. 8.
14. Dewar, "Life," p. 21.
15. *Toronto Globe*, Nov. 3, 1883, p. 16.
16. Jack Naismith interviews; Kerry, "Football," p. 20.
17. "James Naismith: Inventor"; M. Whitcomb Hess, "The Man Who Invented Basketball," *American Scholar*, XVIII (Winter, 1948–1949), p. 87.
18. "James Naismith: Inventor."
19. Howell and Howell, *Sports*, p. 78.
20. Kerry, "Football," p. 20.
21. *Toronto Globe*, Nov. 7, 1887, p. 2.
22. Ibid., Nov. 9, 1885, p. 8.
23. Kerry, "Football," p. 20; Leonard, *Guide*, p. 398.
24. "Kansas University: Items in Its History," III, Watson Collection, University of Kansas.
25. Leonard, *Guide*, p. 399.
26. Kerry, "Football," p. 20.
27. Howell and Howell, *Sports*, p. 78.
28. Kerry, "Football," p. 20.
29. *Toronto Globe*, Nov. 9, 1885, p. 8.
30. Ibid., Nov. 8, 1886, p. 3.
31. Ibid.
32. Ibid., Nov. 15, 1886, p. 3.
33. Ibid., Nov. 9, 1886, p. 3.
34. Interview with Mrs. William J. Naismith, Mrs. Albert Naismith, and Maggie Naismith.
35. Kerry, "Football," p. 21; Leonard, *Guide*, pp. 398–99.

36. Interview with office staff of Almonte High School.
37. Dawe interviews.
38. Jack Naismith interviews.
39. Maggie Naismith interview.
40. Young interview.
41. Jack Naismith interviews.
42. Young interview.
43. "The Mill of Kintail."
44. "James Naismith: Inventor."
45. Dawe interviews.
46. Hussey, *Tait McKenzie*, pp. 7–8.
47. See also Leonard, *Guide*, pp. 397–98.
48. Grace Naismith, "Father Basketball," p. 65.
49. See also "The Mill of Kintail"; Hussey, *Tait McKenzie*, pp. 7–8.
50. Collard, *Oldest McGill*, p. 35.
51. Dodd interview.
52. J. S. Naismith interview.
53. Emil Rath, "Report of Necrology Committee," *Journal of Health and Physical Education*, XI (Feb., 1940), 99; Leonard, *Guide*, p. 475.
54. Jack Naismith interviews.

CHAPTER 5

Great Decision at the Presbyterian College

1. Interview with head of library, the Presbyterian College; Macmillan, *McGill*, p. 234.
2. Dewar, "Life," p. 17.
3. Jack Naismith interviews; Grace Naismith, "Father Basketball," p. 65.
4. Interview with head of library, the Presbyterian College.
5. *Presbyterian College Journal*, monthly issues, 1887–1890.
6. Interview with head of library, the Presbyterian College.
7. Dewar, "Life," p. 23.
8. The discussion in this chapter is based in part on Naismith, *Basketball*, pp. 22–25, 41, 129.
9. "James Naismith: Inventor."
10. Howell and Howell, *Sports*, p. 70.
11. Glenn D. Everett, "The Canadian Who Gave Us Basketball," *Presbyterian Record*, Apr., 1962.
12. Interview with head of library, the Presbyterian College.
13. Stanley interview.
14. Interview with head of library, the Presbyterian College.
15. Dewar, "Life," p. 17.
16. Ibid., p. 28.
17. McKenzie, "Barnjum," p. 80; Howell and Howell, *Sports*, p. 99.
18. McKenzie, "Barnjum," p. 80; Hussey, *Tait McKenzie*, p. 8.
19. McKenzie, "Barnjum," pp. 75–78, 80, and "Reminiscences," p. 21.
20. McKenzie, "Reminiscences," p. 21; Hussey, *Tait McKenzie*, pp. 7–9 and passim; "McKenzie, Robert Tait," in *The Macmillan Dictionary of Canadian Biography*, p. 468.

21. McKenzie, "Reminiscences," p. 21.

22. Stanley interview.

23. Dewar, "Life," p. 26.

24. Interview with head of library, the Presbyterian College.

25. Naismith, *Basketball,* p. 22.

26. Ibid., p. 23.

27. Ibid.

28. Grace Naismith, "Father Basketball," p. 65.

29. "James Naismith: Inventor."

30. Naismith, *Basketball,* pp. 23–24.

31. "Young Men's Christian Association," in *Compton's Pictured Encyclopedia,* XV, 342.

32. "Springfield College," in *Funk & Wagnalls Standard Reference Encyclopedia,* XXII, 8201.

33. "Springfield College" (leaflet).

34. Robert H. Boyle, "Spirit, Mind, Body," *Sports Illustrated,* Dec. 2, 1963, p. 78.

35. Leonard, *Guide,* pp. 315, 322.

36. Interviews with Jack Naismith and head of library, the Presbyterian College.

37. McKenzie, "Reminiscenses," p. 55.

38. Howell and Howell, *Sports,* pp. 69–90.

39. Donnell, "Extracts," p. 6.

40. Naismith, *Basketball,* p. 129.

41. "James Naismith: Inventor."

42. Donnell, "Basketball," pp. 12–13, and interviews; Dewar, "Life," p. 32.

43. Donnell, "Basketball," pp. 12–13, and interview.

44. Naturalization papers, Dr. James Naismith: Declaration of Intention, dated Sept. 11, 1918.

45. "A Master Sportsman Has Completed His Assignment," *Graduate Magazine* (University of Kansas), XXXVIII (Dec., 1939), 5.

CHAPTER 6

Gymnasts South of the Canadian Border

1. Hickox interview; Alexander M. Weyand, *The Cavalcade of Basketball,* p. 6; Jack Naismith interviews.

2. The discussion in this chapter is based in part on the following: Naismith, *Basketball,* pp. 8, 24–42; James Naismith, "How Basketball Started and Why It Grew," in E. Dana Caulkins, ed., *Aims and Methods in School Athletics,* pp. 221–35; "James Naismith: Inventor"; Dewar, "Life," pp. 33–39, 51, 134.

3. J. S. Naismith interview; Boyle, "Spirit," p. 78.

4. Dewar, "Life," p. 134.

5. *Daily Advertiser* (Lafayette, La.), Mar. 18, 1965, p. 10; "Necessity Is the Mother of Invention" (leaflet of the Naismith Memorial Basketball Hall of Fame Committee), p. 1.

6. Naismith, *Basketball,* pp. 25–26.

7. Allen interviews; *Daily Advertiser* (Lafayette, La.), Mar. 18, 1965, p. 10.

8. Leonard, *Guide,* pp. 315, 318–25; Ethel Josephine Dorgan, *Luther Halsey Gulick, 1865–1918,* pp. 6–7, 9, 25–26, 60–70, and passim.

9. T. Duncan Patton, "The First Game: How and When Introduced," *in* "Old Timer's Exhibition" (leaflet of the Naismith Memorial Basketball Hall of Fame Committee).

10. Dorgan, *Gulick,* pp. 25–26.

11. Fred E. Leonard, *Pioneers of Modern Physical Training,* pp. 127–36; Jack Naismith interviews.

12. Hanford M. Burr, "Dr. Luther Halsey Gulick, Missionary," *in* "Dr. Luther Halsey Gulick, 1865–1918: A Symposium," *APER,* XXIII (Oct., 1918), 421; Leonard, *Pioneers,* p. 133.

13. Dorgan, *Gulick,* pp. 35–37; Persis B. McCurdy, "Editorial," *APER,* XXIII (Oct., 1918), 448–49.

14. Naismith, *Basketball,* p. 25.

15. Boyle, "Spirit," p. 78.

16. Ibid.

17. Weyand, *Cavalcade,* p. 5; *New York Times,* Dec. 13, 1890, p. 3.

18. *New York Times,* Dec. 13, 1890, p. 3.

19. Ibid.

20. Weyand, *Cavalcade,* p. 5.

21. *New York Times,* Dec. 13, 1890, p. 3.

22. Weyand, *Cavalcade,* p. 5.

23. "James Naismith: Inventor."

24. Naismith, *Basketball,* pp. 27–28.

25. Hickox interview.

26. Jack Naismith interviews.

27. Stanley, Oakes, Dawe, and J. S. Naismith interviews; letter from Mrs. Edward F. Oakes, July 19, 1964.

28. Oakes interview and letter.

29. Stanley, Dawe, and Oakes interviews.

30. Dodd and Jack Naismith interviews.

31. *Kansas City Star,* Nov. 28, 1939, p. 6.

32. "Naismith, James," in *Dictionary of American Biography,* XXII, Supp. 2 (to Dec. 31, 1940), 484.

33. Weyand, *Cavalcade,* p. 5; Jack Naismith interviews; *New York Times,* Apr. 3, 1936, p. 25.

34. Leonard, *Guide,* pp. 315, 318–25.

35. Ibid., pp. 317–18, 330, 333.

36. Grace Naismith, "Father Basketball," p. 65; Phelps, "National Ceremony," p. 19.

37. Patton, "First Game."

38. Dorgan, *Gulick,* pp. 32–33 and passim.

39. Grace Naismith, "Father Basketball," p. 65.

40. Patton, "First Game"; Frank G. Menke, *The Encyclopedia of Sports,* p. 161; Naismith, *Basketball,* pp. 32–33.

41. Grace Naismith, "Father Basketball," p. 65; "Necessity Is the Mother of Invention," p. 1.

42. Dodd interview.

43. See also "Necessity Is the Mother of Invention," p. 1.

44. W. J. Saunders, "Former Principal of A.H.S. Writes about Naismith," *Almonte Gazette,* Sept. 10, 1964; Patton, "First Game."

45. Naismith, Basketball, pp. 39–40.

46. "Lacrosse," in *Funk & Wagnalls Standard Reference Encyclopedia,* XV, 5470–71.

CHAPTER 7

Peach Baskets at Springfield

1. Letter from J. Halsey Gulick, Dec. 12, 1963.

2. "A Peachbasket Prodigy," *Monsanto Magazine,* Dec., 1961, p. 10.

3. This chapter is based in part on the following: Naismith, *Basketball,* pp. 29–99, and "How Basketball Started," pp. 221–30; "Necessity Is the Mother of Invention."

4. Naismith, *Basketball,* p. 46.

5. Jack Naismith interviews.

6. *Topeka Daily Capital Sunday Magazine,* Mar. 23, 1958, p. 11A; Duke D'Ambra, "The Doctor and the Baskets," *Empire Magazine* (Sunday magazine of the *Denver Post*), Jan. 19, 1958, p. 8; Donnell interviews.

7. G. L. Comba, quoted in *Almonte Gazette* (1953?), from Donnell interview.

8. "James Naismith: Inventor."

9. *New York Times,* Nov. 28, 1939, p. 25; Menke, *Encyclopedia of Sports,* p. 162; "James Naismith: Inventor."

10. "Necessity Is the Mother of Invention," p. 1.

11. Jack Naismith interviews.

12. "James Naismith: Inventor"; cf. Naismith, *Basketball,* pp. 52–53.

13. A first-hand source, relying on memory, states: "For the basket Naismith used the old styled peach basket with the bottom knocked out"—letter from Mrs. Edward F. Oakes, July 19, 1964. Another source describes the baskets used in early games as being placed on their sides, open ends toward the players—W. J. Saunders, in *Almonte Gazette,* Sept. 10, 1964. These descriptions, however, are contradicted by early photographs and drawings.

14. Naismith, *Basketball,* p. 53.

15. Ibid.

16. Ibid., pp. 55–56.

17. See also Patton, "First Game"; "James Naismith: Inventor."

18. Naismith, *Basketball,* pp. 51–52.

19. Published sources offer a choice of three dates for the first basketball game: December 21, 1891, January 15 and January 20, 1892. *New York Times,* Nov. 28, 1939, p. 25. Naismith, however, has stated that the game was first played before Christmas in 1891.

20. Grace Naismith, "Father Basketball," p. 64; Patton, "First Game"; Hickox interview.

21. "Old Timer's Exhibition"; Weyand, *Cavalcade,* p. 8; Patton, "First Game."

22. Grace Naismith, "Father Basketball," p. 64; Weyand, *Cavalcade,* p. 6.

23. Naismith, *Basketball*, pp. 57–60.
24. Jack Naismith interviews; Leonard, *Guide*, p. 472.

CHAPTER 8

Who's Gone Crazy?

1. Hickox interview. This chapter is also based in part on the following: Naismith, *Basketball*, pp. 29–60, 109–70, and "How Basketball Started," pp. 221–35; Weyand, *Cavalcade*, pp. 17–19, 221.
2. See also Patton, "First Game."
3. *New York Times,* Apr. 26, 1892, p. 2.
4. Ibid.
5. Ibid., Dec. 25, 1893, p. 10.
6. Ibid., Nov. 8, 1894, p. 3.
7. Ibid., Dec. 25, 1893, p. 10.
8. *Topeka Daily Capital,* Nov. 29, 1939, p. 9.
9. *Springfield* (Mass.) *Republican,* Mar. 12, 1892.
10. *New York Times,* Apr. 3, 1936, p. 25, and Nov. 28, 1939, p. 25.
11. Ibid., Nov. 28, 1939, p. 25.
12. Naismith, *Basketball,* pp. 164–65; quoted from *Denver News,* Feb. 1, 1896.
13. Margaret H. Meyer and Marguerite M. Schwarz, *Technic of Team Sports for Women* (2d ed., Philadelphia: W. B. Saunders Co., 1948), p. 14.
14. "Necessity Is the Mother of Invention," p. 1.
15. Weyand, *Cavalcade,* p. 18.
16. Ibid., p. 19.
17. John Allen Krout, *Annals of American Sport,* vol. XV of The Pageant of America, p. 267.
18. Ibid., p. 266.
19. Hurt, "Basketball Got Away," p. 5C.
20. "Necessity Is the Mother of Invention," p. 1.
21. "James Naismith: Inventor."
22. Ibid.
23. Everett, "Canadian."
24. Letter from J. Halsey Gulick, Dec. 12, 1963.

CHAPTER 9

Thirteen Rules and Nine Players

1. This chapter is based in part on the following: Naismith, *Basketball,* pp. 61–114, and "How Basketball Started," pp. 228–35.
2. "James Naismith: Inventor"; Jack Naismith interviews.
3. James Naismith, "Basket Ball," *Triangle,* I (Jan. 15, 1892), 144–47, quoted in Weyand, *Cavalcade,* p. 8; "Necessity Is the Mother of Invention," p. 1.
4. Weyand, *Cavalcade,* p. 8.
5. See also Forrest C. Allen, *Better Basketball,* p. 46.
6. Menke, *Encyclopedia of Sports,* p. 161.
7. *Topeka Daily Capital,* Nov. 29, 1939, p. 9.

8. Jack Naismith interviews.
9. Grace Naismith, "Father Basketball," p. 65.
10. Menke, *Encyclopedia of Sports,* p. 160.
11. "Basketball," in *Encyclopaedia Britannica,* III, 248.
12. Menke, *Encyclopedia of Sports,* p. 160.
13. Naismith, *Basketball,* pp. 63–64.
14. Naismith, "How Basketball Started," p. 234.
15. "James Naismith: Inventor."
16. Phelps, "National Ceremony," p. 19.
17. Naismith, *Basketball,* pp. 53–54.
18. *Daily Advertiser* (Lafayette, La.), Feb. 12, 1970, p. 1; *Family Weekly* (Sunday magazine of *Daily Advertiser*), Sept. 7, 1969, p. 2; *Winnipeg Free Press,* Aug. 8, 1964.
19. Naismith, "How Basketball Started," p. 230.
20. Donnell interviews.
21. Weyand, *Cavalcade,* pp. 1–2.
22. Ibid., p. 3.
23. Ibid., p. 4.
24. Ibid., pp. 4–5.
25. Ibid., pp. 1–5.
26. Quoted in *Almonte Gazette* (1953?), from Donnell interview.
27. D'Ambra, "The Doctor," p. 8.
28. Letter from J. Halsey Gulick, Dec. 12, 1963.
29. Weyand, *Cavalcade,* pp. 2–3; also letter from J. Halsey Gulick, March 13, 1972.
30. When James Naismith signed the original copy of the thirteen basketball rules, many years after he had written them, he mistakenly dated the sheets of paper February, 1892, although the rules had been published in the January, 1892, issue of *Triangle.* He retyped the rules on June 28, 1931, adding minor handwritten clarifications, signature, and current date. (Photo and caption in "Naismith Memorial Basketball Hall of Fame," in *Springfield, Massachusetts, Sunday Republican,* Apr. 14, 1968, p. 22A.)

CHAPTER 10

Courtship, Marriage, and Westward Ho

1. Dawe interviews.
2. Letter from Bess S. (Mrs. Edward F.) Oakes, July 19, 1964.
3. Stanley and D'Ambra interviews.
4. J. S. Naismith interviews; Mrs. Oakes's letter; Dawe interviews; "James Naismith: Inventor"; Stanley interview.
5. D'Ambra, Dawe, Stanley, J. S. Naismith, and Oakes interviews.
6. D'Ambra interview.
7. Stanley interview.
8. Ibid.
9. J. S. Naismith interview.
10. Allen interviews.
11. Naismith, *Basketball,* pp. 162–63.
12. "James Naismith: Inventor."

13. Mrs. Oakes's letter.
14. Naismith, *Basketball*, pp. 162–63.
15. Oakes interview; McKenzie, "Reminiscences," p. 55.
16. Leonard, *Guide*, pp. 465–66.
17. Mrs. Oakes's letter.
18. J. S. Naismith and Dawe interviews.
19. Oakes interview and Mrs. Oakes's letter.
20. Oakes interview.
21. Ibid.
22. "James Naismith: Inventor"; Jack Naismith interviews.
23. "McCurdy, James Huff," in *The National Cyclopaedia of American Biography* (1893), XXX, 185.
24. Forrest C. Allen, *Coach "Phog" Allen's Sports Stories for You and Youth,* pp. 109–10; Allen interviews.
25. Leonard, *Guide,* p. 474.
26. Dewar, "Life," pp. 41–42.
27. *Daily Advertiser* (Lafayette, La.), Mar. 18, 1965, p. 10.
28. Weyand, *Cavalcade,* p. 21.
29. Mrs. Oakes's letter and Oakes interview.
30. Stanley interview.
31. Ibid.
32. Jack Naismith interviews.
33. "James Naismith: Inventor"; Phelps, "National Ceremony," p. 19.
34. Grace Naismith, "Father Basketball," p. 65.
35. *Rocky Mountain News* (Denver), June 6, 1897, p. 1.
36. Letter from William A. Douglas, July 15, 1964.
37. Naturalization records of James Naismith: Declaration of Intention, dated Sept. 11, 1918.

CHAPTER 11

Pulpit to Gymnasium to Medical School

1. Menke, *Encyclopedia of Sports,* p. 161.
2. This chapter is based in part on the following issues of *Rocky Mountain News* (Denver) available in the Library of the State Historical Society of Colorado, Denver Public Library: Mar. 30, 1896, p. 5; Sept. 10, 1896, p. 6; May 23, 1897, pp. 13, 16; June 6, 1897, p. 1; June 7, 1897, p. 4; June 8, 1897, p. 10; June 15, 1897, p. 1; July 6, 1897, pp. 1, 7; Dec. 18, 1897, p. 1; Mar. 2, 1898, pp. 4, 7; Apr. 11, 1898, p. 8; Apr. 13, 1898, p. 8; Apr. 14, 1898, p. 8; and *Denver Evening Post,* Sept. 25, 1896, pp. 1, 3, 6, 7.
3. *Rocky Mountain News* (Denver), Mar. 30, 1896, p. 5.
4. Ibid.
5. See also letter from William A. Douglas, July 15, 1964.
6. Naismith, *Basketball*, pp. 124–25.
7. Douglas letter.
8. Ibid.
9. *Rocky Mountain News* (Denver), July 6, 1897, p. 1.
10. Douglas letter.
11. Dawe, Oakes, and Dodd interviews.

12. J. S. Naismith interview.
13. J. S. Naismith, Stanley, and Oakes interviews.
14. Stanley and Dawe interviews.
15. Dawe interviews.
16. *New York Times,* Nov. 28, 1939, p. 25.
17. Stanley interview.
18. Ibid.
19. Stanley, J. S. Naismith, and Jack Naismith interviews.
20. J. S. Naismith interview.
21. Ibid.
22. Jack Naismith interviews; Douglas letter.
23. *Rocky Mountain News* (Denver), Apr. 13, 1898, p. 8.
24. J. S. Naismith interview.
25. "Items about the Faculty Members of the University of Kansas," I, Watson Collection, University of Kansas.
26. Letter from Duke D'Ambra, Aug. 26, 1970.
27. Ibid.
28. Ibid.
29. Ibid.
30. Ibid.
31. Ibid.

CHAPTER 12
To the Halls of Fraser and the Banks of the Kaw

1. This chapter is based in part on the following: Fred Ellsworth, "Our Amazing Chancellors," a series of articles in *Kansas Alumni*: LXIII (Oct., 1964), 6–8, 22–23; LXIII (Nov., 1964), 12–13, 22; LXIII (Dec., 1964), 10–11; Deane Malott, "Sturdy Folks—Our Founding Fathers," *Kansas Alumni,* LXIV (Mar./Apr., 1966), 10–15; Walt Blackledge, "End of an Era," *Kansas Alumni,* LXIV (Nov., 1965), 10–12, 30. See also *University Daily Kansan,* Feb. 25, 1936, p. 2; Clyde Kenneth Hyder, *Snow of Kansas,* pp. 215–16; Allen interviews; Hammig, "Historical Sketch," pp. 10–11.
2. Hyder, *Snow of Kansas,* p. 215; Ellsworth interview.
3. Hurt, "Basketball Got Away," p. 5C; *Lawrence Daily Journal-World,* Nov. 28, 1939, p. 2; Hyder, *Snow of Kansas,* pp. 215–16; Allen and Ellsworth interviews.
4. Dewar, "Life," pp. 55–56.
5. Letter from Shirley Leslie, Aug. 18, 1964; Grace Naismith, "Father Basketball," p. 65.
6. Malott, "Sturdy Folks," p. 11.
7. Ibid.
8. Ellsworth, "Our Amazing Chancellors," *Kansas Alumni,* LXIII (Nov., 1964), 22.
9. Holly Thompson, "KU Profile," *Kansas Alumni,* LXVII (Dec., 1968, Jan., 1969), 31.
10. *University Daily Kansan,* Feb. 25, 1936, p. 2; Dewar, "Life," p. 56.
11. "James Naismith: Inventor"; naturalization records of James Naismith.

12. D[ick] W[intermote], "Chiming In," *Kansas Alumni*, LXVI (Feb., 1968), 12; LXIX (May 16, 1970), 7.

13. "James Naismith: Inventor."

14. Personal observation by author.

15. Malott, "Sturdy Folks," p. 12.

16. Blackledge, "End of an Era," p. 30.

17. Ibid.

18. John Kiely, "Skeletons, Top Hats and the Red Peril," *Kansas Alumni*, LXVIII (Oct., 1969), 20.

19. Ibid.

20. Ibid.

21. "Pictures of the Past," *Kansas Alumni*, LXIV (Mar./Apr., 1966), 6.

22. Dewar, "Life," p. 17.

23. Robert Taft, *Across the Years on Mount Oread, 1886–1941*, p. 80.

24. "Quantrill, William Clarke," in *Funk & Wagnalls Standard Reference Encyclopedia* (1961), XX, 7359.

25. "Along the Jayhawk Walk," *Kansas Alumni*, LXVII (Nov., 1968), 14.

26. Chittenden's Lawrence City Directory, IV (1898), Lawrence, Kans.

27. Ibid.

28. "Lawrence Industry" (leaflet of the Chamber of Commerce of Lawrence, Kans.); "A Last Salute to Faithful Jayhawkers," *Kansas Alumni*, LXIII (Nov., 1964), 37.

29. Chittenden's Lawrence City Directory, IV (1898), Lawrence, Kans.

CHAPTER 13

The Basketball Man on Mount Oread

1. Ed Elbel, "50 Years on the Cinder Path," *Kansas Alumni*, LXIII (Mar., 1965), 8–9.

2. Ibid., p. 8.

3. This chapter is based in part on the following: "James Naismith: Inventor"; "Across the Years: Naismith's Game," *Kansas Alumni*, LXVIII (Jan., 1970), 18; *Kansas University Weekly* (subsequent titles: *Kansan* and *University Daily Kansan*): Dec. 10, 1898, p. 1; Feb. 4, 1899, p. 1; Oct. 30, 1909, p. 3; Mar. 9, 1924, p. 3. See also Hyder, *Snow of Kansas*, p. 214.

4. "Kansas University: Items in Its History," III, 16.

5. "Skiing in Kansas," *Kansas Alumni*, LXVIII (Jan., 1970), 6–7.

6. "Readers Forum: Basketball and Moratoriums," *Kansas Alumni*, LXVIII (Apr., 1970), 2.

7. Dewar, "Life," pp. 61–62.

8. Naismith, *Basketball*, p. 126.

9. *Kansas University Weekly*, Dec. 10, 1898, p. 1.

10. "Across the Years: Naismith's Game," p. 18.

11. Ibid.

12. "Readers Forum: Basketball and Moratoriums," p. 2.

13. Ibid.

14. Ellsworth, "Our Amazing Chancellors," *Kansas Alumni*, LXIII (Dec., 1964), 10.

15. "Robinson Gymnasium," *Kansas Alumni*, LXV (Sept., 1966), 18.

16. City directories, Lawrence, Kans., 1898, 1902–1903, 1905 through 1919; interview with office personnel of New York Cleaners, Lawrence, Kans.

17. *New York Times,* Dec. 25, 1893, p. 10.

18. "James Naismith: Inventor"; "Kansas University: Items in Its History."

19. "Robinson Gymnasium," p. 18.

20. Basketball Program, Allen Field House Dedication, Mar. 1, 1955.

21. James Naismith, "High School Athletics and Gymnastics As an Expression of the Corporate Life of the High School," *in* Charles Hughes Johnston, ed., *The Modern High School,* pp. 447, 450–51.

22. Ibid., p. 462.

23. See also Theodore M. O'Leary, "Basketball a Triumph of Dr. Naismith's Logic," *Kansas City Times,* Nov. 11, 1961.

24. *New York Times,* Apr. 3, 1936, p. 25, and Nov. 28, 1939, p. 25.

25. O'Leary, "Basketball"; "James Naismith: Inventor."

26. See also Allen, *Coach "Phog,"* p. 109; Allen interview.

27. Frank Deford, "In Search of Naismith's Game," *Sports Illustrated,* Mar. 6, 1967, p. 32.

28. Naismith, *Basketball,* facing p. 111.

29. "The Incredible Phog," *Kansas Alumni,* LXVIII (Mar., 1970), pp. 4–5.

CHAPTER 14
Prayers, Sports, and Students

1. This chapter is based in part on the following: Ellsworth, "Our Amazing Chancellors," *Kansas Alumni,* LXIII (Nov., 1964), 12–13, 22, and LXIII (Dec., 1964), 10–11; "James Naismith: Inventor"; *Kansan:* Nov. 2, 1909, p. 1; Mar. 11, 1911; Mar. 18, 1911, p. 3; May 27, 1911, p. 1.

2. Allen interviews.

3. Allen and Ellsworth interviews.

4. Ellsworth interview.

5. Letter from Mildred Clodfelter, May 7, 1970.

6. Malott, "Sturdy Folks," p. 13.

7. Taft, *Across the Years,* p. 82.

8. Interviews with faculty members of the Department of Physical Education, University of Kansas, Aug., 1963.

9. Albert Bushnell Hart, "The Status of Athletics in American Colleges," *Atlantic Monthly,* LXVI (July, 1890), 64.

10. Ibid., p. 66.

11. When the Board of Regents later rescinded the ruling, Naismith had retired. A resolution of the University Athletic Board, drawn up in his honor after his death, states, disregarding any interrupted service, that he was a member of the Board from 1901 until 1937.

12. Interviews with Jack Naismith; "Rugby!" *Kansas Alumni,* LXV (June, 1967), 10; Hyder, *Snow of Kansas,* p. 216.

13. "Kansas University: Items in Its History," I, 105.

14. "Fencing," in *Funk & Wagnalls Standard Reference Encyclopedia* (1962), X, 3439–40.

15. "Kansas University: Items in Its History," I, 105; J. S. Naismith interview; Phelps, "National Ceremony, p. 19.

16. Gardner interview.

17. Stanley interview.

18. "That Wonderful Year—1929," *Kansas Alumni,* LXVII (Feb., 1969), 13.

19. See also "Pictures of the Past," *Kansas Alumni,* LXIV (Mar./Apr., 1966), 7.

20. Elbel, "50 Years," p. 9.

21. Ibid.

22. Ibid., pp. 9, 31.

23. Ibid., p. 31.

24. *Jayhawker,* 1908, unnumbered page facing "The New Gymnasium."

25. Taft, *Across the Years,* p. 80.

26. Stanley interview; Hammig, "Historical Sketch," pp. 12–13 and passim.

27. Ibid.

28. See also letter from a K.U. alumnus, Alumni Office, University of Kansas.

29. Ellsworth interview.

30. Letter from a K.U. alumnus, Alumni Office, University of Kansas.

31. O'Leary, "Basketball," *Kansas City Times,* Nov. 11, 1961; Olinger interview.

32. *Congressional Record,* CVII, pt. 16 (Sept. 22, 1961, to Sept. 26, 1961), Sept. 25, 1961, p. 21199.

33. "Hy-Lo Ball," *APER,* XXII (Nov., 1917), 567–69; James Naismith, "Vrille (Vree) Ball," *APER,* XXIV (Feb., 1919), 116–18; "A New Adaptation of Basket Ball," *APER,* XXII (June, 1917), 385–86; "Naismith Week," *Time,* Feb. 24, 1936, p. 28.

34. M. J. Exner, "Social Hygiene and the War," *Social Hygiene,* V (July, 1919), 293.

35. Stanley interview.

36. "Fraternities Today," *Kansas Alumni,* LXVIII (Mar., 1970), 7.

37. Interview with members of Sigma Phi Epsilon fraternity.

38. Kiely, "Skeletons," p. 20.

39. Taft, *Across the Years,* p. 83.

40. Chris Taylor, "Dodge City's Oldest Practicing Attorney," *Kansas Alumni,* LXVII (June, 1969), 28.

41. Department of Physical Education interviews.

42. See also "Pictures of the Past," *Kansas Alumni,* LXIV (Mar./Apr., 1966), p. 7.

43. Phelps, "National Ceremony," p. 19.

44. J. S. Naismith interview.

45. Ibid.

46. Interviews with residents of Sprague Apartments.

47. *Oberlin* (Kansas) *Herald,* Jan. 15, 1970, p. 2; Malott, "Sturdy Folks," p. 13; "Items about the Faculty Members of the University of Kansas," IV.

48. P. Everett Sperry, *From Sod to Sodom,* p. 23.

49. "Items about the Faculty Members of the University of Kansas," IV.

50. Dodd and Dawe interviews.
51. *Daily Advertiser* (Lafayette, La.), Mar. 18, 1965, p. 10.
52. Leonard, *Guide,* pp. 318–19, 324, 468.

CHAPTER 15
"I'll Lend No More of My Babies"

1. *University Kansan,* Oct. 30, 1909, p. 3.
2. Department of Physical Education interviews; Leonard, *Guide,* pp. 322–23, 465.
3. This chapter is based in part on the following: James Naismith, "An Improved Basis for Judging and Comparing the Physical Development of Children," *Kansas University Bulletin of Education,* III (Dec., 1930), 14–24; records kept by James Naismith, Department of Physical Education, University of Kansas. See also Hart, "Status of Athletics," pp. 65–66; Leonard, *Guide,* pp. 465–66.
4. Alvin D. Ward, Edwin R. Elbel, and Kenneth E. Anderson, "Comparison of Bodily Measurements of Entering University Students," *University of Kansas Bulletin of Education,* VIII (Nov., 1953), 7.
5. Ibid., p. 8.
6. Records kept by James Naismith, Department of Physical Education, University of Kansas.
7. Dawe interviews.
8. J. S. Naismith interview.
9. Ibid.
10. Ibid.
11. Naismith, "An Improved Basis," pp. 20, 23–24.
12. "James Naismith: Inventor"; Department of Physical Education interviews.
13. Naismith, "Basket Ball," *APER,* XIX (May, 1914), 340.
14. Stanley interview.
15. "James Naismith: Inventor."
16. Naismith, *Basketball,* pp. 171–80.
17. J. McKeen Cattell, ed., *Leaders in Education: A Biographical Directory* (1st ed., Lancaster, Pa.: Science Press, 1932), p. 681.
18. Naismith, *Basketball,* pp. 173–74.
19. Department of Physical Education interviews.
20. Ibid.
21. Ward, Elbel, and Anderson, "Comparison," pp. 7, 8, 11, and passim.
22. Ellsworth interview.
23. Jack Naismith interviews.
24. J. S. Naismith interview.
25. "James Naismith: Inventor."
26. Personal observation by author, Almonte, Ont.

CHAPTER 16
Home and Community

1. "Our First One Hundred Years, 1858–1958" (pamphlet issued by First Presbyterian Church, Lawrence, Kans.), p. 13.

2. Ibid., pp. 13–14; church records, First Presbyterian Church, Lawrence, Kans.

3. This chapter is based in part on the following: Dawe, J. S. Naismith, Jack Naismith, and Olinger interviews. See also "James Naismith: Inventor" and "Our First One Hundred Years, 1858–1958," p. 25.

4. "Our First One Hundred Years, 1858–1958," p. 25.

5. Ann Ogden, "KSR Comes of Age," *Kansas Alumni*, LXVI (June, 1968), 8.

6. "Our First One Hundred Years, 1858–1958," pp. 14–16; *Lawrence Today and Yesterday, 1913*, p. 80.

7. Olinger interview.

8. "Young Men's Christian Association," in *Funk & Wagnalls Standard Reference Encyclopedia* (1961), XXV, 9432.

9. Interview with office personnel, New York Cleaners; personal observation by author.

10. "Items about the Faculty Members of the University of Kansas," III, 8–9.

11. "James Naismith: Inventor."

12. Also Allen interviews.

13. Olinger interview.

14. See also "James Naismith: Inventor"; Dodd interview; Dewar, "Life," pp. 102–30.

15. Christine Miller Hetzel, "Cheers & Jeers" (letters to editor), *Kansas Alumni*, LXVI (Oct., 1967), 42.

16. Walt Blackledge, "A Lot of K.U. Wrapped Up in Bronze," *Kansas Alumni*, LXIV (Oct., 1965), 6–7.

17. See also "James Naismith: Inventor."

18. J. S. Naismith interview.

19. D'Ambra interviews.

20. Naturalization records of James Naismith: Petition for Naturalization, Nov. 5, 1924; Certificate of Naturalization #1971558, May 4, 1925.

21. Allen interviews.

22. Letter from Allan Donnell, Aug. 24, 1964; Donnell interviews; Edna Gardner Lowry, "Dr. James Naismith, 1861–1939: Inventor of Basketball."

23. Young interviews.

24. Letters from Edna Gardner Lowry, Aug. 24, 1964, and Aug. 19, 1965; Lowry interview.

25. City directories, Lawrence, Kans., 1902–1903, 1905.

26. Also Dodd interview.

27. Jack Naismith interview.

28. City directory, Lawrence, Kans., VIII, 1907.

29. Ibid.

30. Dawe interviews.

31. Jack Naismith interviews.

32. See also "The Gallopin' Goose," *Jayhawker Magazine Yearbook*, LXXVII (Fall, 1965), 54–55; Ellsworth, "Our Amazing Chancellors," *Kansas Alumni*, LXIII (Dec., 1964), 11; "Pictures of the Past," *Kansas Alumni*, LXIV (Mar./Apr., 1966), p. 8.

33. Dawe interviews.

34. "Items about the Faculty Members of the University of Kansas," IV.
35. Also Dodd interview.
36. Dawe interview.
37. "When Doctor Naismith 'Found' a Star," *Graduate Magazine*, XXII (Feb., 1924), 16–17.
38. Ibid.
39. Hess, "Man Who Invented," p. 90.
40. Stanley interview.
41. Also ibid.
42. Ibid.
43. J. S. Naismith interviews.
44. See also Donnell, "Extracts."
45. Jack Naismith interviews.
46. Oakes and Young interviews.
47. "James Naismith: Inventor"; Allen interviews; letter from Forrest C. Allen to Allan Donnell, May 20, 1953, in "James Naismith: Inventor."
48. Allen interviews; "James Naismith: Inventor."
49. See also Allen letter to Donnell.
50. Donnell letter.

CHAPTER 17

Spare the Rod

1. Ellsworth and Allen interviews.
2. Ibid.
3. Dorgan, *Gulick,* p. 12.
4. This chapter is based in part on the J. S. Naismith, Jack Naismith, and Dawe interviews.
5. Also Ellsworth interview.
6. James Naismith, "Universal Military Training," *APER*, XXIV (Apr., 1919), 202.
7. J. S. Naismith interview.
8. Stanley interview.
9. Also Oakes interview.
10. Also Vanderhoof interview.
11. Ibid.
12. Jack Naismith interviews.
13. Ibid.
14. See also "James Naismith: Inventor."
15. Elmer Verner McCollum, *From Kansas Farm Boy to Scientist* (Lawrence, Kans.: University of Kansas Press, 1964), pp. 71–73, 88; "Study, Think—and Sleep Well, Men," *Kansas Alumni*, LXIV (Dec., 1965, Jan., 1966), 8; "Along the Jayhawk Walk," *Kansas Alumni*, LXIV (Nov., 1965), 14; "A Last Salute," *Kansas Alumni*, LXVI (Dec., 1967, Jan., 1968), 41.
16. McCollum, *From Kansas Farm Boy,* p. 88.
17. "A Last Salute," p. 41; " 'The Best Hope of Humanity' "; "Study, Think—and Sleep Well, Men," p. 8.
18. Naismith, *Basketball,* pp. 17–18.
19. Dawe interviews.

20. Ibid.
21. Jack Naismith interviews.
22. Ibid.
23. Ibid.
24. Allen interviews.
25. Olinger interview.
26. Allen interviews.
27. Dick Williams, "The Boy Who Could Never Run," *Reader's Digest,* XXV (Nov., 1934), 88–90; Walt Blackledge, "Glenn's Second Mile," *Kansas Alumni,* LXVI (May, 1968), 6.
28. J. S. Naismith interview.
29. Ibid.
30. D'Ambra interview.
31. Oakes interview.
32. Ibid.
33. Jack Naismith interviews.
34. "A Master Sportsman Has Completed His Assignment," p. 5.
35. Allen interviews.
36. Jack Naismith interviews.
37. Ibid.
38. Ibid.
39. Dodd interview.
40. Ibid.
41. Dodd and Jack Naismith interviews.
42. Naismith, "Universal Military Training," p. 203.
43. Ibid.
44. Ibid.
45. M. Whitcomb Hess, "And He Called It Basketball," *in* "James Naismith: Inventor."

CHAPTER 18

Chaplain on the Mexican Border

1. This chapter is based in part on the Stanley and Means interviews.
2. Jack Naismith interviews.
3. Stanley interview.
4. J. S. Naismith interview.
5. Church records and interview with minister of First Presbyterian Church, Lawrence, Kans.
6. Ellsworth interview.
7. Military records of James Naismith (Certificate of Service, First Regiment, Kansas National Guard).
8. "Villa, Francisco," in *Funk & Wagnalls Standard Reference Encyclopedia* (1962), XXIV, 9001; Lewis Paul Todd and Merle Curti, *Rise of the American Nation* (2d ed., New York: Harcourt, Brace & World, 1966), p. 590.
9. First Presbyterian Church, Lawrence, Kans.
10. Military records of James Naismith (Certificate of Service, First Regiment, Kansas Volunteer Infantry); Dewar, "Life," p. 65.

11. Jack Naismith interviews; *St. Marys Star,* July 6, 1916, p. 1; interview with office employees of *St. Marys Star.*

12. Dewar, "Life," p. 65.

13. Gerald J. Delcambre, "Memories of Border Clash Recalled," *Advocate Sunday Magazine* (Baton Rouge, La.), June 29, 1969, p. 3E.

14. Ibid.

15. Ibid.

16. Dewar, "Life," p. 66.

17. Dawe interviews; Dewar, "Life," p. 67.

18. Exner, "Social Hygiene," pp. 277–79; Luther H. Gulick, *Morals and Morale,* pp. 5–13.

19. Gulick, *Morals,* pp. 5–13; Exner, "Social Hygiene," pp. 278, 293.

20. Dawe and Allen interviews; "James Naismith: Inventor."

21. "A New Adaptation of Basket Ball," pp. 385–86.

22. Ibid.

23. Means interview.

24. Ellsworth interview.

25. Means interview.

26. Ibid.

27. Dewar, "Life," p. 67.

28. Military records of James Naismith (Certificate of Service, First Regiment, Kansas National Guard).

CHAPTER 19

Sex and Games on Home Soil

1. Malott, "Sturdy Folks," pp. 14–15.

2. This chapter is based in part on Exner, "Social Hygiene," pp. 277–97, and articles in *APER*: XXII (June, 1917), 387; XXII (Oct., 1917), 447–49; XXII (Nov., 1917), 505–8; XXII (Dec., 1917), 558–66 and 567–69; XXIII (Jan., 1918), 51; XXIII (Feb., 1918), 81–90; XXIII (Mar., 1918), 185–86 and 191–93; XXIII (May, 1918), 263–78; XXIII (June, 1918), 383–98; XXIV (Mar., 1919), 125–36; XXIV (Apr., 1919), 191–95; XXIV (May, 1919), 249–54 and 264–71; XXIV (Nov., 1919), 443–48; XXIV (Dec., 1919), 518–19.

3. Exner, "Social Hygiene," p. 293.

4. Military records of James Naismith (Certificate of Service, First Regiment, Kansas National Guard); Means interview.

5. Albert H. Hindman, letter in *Kansas Alumni,* LXIII (Oct., 1964), 38.

6. See also *Summary of World War Work of the American YMCA,* p. 9.

7. "Secretary of War Appoints Recreation Commission," *APER,* XXII (June, 1917), 387.

8. See also Gulick, *Morals,* pp. 5, 9.

9. *Summary of World War Work,* pp. 5–6.

10. See also Gulick, *Morals,* pp. 12–13.

11. Exner, "Social Hygiene," p. 293.

12. "James Naismith: Inventor."

13. Hess, "Man Who Invented," p. 91.

14. Ellsworth, "Our Amazing Chancellors," *Kansas Alumni,* LXIII (Nov., 1964), 12.

15. Thompson, "KU Profile," *Kansas Alumni,* LXVII (Dec., 1968, Jan., 1969), 31.

16. Hess, "Man Who Invented," p. 91.

17. J. S. Naismith interview; "James Naismith: Inventor"; Grace Naismith, "Father Basketball," p. 65.

18. See also Gulick, *Morals,* p. 10.

19. See also *Summary of World War Work,* p. 9.

20. G. L. Meylan, "Athletics and Recreation in the French Army," *APER,* XXIV (May, 1919), 251.

21. Thomas A. Storey, "The State Military Training Camp for Boys, Peekskill, New York, July, 1917," *APER,* XXIII (Feb., 1918), 90.

22. Meylan, "Athletics," pp. 251–52.

23. "The Problem of Athletics in Colleges and Schools under Present War Conditions," *APER,* XXII (Oct., 1917), 448.

24. Ibid., pp. 447–48.

25. John L. Griffith, "The Value of Athletics As Part of Military Training," *APER,* XXIV (Apr., 1919), 191.

26. Ibid., p. 195.

27. F. L. Kleeberger and Earl H. Wight, "War Sports Embracing Grenade Throwing, Boxing, and Athletic Drills, Arranged in Accord with Military Procedure," pt. 2, *APER,* XXIII (June, 1918), 383–85, 387–91, 393–94, 396–98.

28. "Extracts from Occasional Letters from Physical Directors in Army Camps to Dr. George J. Fisher, Director, War Work Council Young Men's Christian Association," *APER,* XXII (Dec., 1917), 563.

29. Grace W. Baxter, "Army and Navy Quickstep," *APER,* XXIV (Dec., 1919), 518–19.

30. "Naismith Week," *Time,* Feb. 24, 1936, p. 28.

31. Military records of James Naismith (Certificate of Service, First Regiment, Kansas National Guard); "James Naismith: Inventor."

CHAPTER 20

Rain and Mud and Cold in France

1. This chapter is based in part on the following: William Howard Taft, ed., *Service with Fighting Men,* I, 119–59, 444–85, 518–21, and II, 27–70, 104–59, 355, 462–64, and passim, and Plates XV, XVI; Gulick, *Morals,* pp. v, 16–77, 141–59; *APER*: XXII (Oct., 1917), 443; XXII (Nov., 1917), 500, 502, 504–5; XXII (Dec., 1917), 555–58; XXIII (Jan., 1918), 50; XXIII (Feb., 1918), 123–26; XXIII (Mar., 1918), 180, 182–83; XXIII (Apr., 1918), 238–40; XXIII (May, 1918), 324–25; XXIII (June, 1918), 341–54, 399–401; XXIII (Oct., 1918), 455–57; XXIV (Apr., 1919), 204–12, 239–42; XXIV (May, 1919), 249–54; XXIV (June, 1919), 343–52; XXIV (Oct., 1919), 380–85.

2. See also "World War I," in *Funk & Wagnalls Standard Reference Encyclopedia* (1961), XXV, 9303.

3. Gulick, *Morals,* p. 141.

4. Luther H. Gulick, "Physical Fitness in the Fighting Armies," *APER,* XXIII (June, 1918), 353.

5. Robert C. Davis and James W. McAndrew, "G.H.Q.," *APER*, XXIV (Apr., 1919), 239–340.

6. Taft, *Service*, II, 35.

7. *Summary of World War Work*, pp. 26–27.

8. Exner, "Social Hygiene," pp. 292–93.

9. Ibid.; "Naismith, James," in *Who's Who in America*, XVII (1932–1933), 1699.

10. Stanley interview.

11. Percy Carpenter, "Latest News from Y.M.C.A. Physical Work in France," *APER*, XXIV (Oct., 1919), 381.

12. Hussey, *Tait McKenzie*, pp. 53–55 ff.

13. Stewart A. McComber, "American Sports in France, *APER*, XXIV (Apr., 1919), 209.

14. Stewart A. McComber, letter in *APER*, XXIV (Apr., 1919), 205.

15. Gulick, *Morals*, p. 145.

16. Carpenter, "Latest News," p. 381.

17. "Wanted! Mature Athletic Directors," *APER*, XXII (Dec., 1917), 555.

18. J. H. McCurdy, "Extracts from Letters Received from Dr. J. H. McCurdy," *APER*, XXII (Dec., 1917), 558.

19. McCurdy, "Extracts," pp. 556–57.

20. Ibid., 556.

21. See also J. H. McCurdy, "Lessons from France," *APER*, XXIV (June, 1919), 344–45.

22. Ibid., p. 345.

23. Carpenter, "Latest News," p. 380.

24. Davis and McAndrew, "G.H.Q.," p. 239.

25. C. J. Surbeck, letter in *APER*, XXIII (Jan., 1918), 50.

26. J. H. McCurdy, "A Patriotic Opportunity for Men over Draft Age," *APER*, XXII (Nov., 1917), 500.

27. Carpenter, "Latest News," p. 381.

28. Taft, *Service*, II, 143, and I, 128.

29. See also *Summary of World War Work*, pp. 26–27; "James Naismith: Inventor."

30. See also *Summary of World War Work*, pp. 119–20.

31. Taft, *Service*, II, 104.

32. Ibid., II, 135.

33. Ibid., I, 472, 485.

34. Exner, "Social Hygiene," p. 293.

35. Records at McGill University, Mar., 1918.

36. Exner, "Social Hygiene," pp. 293–94.

37. Gulick, *Morals*, pp. 74–75.

38. Taft, II, 355, quoting from *For the Millions of Men Now under Arms* (New York: privately printed for the International Committee of Young Men's Christian Associations, 1919), no. 14, pp. 8–9.

39. Gulick, *Morals*, p. 158.

40. Letter from Shirley Leslie, Aug. 18, 1964.

41. Exner, "Social Hygiene," pp. 294–95.

42. A. E. Bradley, "Suggestions," *APER*, XXIII (Feb., 1918), 126.

43. Ibid., p. 125.
44. Ibid.

CHAPTER 21
Games, Bayonets, and Lofty Ideals

1. This chapter is based in part on the following: Taft, *Service*, I, 448, 503, and II, 26–53, 122, 154, 345–46, Plate XVI; *APER*: XXIII (Feb., 1918), 123–24; XXIII (Mar., 1918), 180–86; XXIII (Apr., 1918), 238–40; XXIII (May, 1918), 324–25; XXIII (June, 1918), 341–54, 399–401; XXIII (Oct., 1918), 413–26, 455–57; XXIV (Feb., 1919), 90–92, 116–18; XXIV (Mar., 1919), 125–36; XXIV (Apr., 1919), 197–98, 200–204, 206–12; XXIV (May, 1919), 249–54; XXIV (Oct., 1919), 380–85, 418–20. See also Leonard, *Guide*, p. 462.
2. McCurdy, "Extracts," p. 325.
3. "To Teach Poilus to Play—Recreation Workers to Train at Princeton," *APER*, XXIII (Mar., 1918), 183–84.
4. Fisher, "Extracts," p. 400.
5. Ibid.
6. George J. Fisher, "Points of Emphasis in a Post-War Program of Physical Training," *APER*, XXIV (Mar., 1919), 131.
7. Carpenter, "Latest News," p. 382.
8. "James Naismith: Inventor."
9. Fisher, "Extracts," p. 400.
10. Ibid.
11. "Naismith Week," *Time*, Feb. 24, 1936, p. 28.
12. Ellsworth interview.
13. Hess, "Man Who Invented," pp. 91–92.
14. Leonard, *Guide*, pp. 459–60, 464.
15. McCurdy, "Extracts," p. 180.
16. W. P. Bowen, "The Influence of the War upon Physical Education," *APER*, XXIV (Feb., 1919), 90.
17. Ibid., p. 91.
18. Fisher, "Points of Emphasis," p. 130.
19. Gulick, "Physical Fitness," pp. 342, 346.
20. "Bayonet Drill Has Advantages over Jiu-Jitsu," *APER*, XXIII (Mar., 1918), 181.
21. Gulick, "Physical Fitness," p. 350.
22. Ibid., pp. 344–45.
23. James Naismith, letter in *APER*, XXIV (Apr., 1919), 197–98.
24. Ibid.
25. J. S. Naismith interview.

CHAPTER 22
Season of Armistice

1. Dorgan, pp. 147–48.
2. Ibid.
3. This chapter is based in part on the following: Taft, *Service*, I, 131, 475–85, Plate XII, and II, 38–52, 579, 629; *APER*: XXIII (June, 1918),

402–3; XXIII (Oct., 1918), 413–26, 448–51; XXIV (Apr., 1919), 199–200, 204–12; XXIV (May, 1919), 249–54; XXIV (June, 1919), 343–52; XXIV (Oct., 1919), 380–85, 416. See also Dorgan, *Gulick,* pp. 147–48.

4. "That Wonderful Year—1919," *Kansas Alumni,* LXVII (May, 1969), 12–13.

5. Ibid.; "Pictures of the Past," *Kansas Alumni,* LXIV (Mar./Apr., 1966), 7; John Gillie, "Across the Years: ROTC," *Kansas Alumni,* LXVIII (May, 1970), 20; Ellsworth, "Our Amazing Chancellors," *Kansas Alumni,* LXIII (Dec., 1964), 11.

6. Gillie, "ROTC," p. 20; "That Wonderful Year—1919," p. 13.

7. "That Wonderful Year—1919," pp. 12–13; Ellsworth, "Our Amazing Chancellors," *Kansas Alumni,* LXIII (Dec., 1964), p. 11.

8. McComber, "American Sports," p. 206.

9. Percy R. Carpenter, "Letter from Prof. Percy R. Carpenter," *APER,* XXIV (Apr., 1919), 199.

10. Taft, *Service,* II, 629.

11. Carpenter, "Latest News," p. 385.

12. Leonard, *Guide,* p. 462.

13. McComber, "American Sports," p. 210.

14. See also *Summary of World War Work,* p. 38.

15. Meylan, "Athletics," p. 254.

16. Carpenter, "Latest News," p. 385.

17. Ibid., p. 382.

18. Naismith, *Basketball,* pp. 140, 152–53, 169.

19. McComber, "American Sports," p. 211.

20. Naismith, *Basketball,* pp. 150–51.

21. Ibid., pp. 150–56.

22. See also *Summary of World War Work,* pp. 143–44 and passim; Gulick, *Morals,* pp. 165–69.

23. See also *Summary of World War Work,* pp. 143–44 and passim; "James Naismith: Inventor."

24. *Summary of World War Work,* p. 144; "James Naismith: Inventor."

CHAPTER 23

Sermons in Kansas

1. This chapter is based in part on the following: "That Wonderful Year—1919," *Kansas Alumni,* LXVII (May, 1969), 12–13; Jack Naismith, J. S. Naismith, Dawe, and Olinger interviews; *APER*: XIX (Mar., 1914), 267–76; XXII (Mar., 1917), 179–82; XXIV (Apr., 1919), 197–98; XXIV (June, 1919), 353–60; XXIV (Dec., 1919), 519–20. See also Gillie, "ROTC," p. 20.

2. Ellsworth, "Our Amazing Chancellors," *Kansas Alumni,* LXIII (Oct., 1964), 6, and LXIII (Dec., 1964), 11.

3. Albert H. Hindman, letter in *Kansas Alumni,* LXVI (Dec., 1967, Jan., 1968), 42.

4. Ellsworth, "Our Amazing Chancellors," *Kansas Alumni,* LXIII (Dec., 1964), 10.

5. "Naismith, James," in *Who's Who in America*, XVII (1932–1933), 1699; "James Naismith: Inventor."

6. See also Hammig, "Historical Sketch," p. 14.

7. James Naismith, letter in *APER*, XXIV (Apr., 1919), 197–98.

8. Naturalization records of James Naismith: Declaration of Intention, Sept. 11, 1918.

9. Ibid., and Petition for Naturalization, Nov. 5, 1924, and Certificates of Naturalization #1971557 and #1971558, May 4, 1925.

10. Ogden, "KSR Comes of Age," pp. 7–8.

11. Stanley interview.

12. Ibid.; "Our First One Hundred Years, 1858–1958," pp. 17–19.

13. Also Dodd and Ellsworth interviews.

14. Sign in Vinland, Kans.: "Vinland, Home of Coalcreek Library, Oldest Library in Kansas. Founded, Nov. 22, 1859"; "Library at Coal Creek Is Oldest in Kansas," *Wichita Eagle*, Aug. 22, 1968.

15. Note written by Mrs. H. C. Rumsey, Dec., 1963; letters from Mrs. Erma D. Shank, Jan., 1964, and Mrs. Edith Woods Lindley, Dec. 29, 1963.

16. J. S. Naismith interviews.

17. Jack Naismith interviews.

18. Olinger interview.

19. Also Vanderhoof interview.

20. Also Shank letter; Vanderhoof interview; Lindley letter.

21. Jack Naismith interviews.

22. Ibid.

23. Lindley letter; Vanderhoof interview.

24. Also Shank letter.

25. Also interview with minister, First Presbyterian Church, Lawrence, Kans., Aug., 1963; Phelps, "National Ceremony," p. 19.

CHAPTER 24

Forgotten Man at K.U.

1. This chapter is based in part on the following: "James Naismith: Inventor"; Allen and Stanley interviews; *Kansas Alumni*: LXIII (Jan., 1965), 12–13, 26; LXIII (Feb., 1965), 12, 24; LXIII (Mar., 1965), 8–9, 31; LXV (Sept., 1966), 18, 38; LXVI (Feb., 1968), 16–17; LXVI (July/Aug., 1968), 14–15, 26–27; LXVII (Feb., 1969), 12–13; LXVII (May, 1969), 2–4; LXVIII (Oct., 1969), 23–25; LXVIII (Mar., 1970), 2–5; Naismith, *Basketball,* pp. 61–86, 100–108, 181–98.

2. *University Daily Kansan,* Mar. 9, 1924, p. 3.

3. See also Allen, *Better Basketball,* p. 46; Donald W. Elston, "A Biography of Forrest C. 'Phog' Allen," pp. 5–6.

4. Letter from Mildred Clodfelter, Sept. 20, 1967; "Kansas University: Items in Its History," III.

5. Allen, *Coach "Phog,"* p. 175.

6. Deford, "In Search," p. 32.

7. Clodfelter letter.

8. Ibid.; Weyand, *Cavalcade,* p. 49.

9. See also Weyand, *Cavalcade,* p. 49.

10. Also Jack Naismith interviews. (A resolution of the University of Kansas Athletic Board honoring Naismith states that he coached basketball until 1908.)

11. See also Weyand, *Cavalcade,* p. 49.

12. Elston, "Biography of 'Phog' Allen," p. 11.

13. Allen interviews.

14. Deford, "In Search," p. 32.

15. See also Elston, "Biography of 'Phog' Allen," p. 11.

16. Allen, *Coach "Phog,"* p. 161.

17. Elston, "Biography of 'Phog' Allen," p. 7.

18. See also Clodfelter letter.

19. Also Jack Naismith interviews.

20. See also *Lawrence Daily Journal-World,* Aug. (?), 1964.

21. Letter from Forrest C. Allen to Allan Donnell, May 20, 1953.

22. Allen, *Coach "Phog,"* pp. vii, xv.

23. Naismith, *Basketball,* p. 189.

24. "James Naismith: Inventor."

25. Interviews with residents of Sprague Apartments.

26. Stanley interview.

27. Ibid.

28. Carman interview.

29. Letter from Anna D. McCracken, Feb., 1964.

30. See also records in office of Alumni Association, University of Kansas; D'Ambra interviews; Rath, "Report," p. 99.

31. D'Ambra interviews.

32. *Jayhawker,* 1925, p. 2.

33. Dewar, "Life," p. 76.

34. "Kansas University: Items in Its History," III.

35. "That Wonderful Year—1929," *Kansas Alumni,* LXVII (Feb., 1969), 13.

36. See also *Topeka Daily Capital,* Nov. 29, 1939, p. 9.

37. Ibid.

38. Jack Naismith interviews.

39. Ibid.

40. J. S. Naismith interview; *Topeka Daily Capital,* Nov. 29, 1939, p. 9.

41. Naismith, "How Basketball Started," p. 234.

42. Jack Naismith interviews.

43. See also Naismith, "How Basketball Started," p. 234.

44. *Christian Science Monitor,* Mar. 25, 1963, p. 14.

45. Naismith, "How Basketball Started," p. 235; Tim Cohane, *Bypaths of Glory* (New York, Evanston, and London: Harper & Row, 1963), p. 59.

CHAPTER 25
The Roaring Twenties and the Depressed Thirties

1. Phil Elderkin, "Pro Basketball's First Dynasty," *Christian Science Monitor,* Jan. 25, 1964, p. 4C.

2. This chapter is based in part on the following: *Kansas Alumni*: LXIII (Dec., 1964), 10–11; LXIII (Jan., 1965), 12–13, 26; LXIII (Feb., 1965), 12,

24; LXIV (Mar./Apr., 1966), 6–9; LXV (June, 1967), 16, 24; LXVII (Feb., 1969), 12–13; LXVII (May, 1969), 10–11; LXVII (Sept., 1969), 28; Jack Naismith, J. S. Naismith, and Dawe interviews; "James Naismith: Inventor."

3. See also *University Kansan,* May 27, 1911, p. 1; interviews with residents of Sprague Apartments.

4. "International Young Men's Christian Association College," *APER,* XXIV (Oct., 1919), 413.

5. Ibid.

6. "Famous Olympic Cup Awarded to Springfield Institution," *APER,* XXIV (May, 1919), 318.

7. City directory of Lawrence, Kans., 1923.

8. Also Stanley interview.

9. City directories of Lawrence, Kans., 1923 and 1925; naturalization records of James Naismith: Petition for Naturalization, Nov. 5, 1924.

10. Jack Naismith interviews.

11. The account of Mrs. Naismith's illness is based on statements made by her daughter Ann Naismith Dawe, a nurse.

12. Jack Naismith interviews.

13. Also Young interviews; Donnell, "Basketball," p. 35.

14. Young interviews; letter from John E. Young, postmarked March 28, 1972.

15. Lowry interview; Donnell, "Basketball," p. 35.

16. See also Naismith, *Basketball,* pp. 121–38.

17. Letter from Edna Gardner Lowry, Aug. 19, 1965.

18. Interviews with office staff of Almonte High School; Young interview.

19. Lowry letter.

20. Ibid.

21. Young interviews.

22. Ibid.

23. Allen interviews.

24. Also letter from Mildred Clodfelter, Sept. 20, 1967.

25. Also Clodfelter letter; Stanley interview.

26. Interviews with residents of Sprague Apartments.

27. "Along the Jayhawk Walk," *Kansas Alumni,* LXVII (May, 1969), 10.

28. See also Leonard, *Guide,* p. 475; Rath, "Report," p. 99.

29. Ibid.

30. J. H. McCurdy, "Dr. James Naismith, Inventor of Basketball," *Journal of Health and Physical Education,* IV (Jan., 1933), 55.

31. See also Naismith, "How Basketball Started," pp. 221–35.

32. See also records of Alumni Association, University of Kansas; Olinger interview.

33. See also records of Alumni Association, University of Kansas.

34. See also *Kansan,* Apr. 5, 1934.

35. Letter from Anna D. McCracken, Jan., 1964.

36. Jack Naismith interviews.

37. Allen interview.

38. See also "Our First One Hundred Years, 1858–1958," p. 20.

39. Allen interviews.

40. "Naismith Week," *Time,* Feb. 24, 1936, p. 28.

41. Also Allen interviews.

42. Jack Naismith interviews.

43. See also records of Alumni Association, University of Kansas; Stanley interview.

44. Menke, *Encyclopedia of Sports,* p. 161.

45. See also records at Springfield College, Springfield, Mass.; Hussey, *Tait McKenzie,* pp. 44–45, Plate "Joy of Effort" (facing p. 44).

46. See also Hussey, *Tait McKenzie,* pp. v, vi, 45, and passim.

CHAPTER 26

One Penny . . .

1. This chapter is based in part on the following: "James Naismith: Inventor"; *New York Times:* Feb. 2, 1936, V, p. 2; Mar. 22, 1936, V, p. 3; Mar. 29, 1936, V, p. 4; Apr. 4, 1936, pp. 1–2; Apr. 6, 1936, p. 25; *Lawrence Daily Journal-World:* Feb. 10, 1936, p. 1; Feb. 17, 1936, p. 1; Mar. 12, 1936, p. 10; Mar. 20, 1936, p. 10; Arthur J. Daley (articles in *New York Times*): "Denver Five Is out of Olympic Trials," Apr. 2, 1936, p. 32; "McPherson Oilers Conquer All-Stars," Mar. 12, 1936, p. 25; "M'Pherson Oilers Stop Temple, 56–48," Apr. 4, 1936, p. 20; "M'Pherson Oilers to Oppose Temple," Apr. 3, 1936, p. 32; "Oilers and the Universals Reach Basketball Final," Apr. 5, 1936, V, pp. 1–2; "U.S. Olympic Committee Ousts Ornstein As Member," Apr. 6, 1936, pp. 25, 28; John Kieran, "Sports of the Times," *New York Times,* Apr. 3, 1936, p. 32. See also Hammig, "Historical Sketch," p. 20.

2. Bill Henry, *An Approved History of the Olympic Games,* pp. 16, 26–33; Charles Bonnamaux, "The Contributions of Baron Pierre de Coubertin to Physical Education," *APER,* XXIII (Feb., 1918), 93; Donnell, "Basketball," pp. 31–32.

3. *Lawrence Daily Journal-World,* Feb. 10, 1936, p. 1.

4. Ibid., Feb. 17, 1936, p. 1.

5. Ibid.

6. Ibid.

7. Letter from Forrest C. Allen to Almonte High School, Almonte, Ont., Mar. 11, 1936.

8. *University Daily Kansan,* Feb. 25, 1936, p. 4.

9. Daley, "McPherson Oilers Conquer All-Stars," *New York Times,* Mar. 12, 1936, p. 25.

10. *Lawrence Daily Journal-World,* Mar. 20, 1936, p. 10.

11. Ibid.

12. Kieran, "Sports of the Times," *New York Times,* Apr. 3, 1936, p. 32.

13. Daley, "Oilers and the Universals Reach Basketball Final," *New York Times,* Apr. 5, 1936, V, p. 1.

14. See also Henry, *Approved History,* pp. 229–30.

15. Daley, "M'Pherson Oilers Stop Temple, 56–48," *New York Times,* Apr. 4, 1936, p. 20.

16. Interview with office staff of Almonte High School.

17. Daley, "Oilers and the Universals Reach Basketball Final," p. 1.

18. Interviews with Jack Naismith and with faculty members, Department of Physical Education, University of Kansas.

19. Allen interviews; "The Incredible Phog," p. 4.

20. Jack Naismith interviews.

CHAPTER 27

. . . And a Moment of Glory

1. This chapter is based in part on the following: Dewar, "Life," pp. 81–82; "James Naismith: Inventor"; Henry, *Approved History*, pp. 5, 232–39; Frederick T. Birchall (articles in *New York Times*): "11th Olympics Open Today in Gay and Crowded Berlin," Aug. 1, 1936, pp. 1, 6; "Luck of Nazis with the Weather Failing During the Olympic Games," Aug. 6, 1936, p. 24; "100,000 Hail Hitler; U.S. Athletes Avoid Nazi Salute to Him," Aug. 2, 1936, pp. 1, 33; "Swiss, Briton and German Govern Basketball, Originated in U.S.," Aug. 8, 1936, p. 6; Arthur J. Daley (articles in *New York Times*): "Lovelock Breaks 1,500-Meter Mark in Olympic Games," Aug. 7, 1936, pp. 1, 12; "110,000 See Owens Set World Record at Olympic Games," Aug. 3, 1936, pp. 1, 19; "Owens Captures Olympic Title, Equals World 100-Meter Record," Aug. 4, 1936, pp. 1, 23; "Owens Completes Triple As 5 Olympic Marks Fall," Aug. 6, 1936, pp. 1, 25; "U.S. Captures 4 Events; Owens Sets Jump Record," Aug. 5, 1936, pp. 1, 25; *New York Times:* Apr. 5, 1936, V, p. 2; Aug. 1, 1936, pp. 1–2; Aug. 2, 1936, V, p. 3; Aug. 4, 1936, p. 23; Aug. 5, 1936, pp. 1–2; Aug. 8, 1936, p. 7.

2. J. S. Naismith interview.

3. Robert Daley, *The Bizarre World of European Sports* (New York: William Morrow & Co., 1963), p. 13.

4. See also ibid., pp. 13 ff.

5. Birchall, "100,000 Hail Hitler," pp. 1, 33.

6. Birchall, "Swiss, Briton and German," p. 6.

7. Edward Pinkowski, *Forgotten Fathers*, pp. 97–98.

8. See also Weyand, *Cavalcade,* p. 225; "A Peachbasket Prodigy," p. 13.

9. See also Naismith, *Basketball,* pp. 159–60; Hickox interview; Hurt, "Basketball Got Away," p. 5C.

10. Weyand, *Cavalcade,* p. 225.

11. See also "A Peachbasket Prodigy," p. 13.

12. See also Francis J. O'Riley, "Basketball Rules Undergo Revision," *New York Times,* Apr. 6, 1936, p. 25.

13. See also Weyand, *Cavalcade,* p. 225.

14. See also "A Peachbasket Prodigy," p. 13; Jack Naismith interviews.

15. See also Williams, "The Boy Who Could Never Run," 88–90; Vernon Pizer, "The Man with 8000 Miracles," *Reader's Digest,* LXXXVIII (Feb., 1966), 112–16.

16. Kieran, "Sports of the Times," p. 14.

17. "2800 Campers—and Not One Tent," *Kansas Alumni,* LXVII (Mar./Apr., 1969), 2.

18. Young interviews.

19. Also Stanley interview.

CHAPTER 28
The Ripening Years

1. This chapter is based in part on the following: "James Naismith: Inventor"; Dawe, J. S. Naismith, and Jack Naismith interviews. See also Grace Naismith, "Father Basketball," pp. 64–65; *Lawrence Daily Journal-World,* Nov. 28, 1939, p. 2.

2. Grace Naismith, "Father Basketball," pp. 64–65.

3. Also Olinger interview.

4. Allen and Olinger interviews.

5. Naismith, *Basketball,* pp. 75–76.

6. Ibid., pp. 127–28.

7. Dawe interviews.

8. Also Stanley interview.

9. Olinger and Stanley interviews.

10. Dawe interviews.

11. Olinger interview.

12. Hess, "Man Who Invented," p. 90.

13. Ibid.

14. J. S. Naismith interview.

15. Phelps, "National Ceremony," p. 19.

16. Also Stanley and Allen interviews; Phelps, "National Ceremony," p. 19.

17. Former member of University of Kansas faculty. Name withheld.

18. J. S. Naismith interview.

19. Phelps, "National Ceremony," p. 19.

20. Former member of University of Kansas faculty.

21. D'Ambra interviews.

22. Ibid.

23. Jack Naismith interviews.

24. Also Stanley and Dodd interviews.

25. Dodd interview.

26. "Naismith Week," *Time,* Feb. 24, 1936, p. 28.

27. Dawe interviews.

28. "Kansas University: Items in Its History," III, p. 16; *Kansas City Times,* Feb. 2, 1937, p. 18.

29. Gillie, "ROTC," p. 20.

30. J. S. Naismith interview.

31. Also Florence Naismith interviews.

32. Dawe interviews.

33. Ibid.

34. D'Ambra interviews.

CHAPTER 29
Alone for a While

1. This chapter is based in part on the following: "James Naismith: Inventor"; D'Ambra, Jack Naismith, and Florence Naismith interviews; letters from Duke D'Ambra, Aug. 26, Aug. 31, Nov. 23, 1970.

2. D'Ambra interviews.

3. Also Olinger interview.

4. D'Ambra interviews.

5. Also Olinger interview.

6. D'Ambra interviews.

7. Cohane, *Bypaths of Glory,* pp. 59, 49.

8. See also radio script (Edmonton Grads), Donnell Collection; *Winnipeg Free Press,* Aug. 7, 1965, p. 15; Donnell, "Basketball," pp. 28–29.

9. *Lawrence Daily Journal-World,* July 12, 1937.

10. Donnell, "Basketball," p. 36.

11. See also "The Mill of Kintail."

12. D'Ambra interviews.

13. Ibid.

14. Young interviews.

15. See also *Kansan,* Dec. 3, 1937.

16. Kiely, "Skeletons," p. 22.

17. "Items about the Faculty Members of the University of Kansas," III, pp. 8–9; Donnell, "Basketball," p. 33.

18. Dawe interviews; "Necessity Is the Mother of Invention," p. 1; "Naismith Field House Fund," *Graduate Magazine,* Oct., 1939 (*in* "James Naismith: Inventor").

19. Leonard, *Guide,* p. 471; Stanley interview.

20. Kiely, "Skeletons," p. 22.

21. D'Ambra, "The Doctor," p. 9.

22. Kiely, "Skeletons," p. 22.

23. See also program, Seventy-second Annual Convocation of the Presbyterian College.

24. Jack Naismith interviews.

25. Also Dawe and Allen interviews.

26. Dawe interviews.

27. Jack Naismith interviews.

28. Ibid.

29. See also Louisa Cooke Don-Carlos, "The Writers of Tennessee: A Manual of Tennessee Literature" (Master's thesis, University of Kansas, 1925), pp. 1–3.

30. *Lawrence Today and Yesterday, 1913* (*Lawrence Daily Journal-World Supp.*), p. 103; "Prominent Alumni of the University of Kansas," VII, 5, and X, 56, Watson Collection; *Lawrence Daily Journal-World,* July 12, 1949, pp. 1–2.

31. "Prominent Alumni of the University of Kansas," VII, 5.

32. D'Ambra interviews.

33. See also letters from A. O. Duer, Oct. 6 and Nov. 2, 1967. As Duer explains, in 1940 the National Intercollegiate Basketball Tournament became the National Association of Intercollegiate Basketball, or NAIB. In 1952 the membership voted to include a variety of sports and to change the name. A suggested name was "National Association of Intercollegiate Sports," to be known by the acronym NAIS, the first four letters of James Naismith's surname. Members voted for "athletics," however, rather than

"sports," in the title. Thus, the organization became the National Association of Intercollegiate Athletics, or NAIA.

34. Also J. S. Naismith interviews.
35. Ibid.
36. D'Ambra interviews.
37. Florence Naismith interviews.

CHAPTER 30
Florence and the Doctor

1. This chapter is based in part on the following: Florence Naismith, Jack Naismith, and Dawe interviews; "James Naismith: Inventor"; *Kansas City Star*: June 10, 1939, p. 5; Nov. 28, 1938, p. 6; *New York Times*: Nov. 20, 1939, p. 23; Nov. 22, 1939, p. 13; Nov. 25, 1939, p. 7; Nov. 28, 1939, p. 25.
2. Florence Naismith interviews.
3. Ibid.
4. Olinger interview.
5. Ibid.
6. *Kansas City Star*, June 10, 1939, p. 5.
7. See also *Lawrence Daily Journal-World,* June 10, 1939.
8. See also *Daily Advertiser* (Lafayette, La.), Mar. 18, 1965, p. 10.
9. Radio script (Winnipeg Toilers), Donnell Collection; Wilson interview.
10. Radio script; Wilson interviews; Phelps, "National Ceremony," p. 19.
11. See also Wilson interviews.
12. Florence Naismith interviews.
13. See also Wilson interviews; Phelps, "National Ceremony," p. 19.
14. Florence Naismith interviews.
15. See also Ellsworth, "Our Amazing Chancellors," *Kansas Alumni,* LXIII (Feb., 1965), 12, 24; "Dr. Wescoe Will Leave Mt. Oread," *Kansas Alumni,* LXVII (Oct., 1968), 4.
16. Florence Naismith interviews.
17. Ibid.
18. D'Ambra interviews.
19. Dawe interviews.
20. Gillie, "ROTC," p. 20.
21. "Pictures of the Past," *Kansas Alumni,* LXIV (Mar./Apr., 1966), 8.
22. Florence Naismith interviews.
23. See also Donnell, "Basketball," p. 36.
24. "Naismith Field House Fund," *Graduate Magazine,* Oct., 1939.
25. "The Incredible Phog," pp. 2, 3.
26. Also Olinger interview.
27. Dawe interviews.
28. Ibid.
29. Jack Naismith interviews.
30. Florence Naismith interviews.
31. Ibid.
32. Ibid.
33. Ibid.

364

34. Ibid.
35. See also "Naismith, James," in *Dictionary of American Biography,* XXII, Supp. 2, 484–85.
36. Letter from Duke D'Ambra, Aug. 31, 1970.
37. Letter from Bert Brand to Duke D'Ambra [Nov. 28, 1939].
38. D'Ambra letter.
39. Ibid.
40. Ibid.
41. "James Naismith: Inventor."
42. *Lawrence Daily Journal-World,* Nov. 28, 1939, p. 1.
43. See also Donnell, "Basketball," pp. 2–3.
44. Jack Naismith interviews.
45. "A Master Sportsman Has Completed His Assignment," pp. 4–5.
46. *Emporia Gazette,* Nov. 29, 1939, p. 4.
47. Rath, "Report," p. 99.
48. *Kansas City Star,* Nov. 28, 1939, p. 6.

CHAPTER 31
Pattern for a Man

1. This chapter is based in part on the following: *Kansas Alumni*: LXIII (Mar., 1965), 16; LXIV (Nov., 1965), 10–12, 30; LXV (Sept., 1966), 18, 38; LXVII (Sept., 1968), cover; LXVIII (Mar., 1970), 2–5; personal observation by the author.
2. "James Naismith: Inventor."
3. Personal observation by author, Aug., 1963.
4. *Almonte Gazette,* June 17, 1965, pp. 1, 8, and July 8, 1965, p. 1; letter from Edna Gardner Lowry, Aug. 19, 1965.
5. Interviews with office staff of Almonte High School and with Edna Gardner Lowry.
6. Letter from Edna Gardner Lowry, Aug. 31, 1970.
7. See also "James Naismith: Inventor"; interview with sexton, Memorial Park Cemetery, Lawrence, Kans., Aug., 1963.
8. *Congressional Record,* CVII, pt. 16, Sept. 25, 1961, 21196–99; brochures, Naismith Memorial Basketball Hall of Fame.
9. *Denver Post,* Oct. 4, 1961, p. 65; *New York Times,* Oct. 7, 1961, p. 25; David Lidman, "News of the World of Stamps," *New York Times,* Oct. 8, 1961, II, p. 26, and Oct. 22, 1961, II, p. 23; Naismith commemorative first-day postal cover.
10. *Denver Post,* Mar. 20, 1969, p. 64.
11. "Naismith Memorial Basketball Hall of Fame" (rotogravure section, *Springfield* (Mass.) *Sunday Republican,* Apr. 14, 1968).
12. Letter from Ruth Silvia, May 12, 1969.
13. Allen interviews.
14. Phelps, "National Ceremony," p. 19.
15. D'Ambra interviews.

Bibliography

BOOKS

Allen, Forrest C. *Better Basketball.* New York and London: Whittlesey House, 1937.

———. *Coach "Phog" Allen's Sports Stories for You and Youth.* Lawrence, Kans.: Allen Press, 1947.

———. *My Basketball Bible.* Kansas City, Mo.: Smith-Grieves Co., 1924.

Canniff, William. *History of the Province of Ontario (Upper Canada).* Toronto: A. H. Hovey & Co., 1872.

Collard, Edgar Andrew. *Oldest McGill.* Toronto: Macmillan Co. of Canada, 1946.

Dorgan, Ethel Josephine. *Luther Halsey Gulick, 1865–1918.* Contributions to Education, no. 635. New York: Bureau of Publications, Teachers College, Columbia University, 1934.

Guillet, Edwin C. *Pioneer Days in Upper Canada.* Toronto: University of Toronto Press, 1963.

———. *Pioneer Travel in Upper Canada.* 1933. Reprint. Toronto: University of Toronto Press, 1963.

Gulick, Luther H. *Morals and Morale.* New York: Association Press, 1919.

Henry, Bill. *An Approved History of the Olympic Games.* New York: G. P. Putnam's Sons, 1948.

Howell, Nancy, and Howell, Maxwell L. *Sports and Games in Canadian Life: 1700 to the Present.* Toronto: Macmillan of Canada, 1969.

Hussey, Christopher. *Tait McKenzie: A Sculptor of Youth.* Philadelphia: J. B. Lippincott Co., 1930.

Hyder, Clyde Kenneth. *Snow of Kansas.* Lawrence, Kans.: University of Kansas Press, 1953.

Kane, Joseph Nathan. *Famous First Facts.* 3d ed. New York: H. W. Wilson Co., 1964. ("James Naismith and Luther Gulick—Basket Ball," p. 101.)

Krout, John Allen. *Annals of American Sport. The Pageant of America*, vol. 15. New Haven: Yale University Press, 1929. (Drawing "The First Game," photograph of James Naismith, etc.)

Leonard, Fred E. *Pioneers of Modern Physical Training.* 2d ed. New York, London: Association Press, 1915.

———. *A Guide to the History of Physical Education.* 3d ed., rev. and enlarged by George B. Affleck. Philadelphia: Lea & Febiger, 1947.

Lowry, Edna Gardner, et al. *A Family Record.* Almonte, Ont.: privately printed, 1952.

MacLennan, Hugh, ed. *McGill: The Story of a University.* London: George Allen & Unwin, 1960.

Macmillan, Cyrus. *McGill and Its Story, 1821–1921.* New York: John Lane Co., 1921.

Menke, Frank G. *The Encyclopedia of Sports.* 2d ed., rev. New York: A. S. Barnes & Co., 1944, 1947, 1953, and 1960.

Middleton, Jesse Edgar, and Landon, Fred. *The Province of Ontario— A History.* 1615–1927, vol. 2. Toronto: Dominion Publishing Co., 1927. (Lanark settlement, pp. 929, 1150–53.)

Naismith, James. *Basketball: Its Origin and Development.* New York: Association Press, 1941.

Pinkowski, Edward. *Forgotten Fathers.* Philadelphia: Sunshine Press, 1953. ("Father of Basketball," pp. 82–98; portrait.)

Summary of World War Work of the American YMCA. N.p.: The International Committee of Young Men's Christian Associations, 1920.

Taft, Robert. *Across the Years on Mount Oread, 1866–1941.* Lawrence, Kans.: University of Kansas Press, 1941.

Taft, William Howard, ed. *Service with Fighting Men.* 2 vols. New York: Association Press, 1922.

Weyand, Alexander M. *The Cavalcade of Basketball.* New York: Macmillan Co., 1960.

ARTICLES

"Across the Years: Naismith's Game." *Kansas Alumni* (University of Kansas), LXVIII (Jan., 1970), 18.

"After 40 Years, Still Champs." *Kansas Alumni*, LXVI (July/Aug., 1968), 26–27. (Naismith in group photo.)

Bates, Joseph D., Jr. "Daddy of the Cage Game." *Congressional*

Record, CVII, pt. 16, Sept. 25, 1961, pp. 21196–97. (Reprinted from *Sporting Sportsman*, published by A. G. Spalding & Bros.)

Blackledge, Walt. "End of an Era." *Kansas Alumni*, LXIV (Nov., 1965), 10–12, 30.

Boyle, Robert H. "Spirit, Mind, Body." *Sports Illustrated*, Dec. 2, 1963, pp. 76–78, 81–82, 84, 87–88, 90, 92.

D'Ambra, Duke. "The Doctor and the Baskets." *Empire Magazine* (Sunday Magazine of the *Denver Post*), Jan. 19, 1958, pp. 8–9.

Deford, Frank. "In Search of Naismith's Game." *Sports Illustrated*, Mar. 6, 1967, pp. 24–26, 31–32.

Delcambre, Gerald J. "Memories of Border Clash Recalled." *Advocate Sunday Magazine* (Baton Rouge, La.), June 29, 1969, p. 3E.

Dell, William A. "Dr. Naismith Makes a Basket." *Christian Science Monitor Weekly Magazine Section*, May 27, 1936, p. 6.

"Dr. J. H. McCurdy on Leave of Absence for Work with the Soldiers in France." *American Physical Education Review*, XXII (Oct. 1917), 443.

"Dr. James A. Naismith" (editorial). *Journal of Health and Physical Education*, XI (Jan., 1940), 20.

"Dr. McCurdy in France Sends Word to the Readers of the Review." *American Physical Education Review*, XXII (Nov., 1917), 502.

Elbel, Ed. "50 Years on the Cinder Path." *Kansas Alumni*, LXIII (Mar., 1965), 8–9, 31.

Ellsworth, Fred. "Our Amazing Chancellors." *Kansas Alumni*, LXIII (Oct., 1964), 6–8, 22–23; LXIII (Nov., 1964), 12–13, 22; LXIII (Dec., 1964), 10–11; LXIII (Jan., 1965), 12–13, 26; LXIII (Feb., 1965), 12, 24; LXIII (Mar., 1965), 10–11, 33.

Everett, Glenn D. "The Canadian Who Gave Us Basketball." *Presbyterian Record*, April, 1962.

Exner, M. J. "Social Hygiene and the War. *Social Hygiene*, V (July, 1919), 277–97.

"Famous Olympic Cup Awarded to Springfield Institution." *American Physical Education Review*, XXIV (May, 1919), 318.

"Farewell, Fraser." *Kansas Alumni*, LXIII (Mar., 1965), 16.

Flowers, Paul. "Paul Flowers' Greenhouse." *Commercial Appeal* (Memphis, Tenn.), July 5, 1963, p. 6.

"The Gallopin' Goose." *Jayhawker Magazine Yearbook* (University of Kansas), LXXVII (Fall, 1965), 54–55.

Hess, M. Whitcomb. "The Man Who Invented Basketball." *American Scholar*, XVIII (Winter, 1948–1949), 87–92.

Bibliography

Hicks, Wessely. "Window on the World." *Saturday Night: The Canadian Weekly,* LV (Dec. 9, 1939), 4.

Hurt, Bob. "Basketball Got Away." *Topeka Daily Capital,* Feb. 4, 1962, p. 5C.

"Hy-Lo Ball." *American Physical Education Review,* XXII (Dec., 1917), 567–69.

"The Incredible Phog." *Kansas Alumni,* LXVIII (Mar., 1970), 2–5.

Jayhawker, 1908 (University of Kansas). · (Photographs of basketball and lacrosse teams; pages unnumbered.)

Jayhawker, 1925. (Dedication to Naismith, p. 2; photograph of Naismith, p. 3.)

Kerry, J. G. G. "Football in the Eighties." *McGill News* (McGill University), XXXIV (Summer, 1953), 20–21.

McComber, Stewart A. Letter, Oct. 22, 1918, Paris. No addressee. *American Physical Education Review,* XXIV (Apr., 1919), 204–6.

McCurdy, J. H. "Dr. James Naismith, Inventor of Basketball." *Journal of Health and Physical Education,* IV (Jan., 1933), 55.

———. "Extracts from Dr. McCurdy's Letters." Mar. 23, 27, 28, 1918, Paris. *American Physical Education Review,* XXIII (May, 1918), 324–25.

———. "Extracts from Letters from Dr. J. H. McCurdy to His Family." (Undated, Paris.) *American Physical Education Review,* XXIII (Mar., 1918), 180.

———. "Extracts from Letters Received from Dr. J. H. McCurdy." (Addressed to his family, to Dr. George J. Fisher, to Mr. Berry; undated; 12, rue d'Aguesseau, Paris.) *American Physical Education Review,* XXII (Dec., 1917), 556–58.

———. "Greetings from France to the American Physical Education Association." *American Physical Education Review,* XXIII (Apr., 1918), 238–40.

———. "Lessons from France." *American Physical Education Review,* XXIV (June, 1919), 343–52.

———. "A Patriotic Opportunity for Men over Draft Age." (31, avenue Montaigne, Paris.) *American Physical Education Review,* XXII (Nov., 1917), 500.

McKenzie, R. Tait. "Frederick S. Barnjum and His Work." *American Physical Education Review,* II (June, 1897)), 73–80.

———. "Reminiscences of James Naismith." *Journal of Health and Physical Education,* IV (Jan., 1933), 21, 55.

"A Master Sportsman Has Completed His Assignment." *Graduate Magazine,* XXXVIII (Dec., 1939), 4–5.

"Milestones" (obituary of James Naismith), *Time,* Dec. 11, 1939, p. 40.

Naismith, Grace. "Father Basketball." *Sports Illustrated,* Jan. 31, 1955, pp. 64–65.

Naismith, James. (Letter, Dec. 13, 1918, Paris, addressed to Dr. McCurdy, Paris.) *American Physical Education Review,* XXIV (Apr., 1919), 197–98.

———. "An Improved Basis for Judging and Comparing the Physical Development of Children." *Kansas University Bulletin of Education,* III (Dec., 1930), 14–24.

———. "Basket Ball." *American Physical Education Review,* XIX (May, 1914), 339–51. (Paper read by Dr. Naismith at eighth annual convention, National Collegiate Athletic Association. Reprinted as pamphlet "History and Development of Basketball.")

———. "Basket Ball." *Triangle* (International Y.M.C.A. Training School, Springfield, Mass.), I (Jan. 15, 1892), 144–47. (Basketball rules on pp. 145–46.)

———. "Basketball—A Game the World Plays." *Congressional Record,* CVII, pt. 16, Sept. 25, 1961, pp. 21197–99. (Reprinted from *Rotarian,* LIV [Jan., 1939], 33.)

———. "High School Athletics and Gymnastics As as Expression of the Corporate Life of the High School." Chapter seventeen in *The Modern High School,* edited by Charles Hughes Johnston. New York: Charles Scribner's Sons, 1916, pp. 429–62.

———. "History and Development of Basketball" (pamphlet). Reprint of "Basket Ball," *American Physical Education Review,* XIX (May, 1914), 339–51.

———. "How Basketball Started and Why It Grew." In *Aims and Methods in School Athletics,* edited by E. Dana Caulkins, Wingate Memorial Lectures, 1931–1932. New York: Wingate Memorial Foundation, 1932, pp. 221–35.

———. "The Interrelation of High School and College Athletics, from the Standpoint of the College." *American Physical Education Review,* XIX (Oct., 1914), 528–35. (Paper read by Dr. Naismith at annual convention of the Society of Directors of Physical Education in Colleges, St. Louis, Mo., Apr. 3, 1914. Reprinted as an eight-page pamphlet.)

———. Letter dated Dec. 13, 1918, Paris. Addressed to Dr. McCurdy. *American Physical Education Review,* XXIV (Apr., 1919), 197–98.

———. "Universal Military Training." *American Physical Education Review,* XXIV (Apr., 1919), 200–204.

———. "Vrille (Vree) Ball." *American Physical Education Review,* XXIV (Feb., 1919), 116–18.

"Naismith Field House Fund." *Graduate Magazine,* Oct., 1939.

"Naismith Memorial Basketball Hall of Fame." Rotogravure section of *Springfield* (Mass.) *Sunday Republican,* Apr. 14, 1968. (Photographs of Naismith, original basketball rules, first basketball team, Naismith Cup, Hall of Fame views, etc.; articles.)

"Naismith Week." *Time,* Feb. 24, 1936, pp. 28, 30.

"National Collegiate Athletic Association, Eleventh Annual Convention." *American Physical Education Review,* XXII (Mar., 1917), 179–82.

"National Committees." *American Physical Education Review,* XXIV (June, 1919), 353–60.

"A New Adaptation of Basket Ball." *American Physical Education Review,* XXII (June, 1917), 385 -86.

"Notes from France." *American Physical Education Review,* XXIII (Feb., 1918), 123–24. (Excerpts from interview with Dr. J. H. McCurdy, *Springfield* [Mass.] *Union,* Feb. 14, 1918.)

"A Peachbasket Prodigy." *Monsanto Magazine,* Dec., 1961, pp. 10–13.

Phelps, Grady. "National Ceremony Set for Basketball Founder." *Corpus Christi Caller-Times,* Nov. 5, 1961, p. 19.

"A Physician Invented One of America's Great Sports." *Physicians' Times Magazine,* Oct., 1920. (From James Naismith, "Basket Ball," *American Physical Education Review,* XIX [May, 1914], 339–51.)

"Provisional Recreation Convention Program." *American Physical Education Review,* XXIII (Mar., 1918), 181.

Rath, Emil. "Report of Necrology Committee." *Journal of Health and Physical Education,* XI (Feb., 1940), 99.

"Readers Forum: Basketball and Moratoriums." *Kansas Alumni,* LXVIII (Apr., 1970), pp. 2, 9. (Items by Grace A. Brush, Joe Hambright, et al.)

"Recreation Bulletins for the American Expeditionary Forces." *American Physical Education Review,* XXIII (Feb., 1918), 124–25.

Rice, Grantland. "Golf's Greatest Putt." *Sports Illustrated,* Aug. 16, 1954, pp. 83–84.

"Top K-State Cage Team Is Salute to Kansas' Own Dr. Naismith, Inventor of Game." *Topeka Daily Capital Sunday Magazine,* Mar. 23, 1958, p. 11A.

"Wanted! Mature Athletic Directors." *American Physical Education Review,* XXII (Dec., 1917), 555–56.

Ward, Alvin D.; Elbel, Edwin R.; and Anderson, Kenneth E. "Comparison of Bodily Measurements of Entering University Students." *University of Kansas Bulletin of Education,* VIII (Fall, 1953), 7–11.

"When Doctor Naismith 'Found' a Star." *Graduate Magazine,* XXII (Feb., 1924), 16–17.

PAMPHLETS, MICROPRINT, AND MISCELLANEOUS
PUBLISHED MATERIALS

"Almonte, Ontario." Pamphlet issued by Almonte Industrial Committee, Almonte, Ont.

Dewar, John. "The Life and Professional Contributions of James Naismith." Ed.D. thesis, Florida State University, 1965. Eugene, Ore.: Microcard Publications, School of Health and Physical Education, University of Oregon, 1966.

Gulick, Luther Halsey, and Naismith, James. "Basket Ball." New York: American Sports Publishing Co., 1894. Twenty-four-page handbook (also on microcards, under "Naismith").

"Lawrence Industry." Leaflet prepared and published by the Project 71 Committee, Lawrence Chamber of Commerce, Lawrence, Kans.

"The Mill of Kintail & Robert Tait McKenzie." Leaflet published by What's on in Ottawa Publishing Co.

Naismith, James. "Basket Ball Rules," 1891. Pamphlet.

———. "History and Development of Basket Ball." Pamphlet reprinted from article "Basket Ball," *American Physical Education Review,* XIX (May, 1914), 339–51. Originally a paper read by Dr. Naismith at the eighth annual convention of the National Collegiate Athletic Association.

———. "The Interrelation of High School and College Athletics, from the Standpoint of the College." Pamphlet reprinted from *American Physical Education Review,* XIX (Oct., 1914), 528–35. Originally a paper read by Dr. Naismith at the annual convention of the Society of Directors of Physical Education in Colleges, St. Louis, Mo., Apr. 3, 1914.

———, and Gulick, Luther Halsey. "Basket Ball." Spalding's Athletic Library, II, no. 17. Microcard copy of twenty-four-page handbook by Gulick and Naismith, "Basket Ball."

———, and Johnson, G. E. "The Basis of Clean Living." Pamphlet published by the American Y.M.C.A., 12, rue d'Aguesseau, Paris, Jan., 1919.

Bibliography

———, and ———. "Suggestive Study for Right Standards." Pamphlet published by American Y.M.C.A., 12, rue d'Aguesseau, Paris, Apr., 1919.

"Our First One Hundred Years, 1858–1958." Pamphlet issued by the First Presbyterian Church, Lawrence, Kans.

Patton, T. Duncan. "The First Game: How and When Introduced." In "Old Timer's Exhibition." Leaflet of the Naismith Memorial Basketball Hall of Fame Committee.

UNPUBLISHED MATERIALS

Don-Carlos, Louisa Cooke. "The Writers of Tennessee: A Manual of Tennessee Literature." Master's thesis, University of Kansas, 1925.

Donnell, Allan. "Basketball and Its Inventor, Dr. James Naismith." Unpublished article, June, 1954, Almonte, Ont.

———. "Extracts from a Talk to Almonte Lions, May, 1953." Typescript of selections from address to Almonte Lions Club, Almonte, Ont.

Elston, Donald W. "A Biography of Forrest C. 'Phog' Allen." Master's thesis, University of Kansas, 1967.

Hammig, Jack G. "A Historical Sketch of Doctor James Naismith." Master's thesis, University of Kansas, 1962.

Hartje, George. "Biographical Data of James A. Naismith." Xerox negative from University of Illinois Library.

"Items about the Faculty Members of the University of Kansas," Watson Collection, Spencer Library, University of Kansas.

"James Naismith: Inventor of the Game of Basketball," Watson Collection, Spencer Library, University of Kansas.

Lowry, Edna Gardner. "Dr. James Naismith, 1861–1939: Inventor of Basketball." Unpublished article. Information in it used in *Almonte Gazette,* June 17, 1965, pp. 1, 8. (See "Plaque Will Be Unveiled June 16 to Inventor of Basketball at His Boyhood Home Ramsay Township.")

———. "Some Early Ramsay History." Unpublished article, Almonte, Ont. Mimeographed for private distribution.

Radio scripts (untitled). Subjects, two basketball teams: Edmonton Grads and Winnipeg Toilers. (In the Naismith collection of Allan Donnell, Almonte, Ont.)

Index

JN is used in the Index to refer to James Naismith.

The Basketball Man

James Naismith

Afterword: The Enduring Pattern

Steven Jansen, Ph.D.

Kappelman's Historic Collections
Lawrence, Kansas

Preface – The Afterword

After the publication of *The Basketball Man* (1973), I called the book my "masterpiece." I still do.

Nicknaming the book their "university press best seller," the University Press of Kansas gave it a second printing in 1974. Then, as happen it must, the book eventually went out of print.

After one of my fans in Texas read *The Basketball Man,* the result was years of telephone calls and visits from him, and another chapter in the Naismith story came to be. Nelson Sullivan, a basketball player during James Naismith's last years on the University of Kansas campus, thought the book should be made into a movie. "Impracticable," I demurred. "Out of reach."

Finally, spurred by Sullivan's persisting desire to do further glory to Naismith, I wrote *Two Peach Baskets* for the centenary celebration of the birth of basketball in 1991. In that book I included a summary of *The Basketball Man* (entitling that section "The Little Basketball Man") and an account of Sullivan's experiences on the KU campus ("Phog Allen, Doc Naismith and I"). Now, I told myself, I had something to offer to the persons who had futilely sought a copy of my out-of-print book.

Then something even more gratifying happened. Twenty years after the first printing of *The Basketball Man,* my "masterpiece" has been requested by the Kappelman's Historic Collections for reprint, an author's dream of good fortune come true.

Incidentally, Roy Williams, basketball coach at the University of Kansas, has something to say about good luck. After coaching the KU team into the NCAA Final Four twice in five years, he credits his success in part to his custom of going to Naismith's grave and touching the marker for good luck.

In basketball and books James Naismith lives luckily on.

Bernice Larson Webb
May, 1993

Contents

Acknowledgments

The Afterword is dedicated to my parents, Otto L. Kappelman and Erma Bouse Kappelman, who in the depths of the Great Depression had the foresight and the courage to move their family of five children from a small, rural Kansas town named Richmond to Lawrence in 1932. Only by living in a college town would it be possible economically for all the children to receive a higher education in those bleak and insecure times. But it was basketball specifically that propelled this family move. Francis, the eldest child, had received from the University of Kansas a basketball scholarship, which in those days meant he had a 35¢-per-hour job doing maintenance at the stadium. This job was an important source of support for the family. His athletic career at K.U. included being a starting guard on two Big Six Conference championship teams and the Olympic semi-finalist team of 1936. He was also named to the All-Conference Team in 1936. Younger brother, Lester, played on the K.U. basketball squads of 1937-39. All five Kappelman children – Francis, LaVerne, Lester, Glenn and Karl – went on to graduate from the University of Kansas with a total of seven degrees, spanning the years 1932 to 1950. Thus basketball shaped our family's lives forever.

Thanks and appreciation also go to:

Dr. Bernice Webb, Author of *The Basketball Man*

John Gosset, Director, and Don Rutherford of Naismith Visitor Centre, Almonte, Ontario, Canada

Wayne Patterson, Librarian, Naismith Memorial Basketball Hall of Fame, Springfield, Massachusetts

Matt Kappelman, Technical Assistant

Steve Jansen, Director, Watkins Community Museum

Dr. William Conboy, Professor Emeritus, University of Kansas, Editorial Assistant

Tekgraphics, Inc., Lawrence, Kansas

Judy Sweets, Watkins Community Museum, Technical Assistant

Jon Blumb, Photographer, Lawrence, Kansas

Bob Frederick, Director of Athletics, University of Kansas

Fred Woodward, Director, University Press of Kansas

Jerry Samp, President, Commerce Bank in Lawrence

Ned Kedhe, John Nugent and Barry Bunch at University Archives, University of Kansas

The Board of Directors, Douglas County Historical Society, Lawrence, Kansas

– Glenn L. Kappelman

Afterword:
The Enduring Pattern

1

Introduction: Sites of Honor

Lawrence, Kansas

On January 28, 1938, in a Lawrence school-room, the four-year-old Douglas County Historical Society had as its speaker a long-time resident of the city. A. B. Huddleston, secretary of the society, noted in the minutes that "Dr. James Naismith, father of basketball, was the speaker for the Kansas Day Program. He gave in a very interesting way the 'Growth of Facilities for Physical Education in Lawrence since 1898.' "[1]

Likely, Naismith spoke about a roller skating rink near Eighth and Kentucky that had been used for a few months in 1898-99 as the first home court for the recently formed K.U. basketball team. He might have reminisced about the second floor walk-ups where the team and the local Y.M.C.A. played for several years after the rink burned down in early 1899. Naismith might have described how meager were the first facilities for physical education at K.U., but it would have been uncharacteristic of him to blame such conditions for making him the only basketball coach at the University of Kansas who had a losing record. This piece of trivia is a media favorite – and reflects our preoccupation with how many wins are achieved.

For a pioneer like Naismith, the important accomplishments were the initiating of activities and the providing of facilities for physical education. In his talk to the society, Naismith probably did discuss the building of Robinson Gymnasium in 1907, since he was the key figure in the development of that facility. That achievement by Naismith gave a critical lift to K.U. basketball by providing a great place to play and room for 2,000-plus to watch.

387

Naismith Drive (street sign in inset) is seen in the lower right corner. Behind this street is Allen Field House where the Jayhawks have played since 1955, Parrott Athletic Center (site of James Naismith Room) and Anschutz Sports Pavilion. (Photographs by Jon Blumb).

Two grandsons of Dr. Naismith, Ian Naismith, left, and James J. Dodd, in 1956 with the portrait of their grandfather that hangs in Allen Field House, which was donated by Sigma Phi Epsilon Fraternity. (Courtesy Kansas University Archives).

Another structure he was associated with was the Y.M.C.A. at Eighth and Vermont. Completed in 1906, it provided Lawrence boys a place to compete in many different sports. The Y.M.C.A. gymnasium, for which Naismith was an important sponsor, also increased the supply of local talent for subsequent K.U. basketball coaches. He could also have noted with pride the various gyms which had been built since 1898 in connection with emerging elementary and secondary schools in the city.

It is unfortunate that more lore from Dr. Naismith could not have been collected and preserved. He died in 1939, and the functioning of the historical society was interrupted by the arrival on December 7, 1941, of World War II. The imperatives of the war and the later depletion in the ranks of the leaders from the 1930s kept the historical society from returning to full function until 1963. (Finding a suitable home for the society was also a source of frustration. Lawrence grew from 18,000 people in 1950 to 33,000 in 1960 - stretching existing institutions to the limit, and making heavy demands on the time and talents of persons involved in those institutions.)

Two important events heralded a recommitment to the heritages involved. One was the naming in 1955 of the street east of Allen Field House as Naismith Drive. The other was the reconstitution of the historical society on June 20, 1963. As I write in Lawrence in 1993, the two heritages have come together in several forms: exhibits in Allen Field House, an exhibit detailing Dr. Naismith's career in the Watkins Community Museum, a memorial marker erected at Eighth and Kentucky, and the statue and plaques which are planned for the cemetery where he is buried.

When Mrs. Webb wrote in 1973, she commented that "The place where Naismith would have preferred that any memorial to him be constructed was Lawrence."[2] At that time, she noted that there was a street bearing his name, a portrait of him in Allen Field House, a K.U. private dormitory named for him, and a flower garden in his memory at the cemetery where he is buried. The flower garden is scheduled for a major expansion and will be a significant memorial to Dr. Naismith.

Planned for completion by Memorial Day in 1994 are the Naismith Memorial Gardens in Memorial Park Cemetery in East Lawrence. The project will cost an estimated $250,000 and will involve a nine-foot bronze and granite statue of Naismith. There will be a 645 square foot granite patio, and the Gardens will contain eight benches and three bronze ledgers commemorating K.U. basketball. Six of the eight benches

Naismith's headstone in Memorial Park Cemetery in Lawrence, Kansas. (Photograph by Jon Blumb).

Memorial (proposed) to Dr. James Naismith in Memorial Park Cemetery in Lawrence, Kansas. (Illustration by Matt Kappelman).

will chronicle Naismith's life from his days as a youth in Canada, through his years at the Y.M.C.A. Training School in Springfield, Massachusetts, where he invented the game, to his long career as a coach and professor on Mount Oread at the University of Kansas. The seventh bench will pay tribute to two other K.U. graduates who became successful coaches: John McLendon at Tennessee A&I and Ralph Miller at both Wichita State and Oregon State. The eighth bench will contain a list of all of K.U.'s basketball coaches, from Naismith to Roy Williams and Marian Washington.

The three ledgers will honor coaches Forrest Allen, Adolph Rupp and Dean Smith. Allen coached at Kansas for 39 years, while Rupp and Smith, both of whom played under Allen, went on to spectacular careers at Kentucky and North Carolina respectively.[3]

At Eighth and Kentucky, thanks to Ross Beach, Max Falkenstien and Douglas County Bank, a marker and a plaque were erected in the spring of 1993 to commemorate the site as the home of K.U. basketball in 1898-99. The plaque, featuring an action scene of players around a goal, takes note of the small crowd, the frozen gas line, and the cold night that accompanied Dr. Naismith's introductory game for K.U. and for Lawrence. It will stand as a significant landmark in the history of the sport at the University and in the community.

Springfield, Massachusetts

The Naismith Memorial Basketball Hall of Fame in Springfield, Massachusetts, was the brainchild of the National Association of Basketball Coaches (NABC) following the Berlin Olympics of 1936. Ground was broken in 1959, and on February 17, 1968, at a cost of $650,000, a Hall of Fame was opened on the Springfield College campus.

On June 30, 1985, the present Hall of Fame was opened at a cost of $11,500,000. Its central location in the city and along I-91 – the major highway in New England – has made the three-story museum accessible to more people. In the first five years after its move in 1985, the Hall of Fame welcomed as many visitors from all over the world as had come to see the museum and shrine in 18 years on the Springfield College campus.

The Hall of Fame is one of the nation's major tourist attractions because of ever-growing interest in the sport it documents, honors and

The Springfield, Massachusetts Y.M.C.A. where the first game of basketball was played. It is no longer standing. (Courtesy Naismith Memorial Basketball Hall of Fame).

The Naismith Memorial Basketball Hall of Fame in Springfield, Massachusetts. (Courtesy Naismith Memorial Basketball Hall of Fame).

promotes. Among its popular attractions are various participatory exhibits, interactive videos, feature films, countless memorabilia and the use of modern technology inside the museum.

One display is "Play 52" in the Wilson Action Theatre - where visitors find themselves in the middle of a game that is played on four separate screens. Hall of Fame patrons can test their vertical jumping abilities in the exhibit "How High is Up?" The Hall of Fame's most popular exhibit is the Spalding Shoot-out, where visitors can test their shooting ability.

Three state-of-the-art exhibits new to the Hall of Fame are participatory videos. "The Hall of Fame Challenge" is a multi-level competition where visitors can test their knowledge of basketball since 1891. The most recent addition is the "Hall of Fame/Starter Tip-Off Classic" display. The interactive exhibit contains game highlights and interviews depicting the 15 years of college basketball's opening game. The Hall of Fame's featured attraction is the Honors Court, where 197 men and women plus four teams are formally enshrined. "The Honors Court Comes to Life" is an interactive video setup that enables visitors to view film and access information on many Hall of Fame inductees. All levels of competition are featured in the Hall of Fame – men, women, professional, college, international, scholastic, referees, trainers, coaches and contributors.[4]

Almonte, Ontario (Canada)

Another place where Naismith's impact is still felt is Almonte, Ontario, Canada, his birthplace. On August 1, 1993, the Dr. James Naismith Basketball Foundation officially opened a Visitor and Information Centre on the farm where he was born and raised, as phase one of a three phase project. In its first half season over 3,000 visitors were recorded. The Centre is open May 15 to October 15, 9 a.m. to 5 p.m. Monday through Friday, and 12 to 5 p.m. Saturday and Sunday.

The Foundation, a non-profit, charitable organization, incorporated in 1989, with an active volunteer base, has stated its objectives: "To establish and operate the Naismith International Basketball Centre which will reflect the remarkable heritage and development of Naismith's game in Canada and around the world. To develop programs consistent with Naismith's life, his ideals and his game." The Foundation has acquired through private donations, two acres of land,

The Naismith family home near Almonte, Ontario. James resided here between the ages of nine and 20 with his uncle, Peter Young and sister, Annie. (Courtesy Dr. James Naismith Basketball Foundation).

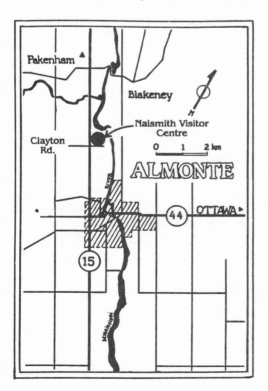

This map shows the Almonte, Ontario area and location of the Visitor Information Centre of the Naismith Basketball International Centre.

Dr. James Naismith Basketball Foundation, Box 1991, Almonte, Ontario, K0A 1A0, Canada

Tel: 613-256-1978

at the back of the original Naismith farm, and has gained the support of both the private and public sectors, with the seed monies and grants necessary to realize its dreams.

The Foundation also has obtained the collaboration of the Government of Canada in the designating Dr. Naismith as a person of National Historic Significance, and in the issuance of a Basketball Centenary stamp set. In addition, an agreement has been initiated with the YM/YWCA, Basketball Canada, Canadian Wheelchair Basketball Association, Federation of International Basketball Associations (FIBA), the Confederation of Pan American Basketball Associations (COPABA), and other sister organizations, to build a year-round multi-dimensional facility. This represents phases two and three of the plan.

The Dr. James Naismith Basketball Foundation is dedicated to preserving the physical and material history of this great Canadian. Dr. Naismith's legacy lives on in Almonte, Ontario, where the birthplace of the inventor of basketball has become an emerging attraction.

2

Then and Now - The Evolving Game

The Hall of Fame has produced a 35-page pamphlet entitled "Basketball Was Born Here." In it there is a brief, valuable section on "Evolution of the Rules." Written by Dennis Phillips of Springfield College, it helps us to evaluate the lasting impact of the original 13 rules developed by Naismith. Phillips notes the great popularity of this American-made sport and attributes much of the popularity to the founder's "inventive genius." He writes: "It is interesting to note that the original 13 rules conceived by Dr. Naismith are still the basis for the game . . . . Basketball rules have not remained static, but have been revised, modified and adapted to the changing needs of the sport, without compromising the values and ideals of its origin."[6]

Physical Specifications

Phillips reports that the 1890s gymnasiums were designed primarily for gymnastic exercise, and there was little uniformity in the size, shape

Basket. Ball.

The ball to be an ordinary Association foot ball.

1. The ball may be thrown in any direction with one or both hands.

2. The ball may be batted in any direction with one or both hands (never with the fist).

3. A player cannot run with the ball, the player must throw it from the spot on which he catches it, allowance to be made for a man who catches the ball when running at a good speed.

4. The ball must be held in or between the hands, the arms or body must not be used for holding it.

5. No shouldering, holding, pushing, tripping or striking in any way the person of an opponent shall be allowed. The first infringement of this rule by any person shall count as a foul, the second shall disqualify him until the next goal is made, or if there was evident intent to injure the person, for the whole of the game , no substitute allowed.

6. A foul is striking at the ball with the fist, violation of rules 3 and 4, and such as described in rule 5.

7. If either side makes three consecutive fouls it shall count a goal for the opponents (consecutive means without the opponents in the meantime making a foul).

8. A goal shall be made when the ball is thrown or batted into the basket from the grounds and stays there, providing those defending the goal do not touch or disturb the goal. If the ball rests on the edge and the opponent moves the basket it shall count as a

First draft of original 13 rules of basketball. (Courtesy Naismith Memorial Basketball Hall of Fame).

goal.

9. When the ball goes out of bounds it shall be thrown into the field, and played by the person first touching it.   In case of a dispute the umpire shall throw it straight into the field. The thrower in is allowed five seconds, if he holds it longer it shall go to the opponent.   If any side persists in delaying the game, the umpire shall call a foul on them.

10. The umpire shall be judge of the men, and shall note the fouls, and notify the referee when three consecutive fouls have been made.   He shall have power to disqualify men according to Rule 5.

11.   The referee shall be judge of the ball and shall decide when the ball is in play, in bounds, and to which side it belongs, and shall keep the time.   He shall decide when a goal has been made, and keep account of the goals with any other duties that are usually performed by a referee.

12.   The time shall be two fifteen minutes halves, with five minutes rest between.

13.   The side making the most goals in that time shall be declared the winners.   In case of a draw the game may, by agreement of the captains, be continued until another goal is made.

First draft of Basket Ball rules.
thing in the gym that the boys might
learn the rules - Dec 1891 James Naismith
6-28-31.

and nature of the floors and walls. In 1896, 3,500 square feet was the largest allowable legal playing area. Now, almost 100 years after those first dimensions, colleges have set a standard of 94 feet long by 50 feet wide, a total of 4,700 square feet. The courts in high schools vary considerably, but the recommended size is 74 feet long by 50 feet wide, a total of 3,700 square feet.

Three notable changes in courts are identified by Phillips: "(a) the increase in the length of the court in 1939 to provide four more feet under each basket, (b) the 1955 expansion of the free throw lane from six feet to 12 feet, and (c) the addition of restraining circles for jump balls in 1935-36."

While there have been no rule changes recently in the square footage of a court, the increasing ability by players to jump and stay suspended in the air has definitely influenced how the game is both played and seen. For example, Rick Telander in his 1976 book on urban basketball, *Heaven Is A Playgound,* describes a Lloyd Hill, the then "master leaper and stuffer of Foster Park" in Brooklyn. Telander tells of a series of dunks by the young man and then goes into detail: "For his final attempt Lloyd walks back an extra ten paces and blows on his hands. He grasps the ball in front of him and takes an all-out sprint at the basket. He cuts sharply through the row of silent boys like a halfback turning upfield and then, nearly ten feet from the hoop, flings himself into the air. As he floats slowly to the rim he rubs the ball on the back of his neck like a man with an itch under his collar and then slams it through the rim so hard it caroms wildly off to another court."[7] While this exhibition was not part of a game, similar actions occur in games played in junior highs and on up the levels of competition in the 1990s.

Perhaps the first player to signal this change was Wilt Chamberlain at Kansas University. In an article entitled "Can Basketball Survive Chamberlain?," Jimmy Breslin made the point in the December 1, 1956, issue of *The Saturday Evening Post.* He described a November 1955 game between freshmen and varsity in Allen Field House during which, "The Stilt drove to the back of the keyhole - or circle - and went up for what appeared to be a one-handed jump shot. But he didn't come down. He kept floating through the air, did a complete twist so that his back was to the basket, shoved his arm behind him, rotated it in helicopter style and dunked the ball behind the net. He landed somewhere behind the basket."[9] It was largely in response to Wilt's prowess that the lane was widened from six to twelve feet in 1956.

Dennis Phillips in his discussion of rule changes notes that as early as 1894 screens six feet by four feet were put in the back of each basket, and that by 1896 "the rules dictated that the inside basket rim should extend six inches from the flat perpendicular surface of the backboard, a rule that has remained ever since."[9] By 1905, it was specified backboards should be solid and the goals were to be one foot from the bottom of the backboard and three feet from each side of the backboard, with the top of the backboard ending three feet above the basket. After 1909, the rules committee said that backboards could be plate glass, and at a later time approval was given to paint on them a target which would give the shooter some idea of how to bank the ball into the goal.

Regarding fan-shaped backboards, they became legal in 1940 and were used by many high schools. Phillips reports that "College coaches, however, did not like the fan-shaped boards, and as time went on, the rules committee ruled the fan-shaped boards out." Now the standard board, as far as all rules are concerned, is the rectangular board.

The backboards on all regulation floors are now four feet in from the end lines. There have been no recent dramatic changes in the rules, but modern athletes are continuing to have a impact on the backboards – not only through dunking, but also by the occasional shattering of a backboard by players like Shaquille O'Neal in his "Shaq Attack."

Dr. James Naismith's original intent was for a large number of players to be able to participate in the game, but as Dennis Phillips observes, "This type of game proved unscientific, with sometimes too many players on a small court . . . . So, in 1893, the number on a side was reduced to five on a small court . . . . The first few years the numbers were in proportion to the playing space . . . . The number of five players on a side was definitely agreed upon in 1895 . . . . This is one rule that so far has not received much criticism down through the years."

In the early rules, "any player disqualified twice was excluded from matched games for the rest of the season. When a player left the game, he could not return. Another rule was that if a player was disqualified, no substitute could take his place in that half of the game." Bill Gutman writes in *The Pictorial History of Basketball* that by 1908 a rule was in place that would disqualify a player after he committed five personal fouls.[10] Prior to 1923, foul shots were awarded for such things as traveling with the ball and double-dribble. But in that year the rules committee changed these breakdowns to violations – meaning only a change of possession, no free throws.

As of 1902, players could only be changed at the half, and this was the case until 1936. Also, 1936 brought the elimination of the center jump after each made basket, and the pace of the game picked up. Bill Gutman comments that "because the clock continued to run during the repeated center jumps, it was estimated that the elimination of the practice would add nine to twelve minutes of play to each game."

Today the rules sanction free and unlimited substitutions. Innovative coaches like Dean Smith and Roy Williams have extended substitution choices beyond themselves. The players, likely the best judges of their own physical condition, may signal to the bench their requests to be replaced.

Peach baskets were not long used as the goals, and by 1893 the coneshaped baskets had been introduced. Since that time, the materials used for them has varied, but the shape has endured. Dennis Phillips notes that "The height of the position of the baskets has remained at 10 feet since the first rules. Suggestions for raising the baskets to 12 feet, because of the advantage for tall players, have not received any definite action from the National Rules Committee, although experimental games have been played under those conditions. The majority of players, officials, coaches and fans seem to approve of the standard 10 foot basket."[11] One who did not and who early on called for the 12-foot height was Forrest Allen. He lobbied long and hard for the change, but he was unsuccessful.

The original hoops were black iron, and the early nets were heavy cord which hung down to 18 inches. Later the net length was shortened to allow the ball to drop through more quickly, and in 1949 the color of the hoops was changed to orange. The most recent major change has been the development of breakaway rims, necessitated by the increased popularity of dunking.

As for the ball, in the first year the ordinary soccer-football was used. By 1892 it was specified that the ball should be round and from 30 to 32 inches in circumference, but in subsequent years the balls used tended to be smaller in response to player preference. In 1934 the rules committee set the size at 29 ½ to 30 inches. In 1984 ball specifications were modified for the women's game – one inch smaller and two and one-half ounces lighter.

According to the rules, a regulation basketball should weigh from 18 to 20 ounces and should carry an air pressure of 13 pounds. A controversy over stitched versus molded types of balls arose in 1942 when molded ones were first recommended by the rules makers. This debate continued until 1950, when the decision was made that the ball should be leather-covered and molded. Improvements continue to be made – wider seams for better grip, and an orange-tan color (replacing the earlier tan) for better visibility. It is interesting to note that athletic abilities have increased to the point where it is common for a player to grasp the ball and throw it much like a baseball or football, despite its greater size.

Scoring Rules and Conditions

Dennis Phillips writes concerning the original rules: "A goal shall be made when the ball is thrown or batted into the basket and stays there, providing those defending the goal do not touch or disturb the goal. If the ball rests on the edges and the opponent moves the basket, it shall count as a goal. If either side makes three consecutive fouls, it shall count as a goal for the opponents . . . . In 1893 field goals counted three points and a foul one point and whenever you committed a foul the point was awarded your opponents . . . . In 1897 the rule was changed so that the field goal counted as two points and the free throw one point."

Important refinements were made in 1894. For the first time, the free throw was added to the rules as the consequence for committing a foul. After one trial at 20 feet in 1895, the line for taking free throws was set at 15 feet. In 1923 it was ruled that each player had to shoot his own free throws.

As early as the 1940s experimental games were played in which three points were awarded for a shot made beyond a 20-foot arc. Dennis Phillips notes that "The three-point field goal was adopted in the professional ranks by Abe Saperstein in the American Basketball League and later in 1967, at 25 feet, by the ABA. Shortly after the ABA and NBA merged, the NBA adopted the shot at the distance of 23 feet 9 inches. The NCAA legislated the three-point field goal in 1986 . . . . Rules editor Dr. Edward Steitz persuasively pushed for acceptance of the rule at a distance of 19 feet 9 inches from the basket despite the opposition of a majority of the nation's coaches. The 'home run' of basketball quickly became a fan favorite, and re-established a balance of inside-outside scoring in the game."

Time Requirements

Originally, in 1891, the contest consisted of two 15-minute halves with a five-minute rest between. In 1893, it was changed to two 20-minute halves with a 10-minute rest between. Phillips reminds us that for a time four 10-minute quarters were played in the colleges and four eight-minute quarters in high schools, with a 15-minute rest in each case between halves. He observes that "Colleges have gone back to the 20-minute halves and 15-minute rest periods while high schools have stayed with the eight minute quarter rule. In professional basketball . . . they play four 12-minute quarters. Original provisions for breaking a tie score at the end of a game included a sudden death overtime. In 1907, the collegiate rules adopted the current five-minute overtime period."

The advent of a style of play called "stalling" in the 1920s grew out of better dribblers and because of bunched five-player defenses close to the basket. By 1893 there had been a rule which assessed a foul penalty for "delay of the game," but "freezing the ball" was still frequently employed.

Two rule changes in 1929 and 1932 respectively required the offensive player to move the ball in five seconds, and, with the court divided into halves, established a 10-second limit for a team to advance the ball from their back court into their front court. This latter rule did aid in the reduction of stalling tactics.

In 1935 the three-second rule went into effect, prohibiting offensive players from staying in the lane for more than that interval. Proposals for a shot-clock limit were strongly opposed by most coaches in the 1940s. They were seen as taking away the strategy of "ball control," and also as attempting to dictate a particular style of play. Still, as Phillips notes "the increase in ball-handling skills, the four-corner delay offense, frequency of inactive, low-scoring games, and previous success with the NBA 24-second and FIBA 30-second shot-clocks led to the ultimate adoption of the shot clock. The 30-second clock for women was accepted in 1971-72 and the 45-second clock for men in 1986." For the 1993-94 season, the rules committee has shortened the men's time span to 35 seconds.

Ball Handling and Management

In 1891-92, the ball could be batted in any direction with one or both hands, but no dribbling was allowed. Inevitably, some way had to be devised to permit players better movement. During Naismith's years at K.U., newspaper references described a "Roly-Boly" technique of rolling the ball on the floor. Yale University was among the first teams to use dribbling and for a time the practice was termed "the Yale game."

Phillips notes that "In 1910, a player could pivot, but the ball had to leave his hand before the pivot foot was lifted; and a player standing still could take one step in any direction, while putting the ball in play in any manner. In starting a dribble, the ball had to leave the hand before the pivot foot came down on the floor again. In 1902 it was a violation to throw for a goal after a dribble . . . . It was not until 1916 that after a dribble a shot for goal was permitted. In 1928 the rules committee changed the rule back, limiting the dribbles to one bounce, but . . . this rule change caused so much discussion, and a lot of arguing and bickering among the college coaches, that the rules committee repealed the change. This discussion and argument caused the formation of the National Association of Basketball Coaches in 1928, so they would have an organized body." Phillips reports that since 1928 debates have continued about dribbling and about how players control the ball while moving with it.

Starting in 1891 and continuing until 1936, the referee put the ball in play at the beginning of a game by throwing it up within a six-foot radius circle at center court. After each score, the ball would again be tossed up at center court. Dennis Phillips states that "In 1936 one of the most revolutionary rule changes was made when the center jump rule was changed. Each time a team scored a field goal or a free throw, their opponents put the ball in play from out of bounds. They now got their chance to advance the ball and to try to score. This change was the great equalizer as it made our game of basketball a game of equal opportunity. Each team had the same opportunity to have possession of the ball and to try to score. Fans, players and coaches all like this rule change as it makes for a more widespread game with equal opportunity for scoring by all teams."

Don Elston, in his 1967 thesis about Forrest Allen, reports that he "fought the elimination of the center jump, and strongly advocated its return for several reasons. First, the elimination of the center jump placed greater 'pressure' on officials. The game was much faster and officials had trouble keeping up with the players . . . . Second, removing the center jump, Dr. Allen believed, penalized the scoring team. After scoring, the scoring team suffered a loss of the ball, with no equal opportunity to score again until the opponents relinquished possession of the ball. With the center jump rule the scoring team would not be penalized. It would have an equal chance of gaining the ball and scoring. To equalize the opportunity of gaining possession of the ball, Dr. Allen proposed that each player on the team would participate in the center jump."[12] Allen, as was the case with the 12-foot goal, lost this battle regarding the rules.

After this review of the evolution of the rules and of the impact of players and coaches, it is apparent that Naismith's game of 1891 still defines most boundaries of the sport. Some journalists may question this point. For example, Fredric C. Klein, in the October 4, 1991, *Wall Street Journal,* remarked that Naismith "wrote that basketball would be basketball as long as four things didn't change: The large, light ball; the elevated, horizontal goal; no personal contact, and no running with the ball. Seems the NBA qualifies on only two of those counts."[13]

Klein did, however, put Naismith's contribution in perspective when he noted that it is "the U.S.'s most important gift to sports. Baseball may be our poets' choice, and football may be No. 1 on the domestic tube, but basketball, with its free-flowing form and abundant opportunities for individual virtuosity, is the American game the world has chosen. FIBA, the Olympic regulator of the sport, recognizes national governing bodies in 176 countries, 10 more than belong to the United Nations. Surveys I've seen identify basketball as the world's foremost spectator sport."

3
Naismith at K.U.

Basketball is the foremost spectator sport at Kansas University and in Lawrence. It has been that way most of the time since Dr. James Naismith arrived here in 1898. As Mrs. Webb noted previously, the *Kansan,* the student newspaper, on December 10, 1898, reported "A new game has sprung into popularity. It is the game of basketball. Every one who is at all interested in athletics is now talking basketball . . . . It is talked at the club; it is discussed in the corridors; it is practiced and played in the gymnasium and on the campus. Even the professors have become actively interested in the game and are giving their time of recreation over to this pastime. At present it appears that the basketball mania would carry all before it."[14] Ninety-five years later, the basketball mania still exists along the banks of the Kaw River.

The Arrival

The chancellor of the University of Kansas in 1898 was Francis H. Snow, and he was the man who hired Naismith. A Reverend Hector Cowan had previously been the Associate Professor of Physical Training and Chapel Director. A historian living in Lawrence, John Peterson, with the help of Snow's great-grandson, Robert H. Brown, has located a May 19, 1898, letter which puts the decision to hire Naismith in a new light. In this 1898 letter written to his wife, Snow tells of a trip first to St. Louis, then to Chicago. In the Illinois city Snow consulted with the president of the University of Chicago, William Harper, about his need for a new faculty member. Harper asked Amos Alonzo Stagg, his athletic director, for suggestions. The previous report was that Stagg sent Snow a brief telegraph recommending his former Y.M.C.A. classmate Naismith as "inventor of basketball, medical doctor, Presbyterian minister, tee-totaler, all-around athlete, non-smoker, and owner of vocabulary without cuss words." But, in the May 1898 letter, Chancellor Snow wrote of the result of his trip, "Have had three very interesting days in Chicago. Have found an apparently first class candidate for Mr. Cowan's place, recommended highly by Director A.A. Stagg of the University of Chicago. He is now at Denver, is a theological grad, also A.B. at McGill University and also a M.D. Have written him. He would be able to fill the bill as *Chapel Director* as well as Physical Culture Professor! He is the man who *invented* the game of basketball."[15] This letter suggests that the Stagg telegram story may have been folklore.

After Naismith arrived on campus in the fall of 1898, it wasn't long before basketball was being played on Mount Oread, the hill on which the University of Kansas is located. Two days after the comment about "basketball mania" on December 12, 1898, the *Lawrence Journal,* under its K.U. notes, stated that the faculties of Snow and Fraser Halls had played the game and among those playing was Naismith himself. It

The Chaplain of the First Kansas Infantry, Dr. James Naismith, in 1916. (Courtesy Kansas University Archives).

Dr. James Naismith and Amos Alonzo Stagg, two pioneers in American sports, at the Kansas University Relays circa 1933. (Courtesy Kansas University Archives).

wasn't long after the holiday break that the first game involving K.U. students was played. It took place in the roller skating rink at 807 Kentucky, close to downtown Lawrence.

The *Journal* on January 19, 1899, told of games between different classes and also that the University Athletic Association had leased the rink for games being arranged. Four days later, the *Journal* told of "An Interesting Public Exhibition" of "A Game of Basketball" in its headlines. The account of the game began, "Lawrence people who were present at the rink Saturday evening were given an opportunity of learning something about basketball, which is being played considerably at Kansas University, as well as nearly every school in the country, and which has been given additional prominence here because of the presence of Dr. James Naismith as physical culture director of the school, who is the inventor of the game. Very few present Saturday night knew what the game was like, and as Dr. Naismith acted as referee and explained the game as it progressed, the occasion was made of greater interest."[16]

The *Journal* further noted, "The game is a vigorous one, and while having all the commendable features of football, has none of its roughness, nor brutality. There are five players on each side, and the players paired off, one man from each side watching a particular man on the other side. The ball is snapped up from the middle of the field, and by passing, striking with the open hand, tossing from side to side or passing in any manner except kicking, from one player to the other, the object is to place the ball in the basket at either end of the field. These baskets are similar to the goal posts of a football field, in that each side has one, and that a man is stationed to guard each one. The players are not allowed to run with the ball, grab it from another player, or indulge in any sort of roughness, and the ball must be kept in motion either by bouncing on the floor, or by passing from one to another. The baskets at each end of the field are at the top of the poles eight feet high, and it is a very difficult task to put the ball in the basket when the ten men are around the player, four trying to help him and five are trying just as hard to knock the ball from his hands, or prevent it being thrown straight. There was an immense amount of activity in the game, and the agility manifested by many of the players was surprising. The game has two twenty-minute halves; each time the ball is thrown through the ring, or into the basket, it counts two for the side that does it, and a ball thrown when the other

side makes a foul counts one." This review from 1899 helps us recapture
how the game appeared to those then on the scene.

The Early Years

The games played between various classes and the faculty were at least
partially intended to identify those who would represent the University.
The *Lawrence Journal* on February 3, 1899, stated that "The following
team plays basket ball in Kansas City with the Y.M.C.A. this evening: F.
Owens, Hess, Avery, Henderson, W.S. Sutton, Coal, Vanderuff and
Yahn." Those eight players were the first basketball players from Kansas
University, and the tradition of achievement began with them.

Max L. Rife in his 1967 M.A. thesis titled "Basketball in its Early Years
at the University of Kansas 1898-1925," tells about the February 10, 1899,
home game against Topeka Y.M.C.A. Rife states "The *Kansas Weekly*
reported that only fifty people were present at this first game 'due to the
fact that the gas line froze up.' "[17] The *Lawrence Journal* wrote about
this spell of cold weather that "There were few business houses that were
warm enough . . . to work inside without wraps on." So the first home
basketball game for K.U. was seen by 50 hardy souls likely bundled up in
their coats. Fortunately, they were rewarded for their attendance with a
victory by the University team.

Rife also notes that K.U. won by a score of 31 to 6 and attributes the
victory to the opponents' unfamiliarity with Jayhawker tactics which
the *Kansan* called the "Roly-Boly" game. The tactic was rolling the
basketball on the floor from one player to another as a means of
advancing it. (Accordingly, it might be said that in gaining its first
victory K.U. was on a roll.) While the Universisty did field a varsity team
for games with outside foes, there were eight other teams organized from
within the faculty and students, as well as the Lawrence Y.M.C.A. In the
contemporary press as much attention was paid to games between these
groups as was given to the outside contests.

On March 20, 1899, the first home for K.U. basketball, at 807
Kentucky, burned to the ground just two days after a game. The loss of
the skating rink brought K.U.'s first home season to an abrupt end. Rife
states that "Various causes of the fire were suggested by the *Kansan*,
among them 'the warmth of the games between the Sophomores and
Seniors.' " During this season the Jayhawkers finished with four wins
and three losses in games between February 3 and April 11 in 1899.

The home for the second season was 936 New Hampshire, the Y.M.C.A., opened on January 1, 1900. Dr. Naismith had been the chairman of the building committeee and had led the conversion of a former agricultural implement store in downtown Lawrence into a gym. Also notable during this first month in 1900 was the naming of Naismith as the general manager of the Athletic Association. The *Lawrence Journal* of January 17, 1900, wrote "So far as the University athletes and students have been sounded on the subject Dr. Naismith has their undivided support in his new position." The student paper of January 20, 1900, commended him, stating "Dr. Naismith is eminently fitted for his new position as general manager. He is in close touch with all athletic interests of the University and will do his best to make them all successful. He did much to make the football team a success this year and will be in a position to do more next year. His election will be especially pleasing to the football men." (Thus Dr. Naismith was saluted at K.U. in 1900 for his support of football.)

The second season of basketball started with a game on January 27, 1900, with the *Weekly* calling on "every one who can to turn out to these games and help the boys. Basket ball became a very popular game last year and the same interest ought to be taken in the games this season." In reports on the March 2, 1900, road game against Nebraska there is no mention of Dr. Naismith having been in attendance. Often during his nine years as coach he did not accompany the team on the road due to many responsibilities.

Another aspect of K.U. basketball in 1900 that was very different from current conditions was the lack of a suitable home on the campus for the sport. The *Weekly* noted in March 1900, "After being shown through Nebraska's beautiful gymnasium, a handsome structure as large as Spooner Library [a K.U. building] fitted with every appliance for the development of physical manhood, the boys were asked how it compared with ours. Someone aptly replied 'We have none. All we have at K.U. is a bath and a hole in the basement of Snow Hall where we have the privilege of storing our apparatus.' " The student paper editorialized on March 10, 1900, about K.U. basketball that "If it had a good gymnasium in which to work it could show us as strong a team as any. Basket ball can never be what it ought to be at Kansas University until this much needed gymnasium is built." In seven years, due largely to the influence and lobbying of Naismith, this deficiency was finally overcome.

In the 1899-1900 basketball season, K.U.'s second try at the sport, the varsity played only seven games, winning three and losing four. The third season began on December 11, 1900, and was notable for K.U.'s only forfeit – due according to the *Weekly* to the referee who "showed an inexcusable lack of knowledge of the rules and our boys were indeed justified in leaving the field." The last game of the 1900-1901 season occurred on March 15, 1901, and the *Lawrence Journal* reported "In a rough and tumble game of basket ball at the Y.M.C.A. gymnasium . . . . Kansas University won from Haskell by a score of 25 to 20. The team work was not of the best on either side and a large share of the goals were pure luck . . . . The Indians' team work was not as good as usual." Unfortunately, luck was not always present, and despite this win the University of Kansas finished with four victories against eight defeats.

Entering the fourth year of competitive play, the Jayhawkers for the third time were looking for a place to play. In 1900 and 1901 home court had been at 936 New Hampshire, but prior to the 1901-02 season that gym had burned. Practice for the year began on October 2, but the *Weekly* on October 5, 1901, told how "The burning of the Y.M.C.A. gymnasium presents a perplexing question to basket ball enthusiasts. Where will the team play? Our university gymnasium is not large enough for practice, to say nothing of playing an inter-collegiate game in it. Dr. Naismith has reserved one end of the gymnasium for the basket ball team, but as there is only enough room for practice in passing the ball, much of the work must be done out of doors." By December 7, 1901, games were being played in Journal Hall at 924-926 Massachusetts, downtown Lawrence.

The position of basketball at K.U. is revealed in a January 25, 1902, comment in the student paper: "The only encouraging aspect of the basket ball situation is that the sport is inexpensive and that the athletic association is not in danger of contracting big debts in support of the game. But the fact that basketball does not entail 1/10th the expense of football and baseball will not insure its success at K.U. The student body must shuffle off its indifference and get on friendly terms with this neglected branch of Kansas athletics. Why not? Do you admire endurance, activity, nerve, a good cool head and a quick eye in an athlete? If so attend the next basket ball game and see a good exhibition of these qualities. Athletics can't thrive on money alone - it must have encouragement." In February of 1902, during a six day trip through

Iowa and Missouri, K.U. played six games, winning two and losing four. For the season, Dr. Naismith's team won five and lost seven.

The 1902-03 season began on December 12, 1902. The *Lawrence Journal* noted, "The Kansas team is greatly strengthened this fall by Allen, who was a member of the crack Independence, Mo., five last year." The Allen mentioned was Harry B. Allen, whose younger brother Forrest would later enroll at K.U. For the year the Jayhawkers won seven and lost eight, and of those 15 only one game was played in Lawrence.

The key stumbling block for K.U. basketball in its early years was finding a suitable place to play. The *Weekly* of September 26, 1903, discussing "The Gymnasium," observed "When the energetic Kansan cannot get what he wants, he makes the best of what he has. The state legislature did not deem it expedient to grant us a gymnasium building when we asked for it last year, yet by extensive remodeling of the basement of Snow Hall, the facilities for gymnasium work have been greatly increased. The large west room has been ceilinged and plastered and its floor lowered 3 feet, thus affording a room 14 feet high with a floor area 38 by 90 feet. One half of this will be used for basket ball and the remainder for general apparatus for physical development." So as the 1903-04 season began K.U. had a gym on campus in the basement of Snow Hall, but the 14-foot height posed obvious problems for those shooting baskets. Also an aggravation was the row of iron columns down the court which gave a turn-of-the-century added meaning to the phrase "Post Up" for the teams playing there.

It is difficult now, given the popular interest in the current Jayhawk baketball program, to relate to conditions in 1904. We have to remember that then the sport was only a six-year project, still largely unnoticed by most on the Mount Oread campus. It was carried on by a manager, then U.S.G. Plank, and an often otherwise-occupied coach, Dr. Naismith. On January 16, 1904, the *Weekly*, in previewing an upcoming series of eight away games in 10 days, cited Plank as the arranger of the schedule and noted, "Either Manager Plank or Dr. Naismith will accompany the team and probably one substitute will be taken along." (A team consisting of six players and an often absent coach was facing eight games in ten days -K.U. basketball in January of 1904!)

On January 21, 1904, in the basement of Snow hall the Haskell basketball team beat the University of Kansas 28 to 12. The student paper, the *Weekly*, reported that "The game was rough and several times evidences of temper were apparent which could have been well done away with. This fault on the part of the K.U. team has kept many people away from the gymnasium and should be kept out of the game. The basket ball games are attracting much more attention here now than ever before, are well attended and with a good team should pay expenses and be able to take just as long trips as a baseball or football team to meet the best teams in the west. The men should remember that their conduct reflects credit or discredit on the University and should play as clean a game as they would in football or baseball." Dr. Naismith's reactions to these incidents is not known.

During the year of 1903-04 only 13 games were played by K.U. Another problem encountered in that season was academic ineligibility, and as a result K.U. fielded two entirely different teams at various points during the year. On February 18, 1904, the Jayhawkers were on the road again, playing the Athletic Club of Kansas City and losing the game 27 to 10. It is likely that one of those playing guard for the Club was Forrest Allen, then 18 years old. The *Weekly* in describing the game noted a brief second-half rally by K.U. which gave rise to improved play by the K.C.A.C. The *Weekly* noted "The Athletics here took a brace. Rickerson and Allen both succeeding in throwing difficult goals." A player named Allen was thus listed as a guard for the K.C. team. K.U. finished the season with five wins and eight losses.

Max Rife in his 1967 thesis tells us, "The disorganized status of the team during the previous year seemed to carry over to the beginning of the 1904-05 season. The ineligibility of players and the absence from school of Captain [Harry] 'Pete' Allen were two factors mentioned by the campus newspaper, now named the *Kansan*. A December 3, 1904, article, stated 'Basket ball is in a rather chaotic condition as far as organization is concerned, but this does not prevent practice. Twice, a week, on Tuesday and Friday nights at 7:30 p.m. players are meeting.' Additional confusion was caused by an incomplete schedule. The Athletic Board hadn't made a decision as to 'backing' the basket ball program for another year. If it did not provide financial backing, the Department of Physical Training would, in which case a much shorter season could be expected." As it turned out, the Athletic Board did not adequately support basketball, and only eleven games were played during that season.

On December 8, 1904, the student paper again complained about the lack of a good gym, stating "The present gymnasium is a discredit to the people of Kansas and to the University. Everything is crowded into half the space it should occupy . . . . The men are forced to work in a small room which is so crowded that those who play basket ball are often injured by falling over apparatus, or against the racks that are standing about the room . . . . What we need are two large combination rooms with plenty of space for indoor games." Add to this description the low ceiling and iron columns and we have a mental picture of the first campus home of K.U. basketball.

The sport accordingly struggled to gain fans among the students on Mount Oread. The *Kansan* editorialized on December 15, 1904, "With the football season at an end, athletes in the University turn their thoughts toward basket ball as the next sport to engage their attention. The prospects for the game this year are very bright, but the team deserves more support than it has received from the student body in the past. Basket ball is a game with as much science in it as there is in football, and ignorance of the fine points of the game is all that keeps the student body from showing a lively interest in the sport. One never enjoys his first game of football, and the same is true of the game under discussion. It is to be hoped that this year the game here will be bettter supported than it has in the past." (It seems clear that interest in the new sport at K.U. was waning despite the presence on campus of its inventor.)

Basketball was in its seventh season of play in 1904-05 at the University of Kansas, and football was definitely the most popular game on campus. The *Kansan* on January 21, 1905, commented "No one will deny that there could be room for improvement in the basket ball team, but whose fault is it? The men now playing are all good players and only lack a little training. On the other hand there are many other larger men and experienced players in the University that should get out and make the team."

One hopeful harbinger in the *Kansan* of January 26, 1905, was the mention that "Dr. Naismith has had plans for the new gymnasium drawn and they are now ready for presentation to the legislature." The respect he had built for physical training on the campus had led to support by the administration and now to an opportunity to present the need to the lawmakers of Kansas.

On February 2, 1905, the student paper told of a seven-game, eight-day road trip by the basketball team through Nebraska and Iowa. The article noted that the players were to be accompanied on this expedition by the manager, U.S.G. Plank, but no mention was made of Naismith making the trip as well. On February 20, 1905, the *Lawrence Journal* stated, "The University basket ball team returned Saturday morning from a successful trip to Osage City and Emporia." That report contradicts the year-by-year scores listed in the official record of the current basketball media guide, which records the final two games of the season as having been played in Lawrence. During the 1904-05 season, out of 11 games played K.U. won five and lost six. Only two of those were played in the Snow Hall gym on campus.

Time of Transition

The *Kansan* on March 9, 1905, told in its headlines of "Plans for Gym" and that the gym was "To Equal Any in the West." In the story which followed it was explained that the original request for $125,000 had been trimmed to $100,000 and accordingly its size had been reduced somewhat but the gym would still include a basement and be two stories tall. The prospective facility was to have both a girls and boys gym, with separate rooms for wrestling, fencing, boxing and a gymnastic apparatus room. All could be merged into one large room by the removal of wire screen partitions. It would have a seating capacity of nearly 3,000 people and the *Kansan* stated, "If these plans are adopted, the University will have a gymnasium second to none in the west."

While the need for a new home for basketball was great, that by itself would not have been sufficient reason to construct the gym. The K.U. *Graduate Magazine* in November 1904 had noted "It is practically impossible for the University to get on further without adequate facilities for the physical care of its young men and women . . . [Students with] none of the opportunities for exercise. . . and under the strain of severe mental work become physically weak and nerveless . . . . There is but one common sense remedy for the great majority of students, and that is regular work in a well-fitted gymnasium."[18] Dr. Naismith, one of the pioneers nationally in physical training, had always sought to advance the interests of all of the students, and he valued the gym primarily as a way to make exercise available to all.

On March 11, 1905, the headline read "University Jubilant," and the *Kansan* told of the enthusiasm generated on Mount Oread at the news of the state legislature's funding for a new gym and auditorium building.

Robinson Gymnasium dedicated in 1907, where Naismith had his office until his death in 1939. It is no longer standing. (Courtesy Kansas University Archives).

A view of the basketball court in Robinson Gymnasium in 1908. With its capacity of over 2,000 persons, this fine facility established a new era for the sport at the University of Kansas. Dr. James Naismith was the key individual in its development. (Courtesy Kansas University Archives).

The *Kansan* noted that it would have been fitting if the legislators "could have heard the old 'Rock Chalk, Jayhawk, K.U.!' ringing through Fraser Hall." Chancellor Frank Strong, at a meeting held to celebrate the appropriation, called on Dr. Naismith, who had developed the plans for the gym. Dr. Naismith stressed that not only would K.U.'s athletes benefit but that it would "make all the students better and stronger men and women."

On May 18, 1905, the student paper featured an article calling for athletic reform, noting student demand for a change in athletics. The *Kansan* stated, "At the present time, the University of Kansas is down, completely down in athletics, and there is no use denying it . . . the most alarming feature of the situation is the apathy and 'don't care spirit' with which a large portion of the students regard athletics. The student body does not support an athletic team as they should, and our teams show the effect of it." The *Kansan* further commented, "Athletics are primarily student activities and the students should, under proper supervision, see that athletics are carried on in a manner staisfactory to the general student body." Dr. Naismith's tenure as basketball coach was during the leanest years at K.U. for athletics. While the lack of good places to practice and play was important, the lack of interest by many, if not most, of the students was also a contributing factor in those "hard times."

The increasing height of men and women in general and of basketball players in particular has been a subject of comment throughout the twentieth century. Much of this increase in height is due to improved nutrition. But there has long been interest in other ways to create taller men and women. The *Kansan* on September 16, 1905, reported a plan by the originator of basketball and the sport's first coach at the University. The student newspaper stated, "Dr. Naismith is contemplating the purchase of a stretching machine or, in other words, an appliance to give additional height to the short individual . . . . there is no doubt that the machine will be popular." Given the perennial debate over the role of height in basketball, Naismith's interest in 1905 seems both ironic and prophetic as we look back.

When the students returned to K.U. for the 1905-06 year, the attention of those following sports was mainly on the football team, but the *Kansan* noted the start in the middle of September of basketball practices. Rife writes that this start marked "the beginning of practice sessions almost two months earlier than usual." Even more important was *who* tried out for the team. Among those on hand was a 19-year old from Independence, Missouri, named Forrest Clare Allen. Max Rife explains that "the 1905-06 basketball season opened with the announcement of a freshman player by the name of Forrest C. Allen, who, with the possible exception of Dr. Naismith, was destined to have a greater impact on Kansas University basketball than any other man." The *Kansan* on October 21, 1905, headlined the account of Allen's appearance as "World's Champion at Basket ball" and then reported, "Forrest Allen made his first appearance at basket ball in the gymnasium Thursday evening. The ceiling was too low for him to show how well he could throw long goals, but he gave the men some good ideas of how to get into the game. Allen will be able to play in the games in this year's schedule, and he will make a strong addition to the team. He is one of the world's champions, and is said to be the best goal thrower in the world."

In his 1967 thesis done on the career of Allen, Donald W. Elston explains why he was referred to as a "World's Champion." Elston tells us that in 1904 three games had been played between the "world champion basket ball team" Buffalo Germans and the Kansas City Athletic Club known as the Blue Diamonds. It was a three-game series, played in Kansas City, and each team won a game before the final decisive contest. Allen later told Elston about those games: "The Germans were tricky. As we would run, they would kick the back of our heels to trip us. They would also run along beside us and would hold our thumb . . . . For the first two games, each team had a referee. Six men on a side so to speak. We didn't like theirs and they didn't like ours. For the final game, we got Dr. Naismith of K.U. and U.S.G. Plank of Haskell and we beat them 45 to 14. We beat the tar out of them."[19] The victory also earned Allen and his K.C. teammates the right to be called "World's Champions." Unfortunately for Allen and his new team, freshmen for the first time were not able to compete in intercollegiate games until after mid-term, February of 1906.

The *Kansan* of January 13, 1906, began with a quote: " 'It will be done by next Christmas,' said Dr. Naismith today while speaking to a *Kansan* reporter about the new gym. Teams and men are already at work excavating for the foundation. The plans for this eleventh edifice to crown the crest of Mount Oread as prepared by the State Architect, John Stanton, and Dr. Naismith are as follows." The story then told of a building to be 178 feet by 70 feet with ample space to play basketball.

During the 1905-06 season, the quality of play was improving because of "a spirited fight for places on the team" according to the student paper, and 10 players were mentioned as distinguishing themselves during the practices. In early February of 1906, preparations were underway for a road trip involving 11 games in 12 days. In the eight years of basketball, there had been similar excursions to Iowa and Nebraska, and in 1906 games in Illinois were also scheduled. The *Kansan* of February 7, 1906, told who was making the challenging journey: "Barlow, W. Miller, and Allen forwards, Siler and Bergen, centers, M. Miller, Winnagle, and Johnson, guards. 'Andy' Brown will probably be taken on the trip for substitute guard and referee. Manager Lansdon will accompany the team." (The Jayhawkers in 1906 brought their own referee but not their coach on this road trip.)

By February 10, 1906, in a victory over the Kansas City Y.M.C.A. the University of Kansas basketball team won its seventh game. This matched the previous high in total wins gained in both the 1898-99 and 1902-03 seasons. The next victory two days later was a milestone achievement. The *Lawrence Journal* on February 13, 1906, told of the victory by K.U. over Nebraska. The headline read "Jayhawkers Outclassed Their Opponents in Basket Ball," and the 37 to 17 victory was recounted: "Kansas University last night played the fastest article of basket ball witnessed in the gymnasium of the Nebraska University . . . . In every phase and department of the contest the Jayhawkers outclassed their opponents and the victory was as meritorious as it was brilliant." It was the fourth meeting of the two teams in seven seasons and in the first three the Cornhuskers had won. The longest continuing rivalry in basketball at K.U. is with the University of Nebraska.

The *Lawrence Journal* further noted that "The laurels of the contest belong to Forrest Allen, right forward of the visiting five. His goals from the floor and free throws alone netted 23 points for the team, six in excess of the combined efforts of the entire Cornhusker quintette." Max Rife identifies this as Allen's first full game. He was initially ineligible, then only played halves in his first two games. It was the first of many great performances by him for K.U., but in only 12 games was he actually on the court. Instead, on the sidelines as a coach he participated in 809 games and gained victories in 590 of those contests.

On February 28, 1906, the student paper called for greater support of basketball, observing that "no University enterprise deserves a more loyal support by students and faculty than the basket ball team. The five is a typical and ideal college organization. The men are all students of the best type, their training and practice is incident only to their school life, and aside from the cost of games they call on the student body for very little financial assistance." The *Kansan* noted that many students had bought tickets for football games and that basketball, baseball and' track "deserve the same sort of loyal backing and need it even more than football. Without money athletic enterprises cannot be carried on."

On March 3, 1906, the *Kansan* headlined "Basket Ball Successful" and reported, "The results of the basket ball season to date show a marked change in the standing of the game as a college sport. Manager W.C. Lansdon has made a financial success of the basketball season so far, to say nothing of the glory and pleasures accorded the University and the team by their victories and trip." During the 11-game trip K.U. had won five and lost six, but the *Kansan* explained "it was not due to the fact that any of the teams were superior to ours." For the year of 1905-06, the Jayhawkers finished with twelve victories against seven defeats.

Max Rife in his 1967 study comments about the ninth and last year of Dr. Naismith's coaching career at the University of Kansas. Rife observes, "The 1906-07 basketball program was faced with certain familiar difficulties, and one important new one. Old problems included the lack of suitable quarters in which to train and a gymnasium to be used for home games. An increasingly apparent problem was the absence of coaching, since Dr. Naismith was becoming so busy with his work as Director of Physical Education that he had very little time to devote to the training of the basketball team. The *Kansan* on [December 10, 1906] affirms, however, that 'time he does spend with them counts.' The new problem presenting itself was the resignation of Allen as captain." Allen had left K.U. to accept the position as basketball coach at Baker University in Baldwin City, Kansas.

In his 1947 book, entitled *Coach 'Phog' Allen's Sports Stories*, Allen recalled what happened: "I became acquainted with Dr. Naismith in 1902. All the rest of my years have been richer for this long association with the gentle Christian gentleman. It is pleasant to recall one meeting with him in old Snow Hall at Kansas University 40 years ago. Dr. Naismith had received a letter from the athletic authorities at Baker University wanting to hire me as basketball coach. With a merry laugh as he met me in the hall, he said 'I've got a good joke on you, you bloody beggar.' He set me back temporarily. I wondered what I'd been doing. Then he laughed aloud, continuing, 'They want you to coach basketball down at Baker.' With surprise, I said 'What's so funny about that?' He replied, 'Why you can't coach basketball! You just play it.' I countered with these words, 'Well, you certainly can teach free-throwing. And you can teach the boys to pass at angles and run in curves.' To this he looked at me wonderingly but didn't reply."[20] (This 1906 encounter between the creator of the game and one of the first to realize the game's finer points gave K.U. basketball one of its greatest stories.)

The *Kansan* of November 14, 1906, offers evidence of what Dr. Naismith was concerned about, reporting "An electric machine for the purpose of curing a 'charley horse' and healing the wounds of bruised athletes is Dr. James Naismith's latest invention. The machine is a simple contrivance, consisting of a motor and a spool which when placed against the wounded part makes several thousand strokes a minute. The machine works on the principle of an electric massage machine. The machine by striking the flesh several thousand quick blows per minute sets up a rapid circulation in the part where the blood has coagulated, reducing the 'charley horse' and as a result cures the bruise. With the machine there will not be nearly so many athletes lying out because of bruises as formerly, as an injury may be healed in much less time than was possible by other treatment." Dr. Naismith was K.U.'s basketball coach, but he was clearly more involved in his other responsibilities.

Dr. Naismith (left) around 1891 wearing an early football helmet of his own invention. (Courtesy Kansas University Archives).

On February 14, 1907, Dr. James Naismith did accompany the team to a game at Baker. This trip is confirmed in the *Kansan* box score, which noted that he was one of the officials and that Allen, the Baker coach, was the other. In their one game coaching against each other the pupil's team won with 37 points to the 24 for the mentor's team, and both were the game officials.

On February 26, 1907, the *Lawrence Journal* told of another invention originated by the Kansas University basketball coach. The *Journal* noted, "Dr. Naismith has invented a piece of apparatus which he says will make short people taller. The machine consists of a horizontal plane with an adjustable extension at the base. The subject is strapped securely to the plane and his feet are attached to the extension which is regulated by the short patient who is trying to grow tall. Dr. Naismith says that a young person may increase his height two inches in six months by thirty minutes daily use of this machine." In September of 1905 Naismith had sought to acquire a comparable device, but by February of 1907 he was devising one of his own.

The *Kansan* on March 13, 1907, commenting on a season-ending road trip during which four games had been lost and two games had been won, asked, "Was the basket ball team playing against luck, or something worse. It would be more satisfactory to believe it was against luck, but it looks suspiciously as if in five of the games the boys were playing against better teams. We feel bad over the result . . . . On the whole we can't say the team did so bad . . . . All K.U. has to say to the victorious teams is, 'you can't do it again.' " In Dr. Naismith's last year as coach, the 1906-07 K.U. basketball team finished with seven wins and eight losses.

The Torch is Passed

The opening of Robinson Gymnasium in the fall of 1907 marked the start of a new era for K.U. basketball. The student newspaper on October 30, 1907, reported, "Robinson Gymnasium, so long the object of the athletes' hopes and the pride of every loyal K.U. student, has at long last been opened to the public. Now the University has a place where visitors may go and we shall not be ashamed to tell them 'this is our gym.' The completion of the magnificent new building will mark a new epoch in the history of this growing institution. The new building is excelled by few such edifices in the west." For Naismith, the opening must have been satisfying indeed.

On November 13, 1907, the *Kansan* told of the rise in interest among students in playing basketball, commenting, "With one hundred men trying out for basket ball and the advantages offered by the new gym, the only thing that stands in the way of a winning team is the lack of a coach." A remedy to this situation was not found for nearly a month, but eventually the large seating capacity of Robinson Gym offered a solution. The *Kansan* on December 11, 1907, announced, "Forrest Allen of K.C.A.C. has been employed by the Athletic Association to coach the team." The possibility of significant revenue from ticket sales to home games in Robinson Gym likely led to this decision to hire Allen. Without Robinson Gym likely there would not have been a way to pay a coach for the team, and Forrest Allen might never have become a legend at K.U. The role of Dr. Naismith in the building of Robinson Gym is clear, but often forgotten is how much having such a large, spacious court, with room for over 2,000 spectators, improved K.U.'s chances for success in the sport he had invented.

For example, the *Kansan* of February 5, 1908, observed, "Although the season started out with a number of defeats the team has shown good form in the last few games and has a splendid chance of winning a large percent of the contests yet to be played. This is the first chance the students have had of supporting a basketball team and they have done well. The crowds have been very large and the game promises to become one of the most popular of college sports. The new gymnasium with its splendid court will encourage more men to come out for the team and Kansas can expect even greater things of her basket ball team in years to come." During the season of 1907-08, K.U. played 24 games, 11 of which were played at home, and won 18 while losing six. In the Naismith era, the most games ever played was 19 in 1905-06, and games at home were few and far between.

During the two seasons of 1907-08 and 1908-09 the Jayhawkers with Forrest Allen as coach won 43 and lost nine. Forrest Allen enrolled in the Central School of Osteopathy in Kansas City in 1909. From 1909-10 until 1918-19 W.O. Hamilton won 125 and lost 59 for a winning percentage of 67.9. Among his best players were several who had previously graduated from Lawrence High School. These hometown products likely resulted from the availability of a basketball court in the Lawrence Y.M.C.A., built with Naismith's help around 1910. Despite the clearly superior record of Hamilton, NCAA records indicate that there were 17 teams which had winning records over 70% nationally. Still, Hamilton's five Missouri Valley championships were a measure of regional dominance.[21]

Forrest Allen returned in September of 1919 as Director of Athletics and Freshman Basketball Coach. In January of 1920 the varsity basketball coach Karl Schlademan resigned his position to devote his full time to coaching the track team, and Allen became the head man. As the coach, Allen continued to include Dr. Naismith in the team photographs out of respect for his contribution to the sport. The first two seasons after Allen's return to Mount Oread resulted respectively in eleven wins and seven losses, and ten wins and eight losses. Then from 1921-1927 K.U. won 97 games and lost only eleven, gaining six conference championships. The 1922 and 1923 teams were subsequently judged by the Helms Foundation to be national champions. During the decade from 1920-1929 K.U. was one of 19 teams to win over 70%.[22]

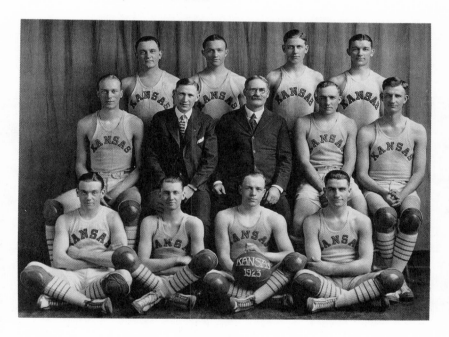

The 1922-23 Kansas University basketball team. Later designated by the Helms Foundation as National Champions. Top Row Left To Right, A. Rupp, B. Mosby, T. Ackerman, V. Wilkin. Middle Row, J. Wulf, Coach F. C. Allen, Dr. J. Naismith, C. Black, B. Frederick. Lower Row, A. Woestemeyer, W. Bowman, P. Endacott, A. McDonald. (Courtesy Kansas University Archives).

James and Maude Naismith circa 1932. (Courtesy Kansas University Archives).

The 1935-36 Kansas University basketball team. Big Six Conference Champions. Top Row Coach, F. C. Allen, Holmer, Hoverstock, Cox, Shaffer, Trainer Dees, Lutton. Middle Row, Rogers, Noble, Kappelman, Allen. Ebling, Pralle. Lower Row, Hormuth, Schmidt, Holliday, Piper. (Courtesy Kansas University Archives).

Allen's efforts in April 1927 to organize opposition to a proposed rule change which would have limited each player to one bounce of the ball led to the formation of the National Association of Basketball Coaches. Allen was its first president and led a successful effort to rescind the proposal. Henry Iba, longtime Oklahoma State coach told Don Elston that, "Dr. Allen, through his type of play, and through his authority as a man in the game of basketball in the early years, almost helped write the rules of basketball."[23] It was this leadership role that led Dr. Naismith to present to Allen a picture of himself inscribed "From the Father of Basketball to the Father of Basketball Coaching."

For the fall of 1927, while practice continued to take place in Robinson Gym, the home game court shifted to Hoch Auditorium, which had more room for spectators. The *Kansan* reported that fall that the lighting was insufficient for viewing satisfactorily. Also, over the years there were problems with players running off court into nearby walls or falling off the stage which supported the court into the Jayhawk faithful. Still, it did allow more spectators to share in the excitement of K.U. basketball.

4
The Naismith Legacies
Decades of Success

Basketball superiority continued into the 1930s for Allen and his teams. From 1930-1939, K.U. won 153 games and lost only 37 to achieve 80.5%, and was one of 20 schools to exceed 70%. During this period K.U. won seven conference championships. Beyond these accomplishments, Allen's successful drive to have basketball included as an Olympic sport in 1936 and his efforts to have Dr. Naismith on hand in Berlin were further examples of leadership beyond his excellent coaching.[24]

In the 1940s K.U. won 155 games and lost 77. Despite this excellent record, K.U. was not one of the 17 teams that won over 70% from 1940-1949.[25] It was during this decade that Allen, irate at the growing dominance of big men, especially one nearby player for Oklahoma State, once again pushed for the adoption of the 12-foot high goal. His push was unsuccessful. Another major effort by Allen was his attacks on gambling and racketeering. Don Elston notes, "In 1944, he claimed that some games in the eastern section of the United States had been 'thrown' by players. He predicted that there would be a 'betting scandal' in college basketball . . . . In general, few people were concerned about the matter . . . . At first, statements by the Kansas basketball coach relative to gambling were not taken seriously. For one, Coach Nat Holman of the City College of New York branded Allen's statements as a lot of 'hogwash.' Subsequent investigation and conviction of a number of persons left no doubt as to the correctness of his accusations. Included among those individuals arrested for 'fixing' games and 'shaving' points were four members of Coach Holman's City College of New York team."[26] In search of an alternative to the NIT post-season tournament which was often linked to these abuses, Allen and other coaches sought another way to determine a champion.

The NCAA Tournament, begun in 1939 as a poorly attended event in Evanston, Illinois, was brought by Allen to Municipal Auditorium in Kansas City, Missouri, in its second year. At this location it was a revenue-producing event for many years, increasingly a popular attraction and controlled by coaches and universities. K.U played in the Final Four in 1940, losing to Indiana in the championship game. In nine of the first ten years of the NCAA Tournament there were teams from the Big Six, later Big Seven, Conference, of which K.U. was a member.[27]

From 1950-1959 K.U. won 177 games and lost 72, but was not one of the 14 schools winning over 70% during the decade. K.U. was the only school to participate in the NCAA Championship Tournament three times during those 10 years, and won the tournament on March 26, 1952, in Seattle, Washington. During the 1950s, Forrest Allen's tenure as coach came to an end and he was succeeded by his longtime assistant Dick Harp. Allen resisted what was then a mandatory retirement and fought hard to continue at K.U. but eventually was forced to retire. During the decade of the 1950s, five conference championships were won. In 1960, A.C. "Dutch" Lonborg, Kansas Athletics Director, retired as the chairman of the basketball committee for the NCAA after serving 13 years and presiding over the expansion of its tournament in the post-gambling-scandal era.[28]

In 1963, Dick Harp stepped down as coach and was succeeded by Ted Owens, who had been an assistant to Harp for three years. From 1960-1969 K.U. won 173 games and lost 91 games. During this decade there were 17 teams with over 70% winning records. During the 1960s K.U. won three conference championships and took part in five years of NCAA and NIT post-season play.

From 1970-1979 K.U. won 178 games and lost 99. Ted Owens was the coach during that time. That record did not place the Jayhawks among the 19 teams that achieved winning marks over 70% during the decade. In the 1970s K.U. won four Big Eight conference championships and were four times involved in post-season NCAA play, twice in the Final Four.

From 1980-1989 the record for the University of Kansas was 219 victories against 106 defeats. After the 1983 season, Ted Owens was replaced by Larry Brown as head basketball coach. During this decade K.U. won one conference championship. The Jayhawks were involved in six NCAA post-season competitions and made the Final Four twice. The second NCAA championship for the University was gained on April 4, 1988, in Kansas City, Missouri.

Since 1988 Roy Williams has been the coach of the team and in five seasons has a winning record of close to 80%. His teams have won three consecutive conference championships and have been involved in NCAA post-season play four times. Twice the Jayhawks have been involved in the Final Four. The tradition of basketball achievement continues at the University of Kansas.

The Honor Roll

This heritage of excellence is well demonstrated by the 13 enrollees from K.U. who are in the Naismith Memorial Basketball Hall of Fame. These include, in order of admission, Dr. James Naismith, Dr. Forrest Allen, Ernest Quigley, John Bunn, Adolph Rupp, Paul Endacott, Arthur Lonborg, William Johnson, John McLendon, Wilt Chamberlain, Dean Smith, Ralph Miller and Clyde Lovellette. Kansas has far more inductees in the Hall of Fame than any other major college basketball program, and is notable for the number of coaches and players enshrined as opposed to rule-makers or officials honored from other universities.[29]

Out of respect for the many who have played the game for K.U. so well, no attempt is here made to discuss individual players beyond those cited for the Hall of Fame. A complete listing would be a long one, and descriptions of their various achievements would exceed available space in this Afterword. Forty-one times Jayhawks have been named consensus

Roy Williams, head basketball coach at the University of Kansas, and portrait of Dr. Naismith in Allen Field House in December 1991. (Courtesy *Lawrence Journal-World* and photographer, Mike Yoder).

All-Americans, and some 25 have been named to NCAA All-Tournament Teams. Four times a Jayhawk has been the National Collegiate Player of the Year, and four times one has been named the Most Outstanding Player in the NCAA Tournament. The players associated with basketball at K.U. have been among the leaders in many nationally ranked categories during the 95 years that the game has been played on the campus.

While many of the top athletes of the 1990s are more concerned with how many times the games played will be televised nationally, it is a source of pride to many of those playing for the Jayhawks to be associated with a school so rich in tradition. Whether they note the **portrait of Dr. Naismith in the entry way to Allen Field House or not, new** players soon realize that the street to its east is named for the game's inventor. Dr. Naismith's legacy is increasingly recognized in the United States, Canada, and the world. Hopefully, more and more people will come to know the ideals and values of this man as he is honored at the place of his birth, at the site where the game was invented, and in the community where he lived the last 40 years of his life.

Notes

1.   Douglas County Historical Society, Minutes (Lawrence, Kansas, Elizabeth M. Watkins Community Museum Library), p.46.

2.   Bernice Larson Webb, *The Basketball Man*. (Lawrence, Kansas: University Press of Kansas, 1973), p.328.

3.   *Lawrence Journal-World,* April 7, 1993.

4.   "Basketball Was Born Here" pamphlet, (Springfield, Massachusetts: Basketball Hall of Fame), pp.32-33.

5.   Pamphlet, "A Memorial to Dr. James Naismith (1861-1939)" (Almonte, Ontario: Dr. James Naismith Foundation).

Dickenson Harrison Associates, *Executive Summary The Naismith Centre,* (Ottawa, Ontario: Dr. James Naismith Basketball Foundation).

Dickenson Harrison Associates, *Final Report, The Naismith Centre,* (Ottawa, Ontario: Dr. James Naismith Basketball Foundation).

6.   "Basketball Was Born Here," p.12.

7.   Rick Telander, *Heaven is a Playgound,* (New York: Simon and Shuster, 1976), p.56.

8.   Jimmy Breslin, "Can Basketball Survive Chamberlain?", *Saturday Evening Post,* December 1, 1956.

9.   "Basketball Was Born Here," p.14.

10.   Bill Gutman, *The Pictorial History of Basketball,* (New York: W.H. Smith Publishers, Inc., 1988).

11.   "Basketball Was Born Here," p.16.

12.   Donald Elston, "Forrest C. Allen," (M.A. Thesis, University of Kansas, 1967).

13.   *Wall Street Journal,* October 4, 1991.

14.   *Kansas University Weekly,* December 10, 1898.

15.   Dr. James Naismith, Subject Files, Watkins Community Museum, Lawrence, Kansas.

16.   *Lawrence Journal,* January 23, 1899.

17.   Max Rife, "Basketball In Its Early Years at the University of Kansas 1898-1925" (M.A. Thesis, University of Kansas, 1967), p.6.

18. *Graduate Magazine,* November 1904.

19. Elston, p.6.

20. Forrest C. Allen, *Coach 'Phog' Allen's Sports Stories,* (Lawrence, Kansas: Allen Press, 1947), pp. 175-176.

21. Sports Information Office, K.U. Athletic Department, *Kansas Basketball 1992-93 Media Guide* (Lawrence, Kansas, K.U. Athletic Department, 1993), p. 169.

22. NCAA Statistics Service, *1988 Men's College Basketball Media Kit* (Mission, Kansas: NCAA Statistics Service, 1988), p. A-2.

23. Elston, p.53.

24. *1992-93 Media Guide* and *1988 Media Kit,* p. A-4.

25. *1988 Media Kit,* p. A-6.

26. Elston, p.49.

27. *1988 Media Kit,* pp.A-5, A-6.

28. *1922-1993 Media Guide* and *1988 Media Kit,* p.A-11.

29. Ibid.

Afterword Index